D0147570

European Integration

European Integration

A Concise History

Mark Gilbert

ROWMAN & LITTLEFIELD PUBLISHERS, INC.
Lanham • Boulder • New York • Toronto • Plymouth, UK

Published by Rowman & Littlefield Publishers, Inc.
A wholly owned subsidiary of The Rowman & Littlefield Publishing Group, Inc.
4501 Forbes Boulevard, Suite 200, Lanham, Maryland 20706
www.rowmanlittlefield.com

Estover Road, Plymouth PL6 7PY, United Kingdom

Copyright © 2012 by Rowman & Littlefield Publishers, Inc.

All rights reserved. No part of this book may be reproduced in any form or by
any electronic or mechanical means, including information storage and retrieval
systems, without written permission from the publisher, except by a reviewer
who may quote passages in a review.

British Library Cataloguing in Publication Information Available

Library of Congress Cataloging-in-Publication Data

Gilbert, Mark, 1961–
  European integration : a concise history / Mark Gilbert. — [rev. and updated ed.]
    p. cm.
  Rev. and updated ed. of: Surpassing realism : the politics of European
integration since 1945. c2003.
  Includes bibliographical references and index.
  ISBN 978-0-7425-6663-7 (cloth : alk. paper) — ISBN 978-0-7425-6664-4 (pbk. :
alk. paper) — ISBN 978-0-7425-6665-1 (ebook)
  1. European Union—History. 2. European Union countries—Politics and
government. 3. Europe—Economic integration—History. I. Gilbert, Mark,
1961– Surpassing realism. II. Title.
  JN30.G55 2012
  341.242'2—dc23

                                                                    2011034445

∞™ The paper used in this publication meets the minimum requirements of
American National Standard for Information Sciences—Permanence of Paper
for Printed Library Materials, ANSI/NISO Z39.48-1992.

Printed in the United States of America

Contents

Acknowledgments

The original edition of this book was written in the academic years 2000 to 2001 and 2001 to 2002, when I was lecturer in Italian history and politics in the department of European Studies at the University of Bath. I made too many friends at Bath to list them here, but I enjoyed the hardworking, dynamic atmosphere of the department.

I subsequently moved to the University of Trento, where, among other things, I taught European integration history at both undergraduate and graduate levels. I learned much from two exceptional colleagues, Marco Brunazzo and Vincent della Sala. They have always been willing to read and comment upon my work and, what is far more important, were good friends in an academic environment that, at times, was anything but easy. Sara Lamberti Moneta, whose PhD research I had the privilege of supervising from 2006 to 2011, was also a great stimulus and has become a friend. I could not list all of the many students of Trento's School of International Studies whom I enjoyed teaching, but Fabio Capano and Benedetta Voltolini are both now embarked on PhD research at universities in the United States and Britain.

I have greatly enjoyed working with colleagues at other universities in Italy: Mario Del Pero, Kiran Klaus Patel, Federico Romero, and Antonio Varsori are just a few of the scholars that make postwar history a lively field in Italy. Elsewhere in Europe, Wolfram Kaiser, Michael Gehler, and Ann-Christina Knudsen invited me to conferences at which I was able to develop some of the ideas that make this book significantly different from the original.

This second edition was prepared over the summer of 2010 and during the fall semester of the academic year 2010 to 2011 at the Johns Hopkins Center for Advanced International Studies in Bologna. I must thank my new colleagues, especially Erik Jones and Veronica Pye, for having made me so welcome, and my students for being so stimulating. A particular expression of thanks (and praise) is due to Marijn Hoijitink, who has been my research assistant. Had she been less diligent and competent, the book would have been finished sooner (but would have been worse).

My intellectual debts will be obvious from my footnotes. I have a particular debt, however, to my brother, Martyn. He is an ardent Euroskeptic, and I have passed many hours arguing with him about the menace that European unification allegedly presents to British liberties. Ultimately, I don't agree with his views, but there is no doubt that it can be useful for a scholar of contemporary politics to hear commonsense opinions robustly expressed.

Most of all I would like to thank my wife, Luciana, and son, Francisco. Francis was an infant when the first edition came out and is now a neoteen with a wicked sense of humor and an encyclopedic knowledge of the Harry Potter stories. This book is dedicated to him.

Abbreviations and Acronyms

ACP	African, Caribbean, and Pacific (countries)
BIS	Bank of International Settlements
CAP	Common Agricultural Policy
CDU-CSU	Christian Democrats (Germany-Bavaria)
CEEC	Committee on European Economic Cooperation (1940s)
	Central and Eastern European Countries (1990s)
CFM	Council of Foreign Ministers
CFSP	Common Foreign and Security Policy
COREPER	Committee of Permanent Representatives
CSDP	Common Security and Defence Policy
DC	Christian Democrats (Italy)
DM	Deutsche Mark
EBRD	European Bank of Reconstruction and Development
EC	European Community
ECA	European Cooperation Agency
ECB	European Central Bank
ECJ	European Court of Justice
ECSC	European Coal and Steel Community
Ecu	European currency unit
EDC	European Defense Community
EDF	European Development Fund
EEA	European Economic Area
EEC	European Economic Community
EFSF	European Financial Stability Facility
EFTA	European Free Trade Agreement

EMI	European Monetary Institute
EMS	European Monetary System
EMU	Economic and Monetary Union
ENP	European Neighbourhood Policy
EP	European Parliament
EPC	European Political Community (1950s)
	European Political Cooperation (1970s–1990s)
EPU	European Payments Union
ERDF	European Regional Development Fund
ERM	Exchange Rate Mechanism
ERP	European Recovery Program
ERRF	European Rapid Reaction Force
ESCB	European System of Central Banks
ESDP	European Security and Defense Policy
EU	European Union
EUA	European Unit of Account
Euratom	European Atomic Energy Community
FPÖ	Austrian Freedom Party
GATT	General Agreement on Trade and Tariffs
IGC	Intergovernmental Conference
IISS	International Institute for Strategic Studies
MCAs	Monetary Compensatory Amounts
MEPs	Members of the European Parliament
MFE	Movimento federalista europeo
MPs	Members of Parliament (Britain)
MRP	Mouvement Républicain Populaire
NATO	North Atlantic Treaty Organization
OECD	Organization for Economic Cooperation and Development
OEEC	Organization for European Economic Cooperation
OPEC	Organization of Petroleum Exporting Countries
PPP	Purchasing Power Parity
PSF	Socialist Party (France)
PSI	Socialist Party (Italy)
PSOE	Socialist Party (Spain)
QMV	Qualified Majority Voting
SEA	Single European Act
SPD	Social Democrats (Germany)
TEU	Treaty on European Union
UEF	Union Européenne des Fédéralistes
UEM	United Europe Movement
USSR	Union of Soviet Socialist Republics
VAT	Value-added Tax
WEF	World Economic Forum
WEU	Western European Union
WTO	World Trade Organization

Chronology 1945–2011

1940s

February 4–11, 1945: Yalta Conference.
July 17–August 12, 1945: Potsdam Conference.
September 19, 1946: Churchill's Zurich speech.
March 12, 1947: Truman Doctrine.
June 5, 1947: George C. Marshall's Harvard address. Beginning of European Recovery Program.
March 17, 1948: Treaty on Western Union (Brussels Pact) signed. Belgium, Britain, France, Luxembourg, and Netherlands form an alliance for mutual defense and economic cooperation.
May 7–11, 1948: Congress of Europe at The Hague.
June 24, 1948: Berlin blockade begins (ends May 12, 1949).
May 5, 1949: Treaty of St. James establishing the Council of Europe.
September 15, 1949: Konrad Adenauer becomes first chancellor of West Germany.

1950s

May 9, 1950: Schuman Plan announced.
October 24, 1950: Announcement of Pleven Plan.
November 4, 1950: Convention for the Protection of Human Rights and Fundamental Freedoms signed in Rome by thirteen European countries. Greece and Sweden sign on November 28.

April 18, 1951: ECSC treaty signed in Paris by Belgium, France, Italy, Luxembourg, Netherlands, and West Germany.

May 27, 1952: EDC treaty signed in Paris by the same countries.

March 10, 1953: EPC proposals presented to the government of The Six by the ECSC Assembly.

August 30, 1954: French Parliament rejects the EDC treaty.

October 23, 1954: WEU treaty signed in Paris.

June 1–2, 1955: Messina conference of The Six delegates to an intergovernmental committee headed by Paul-Henri Spaak the task of drawing up plans for an economic community and a community to govern atomic energy.

October 13, 1955: Jean Monnet forms his Action Committee for a United Europe.

May 29, 1956: Spaak committee presents its report to foreign ministers of The Six in Venice.

October 30–November 6, 1956: Suez Crisis.

March 25, 1957: Treaties of Rome instituting Euratom and the EEC signed by The Six.

January 7, 1958: Walter Hallstein (Germany) becomes the first president of the EEC Commission, which begins operations.

November 14, 1958: French government blocks the British idea of a free trade area encompassing all OEEC countries.

1960s

May 3, 1960: EFTA formed by Austria, Denmark, Great Britain, Norway, Portugal, Sweden, and Switzerland.

July–August 1961: Britain, Denmark, and Ireland apply for EEC membership.

November 2, 1961: Plan for an "indissoluble Union of States" presented by the French government.

January 14, 1962: Agreement on CAP reached. Second stage of EEC begins.

January 14, 1963: De Gaulle's press conference opposing British membership.

January 22, 1963: Franco-German pact of friendship signed in Paris.

January 28, 1963: France vetoes British membership.

July 20, 1963: Association agreement signed with eighteen African states at Yaoundé (Cameroon).

March 31, 1965: The Commission presents its proposals regarding the EEC's "own resources" and the budget question.

April 8, 1965: Merger treaty signed. ECSC, EEC, and Euratom are fused into the EC.

July 6, 1965: Empty Chair Crisis begins. France boycotts the Community.

September 9, 1965: De Gaulle casts doubt on future of EEC if national veto not preserved.

January 28–29, 1966: Luxembourg compromise agreed. France retakes her place at the table.

May 1, 1967: Wilson government formally applies for British membership.

June 30, 1967: The Commission signs the Kennedy Round trade deal on behalf of The Six.

July 6, 1967: Jean Rey (Belgium) becomes second president of the EC Commission.

November 27, 1967: De Gaulle blocks British membership.

July 1, 1968: Customs union begins, eighteen months ahead of the schedule anticipated in the EEC treaty.

December 1–2, 1969: Hague summit of EC leaders.

1970s

July 2, 1970: Franco Maria Malfatti (Italy) becomes third president of the EC Commission.

October 7–8, 1970: Werner Report on monetary union adopted.

October 27, 1970: Luxembourg Report on political cooperation adopted.

August 15, 1971: United States ends dollar convertibility with gold.

January 22, 1972: Britain, Denmark, Ireland, and Norway sign accession treaties. Norway rejects membership in a referendum on September 25.

March 22, 1972: Sicco Mansholt (Netherlands) becomes fourth president of the EC Commission following Malfatti's resignation.

October 19–21, 1972: At Paris, EC Nine commit themselves to creating a European Union by 1980.

January 1, 1973: Britain, Denmark, and Ireland join the EC.

January 6, 1973: François-Xavier Ortoli (France) becomes fifth president of EC Commission.

April 23, 1973: Kissinger announces the "Year of Europe."

December 9–10, 1974: Paris summit of EC leaders establishes European Council.

January 7, 1976: Publication of Tindemans Report.

September 20, 1976: Treaty authorizing direct elections to the European Assembly.

January 6, 1977: Roy Jenkins (Great Britain) becomes sixth president of the EC Commission.

October 27, 1977: Jenkins appeals for monetary union in a speech at the European University Institute.

December 4–5, 1978: Brussels European Council decides to introduce the EMS.

March 13, 1979: EMS enters into operation.

March 16, 1979: Death of Jean Monnet.

June 7–10, 1979: First direct elections to the European Parliament.

November 29–30, 1979: British budgetary question explodes at Dublin European Council.

1980s

January 1, 1981: Greece becomes tenth member state of the EC.

January 6, 1981: Gaston Thorn (Luxembourg) becomes seventh president of the EC Commission.

May 10, 1981: François Mitterrand becomes president of France.

October 4, 1981: French franc devalued within the EMS. Further adjustments follow in February and June 1982 and March 1983.

November 19, 1981: Italian foreign minister Emilio Colombo and his German counterpart, Hans-Dietrich Genscher, explain their proposals for a European Act to the European Parliament.

June 17–19, 1983: Stuttgart European Council ends the Genscher–Colombo process by signing the "Solemn Declaration" on European Union.

February 14, 1984: The European Parliament adopts a proposal for a treaty on European Union.

June 14–17, 1984: Second elections to the European Parliament.

June 25–26, 1984: Fontainebleau European Council. British budgetary problem resolved amid euphoria. Dooge Committee on institutional reform launched.

January 7, 1985: Jacques Delors (France) becomes eighth president of the EC Commission.

June 12, 1985: Portugal and Spain sign their accession treaties. They enter the Community on January 1, 1986.

June 14, 1985: The Commission submits its white paper, *Completing the Internal Market*.

June 28–29, 1985: Milan European Council calls an intergovernmental conference to decide amendments to the EEC treaty.

February 17 and 28, 1986: Single European Act (SEA) signed in Brussels.

May 23, 1986: Death of Altiero Spinelli.

May 29, 1986: The flag of the European Community (twelve gold stars arranged in a circle on a light blue background) is flown for the first time.

February 18, 1987: "Delors Package" proposing big increases in regional development funding presented to European Parliament.

July 1, 1987: SEA becomes law after all twelve member states complete ratification.

June 27–28, 1988: Hanover European Council renews Delors's presidency of the Commission.

September 20, 1988: Bruges speech: Margaret Thatcher warns of a European "super-state."

October 24, 1988: Court of First Instance instituted.

April 12, 1989: Presentation of the Delors Report.

June 15–18, 1989: Third elections to the European Parliament.

November 10, 1989: Fall of the Berlin Wall.

December 8–9, 1989: Strasbourg European Council launches IGC on monetary union and decides to set up a European Bank of Reconstruction and Development (EBRD) to provide loans for the countries of Eastern Europe.

1990s

April 28, 1990: Dublin European Council welcomes German reunification. A second Dublin summit on June 25–26 decides to call a parallel IGC on political union and fixes the date that the two IGCs will begin.

June 19, 1990: Schengen Treaty signed.

October 3, 1990: Reunification of Germany.

October 27–28, 1990: Rome I European Council reveals a deep breach between Britain and the rest of EU.

December 14–15, 1990: Rome II summit launches the two IGCs.

April 14, 1991: The EBRD starts work.

September 7, 1991: Hague peace conference on Yugoslavia begins.

December 9–10, 1991: Maastricht European Council negotiates the Treaty on European Union. Treaty is signed on February 7, 1992.

June 2, 1992: Danes vote against the Maastricht Treaty.

September 20, 1992: French narrowly approve Maastricht Treaty. Vote is preceded by chaos on the financial markets and the elimination of the pound sterling and the lira from the EMS.

December 11–12, 1992: Edinburgh European Council allows Denmark various opt-outs from the EU treaty and gives it a second chance to hold a referendum. "Delors II" regional development package is approved.

May 18, 1993: Danes vote "yes" to Maastricht.

June 21–22, 1993: Copenhagen European Council lays down general principles of entry for would-be members of the EU.

July 28–29, 1993: Final collapse of EMS after speculative attacks on the French franc.

November 1, 1993: Treaty on European Union becomes law.

December 15, 1993: Uruguay Round ends with major accord on liberalization of trade and agreement to establish the World Trade Organization (WTO).

March 30, 1994: Austria, Finland, Norway, and Sweden conclude negotiations for membership. Norway rejects the treaty of accession on November 28; the others ratify and join the EU on January 1, 1995. Membership is now fifteen.

June 9–12, 1994: Fourth elections to the European Parliament.

June 24–25, 1994: Corfu European Council dominated by wrangling over the successor to Jacques Delors. On July 15, Jacques Santer (Luxembourg) is chosen at a special European Council meeting in Brussels.

January 18, 1995: Santer is approved as ninth president of the European Commission by the European Parliament.

March 26, 1995: Passport-free zone between Germany, France, Belgium, Luxembourg, Netherlands, Spain, and Portugal.

July 26, 1995: Europol Convention signed. Begins work in October 1998.

December 15–16, 1995: Madrid European Council decides the name of the single currency: the Euro will enter into operation on January 1, 1999, and will be available in note form from January 1, 2002.

March 29, 1996: IGC on institutional reform begins.

December 13–14, 1996: Stability and Growth Pact agreed by Dublin European Council.

June 16–17, 1997: Amsterdam European Council concludes IGC on institutional reform with a set of amendments, but no great structural alterations, to the Treaty on European Union.

July 16, 1997: The Commission presents Agenda 2000, its opinion on the accession of the ten new democracies of Central and Eastern Europe.

October 2, 1997: Treaty of Amsterdam signed.

March 25, 1998: The Commission gives a passing grade to eleven states for membership of the Euro. Britain and Denmark opt out. European Council confirms decision on May 3.

March 30–31, 1998: Accession negotiations with Cyprus, Czech Republic, Estonia, Hungary, Poland, and Slovenia begin.

June 1, 1998: European Central Bank instituted.

September 27, 1998: Helmut Kohl's sixteen-year leadership of Germany is ended when Gerhard Schröder's SPD win control of the Bundestag.

January 1, 1999: Participant currencies in the Euro fix their exchange rates.

March 15, 1999: European Commission resigns following the publication of a report on fraud, wasteful management, and cronyism. Several commissioners, including Edith Cresson, a former prime minister of France, are criticized by name.

March 24–25, 1999: Extraordinary European Council in Berlin names Romano Prodi (Italy) as its choice to be the tenth president of the Commission. He is approved by the EP on May 5.

May 1, 1999: The Amsterdam Treaty comes into force.

June 3–5, 1999: Javier Solana (Spain) nominated as first EU high representative for foreign policy.

June 10–13, 1999: Fifth elections to the European Parliament. Turnout, at 49 percent, is a record low.

October 15–16, 1999: Tampere European Council in Finland is the first to give most of its time to justice and home affairs.

2000s

January 15, 2000: Accession negotiations begin with Bulgaria, Latvia, Lithuania, Malta, Romania, and Slovakia. IGC on institutional amendments to EU treaty begin in February.

May 12, 2000: Joschka Fischer, German foreign minister, argues in Berlin for a federal European state or else the possibility of a group of states pressing ahead to more advanced forms of integration.

September 28, 2000: Danes vote against joining Euro.

December 7–10, 2000: Nice European Council makes further cosmetic changes to the EU's institutional structures and welcomes a Charter of Fundamental Human Rights without incorporating it into the treaty.

February 26, 2001: Treaty of Nice signed in Brussels.

June 7, 2001: Irish voters reject the Treaty of Nice. They later approve it in a second referendum on October 19, 2002.

September 11, 2001: Destruction of World Trade Center. EU begins work on a draft of antiterrorism measures and proposes the introduction of a "European arrest warrant" to eliminate lengthy extradition procedures.

December 14–15, 2001: Laeken European Council institutes a "Convention," chaired by a former French president, Valéry Giscard d'Estaing, on the EU's institutional and political future.

January 1, 2002: Euro notes and coins begin to circulate throughout most of the Union.

February 28, 2002: The Convention begins work.

December 12–13, 2002: Copenhagen European Council recommends entry of Estonia, Latvia, Lithuania, Poland, Czech Republic, Slovakia, Hungary, Slovenia, Malta, and Cyprus in 2004.

April 16, 2003: Accession treaties signed with Cyprus, Czech Republic, Estonia, Hungary, Latvia, Lithuania, Malta, Poland, Slovakia, and Slovenia in Athens.

July 18, 2003: Convention on the Future of Europe presents the Draft Constitutional Treaty.

October 4, 2003: Constitutional Treaty IGC begins.

May 1, 2004: Cyprus, Czech Republic, Estonia, Hungary, Latvia, Lithuania, Malta, Poland, Slovakia, and Slovenia join the EU. The EU's membership is now twenty-five.

June 10–13, 2004: European Parliament elections are held.

June 18, 2004: IGC ends with an agreement on Constitutional Treaty.

July 22, 2004: The European Parliament approves the appointment of José Manuel Barroso (Portugal) as the Commission's new president.

October 29, 2004: The EU member states sign the treaty establishing a Constitution of Europe in Rome.

April 25, 2005: Accession treaties signed with Bulgaria and Romania in Luxembourg. Actual accessions are scheduled to take place in 2007.

May 29, 2005: French "no" to the Constitutional Treaty.

June 1, 2005: Dutch "nee" to the Constitutional Treaty. European Council begins a "period of reflection" on European Constitution.

October 3, 2005: Accession negotiations with Turkey and Croatia begin.

January 1, 2007: The accession of Bulgaria and Romania completes the fifth enlargement of the EU.

July 23, 2007: Member states' representatives meet in Brussels for an IGC on a draft reform treaty to amend the EU treaties.

December 13, 2007: The Treaty of Lisbon is signed at Mosteiro dos Jerónimos, in Lisbon.

December 21, 2007: The Schengen area is enlarged to include Estonia, the Czech Republic, Lithuania, Hungary, Latvia, Malta, Poland, Slovakia, and Slovenia.

January 1, 2008: Cyprus and Malta adopt the Euro.

June 12, 2008: Ireland rejects the Treaty of Lisbon in a referendum.

September 1, 2008: The EU leaders meet at a summit to discuss the fighting in Georgia and condemn Russia's "disproportionate reaction."

December 12, 2008: The European Council adopts the Economic Recovery Plan.

January 1, 2009: Slovakia adopts the Euro.

June 4–7, 2009: European Parliament elections are held.

July 23, 2009: Iceland applies for EU membership.

September 16, 2009: The European Parliament approves the nomination of José Manuel Barroso for a second five-year term as president of the European Commission.

October 3, 2009: Ireland approves the Lisbon Treaty in a second referendum.

November 20, 2009: The European Council appoints Herman Van Rompuy (Belgium) as the first permanent president of the EU Council.

Catherine Ashton (UK) becomes High Representative of the Union for Foreign Affairs and Security Policy.

December 1, 2009: The Lisbon Treaty comes into effect.

2010

February 9: The European Parliament approves the Barroso II Commission.

May 7: Together with the IMF, EU leaders approve emergency funding, worth up to €750 billion, to bail out members of the Eurozone unable to finance their national debt.

June 17: The European Council decides to open accession negotiations with Iceland. European Council adopts Europe 2020 strategy for "smart, sustainable and inclusive growth."

November 28: The EU agrees to support the Irish economy to help safeguard the stability of the Euro.

2011

January 1: Estonia adopts the Euro, the seventeenth state to do so.

March 25: "Euro Plus" pact adopted by European Council.

May 28: ECB chief Jean-Claude Trichet (France) calls for EU supervision of national finances.

August 16: Chancellor Angela Merkel (Germany) and President Nicolas Sarkozy (France) call for additional biannual meetings of the European Council to provide "true economic government" for the EU.

European Union

1

✠

Introduction

This book is a revised and updated edition of an earlier work, *Surpass-ing Realism: The Politics of European Integration since 1945*, which was published by Rowman & Littlefield in 2003. Like its predecessor, this book is a narrative history that inserts the story of European integration into the wider history of this period. Imperial decline and decolonization; the threat and then fall of communism; the impact of American foreign, fiscal, and monetary policy; and the democratization of the Mediter-ranean countries and the nations of central Europe are just some of the contemporaneous historical developments whose stories intersected with the history of European integration and have been woven into this book's fabric.

What is meant by European integration? We mean the historical process whereby European nation-states have been willing to transfer, or more usually pool, their sovereign powers in a collective enterprise. The European Union (EU), which today counts twenty-seven member states, nearly 500 million inhabitants, an economy larger than that of the United States (U.S.), and a complex institutional structure that includes a supranational central administration (the European Commission), an elected Parliament, a Court of Justice, and a Central Bank, is the out-come of this process.

When one thinks of the economic, political, and moral abyss into which Europe fell in the 1930s and 1940s, the emergence of such an or-ganization can seem like a miracle. Indeed, some partisans of European integration have the unfortunate habit of squashing criticism of the EU's current policies or institutions by evoking the specter of a return to

Europe's totalitarian past if the EU is criticized. Despite such overzeal-ousness, building the EU is an important achievement, of which three generations of European politicians have a right to be proud.

There have, of course, been many efforts to find a root cause for the development of supranational institutions in Europe. The desire to super-sede ruinous nationalism and ensure peace; the original member states' need to provide economic welfare and geopolitical security; the need of European states, prodded by domestic lobbies, to adapt to changes in the global economy; the influence of liberal economic theory on politi-cal elites; the intended and unintended consequences of experiments in supranationalism; and the lingering conviction of the original member states that they could better maximize their relative power (i.e., the extent to which they counted in the world) by uniting are six more or less plau-sible overarching hypotheses. Other hypotheses might be added, but not by this book, which has no pretensions to do anything more than tell a very complex story clearly and concisely.

The one broad observation that this book does advance about Euro-pean integration is that it could not have occurred had West European states not grasped after 1945 that they had to abandon the "autistic power politics" that had dominated their relations hitherto. In other words, West European states, finding themselves in a world dominated by the rival superpowers and longing to rebuild their devastated economies, realized that they could no longer pursue their own short-term interests with scant regard for the consequences of their actions on their neighbors.[1] In an age of nuclear weapons, moreover, war could no longer be regarded as an extension of foreign policy. The aura of moral approbation that has al-ways surrounded the process of European integration, in both the public rhetoric of statesmen and specialist texts in international relations theory, has ultimately derived from this renunciation of realpolitik. Turning their backs on power politics, however, did not mean that nation-states in Europe suddenly became paragons of altruism. They remained protec-tive of their economic, commercial, and political interests and invariably battled hard within the confines of the European Community to secure their goals. Toward the rest of the world, notably over agricultural trade, Europe has also regularly showed that it puts its own interests first, irre-spective of the consequences for its principal partners and allies.[2]

With hindsight, the most striking fact about the history of European integration is the tenacity with which the member states have defended their formal sovereign rights. The number of member states increased from the six original nations to nine in 1973, to ten in 1981, to twelve in 1986, to fifteen in 1995, to twenty-five in 2004, to the current twenty-seven in 2007, and the sheer number of policies decided at European level multiplied even more dramatically, but the essence of the Community's decision-making procedure has remained the same since the 1950s: major new policy departures are almost never made unless the member states have reached collective agreement. Only rarely does a "qualified majority" of member states compel their peers to accept a proposal against their will in the EU's key legislature, the Council of Ministers. This is especially true when the member states negotiate amendments and additions to the treaties that are the EU's de facto "constitution." Such changes must be agreed upon unanimously.

This is not to deny that Community policy possesses an important supranational dimension. It does. The European Commission, a committee of senior officials nominated by the member states, formulates, after consultation with the member states' permanent representatives at Brussels, all proposals for new legislation and also keeps nominal vigil over the member states' implementation of European law. Since the 1992 Treaty on European Union, moreover, the power of the elected European Parliament to ratify and shape the decisions reached by the member states has significantly increased. The sentences of the European Court of Justice have established the supremacy of European law over national law, and the Court provides for judicial review of an overzealous Commission's actions, or, more usually, of member states too indolent in implementing Community law.

Nevertheless, the institutions and procedures of the European Union could not work for a week in the absence of the will to cooperate of the member states, especially the largest ones—Germany and France above all, but also Britain, Italy, Spain, and, since 2004, Poland. This salient fact, which is obvious, but which it is not always fashionable to stress, means that the limit of European integration can be identified with some ease: it is that frontier beyond which lie the policy areas over which the member states of the Union are not prepared to relinquish sovereign power or, put more simply, do not wish the neighbors to intrude upon.

There are good reasons to believe that the process of European integration is bumping at this frontier. Public opinion in nations such as the Netherlands, Germany, and France—countries historically in favor of pooling sovereignty or delegating more powers to central European institutions—seems unwilling to countenance significant further steps in the direction of greater integration. Certainly, it is not favorable to rapid enlargement of the Union in the Balkans and Eastern Europe (Norway or Switzerland, by contrast, would be greeted with open arms).

Since the turn of the century, moreover, some of the EU's most high-profile projects—the Lisbon program to make the EU the most competitive knowledge-based economy in the world by 2010, the would-be EU Constitution rejected by French and Dutch voters in 2005, the idea of a common EU foreign policy, the Euro itself—have met with mixed success or even outright failure. All four projects were hailed as giant steps toward building Europe, but in every case, member states, or their peoples, pulled back from the implications of "more Europe." Member states, especially but not only in the Mediterranean, have been reluctant to introduce the liberalization of services foreseen by the Lisbon plan; the prospect of freer movement of peoples from Central to Western Europe was one of the main reasons why the Constitution failed, and the strict rules imposing fiscal discipline on members of the Euro-zone were evaded (in the case of Greece fraudulently) by some member states since they would have required too much fiscal pain to implement.

Supporters of European integration often say, echoing the words of the first president of the European Commission, the German diplomat Walter Hallstein, that European integration is like riding a bicycle: if you stop, you topple over. But it is also true, to develop the simile, that few cyclists have the muscles or the will to ascend the highest mountains and are quite content to spin along the foothills without breaking sweat. Since the introduction of the Euro, the EU has launched itself at some stiff climbs: in every case, several countries' legs have buckled and the pack of riders has had to freewheel back downhill.

In other words, the aura of success that has enveloped the process of European integration for most (though not all) of the period since the 1950s is dissipating. If it disappears, there will be repercussions for the way in which the story of European integration is told. The process of European integration is no more immune from revision than any other historical process.[3] The years since 2003 have revealed long-standing structural flaws in the so-called European construction and a straightforward narrative of success, which *Surpassing Realism* on the whole was, today looks difficult to justify. A history of the European Union, to be plausible, is one which, as well as capturing the authentic novelty of the process of integration and the indisputable idealism that it has engendered, also looks back from the EU's present and traces the causes of the current malaise—for malaise there is.

The book is structured chronologically. Chapter 2 deals with the five-year period between the war's end in May 1945 and May 1950, when French foreign minister Robert Schuman proposed establishing an economic community for coal and steel products. Why 1945? Why neglect the many intellectuals and statesmen who proselytized for European unity between the wars? The answer to this valid question is that ideas for European unity have been around for centuries, but the will to realize them emerged only after the catastrophe of the Great Depression, fascism, and world war. Had Europe not been laid so low, both morally and economically, by fascism, the ideal of European unification would not have seemed a practical venture to the primarily Christian Democrat leaders of Western Europe.

The third chapter deals with events from 1950 to 1958. These were the years in which the Coal and Steel Community (ECSC) treaty was negotiated by six West European states (Belgium, France, Italy, Luxembourg, the Netherlands, and West Germany), and the Community began its work; they were also years of great tension in the Cold War in which the United States tried and failed to involve these same countries in a defense community working in harmony with NATO. By March 1957, however, "The Six" had nevertheless negotiated a treaty to promote cooperation in the field of nuclear energy and research, and—crucially—to establish a European Economic Community (EEC), which was a customs union for industrial and agricultural products. The negotiation of the EEC was a hard-fought battle and many, notably the British government, underestimated the will of The Six to make the necessary compromises.

Between 1958 and 1969, the EEC was dominated by the personality and ambitions of the president of France, Charles de Gaulle. The great French leader was determined to transform the EEC into a vehicle for French foreign policy and was adamant, too, that the member states should remain the Community's key decision makers. This "intergovernmentalist" approach clashed with the more "federalist" conception of the treaty preferred by the European Commission and other enthusiasts for supranational government, and also led de Gaulle to block the entry into the Community of Great Britain, which he regarded, not entirely falsely, as an American stooge. Chapter 4 deals with the mark that de Gaulle left on the Community's development, which was deeper than many historians of European integration have been wont to acknowledge.

Chapter 5, "Weathering the Storm," is dedicated to the development of the Community in the 1970s. In retrospect, it is something of a miracle and a powerful testament to the sense of cohesion achieved by the European Community (EC) as the EEC began to be called from the late 1960s onward, that Western Europe did not revert to economic nationalism in the 1970s. Wildly swinging exchange rates, rampant inflation, low economic growth, and soaring oil prices were a recipe for protectionism. Instead, cooperation intensified. From December 1974, the EC's heads of state and government began to meet on a regular basis in what became known as the European Council. This quintessentially intergovernmental body swiftly became the EC's strategic decision-making body. The EC admitted Great Britain, Denmark, and Ireland to membership in 1973. The EC also strove to control the damaging effects of fluctuating exchange rates by instituting the European Monetary System (EMS) in 1979, and the member states agreed that the EC Assembly should be directly elected, making its pretensions to be an authentic parliament less risible. A string of sentences by the ECJ had, by the end of the 1970s, established that the Treaty of Rome conferred rights directly on the citizens of the member states and that the regulations and directives made by Community institutions enjoyed supremacy over conflicting national laws. These achievements were remarkable given the economic and political turbulence of the 1970s.

The turning point in the history of European integration nevertheless undoubtedly comes between 1984 and 1992. A citizen transported forward in time from 1963 would have found the EC of 1983 essentially similar to the EEC of twenty years before. Trade was much freer, but even trade in merchandise was still obstructed by a host of nontariff barriers. Physical barriers—passport and customs controls—still blocked the movement of citizens of EC member states from one country to another. The EC was primarily concerned with agriculture. In the early 1980s agriculture took up nearly 80 percent of the Community's budget, and the disagreements provoked by the costs of agricultural policy absorbed (it sometimes seemed) 99 percent of its energies.

Yet just ten years later, in 1993, our time traveller would have been astonished by the degree to which the Single European Act (SEA, 1986) and the Treaty on European Union (1992) were enabling people to move, buy, invest, and sell across the member states of what was now called the European Union. The traveller would, moreover, have been equally astonished at the policy responsibilities that had been transferred to the Community level and at the growing role played by the EU's supranational institutions.

Chapters 6 and 7 describe how this transfer of responsibilities was decided and how and why the member states decided to move forward so far, so fast to "complete the single market" and, in the teeth of fierce British opposition, to complement the single market with a plan for a single currency, an autonomous central bank, and enhanced powers for the directly elected European Parliament. The shock of the unification of Germany was the decisive impulse for this acceleration in the pace and scale of European integration. The French historian Frédéric Bozo has rightly dubbed the Treaty on European Union that emerged at Maastricht a "quantum leap" for the integration project as a whole.[4]

The final two chapters are concerned with the European Union as it has developed since Maastricht. In brief, it is a story of hopes dashed, or at least blunted. After Maastricht, and especially after the introduction of the Euro in 2002, the EU enjoyed an Indian summer of favorable attention from the international punditocracy. The EU was depicted as an emerging superpower that would dominate the twenty-first century; an organization whose postnational institutions, environmental friendliness, commitment to peace and human rights, and general aura of sanctity made it an exemplar for the rest of the world—and especially for the "Toxic Texan" and the neoconservatives lurking within the Washington beltway. The EU would match the United States as a force in the world by virtue of its superior way of life, such commentators asserted boldly.[5]

Such panegyrics to the EU's soft power attributes were taken seriously by some surprising people. The EU in the late 1990s and early 2000s generated a mood of progressivism that recalls, to those who have read both literatures, the enthusiasm of many liberal intellectuals and scholars across Europe for the League of Nations in the 1920s and early 1930s. In both cases, ideals ran into blunt facts. In the 1930s, it was the rise of fascism that exposed the League's weaknesses; in the 2000s, economic issues and recalcitrant voters exposed the shortcomings of what this book has dubbed "EUphoria."

Chapters 8 and 9 deal with both this mood of optimism and with the EU's dashed hopes since 2005. Chapter 8 surveys four of the policy areas in which the EU took major decisions between 1992 and 2005: monetary union, enlargement to Central and Southeast Europe, the negotiation and subsequent electoral defeat of the EU Constitution, and the EU's dissensions over issues of foreign policy, especially the 2003 invasion of Iraq, which split it into two angrily divided camps. Restricting the chapter to these four areas obviously leaves out much of what the EU did in those years, but these areas are nevertheless the ones in which the EU's actions have some claim to the immediate attention of historians.

Chapter 9 concludes the book by examining the mood of crisis that has taken hold in the EU since 2005 and attempts to draw conclusions for the Union's future. These conclusions are necessarily both tentative and limited in scope. The EU's future may be predictable by Madame Sosostris's wicked pack of cards, but lesser mortals without this precious theoretical tool should acknowledge that almost anything, including the disintegration of the EU (but also the transformation of the EU, or a large part of it, into a federal state), is possible over the next five to ten years.[6]

This summary of the book's contents has already given away one point of narrative technique: the book is not what the historian Herbert Butterfield notoriously identified as "Whig history."[7] The study of European integration has sometimes been the last redoubt of history of this kind. In much the same way that scholars once depicted English constitutional history as a seesaw battle between reformist "Whigs" (Liberals) and reactionary "Tories," in which British parliamentary democracy was at length perfected by Whig statesmen despite the low cunning and the self-interested opportunism of the Tories, so many scholars of European integration have portrayed European integration as a historical process whose forward march has been hampered by states and national leaders (de Gaulle and Margaret Thatcher—indeed British leaders more generally—have a starring role as villains) irrationally attached to the principles of national sovereignty, but which has issued nevertheless in a unique polity that is an example to the rest of the world.

The problem with seeing any history in terms of reactionaries versus progressives is that it "abridges"—to use Butterfield's term—the historical process. According to Butterfield, the historian's job is rather the "analysis of all the mediations by which the past was turned into our present." It is to "recapture the richness of the moments, the humanity of the men, the setting of the external circumstances, and the implications of events." When writing general history, which is of necessity a compressed summary of the whole, we have the right to expect, Butterfield adds, that the historian has not, by the selection and organization of the facts, "interpolated a theory . . . particularly one that would never be feasible if all the story were told in all its detail."[8]

I agree with Butterfield's injunctions on how to write general history. I have accordingly concentrated upon capturing much that was contingent about European integration and upon evoking the drama of its many crises. Europe might have taken any number of forks in the road: striving to convey how easily things might have turned out differently at every juncture was the book's major challenge (and the one, whatever the book's defects, which I am most confident of having met). In addition, as I hinted earlier, I have made a deliberate choice not to advance a broad theory to explain the dynamic of European integration but to concentrate upon clarifying the issues at stake at any given moment in the EU's emergence and explaining specific outcomes in such detail as was possible given the amount of space available.

All the same, it is important for a general text not to become too immersed in detail. Detail for the sake of detail is an occupational hazard for professional historians, and European integration history—if a gentle euphemism may be permitted—is not immune from this failing. Just as the EU itself can seem forbidding and opaque to its citizens, so can the EU's history. Specialists who focus on a particular policy or event and conduct intensive archive research with a view to finding out what really happened dominate the corpus of work on the EU's history. This book, by contrast, attempts to identify what European integration has amounted to. I would be the first person to advocate supplementing this book with more detailed studies on individual chapters in the EU's story.

This caveat aside, I hope this book's attempt to represent what the Polish-British historian Lewis Namier called "the nature of the thing" is regarded as plausible. Historiography is ultimately portraiture, not scientific explanation. If a subject is drawn too boldly, it easily becomes a caricature; if drawn too fussily, it loses the character of the sitter. If it is drawn too remorselessly—warts and all—it will likely be relegated to the attic and kept out of public view. This book is not always a flattering portrait, but it is a sincere attempt to capture a very complex character in an impartial way. And if the finished portrait has too many wrinkles for the taste of some, it will at least act as a corrective to the many extant portrayals of a thriving subject blooming with health.

2

✛

Enemies to Partners

The Politics of Cooperation in Western Europe 1945–1950

T he war ended in Europe in May 1945. It left the continent's infrastructure in pieces and its peoples divided by ideological conflict and
nationalist resentments. Yet a mere five years later, six West European
nations, including France and the newborn Federal Republic of Germany,
had begun negotiations to place production of their key coal and steel
industries under the control of a "High Authority" with supranational
decision-making powers. Many leading intellectuals and politicians were
by May 1950 even advocating the creation of a "United States of Europe"
along American lines.

Why were European leaders so susceptible after 1945 to the cause of
promoting European unity? One reason was obvious to anyone who just
looked around. The continent had been devastated. Konrad Adenauer, a
conservative opponent of the Nazis who became chancellor of Germany
in 1949, gave a bleak description in his memoirs of what Cologne looked
like when he returned as mayor in April 1945:

> The task confronting me . . . was a huge and extraordinarily difficult one.
> The extent of the damage suffered by the city in air raids and from the other
> effects of war was enormous . . . more than half the houses and public build-
> ings were totally destroyed . . . only 300 houses had escaped unscathed. . . .
> There was no gas, no water, no electric current, and no means of transport.
> The bridges across the Rhine had been destroyed. There were mountains of
> rubble in the streets. Everywhere there were gigantic areas of debris from
> bombed and shelled buildings. With its razed churches, many of them a
> thousand years old, its bombed-out cathedral . . . Cologne was a ghost city.[1]

Yet Adenauer nevertheless believed that in 1945 "the unification of Europe seemed far more feasible now than in the 1920s. The idea of international cooperation must succeed."[2] This conviction was especially pronounced among Christian Democrats, who emerged after 1945 in France, Italy, West Germany, and several other states as the principal political party. For leaders like Adenauer, or the Italian Alcide De Gasperi, or the Frenchman Robert Schuman, there was no choice but to supersede national rivalries if Europe was ever to return to civilized life again.

In the meantime, however, it was touch and go whether Europe could survive at all. Key economic hubs such as Rotterdam and Hamburg had been blitzed into the preindustrial age. The 1945 harvest was little more than half as large as the last prewar harvest in 1938, and getting it to market was a task of surpassing difficulty since roads, bridges, and canals were blocked with the detritus of war. During the winter of 1945 to 1946, Europe's urban areas were reduced to near-famine conditions.[3] Across Western Europe (in Central and Eastern Europe, conditions were even worse), millions of people survived on one thousand calories a day, or little more. Only Britain and the Nordic countries provided their citizens with the 2,400 to 2,800 calories consumed by the average sedentary man in a normal day—and as Europe rebuilt, few people were living sedentary lives.[4]

At first, the problem of reconstruction meant digging enough coal, growing enough crops, and rebuilding war-blasted infrastructure. It soon became clear, however, that reconstruction necessitated a common market that would guarantee economies of scale and would signal a rejection of the economic nationalism of the 1930s. The economic success of the United States provided a compelling argument for the benefits of a large domestic market. Robert Marjolin, a French economist who became secretary-general of the Organization for European Economic Cooperation (OEEC) in 1948 and was a French representative on the first Commission of the European Economic Community (EEC) in 1958, wrote in his memoirs that in the immediate postwar years, "America hypnotized us, her material success was our ideal; we had almost no other aim than to bridge the gap between European industry and American industry."[5]

U.S. leaders were themselves anxious to promote economic and political integration in Western Europe as the Cold War became a fact of international life in 1946 to 1947. Without postwar American aid, Europe would have had to find the resources to defend itself against the USSR and to rebuild its industrial base entirely from the pockets of its citizens. For this reason, no Western European government could ignore the Americans' vision for the postwar organization of the continent. This vision was postnational in scope. As Diane Kunz has remarked: "European unity continued to appeal to Americans for several reasons, not the least of which was the conviction, tapping deep into the American psyche, that Europe's best course was to imitate the United States as closely as possible."[6]

The reintegration of Germany, even its western rump, was a further factor tending toward integration. The question of how to treat Germany after 1945 was a major cause of the tensions between the United States and the USSR, and it also dominated French foreign policy. France wanted the wartime allies to allow her to substitute Germany as the economic motor of Western Europe. Only when it became clear to Paris that Washington was determined to build up West Germany as a bulwark against the Soviet Union did France encourage the rehabilitation of a democratic Germany in the context of wider European integration. Without Franco-German rapprochement, no step toward European unity was imaginable, and it is for this reason that the French statesmen most responsible for seeking better relations with Germany, Robert Schuman and Jean Monnet, are regarded as the founding fathers of the European Community.

By the early 1950s, in fact, France had established itself as the key political actor in Western Europe. This position ought, logically, to have belonged to Britain. An additional factor structuring the development of Western Europe after 1945 was Britain's political ambivalence to European projects. Britain enjoyed moral authority as the nation that had led the fight against fascism and which had elected in July 1945 a government committed to far-reaching socialist reforms, but it was suspicious of schemes for European integration. Britain's politicians, Labour and Conservative alike, saw Britain as a world power, not a regional leader, and dismissed all plans that required Britain to concede any portion of its national sovereignty to common European institutions.

This condescending attitude had important consequences. Had London been more open to European integration in the late 1940s, Britain might have led a commonwealth of European nations in the 1950s, instead of failing expensively to maintain itself as a world power. Britain's economy would also have received a salutary dose of competition from cheaper competitors that might have prevented its slide in the 1950s and 1960s into relative decline. Britain's leaders had good reasons for their choices, but it is hard to acquit them of having been shortsighted in their European policy.

THE AMERICAN VISION FOR EUROPE: THE MARSHALL PLAN AND THE OEEC

It was not until the end of 1947 that East–West relations broke down and the Cold War began. Yet throughout the first two years of peace, ideological competition with communism was an ever-present factor in the calculations of European statesmen. The fact that European (and American) leaders had constantly to remember in the postwar years was that for millions of Western Europeans, Soviet Russia was a model of economic modernization, not ruthless dictatorship, and in the event of economic failure in Western Europe, the USSR might exert an attraction for millions more.

After a decade and a half of economic depression and war, Europe's voters wanted above all else work, welfare, and homes: the only question was which political system would provide these basic social needs. In the first postwar elections, the voters of Western Europe mostly opted for social democracy (in Britain, most dramatically) or Christian democracy (in Italy, after the ideologically charged April 1948 elections; in Germany, where Konrad Adenauer emerged as democratic Germany's most important statesman; in Belgium, where the Christelijke Volspartij/Parti Social Chrétien took 42 percent of the vote in 1946). In France, the Christian Democratic Mouvement Républicain Populaire (MRP) was an important component of the coalition of centrist parties that formed governments in the immediate postwar years, and the MRP controlled the foreign ministry between 1945 and 1953.[7] Yet the Communists emerged as the second party in France in the 1946 elections and, in April 1948, as the dominant party of the left in Italy, too. In both countries, they commanded key government ministries until May 1947, when they were maneuvered from power.[8] Tightly disciplined, with a huge mass membership and a powerful role in key trade unions, Communist parties were potent political rivals to the parties of the democratic mainstream.

The provision of a higher standard of living was therefore a political imperative. But raising living standards required vast capital spending, the money for which could be raised in any or all of three ways: by diverting as much as possible of national income to investment rather than consumption; by stimulating exports to bring in money from abroad; and by receiving foreign aid or investment. France, most famously, took the first course. The French five-year postwar modernization plan sought to direct capital investment into selected industries such as coal mining, steel, cement, and transport.[9] Large segments of the French economy were taken into public ownership as the planners channeled national income toward the development of heavy industry. To a greater or lesser extent, the Netherlands, the Scandinavian countries, and Italy followed suit.[10]

Britain was constrained by circumstances to take a different approach. The Attlee government's spending plans for health and housing, in addition to its substantial military commitments in Germany and the Far East, reduced its investment in industry. In February 1947, the Labour government had to tell Washington that it no longer had the resources to maintain troops in Greece (where withdrawal might have led to a Communist seizure of power). This decision, which provoked the "Truman Doctrine," a commitment to defend democracy from totalitarian subversion, also persuaded U.S. policymakers that Europe was on the verge of economic collapse. The United States had given Britain hefty postwar loans (over $4 billion) in the expectation that Britain would soon be able to act as the chief economic motor for Western Europe. This illusion was now dispelled.

By the spring of 1947, Washington feared that Western Europe's stuttering recovery was providing fertile soil for Communist flowers to bloom. A memorandum from Will Clayton, undersecretary of economic affairs in the State Department, at the end of May 1947 stated baldly that Europe was "slowly starving" and on the brink of disintegration and social revolution.[11] Clayton's memorandum was seemingly decisive in persuading U.S. Secretary of State George Marshall to make his famous Harvard speech on June 5, 1947, promising that America would fund a "program to put Europe on its feet economically." For only a healthy economy, Marshall sustained, could "permit the emergence of political and social conditions in which free institutions can exist."

The British economic historian Alan Milward has convincingly shown that opinions like Clayton's were alarmist. In Milward's view, the European economies' dash for industrial growth had merely precipitated an entirely predictable balance-of-payments crisis with the United States. Europe did not have enough dollars to maintain the high levels of investment in industrialization and social services that her peoples were demanding.

Unable to buy capital goods and manufactures from Germany, the traditional producer of engineering products, and with Britain slow to fill the gap that Germany had left, the European nations had turned to the United States for the ships, airplanes, tractors, machinery, industrial plant, and raw materials they needed to maintain their ambitious investment programs. Unfortunately, they had little to sell the Americans in return. Most European exports to the United States were luxury goods. It takes a lot of olive oil, perfume, or whisky to buy a ship or an airplane. France's deficit on merchandise trade with the United States increased from $649 million in 1946 to $956 million in 1947. The Netherlands' deficit more than doubled from $187 million to $431 million. Italy's more than tripled from $112 million in 1946 to $350 million in 1947. Britain, like France, had a $1 billion shortfall in 1947.[12] Western Europe as a whole accumulated a deficit of $7 billion in the first two peacetime years.

European governments, in short, were living far beyond their means: "In both Britain and France policy seems to have gone ahead fatalistically based upon an unspoken, perhaps unutterable assumption that the

United States would . . . have to lend or give the necessary sums of hard currency to make their postwar economic policies feasible."[13]

Marshall insisted in his Harvard address that the Europeans themselves should draw up a plan for economic recovery. Britain and France responded by calling a conference of foreign ministers in Paris in July 1947. Sixteen North and West European states attended. The Soviet Union, to the relief of everybody but the satellite nations of Eastern Europe, which were compelled to follow the Soviet example, distanced herself from the Anglo-French initiative. The conference established the so-called CEEC (Committee on European Economic Cooperation) and entrusted it with the task of estimating the size of Europe's economic needs for the period from 1948 to 1952, by when, the Americans insisted, Europe should be self-sufficient. Despite intense American pressure for something other than sixteen "shopping lists," the CEEC's initial report in August 1947 requested for $29 billion in American aid by 1952. Michael Hogan, in his magisterial history of the Marshall Plan, states that this figure "stunned the Europeans as much as the Americans."[14]

Secretary of State Marshall had previously been reluctant to impose conditions upon the would-be recipients of aid. However, the giant CEEC request precipitated matters. American policymakers urged the governments of Western Europe to devote more resources to reviving production, even if this meant cutting back on cherished social programs; to liberalize trade by slashing tariffs and ending exchange controls; to move to a customs union as quickly as possible; and to establish a "continuing European organization" with sovereign powers over the direction of the European reconstruction effort.[15]

The European reaction to these prescriptions was unenthusiastic. British Foreign Secretary Ernest Bevin lamented the "unfortunate impression of high-handedness" left by the Americans' approach.[16] The Europeans refused to abandon social programs or jeopardize employment levels. Led by Britain and France, they also refused to accept that the proposed supranational economic organization should have sovereign powers. On the other hand, they were obliged to accept a reduced aid package of just over $19 billion. Hogan comments: "Europeans . . . sought a recovery program that would limit the scope of collective action, meet their separate requirements and preserve the greatest degree of national self-sufficiency and autonomy. Americans, on the other hand, wanted to refashion Western Europe in the image of the United States."[17]

The Americans could not simply impose their social and political model, however. The dollar, mighty though it was, was much less influential than the Red Army. Just as negotiations in the CEEC reached their climax in September 1947, Britain defaulted on the terms of the

$4 billion loan extended to her in 1946 by suspending convertibility of the pound sterling into dollars. France and Italy also wobbled on the verge of bankruptcy in the autumn of 1947. The fragility of Europe's economies, paradoxically, was a political strength: it heightened the conviction in Washington that U.S. aid was necessary to stave off the threat of left-wing electoral success.

In April 1948, by large majorities in both chambers, Congress authorized the first $5 billion of recovery spending for Europe. It also established the Economic Cooperation Agency (ECA), with branches in every Western European country, to oversee the distribution of Marshall aid. The first director of the ECA was a prominent businessman strongly sympathetic to the idea of European political unity, Paul Hoffman; day-to-day relations with the Europeans were entrusted to a presidential special representative based in Paris. W. Averell Harriman was appointed to this post.

In parallel to the ECA, the European countries set up the OEEC, the "continuing organization" that would plan the division of Marshall Plan aid among its member states as well as act as the forum for intra-European negotiations to liberalize trade. Essentially a ministerial council of sovereign states, the OEEC was served by a secretariat of officials, planners, and economists and by an executive committee of civil servants from the nation-states that formulated the Council's final decisions. The work of the secretariat was placed in the hands of a youthful French economist, Robert Marjolin; the executive committee was chaired by a British official, Sir Edmund Hall-Patch. Marjolin has written, "France and Britain called the tune in the OEEC."[18] Nevertheless, every country (even small nations such as Iceland and Luxembourg) had a right of veto in the Council, and no country was obliged to implement Council decisions against its will.

Despite the intergovernmental character of the OEEC, and thus the difficulty of securing unified action, Hoffman's opening address to the Council on July 25, 1948, called upon the nation-states of Europe to devise a "master plan of action" for the rebirth of European economic and political life. He called for the OEEC nations to "face up to readjustments to satisfy the requirements of a new world." In particular, nations should avoid thinking along "the old separatist lines." Hoffman urged his listeners to think in terms of "the economic capacity and the economic strength of Europe as a whole."[19] What the Americans had in mind for Europe has been dubbed since "the politics of productivity"—the creation of a free trade area administered (at least in the first instance) by supranational planning bodies that would make boosting production their fundamental goal and lead to political unity in friendship with the United States.[20]

A "HARMONIOUS SOCIETY":
THE VISION OF THE EUROPEAN MOVEMENT

The primary impulse for supranational government in Europe has always been the pressing need to stop members of the European family from slaughtering one other. Before, during, and after World War I, liberal thinkers in Britain argued that peace in Europe required the creation of an international organization that would enable the nations of the world to resolve their disputes peacefully and provide a forum for planning their economic development. Similar ideas were influential in the United States, where they provided the intellectual ballast for President Woodrow Wilson's scheme for a League of Nations, and in Italy, where the country's leading economist, the Turin professor Luigi Einaudi, was a proponent of greater political and economic integration.[21] In the 1920s, such developments as the Locarno Pact (1925), whereby the nations of Western Europe promised to resolve their differences through the League of Nations and to respect the borders established by the 1919 Versailles Treaty, were hailed as a major step toward greater European unity by its chief architects, Aristide Briand and Gustav Stresemann, the foreign ministers of France and Germany. Briand, in 1931, even advanced the idea of a European Confederation of nation-states, although by that date many of the high hopes of the Locarno period had already evaporated.[22]

The subsequent failure of the League of Nations in the 1930s strengthened the search for internationalist solutions to the eternal problems posed by national sovereignty. The doctrine that wars broke out because of the insecurity engendered by the nature of the state system and by the economic conflicts intrinsic to international capitalism continued to hold sway. A "New League" of socialist states, the radical journalist H. N. Brailsford contended in 1936, dedicated to raising the standards of living of its citizens by economic planning on a Soviet scale but via British standards of parliamentary government, would set in motion a dynamic that would entice the peoples of Italy and Germany back to the path of democracy. The institutions Brailsford envisaged for the "League"—a parliament of delegates drawn from national assemblies and a technocratic central directorate—bore a remarkable resemblance to those subsequently proposed by Jean Monnet for the European Coal and Steel Community.[23]

When war broke out, drafting schemes for European integration became every British intellectual's favorite pastime.[24] Some of these schemes today seem far-fetched. But political thinkers like Harold J. Laski, G. D. H. Cole, and E. H. Carr were making a serious point that would have to be addressed once the war was over. This point was that dictatorship had thriven in the context of the Depression and the concomitant economic nationalism of the 1930s. If Europe was to avoid a return to fascism in the future, such thinkers reasoned, its countries should make boosting production and the welfare of their citizens the centerpiece of their postwar economic strategy. Cooperation in this endeavor, via pan-European institutions, would greatly increase the chances of success.[25] At a time when the Allies, including the United States, were contemplating the "pastoralization" of defeated Germany (resolving the problem of postwar security by depriving Germany of its heavy industrial capacity), this understanding of how Europe would have to be rebuilt was very farsighted.[26]

Similar arguments were being made by the Federal Union movement, an organization started by mostly British academics, thinkers, and churchmen at the beginning of 1939. British intellectuals associated with Federal Union produced pamphlets that enjoyed great intellectual influence and, by the standards of political texts, a very large sale. W. B. Curry's *The Case for Federal Union* (1939) sold 100,000 copies, while Barbara Wootton's *Socialism and Federalism* (1941) launched the powerful idea that socialism could only be carried out on a pan-European scale.[27]

The debate in Britain is important because it influenced a generation of continental intellectuals active in the resistance against fascism. Altiero Spinelli and Ernesto Rossi, the imprisoned antifascist authors of the *Manifesto di Ventotene* (1941), one of the canonical documents of the European integration movement, took the debate in Britain as the starting point for their powerful appeal to the socialist movements of Europe to make the struggle for revolution across Europe and the establishment of a socialist federation of Europe the cardinal purpose of their political action. In the *Manifesto*, a socialist federation was represented as being a moral and historical imperative that even justified the use of dictatorial methods against advocates of a return to the traditional nation states of the pretotalitarian period. After the fall of Benito Mussolini in July 1943, one of the leading components of the partisan movement in Italy, the Partito d'Azione (Action Party), made European unity the core of its political program. Action Party intellectuals were prominent in the Movimento federalista europeo (MFE), which was founded in August 1943 and contributed to the movement's journal, *L'unità europea*. Italian federalists successfully managed to diffuse their ideas. A pamphlet, *L'Europe de demain*, was smuggled into the rest of occupied Europe in 1944, and a conference of federalists, with delegations from resistance movements across Europe, was held by the MFE in Geneva in May 1944.[28]

By 1946, every country in Western Europe could boast a federalist movement of greater or lesser size—some countries, notably France, had more than one. In April 1947, these bodies federated themselves into the Union Européenne des fédéralistes (UEF). The new association, which had a collective membership of some 150,000 people, declared its purpose was "to work for the creation of a European federation which shall be a constitutive element of a world federation."[29] As this declaration suggests, the UEF was not without its utopian aspects. Its main goal, however, was one that inspired intellectuals all over the continent in the early months of the Cold War—the creation of a European "Third Force" that could act as a bridge between Soviet communism and the West European tradition of democratic socialism.[30] Intellectuals argued that a European federation offered the opportunity of building a progressive socialism that would assuage Soviet fears of capitalist aggression and would, over time, lead to totalitarian and federalist forms of socialism, converging into a single democratic model.[31]

Some left-wing intellectuals—the British novelist and political writer George Orwell and Altiero Spinelli being the most famous examples— were less optimistic about relations between a United States of Europe, even one that followed socialist precepts, and Soviet totalitarianism. Spinelli, breaking decisively with the two mass parties of the Italian Left (the Communists and the Socialists), was arguing by 1947 that the Soviet Union regarded Western Europe as a "vital space" that it was hoping to "exploit" economically to relieve the Soviet people's misery.[32] The United States, by contrast, while it possessed "imperialist temptations and ambitions," also possessed a "sincere desire" to see Europe emerge as an independent liberal state. Insofar as there was a risk of American hegemony, Spinelli contended on many occasions it came from the shortsighted nationalism of Europe's leaders, who refused to admit that the day of independent nation-states was over.[33]

Federalist ideas might have remained isolated in an intellectual ghetto had it not been for the intervention of Winston Churchill, the internationally renowned British war leader whose Conservative Party had been defeated in the general elections of July 1945. At the University of Zurich on September 19, 1946, Churchill argued that the countries of Western Europe should "re-create the European family, or as much of it as we can . . . we must build a kind of United States of Europe." According to Churchill, the rock upon which this new federation should be founded was not Britain—"We British have our Commonwealth of Nations . . . why should there not be a European group which could give a sense of enlarged patriotism and common citizenship to the distracted peoples of this turbulent and mighty continent"—but a "partnership between France and Germany." This was the only way, Churchill thought, that France could "recover the moral leadership of Europe."[34]

Subsequently, in May 1947, Churchill became the founder of the United Europe Movement (UEM).[35] Its three thousand members included numerous MPs, especially Conservatives, and many prominent academics, journalists, and clergymen. Relations with the UEF were not easy at first. Whereas the UEF saw European federalism as an opportunity to reassure the Soviets, the UEM regarded it as a way of reinforcing Europe's ability to resist the encroachments of the USSR. Nevertheless, together with several other influential movements such as the French Council for a United

Europe, the European Parliamentary Union, the Economic League for European Cooperation, and the Christian Democrat Nouvelles Équipes Internationales, the two principal associations agreed in December 1947 to form a coordinating committee that would call a "Congress of Europe" at The Hague (Netherlands).[36]

The Congress, which was attended by over 1,200 dignitaries—including seven hundred parliamentary deputies—from every free country in Europe, took place in May 1948 in the aftermath of the Soviet takeover of Czechoslovakia in February 1948 and the ideologically charged elections in Italy in April. In addition to Churchill, the Christian Democrat prime ministers of Italy (Alcide De Gasperi) and France (Georges Bidault) took part, as did such statesmen as Leon Blum, the Socialist prewar premier of the Popular Front government in France; Paul Reynaud, the last premier of France before the Nazi victory; and Paul Van Zeeland, a Princeton-educated economist who was a former premier of Belgium.

The Congress, after an initial address from Churchill, divided into three committees—the Political Committee, chaired by another former French prime minister, Paul Ramadier; the Economic and Social Committee, chaired by Van Zeeland; and the Cultural Committee, chaired by an exiled Spanish liberal, Salvador de Madariaga. These committees drew up three broad resolutions. The Political Committee asserted that it was the "urgent duty" of the nations of Europe to create "an economic and political union" that would "assure security and social progress." It maintained that the "integration of Germany in a United or Federated Europe" was the only "solution to both the economic and political aspects of the German problem." Its main practical recommendation was the convening of a "European Assembly," composed of delegations from the national parliaments, which would act as a constituent assembly for the creation of a federal state in Western Europe. It also proposed that a Commission should draw up a Charter of Human Rights, adherence to which would be a precondition for membership in the European Federation.[37]

The Economic and Social Committee made pragmatic recommendations for economic policy. Trade restrictions of all kinds should be abolished "step by step"; coordinated action should be taken to "pave the way for the free convertibility of currencies"; a common program should be established to develop agriculture; Europe-wide planning was urged for the development of core industries such as coal and electricity generation; employment policy should be coordinated so as to produce full employment. The "mobility of labor" should be promoted to the "maximum possible extent." In addition, it advised that these measures should be only the prelude to an Economic Union in which capital could move freely, currencies were unified, budgetary and credit policy were centrally coordinated, a full customs union with a common tariff was established, and social legislation was coordinated to common standards.

The greater prosperity engendered by these economic measures was held to be an essential precondition for "the development of a harmonious society in Europe."[38]

The Cultural Committee recommended the creation of a "European Cultural Centre," whose task would be to promote cultural exchanges, promote awareness of European unity, encourage the federation of the continent's universities, and facilitate scientific research into "the condition of twentieth-century man." A "European Institute for Childhood and Youth Questions" was also to be established: one of its tasks, since partially realized in the Erasmus and Socrates programs of the European Union, would have been to "encourage exchanges between the young people of all classes in Europe, by providing finance and accommodation for their study, apprenticeship and travel." Like the Political Committee, the Cultural Committee recommended that a Charter of Human Rights should be drawn up and a European Supreme Court, with supranational jurisdiction, should be established to ensure the Charter's implementation.[39]

The Congress had two main institutional outcomes. In October 1948, a unified "European Movement" was formally inaugurated in the City Hall of Brussels. The new movement's "Presidents of Honor" were Churchill, Blum, De Gasperi, and the prime minister of Belgium, Paul-Henri Spaak. In August 1948, detailed projects for unification were presented to the Permanent Commission of the Western Union.[40]

COOPERATION BETWEEN GOVERNMENTS: THE BRITISH VISION

The Treaty on Western Union (the Brussels Pact) had been signed in Brussels in March 1948 between the governments of Britain, France, Belgium, Luxembourg, and the Netherlands. The treaty, as well as being a military alliance, bound its participants to develop and harmonize the economic recovery of Europe and to raise the standards of living of their populations. The Permanent Commission was supposed to be the forum for such mutual cooperation between governments in the economic field.

The Treaty on Western Union was a far cry from the much greater degree of integration wished for by the European Movement, but its provisions, like the equally intergovernmental structure of the OEEC, accurately reflected how far Britain was prepared to move down the road toward supranational cooperation in the spring of 1948.

British hostility to a federal state in Europe might seem a foregone conclusion. Interestingly, however, Foreign Secretary Bevin himself had been, for much of 1947, intrigued by the notion of a European Customs

Union and was seemingly prepared to acquiesce to the loss of sovereignty such an institution implied. The problem with a customs union was that while greater economic integration in Western Europe would lead to a rationalization of British heavy industry and expand trade and strengthen the continent politically, it would also lead to damaging short-run competition for the iron and steel industry and would end Britain's advantageous trade relationship with the countries of the Commonwealth. A customs union seemed likely, moreover, to lead to a fully fledged economic union governed by supranational institutions. The notion of conferring sovereignty over the economy to an external body was even harder for a socialist government to accept than it would have been for the Conservatives. Labour ministers were in no mood to subordinate their socialist vision for British society to the economic priorities of foreigners.

In December 1947, however, the disastrous outcome of the London meeting of the Council of Foreign Ministers (CFM) placed European cooperation firmly on the agenda. The CFM was the forum through which the United States, the USSR, and Great Britain, together with France and China, should have agreed on a postwar settlement. Its meetings, however, became steadily more acrimonious as mutual perceptions of ideological enmity grew. The London meeting, which was preceded by vituperative Soviet propaganda against the Americans' plans to "enslave" Europe, left free Europe's leaders in no doubt that, as Bevin expressed the situation in a paper entitled "The First Aim of British Foreign Policy" to the Cabinet in January 1948, "We shall be hard put to it to stem further encroachments of the Soviet tide" in the absence of "some form of union in Western Europe, whether of a formal or informal character."[41]

The discussion in the Cabinet of this paper led to Bevin's famous "Western Union" speech to the House of Commons on January 22, 1948, which included the telling remark, "Great Britain cannot stand outside Europe and regard her problems as quite separate from those of her European neighbors." In Europe, this comment, not unreasonably, was taken as a sign that Britain was preparing to throw her prestige behind the concept of European unity. Certainly, it was the decisive impulse that led to the signature of the Brussels Pact.[42]

Britain regarded her promotion of the Western Union as a major development in her foreign policy, but, in fact, her attitude to European integration satisfied neither the Americans nor her European neighbors. British behavior was "a great source of irritation" to the Americans between 1947 and 1951, but there was a limit to how tough America could get with Britain.[43] Britain had taken the lead in the spring of 1948, even before the signature of the Treaty on Western Union, to formalize military cooperation between the United States and Western Europe in a military alliance. In early 1949, these negotiations, which led to the signature in April 1949 of the North Atlantic Treaty, were at a critical stage. American policymakers were afraid that Soviet tanks would roll across the North European plain. Their only ally of any substance was Britain. Article Five of the Treaty committed its member states to regarding an armed attack against any one of them as an attack against them all. In practice, this meant that Britain and the United States were giving a guarantee that they would risk a Third World conflict to defend the Rhine.

With their fellow Europeans, the British could be more obdurate. Britain tried to restrain all attempts to implement the resolutions agreed at the Congress of Europe. The British were reluctant to go further than the creation of a council of European governments without any form of parliamentary supervision. In January 1949, however, Bevin agreed to a compromise by which decision-making power was to be reserved for a Committee of Ministers (as it was named), but an assembly with consultative powers was to be created in tandem. Five nations who had not signed the Brussels Pact—Italy, Ireland, Denmark, Norway, and Sweden—were invited to join the new "Council of Europe."[44] This invitation, together with Italy's parallel signature of the North Atlantic Treaty, marked the end of Italy's postwar isolation. Italy's foreign minister, Count Carlo Sforza, immediately pressed the other nations to adopt a more "federal" conception of the Council of Europe. Italy even recommended that the new body be called the "European Union." Bevin swatted aside Sforza's bumptious diplomacy without difficulty.[45] The Treaty of St. James Palace (London, May 15, 1949) instituting the Council of Europe was rigorously intergovernmental in scope.

The Council's purpose was to constitute a "closer unity" between the member states through joint action in economic, social, scientific, judicial, and administrative fields. Its main institutions, the Committee of Ministers and the Assembly, were both consultative in character. The Committee of Ministers, in which each country possessed one vote and in which votes required unanimity, was a forum for member states to debate measures proposed by the member states or the assembly, not an executive committee whose decisions were binding upon governments. The Committee had the power only to recommend measures to the governments of the member states. The Consultative Assembly, meanwhile, was able to propose items for debate by the Ministerial committee if they were passed by a two-thirds majority, but it had no legislative power whatever. Paul-Henri Spaak, who was elected first president of the Assembly on August 10, 1949, later said of the Ministerial committee in particular, "Of all the international bodies I have known, I have never found any more timorous or more ineffectual."[46]

Yet the Assembly opened its first session in Strasbourg amid scenes of great enthusiasm for European unity. The Assembly seized the initiative by proposing a "supranational political organization" for Western Europe; Britain and the Nordic states vetoed this idea in the Committee.

Another initiative launched by the European Movement in July 1949 had more success. This was the submission of a draft European Convention on Human Rights to the Council. After just over a year's debate and redrafting, the Convention for the Protection of Human Rights and Fundamental Freedoms was signed in Rome on November 4, 1950, by thirteen European states or territories: Belgium, Denmark, France, Iceland, Ireland, Italy, Luxembourg, the Netherlands, Norway, the Saarland, Turkey, the United Kingdom (which, however, specifically refused to ratify two clauses of the treaty that were particularly invasive of national sovereignty), and West Germany. Greece and Sweden signed a few weeks later.

The Charter guaranteed the traditional liberal freedoms of person, property, and conscience: it did not include specific guarantees for social rights such as the right to work. To evaluate and adjudicate if breaches of the Convention had occurred, the document created two institutions: the Commission and the Court of Human Rights. The Commission's task was to screen would-be cases according to strict criteria; the Court then judged on the merits of the case. Article 53 of the Convention committed the signatories to the Convention to "abide by the decision of the Court," although no concrete sanctions could be applied in the event of noncompliance. European states have generally tried very hard not to be cited before the Court in the postwar years. The Court's sentences have carried an explicit moral condemnation that democracies have wished to avoid.[47]

Nevertheless, by early 1950, it was evident that hopes of leaping to a federal state in a single bound had fallen at the first fence. There would be no constitutional convention to found a "European Union." To this extent, the British, with the help of the Scandinavians and the tacit acquiescence of other important states such as France, had imposed their vision of ad hoc cooperation between governments.

Plans for greater European unity were, however, soon to find a new outlet in the functional integration of economic sectors such as coal and steel. Important intellectuals such as E. H. Carr, from 1941 to 1946 the deputy editor of *The Times*, had been advocating this approach since 1942. Yet it was not merely, or even mainly, enthusiasm for greater European unity that motivated this new approach. The growing economic strength and political independence of West Germany was the decisive factor that drove the nations of Western Europe to delegate the management of heavy industry to pan-European institutions.

THE GERMAN QUESTION AND THE SCHUMAN PLAN

No question troubled postwar statesmen more than how Germany should be governed. In 1945, Germany was divided into four zones by the Allied powers. Britain occupied the northwest part of the country, a zone that included the large cities of Cologne and Hamburg and the Ruhr industrial belt. The United States administered the center-south, including Frankfurt-am-Main and Munich. The French occupied the Black Forest region and the Rhineland, as well as the Saarland, while the Russians occupied Prussia and Saxony. Austria was similarly divided between the powers until the 1955 State Treaty. From the point of view of administration, Berlin (and Vienna) was a miniature replica of the country as a whole.

At the Potsdam conference (July–August 1945), the "big three" powers reached broad agreement on how to treat defeated Germany pending a final treaty of peace. They decided that Germany should be subjected to "denazification, demilitarization, democratization, decentralization and decartelization."[48] Germany was to be regarded as a single economic entity, governed by an Allied Control Commission in which each of the three powers, plus France, would possess a veto. The Allies would establish democratically elected governments in the zones they controlled. The thorny issue of reparations—the Russians had already looted eastern Germany of much of its industrial plant and machinery by August 1945—was resolved by allowing each power to take industrial equipment from the zone it occupied. The Soviet Union would receive additional reparations from the heavily industrialized British zone and from the zone controlled by the Americans. In return, the USSR promised to divert foodstuffs from its zone to feed the large cities in the West.

This broad deal never resulted in a final peace treaty. Neither Britain and the United States nor the USSR was able to keep its word. The Soviet Union obstructed democratic competition in its zone and also reneged on its promised shipments of agricultural produce to the West. Britain and the United States responded by suspending shipments of industrial plant to the USSR in the spring of 1946. So long as the shipments continued, the western zones of Germany, particularly the densely populated industrial area controlled by the British, could not resume production at a high enough level to buy food to feed themselves and had to rely on the charity of the occupying authorities. This was costly enough for the United States, but for war-enfeebled Britain it was an impossible burden. In the winter of 1946 to 1947, British rations were cut to feed the people of Germany—hardly a popular move so soon after the end of the war. In January 1947, Britain and the United States merged their zones to create "Bizonia," which was organized as a self-governing federal state under the supervision of the occupying authorities. To the Soviet

Union it must have looked as if the "capitalist" powers were rebuilding Germany against her.

These fears provided the background to the London Council of Foreign Ministers in November–December 1947 mentioned above. After the breakdown of the London talks, the Cold War began in earnest. The Communist coup in Czechoslovakia in February 1948, the signature of the Brussels Pact, and the ideologically charged April 1948 elections in Italy followed in swift succession. In this context, consolidating the West's hold on western Germany became a strategic imperative. The United States extended Marshall Plan aid to Germany and called for the formation of a West German government (an idea that was greeted with great caution by the Germans themselves, who feared—rightly—that it would lead to the dismemberment of their nation). In June 1948, currency unification of the three western zones took place, and the Deutsche Mark (DM) was introduced. The USSR responded by cutting off road, rail, and river transport to Berlin. Only the miraculous Anglo-American airlift kept two million Berliners alive over the following winter. By the time the Soviet blockade was called off in May 1949, some 277,000 flights had been made and some 2.4 million tons of cargo delivered.[49]

France acquiesced in Anglo-American policy toward Germany from June 1948 onward largely because she had no choice. America had decided that European recovery and security required a strong Germany. France's agreement nevertheless marked a drastic U-turn in her foreign policy. After Potsdam, successive French governments had argued for the independence of the Rhineland from the rest of Germany (which would have provided France with a useful buffer against the revival of a strong Germany), for the internationalization of the Ruhr, and for the diversion of German coal and steel production to the French economy. But the events of the spring of 1948 made French statesmen aware that the main military danger to France was presented by the USSR, not Germany. France therefore needed U.S. aid, and that was not guaranteed unless France cooperated with the nascent West German political authorities. As the French statesman Georges Bidault, with a copious spoonful of rhetoric to help the medicine go down, told a disgruntled French National Assembly on June 11, 1948:

> We must build up Europe, and we must find some place in it for Germany. We will do all we can to create a united Europe, for this is the only way we can reconcile the countries of Europe. I wish to say that France would be wise to reconcile itself eventually with the presence of Germany in Europe and the free world, for no other reconciliation would be possible.[50]

The price for French acquiescence was a share in the direction of the Ruhr coalfield. Before 1939, a cartel of German producers had prevented

France from buying the coal she needed to fuel her own steel industry. After the collapse of the CFM in London, France battled hard in negotiations between the three Western Allies on the future of West Germany to ensure that "access to the coal, coke and steel of the Ruhr, which was previously subject to the exclusive control of Germany, [should] be in the future guaranteed without discrimination to the countries of Europe cooperating in the common good."[51]

To this end, France urged the establishment of an "International Authority" for the Ruhr. But this solution was unpopular three times over. The French were unsatisfied with the substantive powers accorded to the Authority to manage German heavy industry directly; the Americans doubted its necessity; and the Germans resented the restriction of their national sovereignty over industrial policy.[52] The Authority came into being in December 1948, but it was too weak to plan or control the growth of German industrial production. West German steel production, which had been restricted to less than three million metric tons in 1947 (France produced nearly six million), surged to over nine million tons in 1949 (the same as France). In 1950, Germany produced twelve million tons; France, less than nine million.[53] The *Wirtschaftswunder* (economic miracle) that would return Germany to its position as the economic powerhouse of Europe had begun.

Contemporaneously, West Germany achieved provisional nationhood. The Basic Law (Constitution) was adopted in May 1949, and the first West German elections took place in August of that year, resulting in a narrow victory for the Christian Democrats (CDU-CSU) who took 139 seats in the Bundestag to the 131 of the Social Democrats (SPD). The CDU formed a coalition government with the Liberals (FDP) and the nationalist "German Party."

The chancellor of the new German state was Adenauer, who had emerged as the leader of the CDU. A veteran politician from the Rhineland (he was almost seventy-four when he took office), Adenauer was convinced of the need for a Franco-German rapprochement: indeed, he had supported the creation of a customs union between the two countries as long ago as 1925. In two interviews with an American journalist in March 1950, Adenauer openly proposed a Franco-German economic union, with a legislature drawn from the two countries' parliaments and an executive "organ" responsible to the legislature. Europe, Adenauer argued, should remember how the 1834 Zollverein customs union had been the prelude to German unification.[54]

The Americans were also pressing for improved Franco-German relations. American efforts to assist Europe intensified in the wake of the Berlin crisis. Marshall Plan aid for April 1949 to June 1950 was over $5 billion; in September 1949, Congress approved the Military Assistance Act and doled out a further $1 billion in military aid to Europe. The quid pro quo for this largesse was the reintegration of Germany into Western Europe. In the fall of 1949, Secretary of State Dean Acheson urged France to normalize relations with West Germany by the spring of 1950.[55] Improving relations with Germany became an "obsession" for French foreign minister Robert Schuman, who, as a native of Lorraine, an area of France occupied by Germany after the Franco-Prussian War of 1870, had only become a French citizen in 1919 at the age of thirty-two.[56]

Schuman gave his name to an initiative at the beginning of May 1950 that has been called "one of the key moments of the century": the plan for the creation of a coal and steel community between France and Germany.[57] This plan was the brainchild of Jean Monnet, an administrator from a brandy-making family in the southern town of Cognac who had been an important figure in the League of Nations and possessed a long list of influential American friends as a result of his wartime service in Washington. Monnet became an influential adviser to President Roosevelt and consequently knew everybody worth knowing in the Truman administration. In 1946, Monnet, as the quintessential planner, was placed in charge of the French five-year modernization and reconstruction effort. The idea of the coal and steel community bore his trademark preference for the technocratic and supranational resolution of complex political issues. Monnet approached Schuman in April 1950 proposing that the French and German coal and steel industries should be subjected to a supranational "High Authority" with sovereign powers to plan and develop economic activity. Schuman agreed, and Monnet and his advisers drew up the text of the declaration, announcing the plan in conditions of great secrecy.[58] Adenauer and the German government were told only on the eve of the plan's announcement through a personal letter from Schuman to the German chancellor, hand-delivered by a senior French foreign ministry official, that made explicit reference to Adenauer's March interviews.[59] The Americans were informed only on May 7, 1950, when Acheson visited Paris. The American secretary of state recorded his reactions in one of his memoirs:

> After a few words of greeting . . . Schuman began to expound what later became known as the "Schuman plan," so breath-taking a step towards the unification of Europe that at first I did not grasp it. . . . Schuman implored us to treat what he was about to tell us in the greatest of confidence, not to speak to any of our colleagues about it, not to send cables, or to have memoranda transcribed. For he had discussed the proposal only with the Premier (Bidault) and one or two members of the Cabinet. The next step would be to consult the whole Cabinet, and, if it approved, then to make some public statement . . . after that, France's neighbors would be approached.[60]

Secrecy was necessary. French politics was unsettled, and untimely disclosure might have set off a damaging political crisis. Even more important, Schuman and Monnet were determined that the British would not sabotage the supranational dimension of the scheme. Only countries that acknowledged the principle of supranational government would be allowed to participate in the detailed negotiations. Their insistence on this point soothed the Americans' disappointment at being excluded from the plan's formulation. John Foster Dulles, a committed supporter of European unity who would become secretary of state during the presidency of Dwight D. Eisenhower, described Schuman's initiative as "brilliantly creative"; President Truman himself lauded the plan as an "act of constructive statesmanship."[61] This was despite the fact that many American industrialists were worried that the putative community might be a protectionist steel cartel under another name.

On May 9, 1950, Schuman made his famous declaration. In addition to its historic proposal to "place the whole of Franco-German coal and steel production . . . under a common 'High Authority' within the framework of an organization open to participation by the other countries of Europe," Schuman's speech implied a breach with the federalist approach. In his view, Europe should advance step-by-step through economic integration: "Europe will not be made all at once, or according to a single, general plan. It will be built through concrete achievements, which first create a de facto solidarity." A "wider and deeper community" would emerge once economies were more fully integrated: action on the "limited but decisive point" of coal and steel production was the best starting point since "the pooling of coal and steel production" would ensure that "any war between France and Germany" was "not merely unthinkable, but materially impossible."[62]

Beneath the high moral tone of the declaration, French national interest was alive and well. Among other things, the declaration insisted that "the task" of the High Authority would be to secure "the supply of coal and steel on identical terms to the French and German markets, as well as the markets of the other member countries." Monnet argued that the Americans were intent on building up Germany as an ally in the Cold War. Sooner or later German industrial competition would present France with the grim choice of protecting its steel industry or accepting German superiority in this field. Monnet favored making a deal with West Germany while she was still weak and using the proposed High Authority to ensure that there was a balanced industrial relationship between the two countries.[63]

According to Adenauer's most comprehensive biographer, the chancellor was initially suspicious of French motives. Monnet was the personification of international cooperation against Germany in the two wars. Might not the Schuman Plan be a subtle plot to retard German economic growth, rather than a mutually beneficial opportunity?[64] Once the two men had met each other on May 23, suspicion disappeared. In their talks, Adenauer approved Monnet's insistence that nations should adhere to the plan on the basis of what Schuman had called "a leap in the dark" during questioning on May 9. That is to say, to have a place at the negotiating table, all would-be members of the proposed community would have to accept the role of the High Authority in advance.

It was precisely this point, as Monnet had foreseen, that was the sticking point for the British. The Schuman Plan placed before Britain a tricky dilemma. In 1950, Britain was still the largest producer of both coal and steel in Western Europe. If Britain stayed out of the Community, her coal and steel would inevitably be excluded from the markets of Western Europe. On the other hand, if she entered the Community, her coal and steel industries would feel the full brunt of low-wage competition from the continent. The mere fact of her joining, moreover, would signal to the world that Britain was a diminished force; that she was no longer an imperial power, but merely first among equals in Western Europe.

As so often, purely contingent factors played a role. Bevin and the treasury minister, Sir Stafford Cripps—the key ministers, and the two most considerable figures in the government—were both critically ill (both died within a few months of the Schuman announcement), but Clement Attlee, the premier, was reluctant to substitute them. Negotiations with Monnet were thus carried on throughout May 1950 by senior civil servants, at least one of whom, Roger Makins, has since been anachronistically described as a "rabid Euro-sceptic."[65] Monnet himself found the British officials to be viscerally anti-European. In his memoirs, he noted that the British seemed to have no confidence in the ability of the continental countries to resist communism. Certainly, they were not prepared to make the "leap in the dark" required of them.[66]

Two leading civil servants, Sir Edward Bridges (permanent secretary to the Treasury) and Sir William Strang (permanent secretary at the Foreign Office) eventually reported to Attlee that agreement was impossible on Monnet's terms, and on June 3, 1950, the Cabinet, presided over by the deputy prime minister, Herbert Morrison, concurred. Morrison's own contribution to the debate over the Schuman Plan was notoriously to say: "It's no good. We can't do it. The Durham miners would never wear it."[67]

In the subsequent Commons debate on June 26–27, 1950, Attlee stated that the British government could not accept the principle that the most vital economic forces of the country should be transferred to "an irresponsible body that is appointed by no-one and responsible to no-one."[68] Few MPs dissented from the government's view that staying out was the wisest course of action. A rare exception was a Conservative making his maiden speech—Edward Heath, the man who would eventually take Britain into the European Economic Community (EEC) in 1973.

Attlee's comment was in fact a reasonable objection to the Schuman Plan as it was originally formulated. If, however, Britain had yielded on the issue of the High Authority, she might have inserted safeguards into the treaty, as well as obtaining a measure of protection for her coal and steel industries. This is exactly what the Dutch and Italian governments did, and Britain, who would have been offering to open her massive coal and steel industry to competition, would have been in a far stronger position to get its own way than either country.

Edmund Dell, a former Labour minister turned historian, regards Britain's refusal to join the negotiations as a disastrous misjudgment—"the British abdication of leadership in Europe." In Dell's opinion, negotiations with Monnet were handled astonishingly badly: "Unprepared officials led unprepared ministers."[69] In his view—and after reading his closely researched account, it is difficult to disagree—the top civil servants convinced themselves that the plan was unacceptable both on grounds of national principle and of feasibility, and they briefed an exhausted government to that effect. Yet even without the historian's privileged vantage point, it ought to have been obvious that there were powerful forces tending to the scheme's success. The plan removed the main cause of friction between Germany and France, had won the immediate and enthusiastic support of the Americans, enlarged the domestic market for the Benelux countries, and was Germany and Italy's return ticket to the society of civilized nations.

But the problem was not just abstract issues of sovereignty, or the plan's likelihood of economic success. Britain's politicians, as Morrison's remark hints, had to take public opinion into account. *The Daily Express*, then Britain's most influential mass circulation newspaper, argued on May 11, 1950, that the Schuman Plan was "a deliberate and concerted attempt to oblige us to accept the United States of Europe"—rhetoric that has a familiar ring to anybody who has lived through the heart searching provoked in Britain by the Treaty on European Union.

But even without a hostile press baying against any concession to the Europeans, it seems unlikely that a Labour government would have surrendered even partial control over the recently nationalized coal and steel industries to a High Authority nominated by largely Christian Democratic governments. Labour believed it was in politics to abolish capitalism, not to make capitalism work better. With what *The Economist* called the Labour Party's "almost phenomenal gift for bad timing"—if bad timing it was—the Labour Party published, in mid-June 1950, its official statement of policy on the European question, a pamphlet called *European Unity*.[70] This document unambiguously asserted that Britain would only cooperate in schemes of European unification with countries that had adopted the key socialist policies of public ownership, full employment, and economic planning. Socialism came first in the order of values; Europe a poor second. Besides, the pamphlet added:

> In every respect except distance we in Britain are closer to our kinsmen in Australia and New Zealand on the far side of the world than we are to Europe. We are closer in language and origins, in social habits and institutions, in political outlook and economic interest. The economies of the Commonwealth countries are complementary to that of Britain to a degree which those of Western Europe could never equal.[71]

Robert Marjolin—who had an excellent vantage point—insisted in his memoirs that the Europeans would have gone "much further in the direction wanted by the Americans had it not been for the stubborn resistance of the British to the idea of committing themselves irrevocably to the Continent."[72] At the very least, a customs union would have been formed. Given the wide agreement on economic issues reached at the Congress of Europe and the enthusiasm generated by the Schuman Plan, this assessment seems plausible. But though Britain had the power to obstruct the path of European integration, she was too much in debt to the United States to insist on having a free hand in Western Europe. Had Britain emerged from the war with a booming economy and her overseas investments intact, Britain would have taken the leadership of Europe by default. The other European countries would have looked to her for loans and export markets. But by 1950 Britain was not strong enough to overcome the profound belief of both the European political class and the Washington élite that—in Schuman's words—*le morcellement de l'Europe est devenu un absurde anachronisme.*[73]

This weakness became crucial in May 1950. The Schuman Plan exposed the limitations of British power. Unlike the Council of Europe, it was a concrete initiative that made sound economic and political sense. The national interests of the United States, France, and West Germany, and the supranationalist instincts of their chief policymakers coincided. The Labour Party's determination not to compromise its socialist program, the ingrained mentalities of upper officialdom, deep fear of economic competition, and a misplaced sense of grandeur prevented Britain from seeing this critical fact. As Diane Kunz argues, Britain's leaders "persisted in seeing Britain lodged within three interlocking circles: with the Continent, with the Empire and Commonwealth, and with the United States. To join a European union would be to favor one relationship to the detriment of others."[74]

The result of this understanding of Britain's place in the world was to ensure that British national influence declined. The experienced American policymaker George W. Ball, a close friend and collaborator of Jean Monnet, was surely right when he said, "Had Britain embraced the original Schuman proposal, it could have dominated the evolution not merely of the Coal and Steel Community, but also of the European Economic Community."[75] In the following two decades, France and West Germany, putting aside their secular rivalry, emerged as Britain's equals, or even superiors. Britain, after her refusal to make the "leap in the dark," carped from the sidelines and was forced to watch as her increasingly cooperative neighbors superseded her in economic performance and matched her in international prestige.

3

✝

Ever Closer Union

From the Schuman Plan to the Economic Community 1950–1958

The Schuman Plan led to the signature of the European Coal and Steel Community Treaty in April 1951 by a core group of six nations: France, West Germany, Belgium, Italy, Luxembourg, and the Netherlands all adhered to Schuman's invitation. The ECSC was ratified by the parliaments of the six nations in the spring of 1952 and began operations in August 1952. It seemed as if, to quote Jean Monnet's famous address to the first ECSC assembly, "the United States of Europe have begun."[1]

Euphoria, however, was short lived. Following the outbreak of war in Korea in June 1950, the United States pushed hard for West Germany's rearmament and integration into the defense effort of the Western democracies. France fought, shy of such rapid normalization of the West German state. In October 1950, the French prime minister, René Pleven, prompted by Monnet, proposed the establishment of a European Defense Community (EDC) as a way of resolving the problem. This suggestion was less fortunate than the Schuman Plan. The EDC treaty was signed by the six member states of the ECSC in Paris in May 1952. Unlike the ECSC treaty, however, the EDC became the object of a political clash in the country that had originally sponsored it. In August 1954, to the despair of European federalists, a coalition of Gaullists and Communists blocked the EDC's ratification in the French National Assembly.

The differing fates of the ECSC and the EDC underline an important point. The nations of Western Europe were cautious about the amount of national sovereignty that they were prepared to pool in European institutions. The ECSC treaty was ratified because, compared to the original

Schuman–Monnet plan, a considerable degree of supervision by national governments was built into the treaty. The EDC treaty, by contrast, represented a remarkable voluntary surrender of sovereignty by the six countries. The treaty passed effective command over national armed forces to the NATO commander in Europe, envisaged a common authority in charge of planning military procurement policy, and anticipated the birth of a European Political Community (EPC): in effect, a federal government for the six nations. The EDC was a bridge too far—and not only for the French. What its failure taught European governments was that integration was easier in the economic sphere than in those areas, such as defense and foreign affairs, that went to the heart of national sovereignty, and that even within the economic sphere, national governments were not going to leave supranational institutions to operate unsupervised.

The treaty establishing the European Economic Community (EEC), signed in Rome in March 1957, reflected this lesson. The EEC treaty built upon the liberalization of trade launched at the beginning of the 1950s by the creation, under the auspices of the OEEC, of the European Payments Union (EPU), by setting up a customs union. The economic area thus created was to be governed, for the most part, through institutionally enshrined interstate negotiations. Nevertheless, the EEC treaty was broadcast as a new step in a process that would lead to "ever closer union" and eventually to "political union," a phrase whose meaning would remain hazy, or at any rate contested, for the next fifty years.

Statesmen doubtless believed their own rhetoric. Academic theorists might have been expected to keep a cooler head. Instead, the "functionalist" school of international relations, whose leading figure was the American scholar Ernst Haas, discerned an irreversible trend toward greater political integration among the countries of Western Europe. As Europe's institutions began to influence daily economic life across The Six, Haas argued, a process of "spillover" would occur: Community institutions would substitute national institutions as the point of reference for political action, and the nation-states would—it is tempting to say—wither away.

This teleological interpretation of European integration has influenced scholarly interpretations of European integration ever since, although, with hindsight, it is as much a 1950s period piece as automobiles with fins or the hula hoop. The member states had no intention of giving up their prerogatives—but were genuinely minded to cooperate with one another, for very good, mostly economic, reasons. In the 1950s, taking full advantage of the benign American attitude to their endeavors, they tentatively experimented with different forms of cooperation, some of which found favor, others of which did not.

THE COAL AND STEEL COMMUNITY

The treaty instituting the ECSC was signed in Paris on April 18, 1951, after an acrimonious negotiation. Even after the treaty was signed, the wrangling continued. The decision over where to base the High Authority was particularly fierce. Liège, Strasbourg, Saarbrücken, and Turin were all mooted. Luxembourg, 80 percent of whose economic production was derived from its coal and steel industries, was the compromise eventually arrived at in a July 1951 meeting of The Six's foreign ministers. It was during this meeting that Konrad Adenauer was overheard by journalists to mutter "poor Europe, poor Europe" as he stalked out of the talks for a reviving cup of coffee.[2] The pattern for all future negotiations involving a significant reduction of national prerogatives had been set.

The preamble to the ECSC treaty expressed lofty sentiments in striking contrast to the jockeying for national advantage that characterized negotiations both before and after the ratification of the treaty. The "High Contracting Parties" recognized that "Europe can be built only through practical achievements which will first of all create real solidarity and through the establishment of common bases for economic development" and hence resolved to "substitute for age-old rivalries the merging of their essential interests." Their intention was to create "the basis for a broader and deeper community among peoples long divided by bloody conflicts and to lay the foundations for institutions which will give a direction to a destiny henceforth shared."

The economic philosophy of the new organization recalled the proposals made by the economic subcommittee of the Congress of Europe. The ECSC was intended to ensure the twin goals of economic liberalism and social solidarity. On the one hand, the ECSC was an effort to prevent protectionist cartels in the coal and steel industries; on the other hand, it was a planning body charged with softening the social costs of modernizing the industries.

The treaty defined the ECSC's tasks, among other things, as ensuring a steady supply of coal and steel to the market, guaranteeing equality of access to the sources of production for all consumers, monitoring prices, providing a climate that would encourage companies to expand and improve production, and promoting "improved working conditions and an improved standard of living for the workers in each of the industries for which it is responsible." More generally, it was to "promote the orderly expansion and modernization of production, and the improvement in quality, with no protection against competing industries that is not justified by improper action on their part or in their favor." Article 4 of the treaty specifically banned import and export duties, quantitative restrictions, discriminatory deals, state subsidies, and market-sharing deals between companies.

The most distinctive institution of the new Community was the High Authority. Consisting of nine members, it was "responsible for initiating and framing most of the measures needed to administer the common market."[3] Eight of these nine members were nominated by governments (France and Germany choosing two, the other four countries nominating one); the ninth member was selected by the eight nominees. All members served six-year terms and elected a president and two vice presidents from among their own number. The first president, unsurprisingly, was Jean Monnet; his two deputies were the German Christian Democrat Franz Etzel and the Belgian Albert Coppé, who became one of Monnet's most steadfast supporters.[4] The treaty bound the nine members of the Authority to "exercise their functions in complete independence, in the general interest of the Community. In the fulfillment of their duties, they shall neither solicit nor accept instructions from any government or any organization. They will abstain from all conduct incompatible with the supranational character of their functions."

Monnet's favorite way of disparaging an institution was to compare it to the OEEC, which he regarded as a byword for futility.[5] The High Authority that emerged from the ECSC treaty was, by contrast with the OEEC Secretariat, a body with far-reaching independent powers. It could impose fines upon firms that defied its decisions or recommendations; it could facilitate investment by floating loans on the capital markets and then relending the money for investment purposes; it could soften the social costs of industrial modernization by financing vocational retraining, resettlement programs, and "tide over" allowances to workers; during times of "manifest crisis," it was free to set production quotas in order to prop up demand. In addition to these wide-ranging powers, the High Authority held a broad antitrust brief and was charged with protecting the common market from anticompetitive mergers, pricing policies, or wage reductions. A Consultative Committee of fifty leading producers, trade unionists, and consumers dispensed advice to the High Authority whenever it asked for it.

There were three principal checks on the High Authority's powers. The Authority's actions and decisions were second-guessed in many areas by the Council of Ministers, which was given the task of harmonizing "the action of the High Authority and that of the governments, which are responsible for the general economic policies of their countries." The Council's approval was necessary for a broad range of policy actions by the High Authority, especially labor issues, transport, and the sale of coal and steel products. The Council was given a limited power to set the High Authority's agenda and exercised a tight control over its budget. The Council, at which the national governments were usually represented by their economics or industry ministers, thus became a powerful de facto legislature able to block (though not amend) the High Authority's initiatives.

The second political check on the High Authority was the Assembly, which consisted of seventy-eight "representatives of the peoples of the States" drawn from national parliaments. The Assembly's powers were "supervisory." It had no legislative function. The Assembly was able to demand oral or written replies from members of the High Authority and possessed the power, under article 24 of the treaty, to censure the High Authority's annual report. In the event of such a motion of censure being passed by a two-thirds majority of votes cast, the High Authority was obliged to resign en bloc. The Assembly was also able to intervene in the budget process. The budget was funded by a levy not exceeding 1 percent on the "average value" of production within the Community, although only under Monnet's presidency (1952–1955) did it come close to raising and spending such a portion of the industries' income.

The third checking institution was the Court of Justice. The Court was originally composed of seven judges appointed by the governments of the member states for a period of six years. The treaty was explicit in stating that the judges should be people "whose independence is beyond doubt." The Court's powers were very precisely detailed in article 33 of the treaty:

> The Court shall have jurisdiction in actions brought by a Member State or by the Council to have decisions or recommendations of the High Authority declared void on grounds of lack of legal competence, major violations of procedure, violations of this Treaty or of any rule of law relating to its application, or abuse of power.

The Court, in other words, was to be a watchdog over the High Authority. Within the Community, its word was law. But its power was unidirectional: firms, citizens, and the High Authority itself could not have recourse to the Court to have national law or administrative directives declared invalid. Despite this caveat, the Court was soon busy and settled several important complaints against the High Authority within the first few years of the ECSC's life.[6]

The novelty of the ECSC treaty was indisputable. Instead of national governments making decisions in the short-term interest of their domestic industries, with little or no thought for the knock-on effects over their borders, the six member states had delegated executive powers to an independent authority. The states were merely reserving to themselves a circumscribed right of veto over the High Authority's decisions and the right to ask for judicial review of the Authority's actions. The egoism of nation-states was to be substituted, in the economic sphere at least, with enlightened planning in a specially created institutional forum. It was this commitment to internationalist principle, not the actual experience of the Community in its first few years of existence, which guaranteed the ECSC the laudatory reception it enjoyed in the halls of academe, especially in the United States.[7]

The truth is more prosaic. If one looks at the activities of the ECSC between February 1953 (when the common market in coal was instituted) and February 1958 (the end of the five-year "transitional period" during which all market-deforming practices were supposed to be eliminated), one sees that the Community played a useful, though limited, role in enabling the six member states to wrestle with the social and economic problems presented by two industries of great importance. The High Authority, which Monnet presided over until 1955 when he resigned and was substituted by the senior French politician René Mayer, propped up high-cost Belgian mining areas until 1958 by imposing an equalizing levy on the sales of cheaper German and Dutch coal (but still took the blame when the mines eventually had to be rationalized) and made notable attempts to inject a degree of competition into the market for coal purchasing, a politically sensitive question. It also successfully managed to obtain a generous loan from the American government and to float other loans on the American capital markets. These loans were then used for investment purposes, although the amount of ECSC investment was only a small fraction of private investment in the same period. Overall, steel production rose by over 40 percent during the transitional period, and trade in steel products and scrap also increased greatly. These last successes, however, owe more to the general rapid expansion of the European economy in these years than to the activities of the ECSC.

On the other hand, the market for coal and steel products was still anything but free in 1958. The High Authority rapidly discovered that it could not establish a common market by decree. Italy's domestic market in steel was still highly protected (Italy having won a five-year exemption in a protocol to the original treaty), and governments possessed an array of devices—currency devaluation, sales taxes, rebates, and subsidies of all kinds—that enabled them to advantage domestic producers.[8] Governments defended national champions tenaciously. The French national coal import agency, for instance, which restricted permits to a handful of dealers purchasing large quantities of coal and coke, was defended tooth and nail by the French government before the Court of Justice and in 1958 still had its powers intact. Overall, as the transitional period wore on, the High Authority became more and more reluctant to take initiatives without the prior approval of the Council of Ministers. The worsening situation of the coal industry, which was in decline as industry increasingly switched to oil, posed severe social problems that the High Authority had neither the financial resources nor the will to handle on its own.[9]

THE DEFENSE COMMUNITY

Like the ECSC, the European Defense Community (EDC) began life as a French improvisation to the rehabilitation of West Germany. The Bundesrepublik was founded in August 1949, but it remained under the tutelage of the so-called High Commission for Germany. This body's task was to keep vigil over the actions of the new German government. West Germany was denied the right to maintain armed forces, could not join NATO or the Brussels Pact, and was excluded from the United Nations. France was willing to remove Germany's pariah status in economic matters, but defense issues were altogether more sensitive for the French government, which had to be mindful of the French Communist Party's capacity to stir up mischief among public opinion on such a delicate subject. Nevertheless, if one assumed—and both French and American policymakers did—that the Soviet Union's intentions were aggressive, then West Germany's strategic importance was undeniable. The Soviet Union had superior ground forces and was in a position to strike across the north German plain at a moment's notice. This mattered less while the United States possessed a nuclear monopoly, but after the USSR exploded its first A-bomb in the summer of 1949, the West's front line effectively became the Rhine. U.S. policymakers decided that the only logical course of action was to rearm Germany as fast as possible.[10]

The United States was unwilling to press the French too hard to accept German rearmament until June 1950, when North Korea invaded its southern neighbor. The similarity of Korea to Germany—a country divided between communist and pro-American halves—could not but arouse alarm in the NATO countries. The invasion seemed like a prelude to an attack in Europe. In September 1950, at a meeting of the NATO foreign ministers, the United States committed itself to sending six fully equipped divisions to Europe, but asked its European allies, as a quid pro quo, to drop opposition to the militarization of West Germany. The French government, stuck, turned to Monnet for help. Monnet reverted to a tried (though not yet tested) formula: a European Community for defense matters similar to the one then under negotiation for coal and steel. Instead of Schuman, the spokesman for Monnet's ideas was, this time, the prime minister, René Pleven.

The Pleven Plan was announced on October 24, 1950. The plan envisaged the creation of a European Ministry of Defense responsible to an assembly and to a council of national defense ministers. The Ministry of

Defense was to organize defense administration (procurement, planning, links with the war industries), not strategic questions; all national governments except West Germany were to retain independent military forces. Germans would, however, have participated in so-called integrated units, though not at more than battalion strength.

American policymakers initially reacted with "consternation and despair" to the Pleven Plan. General Dwight D. Eisenhower said that it contained "every kind of obstacle, difficulty and fantastic notion that misguided humans could put into one package."[11] Naturally, as president, he later became one of the Defense Community's most passionate defenders, although, in fairness, the Pleven Plan had been redesigned by then.

The process of redesign began in Paris between January and July 1951 when delegations from all the ECSC countries except the Netherlands (which, along with Britain, Canada, Denmark, and Portugal, sent observers) agreed to create a European Authority for defense questions. Adenauer, however, insisted that West Germany should participate on the same basis as everybody else and that the Occupation Statute, which gave the High Commission its supervisory authority, should be scrapped. The Americans, in the meantime, had been convinced by Monnet's personal diplomacy to back the scheme. They insisted on explicit guarantees that the new Community would be subject to NATO at the operational level. Britain, which was governed by the Conservatives from the autumn of 1951, never thought of entering the Community.[12]

Between the autumn of 1951 and the spring of 1952, two separate negotiations to abolish the Occupation Statute and to create the Defense Community were conducted. At a meeting of NATO foreign ministers at Lisbon in January 1952, France finally dropped her opposition to the formation of a German army. It was agreed that the Community would place forty-three divisions of approximately thirteen thousand men each at NATO's disposal, of which Bonn would contribute twelve. Despite a determined effort to block the creation of a European army by the USSR, which proposed the neutralization of Germany in a diplomatic note on March 10, 1952, the treaty establishing the European Defense Community was signed by the six ECSC nations (the Netherlands had chosen to participate) in Paris on May 25, 1952; the Occupation Statute was ended, subject to the ratification of the EDC treaty, in Bonn the following day.

The EDC treaty represented the largest single cession of sovereignty made by the countries of Western Europe until the Treaty on European Union in 1992 (see chapter 7). Sovereignty over defense policy was surrendered on the one hand to the EDC, which was described as "supranational in character, comprising common institutions, common armed forces [article 15 specified that they would wear a common uniform] and a common budget," and on the other hand to the United States, which under the treaty would have taken over the day-to-day control of all armed forces within the European theater of war. Article 18 of the treaty stated that "the competent supreme commander responsible to NATO [who was perforce an American] shall . . . be empowered to satisfy that the European Defense Forces are organized, equipped, trained and prepared for their duties in a satisfactory manner." Member states could "recruit and maintain" independent of the EDC only armed forces that were destined for "a serious emergency affecting a non-European territory for which a member state assumes responsibilities of defense" or else were intended for the maintenance of "internal order" (i.e., French gendarmes or Italian carabinieri). Deployment outside Europe, the treaty stressed, must not affect any nation's contribution to the common defense effort.

The Defense Community was given basically the same institutional structure as the ECSC. A nine-member "Commissariat" was to act as the Community's executive and was to report to an Assembly and a Council of Ministers. There was, however, no figure corresponding to the president of the ECSC High Authority, since such an office would have been tantamount to creating a minister for European defense. The Council, too, was stronger than its ECSC equivalent (the Commissariat could not make decisions or make recommendations without its consent) and would inevitably have become the Community's dominant decision-making force. This institutional structure was, however, specifically stated to be "provisional" in character. Article 38 of the treaty, inserted at Italian insistence, asserted that the EDC was only a prelude to the establishment of "a subsequent federal or confederate structure."[13] In August 1952, the Assembly of the ECSC began drawing up a blueprint for a European Political Community (EPC) that would have coordinated the foreign policies of the member states and would have gradually absorbed the functions of the ECSC and the EDC.

By March 1953, the Assembly had completed this job. The EPC was to have consisted of a bicameral Parliament, an Executive Council, a Council of Ministers, and an empowered Court of Justice. The Parliament was to have been composed of a Chamber of Peoples (a directly elected assembly) and a Senate, which would have been drawn from the national parliaments. The Senate would have had the key power of nominating, in a secret ballot, the president of the Executive Council. The president would then have had a free hand to choose a cabinet of ministers. The Executive Council would then have become the federal government of the Community. All its major decisions, however, to be promulgated as law, would have had to be submitted and approved by a simple majority of the Chamber of Peoples and the Senate. The Court of Justice would have provided the nation-states with judicial review of the constitutionality of the EPC's laws.[14]

The boldness of this vision testifies to the mind-set of the European federalists at this time. In their view, the challenge of organizing a common defense for Europe and planning Europe's economy necessitated "a great 'contractualist' effort to overcome the gradual and sectoral character of European integration in order to arrive at the political union of Western Europe."[15] Even though the member states, in a series of meetings between their foreign ministers, immediately tinkered with the Assembly's proposals in order to strengthen the role of the member states, it remains true that the EPC was a bold expression of the federalist ideal.

Washington was delighted with these developments. Both Eisenhower, who became president in January 1953, and Secretary of State John Foster Dulles were committed supporters of European unification.[16] Dulles, moreover, was more willing than Acheson to prod the Europeans. Between 1949 and 1952, the United States had committed $12 billion in military and civil aid to Europe and had placed procurement contracts worth hundreds of millions more.[17] Dulles thought that it was time that the United States was paid back by concrete steps toward political unity.

The process of ratification met opposition in France. Getting the treaty through the National Assembly, where there was strong Gaullist (the supporters of the Free French war leader, Charles de Gaulle) and Communist opposition, and much anti-German feeling, required strong leadership. But this was in short supply. Between May 1952 and May 1954, when the army protecting France's colonial holdings in Indochina was humbled by the Vietnamese at the battle of Dien Bien Phu, France had three premiers (Antoine Pinay, René Mayer, and Joseph Laniel) who preferred to postpone ratification of the EDC treaty. French procrastination eventually caused the Eisenhower administration to lose patience. In December 1953, Dulles warned that the United States would have to undertake an "agonizing reappraisal" of its defense commitments if France did not pass the EDC treaty.[18]

Matters were complicated by the French defeat in Vietnam, which drove the pro-European Mouvement Républicain Populaire (MRP) from power in Paris and led to the austere figure of Pierre Mendès-France becoming prime minister. Aside from de Gaulle, Mendès-France was "the strongest political personality to have emerged in France since the war."[19] Mendès-France, moreover, was suspected in Washington of being a Cold War neutral. Dulles nevertheless was determined to put the case for immediate ratification of the EDC treaty as strongly as he could. On July 13, 1954, he visited Paris, where he bluntly told the French premier that the United States could always opt to defend the European periphery (Britain, Spain, Greece, Turkey) and leave France to face the USSR on her own. Mendès-France responded that the National Assembly would never pass the treaty in its then form. Rejection would be a propaganda disaster. It was better to amend the treaty in order to win over undecided members of the National Assembly.[20]

Mendès-France put forward a list of amendments to a meeting of the EDC powers in Brussels on August 19, 1954. Among other things, he proposed introducing an eight-year national veto over the Board of Commissioners' actions; asked that article 38 (authorizing the EPC) be deleted; and requested the right to withdraw from the treaty if Germany were reunited. These amendments infuriated France's partners, especially West Germany, where the government was under pressure to get results from its controversial policy of Westpolitik (as Adenauer's opening to the French since 1950 was known). The German foreign minister Walter Hallstein vented his feelings at the French move by saying, "Mendès has just presented us with the corpse of Europe."[21]

Mendès-France eventually allowed the unamended EDC treaty to be debated in the National Assembly at the end of August 1954. It was rejected by 319 votes to 264 after a debate whose chauvinism shocked free Europe. Opponents of the treaty used four main arguments. First, they feared that France would be swallowed up in a European superstate if they voted for the treaty. Edouard Herriot, who had been the patron of the French Council for a United Europe and had attended the Congress of Europe in 1948, proclaimed that "for us the European Community is the end of France . . . it is a question of the life and death of France." The treaty was held to be the work of a handful of technocrats (de Gaulle had darkly called Monnet "the inspirer" in a November 1953 press conference and had condemned the EDC treaty for good measure as "an artificial monster" and a "Frankenstein") who were working behind the scenes to reduce France's independence.[22] Second, French legislators worried that the proposed European army would rapidly be Germanized. Distrust of German motives was voiced openly. Third, many deputies thought that the treaty would cut France off from the French Union, as its empire in Africa was now renamed. Fourth, national pride was a major factor. Britain had not signed the EDC treaty, and the United States did not seem to expect her to. France should not lower herself to the level of what one deputy called "two defeated and three tiny countries" if Britain and America did not do the same.[23]

When the result was announced, the anti-*cédistes*—Communists, Gaullists, renegade Christian Democrats, and Socialists—burst into a spirited rendition of "La Marseilleise." In response, Dulles sourly commented, "It is a tragedy that in one country nationalism, abetted by communism, has asserted itself so as to endanger the whole of Europe."[24]

Jean Monnet wrote that the EDC "quarrel" had been a "harrowing split" (*déchirement*) for France.[25] But France, in a sense, was the least of the problems. Germany was left, four years on from the Pleven Plan, without statehood, the Americans were bereft of ideas, and European federalists had been reminded that rumors of the death of national sovereignty were greatly exaggerated.

Britain, in the person of Foreign Secretary Anthony Eden, stepped into the breach with a burst of intelligent diplomacy. The British solution was to extend the Brussels Pact to Germany and Italy.[26] On October 23, 1954, the Brussels powers agreed to terminate the occupation of Germany, to establish a new body called the Western European Union (WEU) with Italy and West Germany as members, to permit West Germany to join NATO, and to draw up a "European Statute" for the Saarland (which had been a bone of contention between France and West Germany throughout the EDC saga). Britain pledged it would maintain military forces in West Germany, while Germany pledged it would abstain from possessing certain categories of weapons (nuclear bombs, guided missiles, capital ships). An agency to monitor and audit national stocks of armaments was set up.

The treaty setting up the WEU retained the Brussels Pact's preamble, stating that one of its goals was "to encourage the progressive integration of Europe," but nobody was fooled. Monnet later described the new body as "a typical military alliance" and a "weak coordination structure" destined to "vegetate," but it would be more accurate to describe it as talking shop.[27] The WEU did draw up a plan to "Europeanize" the Saarland, but it was rejected by popular referendum on October 23, 1955, and the region eventually became part of West Germany.

The EDC debacle persuaded Monnet that he should devote his main activity to proselytizing for European unity among the political class of The Six. He left his post as president of the High Authority to do so. Other prointegration statesmen concluded that the best way of relaunching the European project was to work for trade liberalization.

FROM MESSINA TO ROME

Trade liberalization was a natural outlet for the energies of supporters of European integration. Unlike defense, trade was an area in which integration was already proceeding apace. This was largely due to the much-derided OEEC. In the immediate postwar years, most trade was conducted on the basis of bilateral deals between countries. As Robert Marjolin pointed out in his memoirs, such deals stifled economic growth. If France, for example, derestricted imports from Belgium and

Belgium's trade balance with France moved into surplus as a result, for trade as a whole to continue to grow, Belgium had to be able to use her credit with France to buy goods from other countries.[28] Europe's producers were in effect being limited to their own, relatively small, domestic markets or to such markets abroad as their national governments could negotiate for them. Bureaucrats, rather than the market, were determining the volume of trade.

Liberalizing the market was one of the OEEC's primary tasks, along with disbursing Marshall Plan aid. The biggest step in the pursuit of freer trade brokered by the OEEC was the establishment of the European Payments Union (EPU) in September 1950. The EPU is usually described as a "multilateral clearinghouse"—in effect, a kind of bank. To join, each OEEC member state contributed a fixed quota of capital, in its own currency, equal to 15 percent of its total visible and invisible trade with other OEEC countries. The United States also contributed $350 million to the EPU's capital. Each month, the central banks of the OEEC member states were required to keep a tally of their payments to other OEEC countries and the payments of others to them. At the end of every month, they communicated this information to the EPU's agent, the Swiss-based Bank of International Settlements (BIS), which summed up the aggregate balance of payments of each of its member states and made a deposit, partly in credits redeemable in any OEEC currency, partly in gold and dollars, to the states that had an overall surplus. It made a parallel deduction from the balance of the debtor states. The member states were entitled to an "overdraft" in credits of up to 20 percent of their quota at any one time; thereafter, the Union increasingly demanded payment in gold or dollars. No country was allowed to run up debits exceeding 60 percent of its original quota. Countries with persistent balance-of-payment deficits were therefore compelled either to follow domestic austerity to reduce demand for imports or to devalue their currency—in other words, to reduce their citizens' standard of living.[29]

The EPU thus introduced greater flexibility into European trade. Countries could run deficits with countries that had products or raw materials they needed to boost production. In the meantime, the OEEC presided over the gradual elimination of nontariff barriers such as quotas. By the mid-1950s, quotas on trade in manufactured goods had been almost abolished across the OEEC.

Equally important, mental barriers were dismantled. Countries with long protectionist traditions such as Italy—under fascism, outright autarky had been the regime's goal—were persuaded that a liberal trade policy would enable them to modernize more rapidly. The Italian foreign trade minister in the early 1950s, Ugo La Malfa, lowered or eliminated tariffs on imported goods from other OEEC countries, calculating, correctly, that this policy would make Italian industry more efficient and pay for itself by boosting exports. By the mid-1950s, Italy had won a reputation as one of the most determined liberalizers in the OEEC. This outcome owed much to La Malfa's drive, but much also to the environment created by the OEEC, which enabled La Malfa to make the case for freer trade to government colleagues whose mind-set was instinctively protectionist.[30] Cases such as that of Italy explains why Robert Marjolin insisted in his memoirs that without the trade liberalization set in motion by the activities of the OEEC, it was "unlikely that the Common Market would have seen the light of day."[31]

Nevertheless, although quotas on manufactured goods had been sharply reduced, tariffs on industrial goods remained very high, subsidies abounded, and agriculture was jealously protected. After the debacle of the EDC, further action to boost trade seemed the most promising avenue for cooperation within The Six. The initiative was taken by the Dutch, whose foreign minister, Jan Willem Beyen, was a convinced enthusiast of free markets. In 1954, Beyen began to press for the creation of a customs union between The Six in which all forms of trade discrimination were abolished.[32]

Beyen's proposals were flanked by new initiatives from Monnet and Paul-Henri Spaak to promote ECSC-like integration in the fields of transport and, above all, nuclear energy. On May 18, 1955, the Benelux countries submitted a memorandum incorporating both Beyen's and Monnet's ideas to the foreign ministers of The Six. The memorandum became the agenda for the foreign ministers' summit meeting at Messina in Sicily on June 1–2, 1955. At Messina, the foreign ministers rhetorically agreed that the time had come to make "a fresh advance towards the building of Europe." This advance would be achieved by progress in three fields: sectoral integration in transport and nuclear energy; "the establishment of a European market, free from all customs duties and all quantitative restrictions"; and the "progressive harmonization" of social policies.[33] A committee of governmental representatives, chaired by Paul-Henri Spaak, was charged with the "preparatory work" for these new moves toward integration, to which Britain was also invited to contribute.

To many in Europe, Messina seemed a damp squib. For all the rhetoric of a "European advance," the nations of The Six were plainly reserving their position until Spaak had produced concrete proposals. Monnet, however, was determined to keep the pressure on the national governments. To this end, he established an "Action Committee" composed of leading members of all of Europe's Social Democratic, Liberal, and Christian Democratic political parties, plus representatives of the organized workers.

This body held its inaugural meeting in October 1955. All its founding members pledged themselves to three broad promises. First, they would all ask their own parties or unions to affiliate to the Action Committee and would act as delegates to the Committee on behalf of their own organizations. Second, they stated that they would use their institutional position to ensure that the Messina conference's resolution became a "real step towards the United States of Europe." Third, they would put aside all "specious solutions" to Europe's problems that were based upon "mere cooperation between governments." The Committee's founders agreed that it was "indispensable for states to delegate certain of their powers to European federal institutions." The "close association" of Great Britain with such "achievements" was greatly to be desired.[34]

In practice, the Action Committee became a lobbyist for supranational supervision and the development of nuclear energy. Between its first meeting in October 1955 and the signature of the Treaties of Rome in March 1957, the Action Committee met twice (in January and September 1956). The final "resolutions" of both meetings stressed almost exclusively the potential of atomic energy for the future of Europe and relegated the construction of the common market almost to a footnote.

The Action Committee's reasons are easy enough to understand. Its members believed that Europe was facing an energy crunch in the near future. The "growing deficit in power supplies," they argued during their September 1956 meeting, was "the most grave and urgent problem for our countries" and exposed them to "dangerous threats to peace." Unlike the United States or the USSR, Western Europe was the "only great industrial region of the world that does not produce the power necessary to its development." The September 1956 resolution stated that fuel dependency of this order would result in "insecurity and permanent risks of conflict."[35] Monnet, advised by the French scientist Louis Armand, believed that investment in nuclear energy could fill this gap, if The Six were prepared to pool their resources.

Nuclear energy did indeed occupy an important place in the discussions of Spaak's intergovernmental committee and in the bargaining between national governments that followed the submission of his committee's report in April 1956. Spaak's report combined recommending the establishment of a customs union between The Six, with full backing for Monnet's ideas for a nuclear energy authority to plan and develop the nonmilitary use of nuclear energy (Euratom). The two new communities, the report proposed, should be administered by commissions of government-nominated officials. The ECSC Assembly and Court of Justice would serve both of the new organizations.[36]

The Spaak Report was accepted in principle at a meeting of The Six's foreign ministers in Venice on May 29–30, 1956.[37] An intergovernmental conference was established under Spaak's chairmanship and began its work at the end of June 1956. During the conference, France, which had big ambitions for the civil and military use of nuclear power, pressed for acceptance of Euratom, but dragged its feet over the customs union. The German government, by contrast, believed that The Six should collectively refrain from the military use of uranium and insisted that there was a *Junktim* (link) between a deal on trade and a deal on nuclear power. Bonn was not prepared to let Paris have one treaty without the other.[38]

So far as trade in manufactured products was concerned, the Benelux countries and West Germany were free traders, while France was protectionist. Italy hovered between the two. Economics minister Ludwig Erhard favored opening Europe's markets for industrial products as fast as possible. Marjolin describes him as "a universalist, a fervent advocate of total freedom of trade on a world scale."[39] Influential sections of German business supported him by pressing for the full liberalization of trade in manufactured goods throughout the OEEC.[40]

Erhard, however, did not set Germany's negotiating position. Chancellor Adenauer, who had risked much for Westpolitik, was not prepared to press the French government further than she would go. The negotiation, as Marjolin (one of the chief French negotiators) records, thus "depended on us." With France's agreement, anything was possible, "including a common market based upon the principles of liberalism." Without France, "all roads were barred."[41]

The initial reaction of French officialdom to the Spaak Report was "icy."[42] Powerful industrial lobbies and entrenched state bureaucracies all foresaw a loss of influence if the Spaak proposals were accepted. The French government's official response to the Spaak Report, circulated in May 1956, insisted that liberalization of trade between The Six would be contingent upon welfare arrangements being harmonized upward until they were on a par with the most generous system within the Community—France's, naturally. France insisted that the common market should cover agricultural goods (a recommendation of the Spaak Report, but an unpopular one with West Germany) and highlighted the special difficulties that a customs union would imply for France, with its large number of dependent colonies. Marjolin notes that the agenda of all subsequent talks was chiefly concerned with the need to get France to drop its more obstructive positions.[43]

French reservations to the Spaak Report were such that it seems almost miraculous that a compromise was eventually found. Britain, for one, believed almost to the last that no agreement would be reached. The leading British politicians were too concerned with Britain's global role to worry about her neighbors, and the civil servants, as in 1950, were convinced that the post-Messina talks "would not lead anywhere."[44]

Britain nevertheless participated in the original committee set up at Messina, sending, at the behest of Foreign Secretary Harold Macmillan, an observer, albeit one without plenipotentiary powers. The British representative, a former Oxford don named Russell Bretherton, was a mere undersecretary in the Department of Trade. Bretherton, who was a gifted economist, made matters more complicated for Whitehall by contradicting received wisdom. The process begun at Messina, he argued privately, was serious, "indistinguishable from the OEEC," and likely to succeed. Whitehall refused to listen. Bretherton was recalled from the talks in November 1955. Upon leaving, he stated the official British position succinctly: "The treaty has no chance of being concluded; if it is concluded, it has no chance of being ratified; and if it is ratified, it has no chance of being applied."[45]

As the multiple French objections to the Spaak Report became clear in the summer of 1956, Britain sought to take advantage of the stall in the talks. In October 1956, in a move that has often been interpreted as an attempt to sabotage the construction of an Economic Community, Britain floated a proposal to create a Free Trade Area (FTA) in manufactured goods throughout the seventeen states of the OEEC. "Plan G," as the scheme was known inside the British government, would have put Britain at the center of two preferential trading systems (the Commonwealth and the proposed FTA). Britain would have been free to import wool from Australia and sell expensive sweaters, tariff free, to the continent. The scheme nevertheless appealed to the many free traders in the Netherlands and Germany, who objected to "little Europe" separatism.[46]

The deadlock between The Six was broken, however, in the wake of a disastrous outcome of an Anglo-French military adventure: Suez. On October 31, 1956, British and French troops, ostensibly acting to "separate" clashing Israeli and Egyptian forces, began air attacks on Egyptian forces guarding the Suez Canal, which Egyptian president Gamal Abdel Nasser had nationalized in July. Troop landings followed on November 5–6. Both the United States and the Soviet Union (which was itself crushing revolt against Communist rule in Budapest) condemned the Anglo-French attack, and the world currency markets were spooked. A run on the pound began, and along with America's hostility to the invasion, the financial panic caused the Eden government to lose its nerve on the night of November 6–7 and concede a cease-fire, even though military objectives were being successfully achieved.[47]

The French government, presided over by the Socialist Guy Mollet, was left high and dry. Only as part of a united Europe, Mollet argued, could France be on an equal footing with the Americans.[48] Marjolin says that Mollet "felt that the only way to erase, or at least lessen, the humiliation

France had just suffered from the Suez affair was to conclude a European treaty quickly."[49] The French premier was encouraged in such views by Chancellor Adenauer of Germany, who visited Paris at the height of the crisis.[50] Adenauer allegedly told Mollet, "Europe will be your revenge."[51] After the chancellor's visit, France modified its insistence upon the harmonization of social and labor market policy as a prerequisite for a full customs union. She now accepted that member states would merely be obliged to do what they could to bring about such harmonization.[52] By early 1957, the Germans had also conceded that France could develop an independent nuclear policy for military purposes and were agreed on Community financing of France's overseas empire. The way was open for the signature of both the Euratom and EEC treaties. As Winand has wryly observed, Dulles "probably contributed more to European unification by refusing to back the French and British at Suez than by vigorously pushing for the EDC."[53]

For Britain, therefore, Suez was a dual foreign policy catastrophe. She had incensed the United States, her closest ally, but had also given an unwelcome shot in the arm to the negotiations started at Messina. Eden resigned in disgrace in January 1957, and Harold Macmillan took his place as prime minister. Macmillan faced a difficult dilemma. Britain would shortly find herself outside the common tariff wall erected by The Six upon the establishment of a customs union. Although Britain only sent 13 percent of her total exports to The Six and more than 50 percent to the Commonwealth, The Six was the fastest-growing economic area in the world. British industry could not afford to be driven out of the West European market.[54] On the other hand, joining was not an option either.

The Macmillan government squared the circle by strongly pushing the idea of an FTA, despite a clear U.S. preference for the EEC. Negotiations on the FTA continued until the summer of 1958 when de Gaulle, who had swept to power in Paris, brusquely indicated his preference for "little Europe." Macmillan, who had warned that such a move might lead to British troop withdrawals from Germany and the imposition of a high-tariff "fortress Britain" policy, was left looking foolish. Without American support, Britain was in no position to dictate terms on trade.

Subsequently, Britain negotiated the European Free Trade Agreement (EFTA) with Denmark, Norway, Sweden, Switzerland, Portugal, and Austria, the so-called "Seven." These countries were at least as affected as Britain by the creation of the EEC. Yet all of them, for different reasons, were unwilling or unable to join the EEC. Neutral Austria's and Sweden's sensitive diplomatic status, Switzerland's traditional reluctance to enter international agreements, Denmark's preference for the "Nordic Union," and Portugal's still authoritarian government were all barriers in one way or another to entry. The erection of the common external tariff threatened them with acute issues of economic adjustment. All of them sent between 25 to 50 percent of their exports to the EEC Six and took between 35 to 60 percent of their imports from the new customs union. As a contemporary economist pointed out, "easy trade with the Six" was a "vital matter" both for them and, indeed, for all the eleven OEEC states that were not members of the EEC.[55]

EFTA came into operation in May 1960. Its own members regarded it as primarily a bridge to the EEC: as a way, in the long term, to negotiate with the EEC bloc-to-bloc. Its overall effects were nevertheless mostly good. Intra-Nordic trade grew sharply in the following decade, but most important of all, EFTA set off a virtuous race with the EEC to prove to the United States which of the two blocs was more liberal on trade questions. This unquestionably made the international climate for reducing obstacles to trade favorable and also exercised a real pressure on the EEC to take a liberal direction.[56]

THE TREATIES OF ROME: MARCH 25, 1957

Although it attracted a great deal of contemporary attention and received exceptional political support from the American government, the Euratom treaty was less complex, and, in retrospect, much less important than the parallel treaty establishing an economic community.[57] It identified eight main policy areas in the field of nuclear energy that would be coordinated by the new Community. Euratom was (1) "to research and ensure the dissemination of technical knowledge" by promoting and supplementing research being undertaken at the national level. It was (2) "to establish and ensure the application of" common safety standards throughout The Six and (3) "to facilitate investment" in the industry. Annex Two of the treaty made consulting the five-member Commission of Euratom obligatory whenever investment plans were being made for any aspect of the nuclear industry. Euratom was also (4) "to ensure a regular and equitable supply of ores and nuclear fuels to all users in the Community." The Commission was empowered to set up a purchasing and distribution "agency" that would have had a "right of option" on all "ores, source materials or fissionable materials" produced within the Community. In addition to these powers, Euratom was (5) to supervise the use of nuclear fuels and ensure that "nuclear materials are not diverted for purposes other than those for which they are intended"; (6) to own all "special fissionable materials" (bomb-grade uranium and plutonium) not intended for defense purposes; (7) to establish a common market in materials, capital, and employment for the nuclear industry. Its eighth and final task was to make agreements "likely to promote progress in the peaceful use of nuclear energy" with other countries and organizations. Member states were not precluded from making similar agreements on their own initiative, but the Euratom Commission was entitled to scrutinize any such proposed agreement to see if it harmonized with the aims and objectives of the new Community.

Monnet's Action Committee greeted the Euratom treaty with great fanfare. The resolution of its fourth meeting (May 6–7, 1957) welcomed the signature of the two Treaties of Rome, but especially that of Euratom, as "an event of capital importance."[58] In between the Committee's September 1956 meeting and the meeting in May 1957, a committee of three "Wise Men," chaired by Monnet's adviser Armand (who also became first president of the Euratom Commission), had reported. It asserted that The Six could be producing fifteen million kilowatts (kW) of power from nuclear energy by 1967—"an electricity production greater than those of all the conventional power stations and dams which exist today in France and Germany."[59]

Such rhetoric was always going to be hard to live up to. And in fact Euratom did not live up to the hopes of its sponsors. Its work was soon restricted to norm setting, monitoring, and brokering the actions of governments who were, at least in the case of France, as interested in the military applications of nuclear power as the peaceful ones. Europe, in the meantime, continued to import more and more oil from the Middle East. In this respect, Monnet's geopolitical justification for Euratom was eventually vindicated. Dependency upon the Middle East oil supplies was destined to have major consequences for The Six's foreign policy in the 1970s.

The EEC treaty was far more decisive for the future of European integration than Euratom, although some of the most earnest supporters of European unity nevertheless regarded it as a "gigantic fraud."[60] The treaty's protocol stated that its signatories, being "determined" (among several other worthy objectives) to "lay the foundations of an ever closer union among the peoples of Europe," had decided to create an "Economic Community." The EEC's task, according to article 2, was, "by establishing a common market and progressively approximating the economic policies of the Member States," to "promote throughout the Community a harmonious development of economic activities, an increase in stability, an accelerated raising of the standard of living and closer relations between the States belonging to it."

Specifically, The Six contracted themselves to complete a list of policy objectives. They would abolish all quantitative restrictions on trade among themselves, establish a common external tariff and a common commercial policy toward third countries, and eliminate "obstacles to freedom of movement for persons, services and capital." A "common policy in the sphere of agriculture" would be adopted, as would a common policy on transport. To these ends, The Six bound themselves both to institute a "system" that would ensure that competition was not distorted and to apply procedures that would coordinate their economic policies and remedy "disequilibria" in their balances of payments. They further promised to "approximate" their domestic laws "to the extent required for the proper functioning of the common market." A European Social Fund and a European Investment Bank would be set up, and an "association" agreement for overseas "countries and territories" would be introduced. The common external tariff—the key provision of the customs union—was set at the "arithmetical average of the duties applied in the four customs territories [Benelux, France, Germany, and Italy] comprised in the Community."

The timetable set for this ambitious program was twelve years. This "transitional period" was subdivided into three "stages" of four years (although some slippage was both envisaged and allowed), each of which was assigned a set of actions that had to be fulfilled before the stage came to an end. Revenue raised by tariffs on commerce between member states, for example, would be reduced by 10 percent one year after the treaty came into force; 10 percent eighteen months later, and a further 10 percent upon the conclusion of the first four-year phase. Further precise reductions were specified for the second and third stage. Duties on individual products were to have been reduced by at least 25 percent during the first stage, and a further 25 percent during the second stage. It was this article of the treaty that attracted the most attention from *The Economist*, which printed a derisive analysis in the "Notes of the Week" column of its March 30, 1957, edition. Ironically headed a "Red Letter Day for Shoppers," the paper commented scornfully that "in twelve years' time, if things go well, or seventeen years, if not," Italians wanting to buy a Volkswagen would be able to do so at German prices.

The Six also promised to establish a common market in "the products of the soil, of stockfarming, and of fisheries and products of first stage processing directly related to these products" within the same twelve-year framework. The operation and development of the common market in agricultural products, however, was to be "accompanied by the establishment of a common agricultural policy among the member states." Article 39 clarified that the objectives of this policy would be

1. To increase agricultural productivity by promoting technical progress and by ensuring the rational development of agricultural production and the optimum utilization of the factors of production, in particular labor

2. Thus to ensure a fair standard of living for the agricultural community, in particular by increasing the individual earnings of persons engaged in agriculture
3. To stabilize markets
4. To assure the availability of supplies
5. To ensure that supplies reach consumers at reasonable prices

In other words, the policy in its final form was intended to benefit agricultural producers while guaranteeing reasonable (not world market) prices for consumers. In his memoirs, Marjolin stated bluntly: "France would never have accepted a Customs Union that did not include agriculture and did not guarantee French producers protection comparable to that which they were receiving under French law. Without a common agricultural policy, there would never have been a common market."[61] The Commission of the EEC was charged with the task of "working out and implementing" the common agricultural policy (or CAP, as it became known) by the end of the first stage of the EEC's development (i.e., by December 31, 1961). The Council of Ministers, by unanimous vote during the first two stages of the transitional period, and by qualified majority thereafter, was to make all regulations, issue directives, and take all decisions pertaining to agriculture.

Just as important for France, the EEC treaty provided for a preferential policy of trade and development aid toward the countries of the French Union. Member states' colonies were to have the same access to the common market as the member states' themselves. The Six, moreover, promised to "contribute to the investments required for the progressive development of these countries or territories." In practical terms, The Six promised to invest 580 million EPU "units of account" (i.e., dollars) over five years, with France and Germany each contributing 200 million apiece. French overseas territories, however, would benefit from 511.25 million of this investment. In essence, the other five members of the EEC pledged themselves to subsidize the French empire to the tune of $60 million per year until 1963. France negotiated very hard for this outcome: in the opinion of some scholars it was as important for France as the deal on agriculture. French Premier Guy Mollet made no secret of the advantages for France of this aspect of the EEC treaty: "By opening our overseas populations to the broad opportunities offered by a union with Europe, by enabling them, through our good offices, to enter in this vast collectivity, we adroitly maintain our influence."[62]

The Commission and the Council of Ministers were the unique institutions possessed by the EEC. Unlike the ECSC, in which the High Authority was an executive committee accountable to the Assembly (but not supervised by it) that required on many occasions the consent of the Council of Ministers (which thus functioned as a kind of restraining legislature), in the EEC treaty policymaking power was concentrated in the hands of the Council. While the Commission, which was composed of nine independent individuals nominated by national governments for a four-year term, had the exclusive power to propose regulations, directives, or decisions and was responsible for implementing them, the Council alone could give legal force to the measures emanating from the Commission. During the first two stages of the transitional period, the Council's approval was to be by unanimous vote for major policy areas, thereafter by a qualified majority of twelve votes out of seventeen for measures proposed by the Commission, and twelve votes by at least four states for proposals emanating from a member state. France, Germany, and Italy each possessed four votes, Belgium and the Netherlands two, and Luxembourg one. Council amendments to Commission proposals were only possible by unanimous agreement: a clause clearly designed to prevent denaturing compromises that would benefit a minority of member states.

The Commission, however, rapidly became a more powerful institution than the ECSC High Authority. There were three main reasons for this. The first reason was the exceptional quality of some of the individuals composing the first Commission. The first president of the Commission was Walter Hallstein, a committed European federalist who, as we have seen, had also been German foreign minister. His Commission included Sicco Mansholt, a Dutch agriculture expert who became the father of the CAP; Jean Rey, a protégé of Paul-Henri Spaak, who had been minister for the economy in the Belgian government; and the inevitable Robert Marjolin. These four men brought formidable intellectual and organizational talents to the Commission and had accumulated great experience at the top levels of international negotiation over the previous decade. Their collaboration, it should be added, was far from idyllic. They were strong personalities with different ideas about how "Europe" should be made.[63]

The second reason was the Commission's role as market invigilator. The EEC treaty was, among other things, a supranational antitrust agreement. Articles 85 through 89 of the treaty clearly established that cartels were to be outlawed within The Six, and the Commission was given the task of proposing how. The Commission was, in short, designed to be both a watchdog that barked whenever mercantilist tendencies tried to sneak into the market by the back door and a bloodhound employed to sniff them out. Following on from this, the third reason for the Commission's higher-than-expected profile was its clear remit. The EEC treaty set it numerous tasks and gave it a timetable to fulfill them in. The power of proposal, in this context, became an important tool. An efficient

decision-making cycle was established whereby the Commission researched and put forward new initiatives and the Council of Ministers
said yea or nay. There was, in short, a Whitehall-like division between officials and politicians that could only be upset by either of the two categories deciding to invade the other's turf. The major crisis of the mid-1960s
(see chapter 4) was caused by de Gaulle, on the one hand, and Hallstein,
on the other, forgetting this division of labor.

The EEC shared the Common Assembly and the Court of Justice with
the ECSC (and Euratom). The former of these institutions was as much a
cipher in the new treaty as the old. The latter institution, however, gained
important new powers. Whereas under the ECSC treaty, rulings of the
Court of Justice could only be invoked by states objecting to the actions of
the High Authority, in the EEC treaty both the Commission and member
states could ask the Court to rule whether the domestic regulations of
the member states were infringing the provisions of the treaty. Member
states judged to be guilty were "required to take the necessary measures
to comply with the judgment of the Court" (article 171), although no explicit sanctions were available to the Court in the event of noncompliance.
Article 177, moreover, empowered the Court, upon request of a tribunal
or court within any of the member states, to rule whether the Treaty of
Rome was being infringed by a case being decided under national law.

The crucial issue was whether or not these provisions empowered the
Court to rule national laws and regulations incompatible with the treaty.
International law holds that agreements between nation-states are binding upon the states themselves and should be implemented in good faith,
but that their "direct effect" is a matter for domestic legal procedures. In
other words, a Court ruling that a provision of the EEC treaty was being
violated by a specific regulation in force in a particular member state
would not by itself annul the offending regulation but merely act as judicial signal to the Community in general that one of its members was not
keeping its promises. The problem with this interpretation of the Court's
role, of course, was that it made enforcement of the treaty a question of
politics and hence multiplied the likelihood that the member states would
permit the continuation of regulations contrary to the laissez-faire letter
and spirit of the EEC treaty.

The first landmark case in the ECJ's history, *Van Gend en Loos v. Neder-
landse Administratie der Berlastingen* (no. 26/1962), addressed precisely this
point. *Van Gend en Loos* was a dispute in which a Dutch company import-
ing chemicals from West Germany was charged a higher rate of tariff,
under a Dutch law of December 1959, than had been in force on January 1,
1958. The company's lawyers complained that this breached article 12 of
the EEC treaty, which instructed member states to "refrain from introducing between themselves any new customs duties on imports or exports,

or any charges having equivalent effect, and from increasing those which they already apply in their trade with each other." The Dutch government referred the matter to the Court and asked it to decide (a) whether article 12 conferred individual rights that the domestic legal systems of the member states were bound to respect, and (b) whether, in this particular case, Dutch law actually had infringed article 12. When the case came before the Court, only the Commission supported the company. The Dutch, Belgian, and German governments all took the view that article 12 "was intended by the authors of the Treaty to be binding on the international plane only and that it could not be invoked directly in the national courts."[64] The advocate-general to the Court (the lawyer charged with presenting an impartial summary of the case to the Court and with providing a preliminary opinion) by and large backed the three governments, ruling that "large parts of the Treaty" (including article 12) "contain only obligations of member-states and do not contain rules having a direct internal effect."[65] The Court, citing the sentiments of the EEC treaty's preamble as evidence of the supranationalist intent of the treaty's makers, ruled to the contrary. According to the ruling of the seven judges:

> The Community constitutes a new legal order of international law for the benefit of which the states have limited their sovereign rights, albeit within limited fields, and the subjects of which comprise not only Member States but also their nationals. Independently of the legislation of the member states, Community law therefore not only imposes obligations on individuals but is intended to confer upon them rights which become part of their legal heritage.[66]

WASHINGTON'S BENEVOLENT GAZE

The historian Alan Milward sustained that the construction of the EEC was "an integral part of the reassertion of the nation-state as an organizational concept."[67] Nation-states throughout Western Europe needed to prove that they could deliver the goods to their citizens—not least because they feared that the lesson of twentieth-century European history was that without high levels of welfare, democracy would not survive. Europeanization, to use an anachronism, was a by-product of the urge to produce welfare. A customs union was agreed, against all odds, because The Six's economic growth was being dragged along by rapid West German economic growth. The other five were anxious both to continue to profit from the German boom and to bind Germany into the Western camp. The EEC treaty was a means of satisfying this dual objective.[68]

If, moreover, we read what Milward, tongue firmly in cheek, calls the "lives and teachings of the European saints" (De Gasperi, Adenauer,

Schuman, Van Zeeland, and so forth), we apprehend that the central preoccupation of Europe's "founding fathers" was less idealism for the European cause than fear that "democracy and christianity could not be defended" against the forces of darkness unless there was a "joint economic and spiritual renewal of liberal capitalism."[69]

Milward's realism is too uncompromising for many: it seems to reduce or even deny the idealism that accompanied the early years of European integration. However, by placing a powerful emphasis on the extent to which the process of European integration required a constant act of will on the part of national leaders, it was a useful corrective to the so-called functionalist interpretation, laid out in the political scientist Ernst Haas's 1958 book, *The Uniting of Europe*, which implied that the creation of the ECSC and the EEC was an almost passive process whereby "political actors in several distinct national settings are persuaded to shift their loyalties, expectations and political activities toward a new center, whose institutions possess or demand jurisdiction over the pre-existing national states."[70]

Haas was confident, moreover, that this process was bound to continue since each new move toward economic integration occasioned policy "spillover" into other areas, with the center accruing to itself more and more competences and hence substituting the national capitals as the principal locus of political activity. By 1958, Haas argued, this process had already led to a new instrument of governance that was neither an outright intergovernmental organization nor a federal state, but a "hybrid in which neither the federal nor the intergovernmental tendency has clearly triumphed."[71] Haas nevertheless left little doubt that he believed that the federating principle would win out in the long run and that Europe would become an organized political community administered by central institutions on the model of the United States. "The spill-over may make a political community of Europe before the end of the transitional period."[72] The book's last sentence was, "The vision of Jean Monnet has been clearly justified by events."[73]

Milward speculated derisively that Haas was semiconsciously fulfilling his Cold War duty by propagating this vision of the inexorable merging of the democratic world into a single system of government.[74] It would perhaps be fairer to say that Haas was echoing the mind-set of the U.S. political establishment. No account of European integration in the 1950s is complete unless one remembers the extent to which the Europeans' efforts to achieve greater integration were nurtured and encouraged by the Eisenhower administration, which was extraordinarily committed to European unity, and not only rhetorically. As we have seen in this chapter, the United States funded the EPU and pressed for trade liberalization through the OEEC, backed the ECSC despite its detrimental effect on

American steel exports, committed itself almost aggressively to the notion of a Defense Community, and facilitated the creation of Euratom against the interests of its own atomic energy industry. Washington, doubtless comforted by the fact that its trade surplus with The Six remained comfortably wide, also backed the concept of the EEC against the British notion of an FTA—this despite the fact that U.S. policy since 1945 had been to encourage multilateral trade liberalization through the GATT. More generally, European integration was taking place under the aegis of the American military guarantee and with the benefit of a stable and prospering transatlantic trade relationship. European integration, like most exotic blooms, needed a favorable climate to be able to grow: the United States built and maintained the glass house necessary for its survival.

This is emphatically not to suggest that European integration was imposed from without: quite the opposite. European integration was in the interests of The Six and was achieved overwhelmingly through the ideas, efforts, and hard work of The Six's leaders. It is nevertheless worthwhile asking whether West European nations would or could have proceeded so far, so fast toward integration in the absence of the relatively benign environment created by the United States' protective shield. When one thinks of the centuries of distrust and suspicion dividing The Six, especially France and Germany, and the jealousy with which The Six—especially France—continued to defend national prerogatives throughout the 1950s, it seems unlikely. European integration was a luxury that postwar American hegemony made thinkable.

4

✛

In the Shadow of the General
De Gaulle and the EEC 1958–1969

Charles de Gaulle is often depicted as an ardent nationalist, a man who used France's unique position within the EEC to put a brake on the process of gradual integration begun by the ECSC and accelerated by the Treaties of Rome. There is, of course, some truth in this picture. Yet de Gaulle's arrival in power was arguably also a necessary condition for the EEC's success. The EEC treaty demanded huge alterations in the economic behavior of the member states. France, with heavily protected manufacturers and a comparatively lavish welfare state, was the nation that needed to make the greatest adjustments of all. Without de Gaulle's personal leadership and the institutional power devolved upon the president by the Constitution of the Fifth Republic in France, it is probable that France would have rescinded from its obligations under the EEC treaty. Hans von der Groeben, the second German nominee to the original Commission and, like Walter Hallstein, an ardent federalist, summarized the point well when he said that the last governments of the Fourth Republic would have been willing to "exhaust the political opportunities of the Treaty of Rome" but would "scarcely have been able" to enforce the "radical domestic reforms" that the EEC treaty stipulated.[1]

When de Gaulle came to power at the beginning of June 1958, France was suffering from rapid inflation and a ballooning balance-of-payments deficit. De Gaulle, once his constitutional position had been fortified, acted decisively to prepare France for the first round of tariff reductions envisaged by the EEC treaty. The franc was devalued by 17.5 percent in December 1958, government expenditure was cut sharply back, and taxes were raised.[2]

61

De Gaulle, in short, backed the EEC from the first. He merely had a restrictive interpretation of what it was supposed to lead to. De Gaulle wanted to extend the free market to agriculture, liberalize trade in manufactures gradually within the context of the customs union, preserve The Six from "Anglo-Saxon" contamination, and raise The Six's profile in world politics. It was to be a trading bloc, whose geopolitical stand was to be set by the French government. This concept of European unity was simply different (although hardly less ambitious) from that of Jean Monnet, Walter Hallstein, and supporters of a federal Europe. It was one that entrenched national governments, and especially the government of France, as the driving force of the Community. *"Une Europe des patries"* was not a mere slogan for de Gaulle. But his vision of an activist Europe cutting a dash on the world stage alarmed the more timid member states of The Six. Germany, Italy, and the Netherlands did not regard French *gloire* as a substitute for American strategic leadership and became increasingly frustrated with French high-handedness within the Community itself.

THE EEC'S FIRST FOUR YEARS

De Gaulle's first act in defense of a restrictive interpretation of the EEC treaty was to block negotiations for a wider FTA on November 14, 1958. The Commission welcomed de Gaulle's abrupt termination of the FTA talks since it feared that the EEC might dissolve like a lump of sugar in a cup of tea in a wider trade bloc. A useful consequence of de Gaulle's decision was that liberalization within The Six proceeded apace. Quantitative restrictions on intra-Community trade had been entirely suppressed by December 1961. Intra-Community trade barriers were lowered faster than specified by the EEC treaty, and the common external tariff, in part to reassure the United States, whose exports had been affected by growing intra-Six trade after January 1958, was set at a lower level than Britain's for industrial goods. The EEC also agreed to a large number of bilateral tariff reductions with the United States during the so-called Dillon Round of trade talks from 1958 to 1960.

This substantive progress on trade was matched in another area important for France: the relationship between the EEC and the non-European countries and territories that had special relations with Belgium, France, Italy, and the Netherlands. For the most part, these countries were France's African "dependencies" (to use the patronizing phrase then common). Initially at least, the convention with the associated countries was one of the EEC's "signal successes."[3] Between 1959 and 1962, most of the EEC's associates became independent, but in a sense this only enhanced the EEC's role. The fact that European aid was nominally being dispensed by a supranational organization rather than by the former colonial powers directly undoubtedly rendered such funds more acceptable to the African countries' new leaders. In July 1963, the Yaoundé Convention provided for a further $730 million in aid. An Association Council, composed of ministers from The Six and from the African nations, and a Parliamentary Conference provided the Convention with an institutional framework.[4]

The consolidation of The Six as a cohesive customs union and the successful opening to France's former colonies were chalked up to the EEC's credit in Paris. However, these issues were small beer compared with agriculture. Failure to reach agreement on a Community-wide regime for agriculture would have smashed the EEC as a whole. Yet agriculture was the thorniest of subjects. Producer groups were well organized and politically influential; farmers still constituted a large segment of the electorate (in 1958, agricultural workers constituted 23 percent of the workforce in France, 35 percent in Italy, and 15 percent even in West Germany); and agricultural incomes, depressed by a decade of falling prices, were already very low and were provoking a drift to the towns that was imperiling the rural way of life. The picture was particularly bleak in France, whose rural areas were in deep crisis by 1960. De Gaulle even warned that France would have an "Algeria on our own soil" if the problems of agriculture were not soon resolved.[5]

These factors, taken together, meant that the CAP could not reflect the liberal principles prevailing in the rest of the EEC treaty. The governments of all six countries were determined to keep "farmers on welfare," to quote the title of the most comprehensive book on the agriculture policy of the EEC.[6] With such a starting point, negotiations on the proposals put forward by the Commission inevitably became fraught. On December 9, 1961, de Gaulle flatly warned the rest of the Community that France would not implement the next round of tariff cuts on manufactured goods if the CAP deadline set by the Treaty of Rome was breached. That deadline was December 31, 1961: in the end, an accord was only reached on January 14, 1962, after The Six "stopped the clock" and carried on bargaining.

The accord specified that a common market in agricultural products would be gradually introduced between August 1, 1962, and December 31, 1969. A common system of tariffs on foreign imports was to be introduced to ensure that prices were not undercut by outside competitors, and an export subsidy regime was to be implemented. The CAP, in other words, although fiendishly complicated in its detail, was simple in conception. The EEC intended to solve the economic and social problems of agriculture within The Six as a whole by guaranteeing high domestic prices and subsidizing exports rather than encouraging cheap food and compelling a shakeout among domestic producers.

The devil, however, was in the details. Agricultural production was divided into three main categories: grains and dairy products; pig meat and eggs; and fruit, vegetables, and wines. The first of these categories was the most sensitive since the price of grain had a knock-on effect throughout the entire agricultural economy. During the seven-year transitional phase, each country would set target prices for wheat and barley production. High-cost countries such as Germany would be entitled to impose levies at their frontiers on grain coming from other EEC members and to grant subsidies to allow their domestic producers to export production elsewhere in The Six. The target prices would gradually be reduced until prices were harmonized throughout the Community at the end of the transitional period. Thereafter target prices would be set at Community level.

To prevent target prices from falling, The Six set up the so-called Guidance and Guarantee Fund to buy surplus production from producers at the so-called support price (about 10 percent less than the target price) and to subsidize exports. No cap was placed on the amount that the Community would buy, and thus producers were potentially handed a blank check to increase harvests at the taxpayers' expense. Nobody knew in 1962 how much the CAP would cost. But it was clear that it would not be cheap. It was agreed in principle during the 1962 negotiation that costs would eventually be paid out of the Community's "own resources," but there was then no agreement on what exactly that phrase meant. In the meantime, until June 1965, the CAP was to be financed by contributions from the member states.

Markets in pig meat and poultry and in fruit and vegetables were less tightly regulated. The pig meat and poultry sectors were defended from foreign competition by a tariff on imports. There was no Community support price regime, however, in this sector. Fruits and vegetables were to be regulated by quality standards only, and by January 1966 produce was supposed to circulate freely, with member states being entitled to impose border checks to ensure that quality standards were being maintained.[7]

At bottom, the CAP was a bargain between France and Germany. France wielded the potent threat of postponing the EEC's transition to its second stage—which would have been a severe setback for German industry—in order to unload much of the cost of subsidizing French agriculture onto the Community as a whole. France was "largely uncompetitive on the world market, yet competitive within Europe."[8] The CAP enabled France to dispose of its surpluses within The Six at artificial prices while building up its export trade on the back of Community subsidies. It was a major achievement for de Gaulle, and while Moravcsik arguably exaggerates when he claims that it was less the pursuit of French grandeur than the "price of French wheat" that was driving de Gaulle's EEC policy, the general's concern for agriculture cannot be disputed.[9]

THE "UNION OF STATES"

De Gaulle's determination to restore France's place in the world was shown within weeks of his taking office. In the autumn of 1958, he wrote to Macmillan and Eisenhower proposing that NATO should be put under the joint leadership of a "directory" of the three nuclear (or, in the case of France, which exploded its first atomic bomb in February 1960, soon-to-be nuclear) powers. Both Britain and the United States rejected this proposal as diplomatically as they could.[10] The episode seems to have convinced de Gaulle, however, that France, if it wanted to exercise its rightful role on the world stage, would have to do so as the de facto head of a European "Third Force." But to perform this role, The Six needed institutions capable of making decisions on major questions of foreign policy and military strategy. In the summer of 1959, de Gaulle proposed that The Six's foreign ministers should meet three times a year to coordinate the EEC's foreign policy; in September 1960, at one of his frequent policymaking press conferences, he outlined a vision of a committee of The Six's heads of government making policy in foreign policy, defense, cultural, and economic fields. He also proposed that the plan should be submitted to the peoples of Europe in a Community-wide referendum as a way of giving it greater legitimacy. In short, he was putting forward "a total change in the objectives and methods of European unification."[11]

In March 1961, a committee chaired by Christian Fouchet, a French diplomat who had been a "Gaullist of the first hour"—one of the gallant handful of officials and soldiers who had joined de Gaulle in exile in 1940—was given the task of putting flesh onto the bare bones of this statement. The process was pushed along by the heads of government of The Six at a summit meeting at Bad Godesberg on July 18, 1961. The summit's final communiqué spoke of The Six's "determination" to press ahead with "the desire for political unification implicit in the EEC treaty" by instituting "regular summits between the Six's heads of government."

What the French aspired to achieving is indicated by a draft treaty proposed by Fouchet on November 2, 1961. This document proposed the establishment of an "indissoluble" Union of States. The Union's aims were to "bring about the adoption of a common foreign policy" and to ensure the "continued development" of the member states' "common heritage" and the "protection of the values on which their civilization rests." The Union would contribute to "the defense of human rights, the fundamental freedoms and democracy" and adopt a common policy for defense "in co-operation with the other free nations." Under Fouchet's scheme, the Union was to be provided with three main institutions: the Council, the Parliament, and the Political Commission (PC).

The Council was to be composed of the heads of government of The Six's member states, who would meet three times a year to "deliberate on all questions whose inclusion on its agenda is requested by one or more of the member states." Decisions were to be made by unanimity, with member states being granted the possibility of abstention, and were to be binding upon all states that had not abstained. The Council's president was to be chosen by the member states at each meeting and was to "take up his duties two months before the subsequent meeting and continue to exercise them for two months after the meeting." The Council was not necessarily to have, therefore, a revolving presidency.

Nominal parliamentary scrutiny of the Council was to be provided by the Assembly of the European Communities. Administratively, the Council was to be served by the PC, which was to consist of "senior officials of the Foreign Affairs departments of each member state." It was to be based in Paris and was to be presided over by the representative of the member state holding the presidency of the Council.

The French draft envisaged a period of three years in which the Union of States would work in conjunction with the other European Communities. Article 16 foresaw, however, a "general review" whose "main objects" would be "the introduction of a unified foreign policy and the gradual establishment of an organization centralizing, within the Union, the European Communities." De Gaulle's idea, seemingly, was to merge the three economic Communities into a single body and have the unified "economic" Commission report to the Council of the Union in the same way as the Political Commission was intended to do. The national governments would have reasserted their primacy over the Communities' supranational institutions, and France would probably have asserted its primacy over the other governments of The Six.[12]

It is a mistake, however, to think of the Fouchet Plan purely as a ruse to enhance the greater glory of France. It was a genuine attempt to avert the EEC's degeneration into what Hedley Bull would subsequently call "Civilian Power Europe."[13] Stanley Hoffmann provided an insightful contemporary analysis of de Gaulle's goals for Europe:

> The General, a French nationalist, is also a "European nationalist." His concern for Europe is least understood in the United States, where people tend to assume that only the "Europeans" of Mr. Monnet's persuasion really care about uniting Europe. Just as he wants to prevent France from being a mere pawn on the international chessboard, the General wants to assure that

Europe—which he sees as being the mother of civilization—can again become one of the principal players after having for more than twenty years
been just a stake through the fault of its own divisions.[14]

The French plans were audacious, especially when one remembers that
they were put forward just weeks after the construction of the Berlin Wall.
The East–West conflict had reached its tensest moment since the Berlin
airlift. The USSR was building an intercontinental missile force to rival
that of the United States, a fact that had set off alarm bells among West
European leaders. Would the United States be prepared to use its still superior nuclear forces in defense of Europe, if it risked a devastating Soviet
counterattack? Newly elected President John Kennedy's doctrine of "flexible response," which in substance proposed that the NATO countries in
Europe should build up their conventional forces to deter the USSR and
leave a monopoly on nuclear arms to the United States, had not soothed
the Europeans' worries.[15]

De Gaulle did not trust the Americans. On May 10, 1961, he had announced his intention to build a French *force de frappe*. The French leader
saw two main advantages in having independent nuclear forces. First, as
he had explained to President Eisenhower in 1959, even a small nuclear
force had a deterrent effect—an enemy's power to kill you ten times over
lost all force if he himself had been obliterated once.[16] Second, by threatening to go nuclear, France would have the leverage to ensure that the
United States maintained its European commitments.

When they met at Bad Godesberg, therefore, in July 1961, the other
members of The Six knew perfectly well that moves toward European
political union might mean signing up to a much more self-reliant vision
of Western European security.

It was for this reason that the plan foundered. In the fall of 1961 and
in January 1962, intergovernmental talks on political union stalled, with
the Dutch arguing that it was pointless to go ahead with political union
until Britain's application to join the EEC (Britain had applied on July 31,
1961) had been decided. France's ambitious ideas were watered down
to ensure that the proposed union was subordinate in military matters
to NATO and to underline the independence of the institutions of the
three European communities. This resolute opposition caused de Gaulle's
patience to snap. On January 18, 1962, flushed with his victory in the agriculture negotiations, de Gaulle introduced a new draft treaty that struck
out all mentions of NATO and incorporated trade and industry (the chief
prerogatives of the EEC) into the Union's responsibilities. The Five "were
filled with consternation" at the French government's "blunt way of issu-
ing ultimatums."[17]

American diplomacy chose this moment to make its case. On January 25, 1962, President Kennedy asked Congress for authorization to conclude a wide-ranging free trade agreement with Western Europe. The United States needed such an agreement because the creation of The Six had led to a substantial fall in American exports to the EEC, but the primary motive was political. The "Grand Design," as Kennedy called it, was predicated upon free trade, British membership of the EEC, and American leadership in defense matters. Its most famous evocation came on July 4, 1962, when Kennedy made at Philadelphia what was described as the "declaration of interdependence":

> We believe that a united Europe will be capable of playing a greater role in the common defense, of responding more generously to the needs of the poorer nations, of joining the United States and others in lowering trade barriers, resolving problems of commerce, commodities and currency, and developing coordinated policies in all economic, political and diplomatic areas. We see in such a Europe a partner with whom we can deal on a basis of full equality in all the great and burdensome tasks of building and defending a community of free nations.[18]

Long before the Philadelphia speech, however, American diplomats were spreading the message that the future of The Six was with the United States. The choice, the Kennedy administration argued, was between an "Atlantic Community" protected by NATO, in which the United States and The Six collaborated on equal terms, and a precarious new venture into geopolitics with de Gaulle at the helm.[19]

The smaller nations of the EEC obviously preferred the American option. Between February and April 1962, the Italian premier Amintore Fanfani, a committed Atlanticist not least because he needed U.S. approval of his integration of the still-Marxist Italian Socialist Party (PSI) into his government, strove to find common ground between what the French foreign minister called the "proverbial obstinacy of the Dutch" and the general, whose own obstinacy was of course a thing of legend. It is no small tribute to Fanfani's negotiating skills, honed in the Machiavellian world of domestic Italian politics, that he persuaded de Gaulle to soften the French position considerably, although the backing of Chancellor Konrad Adenauer for de Gaulle's position strengthened France's hand. Thanks to Fanfani's efforts, in April France seemingly began to envisage the Union of States as a coordinating, not commanding institution that would work with the EEC and NATO rather than against it. De Gaulle nevertheless remained trenchant—and, in the long-term, prophetic—about the prospect of supranational government for Europe. At a summit in Turin on April 4, 1962, the general, in good world-historical form, told Fanfani that the ideal of a common European government and parliament was "touching" but merely a "dream." The "states alone were real," he asserted. It is a point of view that has lost none of its relevance in the interim.

The French concessions, however, did not win over the Dutch and the Belgians. To begin with, they resented the fact that *les grands* had been negotiating among themselves without their involvement: a "Franco-Italo-German front" was, for them, an ominous harbinger of the way that the EEC itself might be run in the future. The Netherlands, though its internal debates on the issue of political union were sharp and its cabinet was divided, broadly wanted Britain in the EEC precisely because it believed that the British would be a useful ally against French hegemony. France, moreover, had still not given cast iron guarantees that the Union of States would work within the framework of the NATO alliance and would not supersede the EEC. Since 1959, Dutch Foreign Minister Joseph Luns had regarded building a European political bloc in opposition to the Netherlands' "Anglo-Saxon allies" as "insane," and he remained as stubborn in this conviction as ever in April 1962.[20]

The Dutch eventually pulled the plug on the Fouchet negotiations at a summit of The Six on April 17, 1962, when it became clear that France would not go along with the supranational dimensions of the European Union proposed by the Netherlands and would not delay the implementation of the treaty until after Britain had joined the EEC.

De Gaulle's response was given, as usual, at a press conference. On May 15, 1962, he warned darkly that Europe was far too dependent upon the United States and dismissed the idea that Europe could be governed through supranational institutions as a fantasy worthy of the "thousand and one nights."[21] He was to dedicate the next four years to proving himself right.

THE FIRST BRITISH NEGOTIATION FOR ENTRY

The British decision to apply for entry to the EEC had partly been provoked by its poor economic performance relative to The Six. Between 1950 and 1958, Britain's economy grew at an annual rate of 2.7 percent per year: good by the standards of the 1970s and 1980s, but far behind West Germany (7.8 percent), Italy (5.8 percent), and France (4.6 percent). Even more significantly, the former "workshop of the world" was losing prominence as an exporter of manufactured goods. Britain's export trade grew by just 1.8 percent a year in this period; Germany's by 15 percent. In 1958, Germany's economy overtook Britain in size, and her share of world export trade also exceeded Britain's.[22]

Geopolitical considerations were nevertheless decisive. When Britain applied for membership, the policy of decolonization inaugurated by Prime Minister Harold Macmillan in his February 1960 "Winds of Change" speech was ending Britain's role as an imperial power. Suez had also taught Britain that the "special relationship" with the United States was a somewhat one-sided affair. The Six loomed in the minds of British diplomats as a potential vehicle for the German domination of Europe, or else as a "Napoleonic" bloc, against which Britain was bound to organize her diplomatic efforts. According to de Gaulle, Macmillan told him in the summer of 1958 that the common market was "the continental system all over again." Macmillan somewhat hysterically remarked that "Britain cannot accept it. I beg you to give it up. Otherwise we shall be embarking on a war which will doubtless be economic at first but which runs the risk of gradually spreading into other fields [*sic*]."[23]

In December 1960, Macmillan spent the Christmas holidays drafting a "Grand Design" for the future of British foreign and economic policy. Its key passage stated that exclusion from the "strongest economic group in the civilized world must injure us." Exclusion was "primarily a political problem" that had to be "dealt with" by making a "supreme effort to reach a settlement" while de Gaulle was in power in France. From then on, Macmillan was unequivocally committed to pressing for outright membership of the Community.[24] Britain formally applied for membership in August 1961, along with Denmark. Ireland had anticipated both by a handful of days. Norway followed suit on April 30, 1962. From the start, it was clear that British entry would mean a significant enlargement of "little Europe," as The Six was often called.

Edward Heath, the chief British negotiator, made the thinking behind Britain's position clear in his opening speech at the negotiations on October 10, 1961. Britain, Heath said, recognized that the decision to seek entry to the EEC was "a turning point in our history." Three considerations had been important in persuading Britain to take such a drastic step. First, according to Heath, was Britain's "strong desire to play a full part in the development of European institutions." The "second consideration" propelling Britain's application for membership, according to Heath, was the "increasing realization" that "a larger European unity had become essential" in a world where "political and economic power is becoming concentrated to such a great extent." The "third factor" influencing Britain's decision was the "remarkable success of your Community." Heath stated that Britain wished to "unite our efforts with yours; and to join in promoting, through the EEC, the fullest possible measure of European unity."[25]

Heath's remarks provided an impressive rhetorical garnish for the clear-cut pragmatic bargain that he subsequently offered The Six. Heath stated that the British were willing to "subscribe fully" to articles 2 and

3 of the EEC treaty and accept a common tariff, the abolition of internal tariffs, a common commercial policy, and a common agricultural policy if The Six were prepared to meet Britain halfway over "three major problems." These problems were Commonwealth trade, UK agriculture, and "the arrangements which could be made for our partners in EFTA." The third of these problems was largely pro forma. The concerns of the other EFTA nations would never have dissuaded Britain from concluding an agreement with the EEC that was in Britain's national economic interest. The first two, however, were not. Heath warned that he would be misleading his listeners if he "failed to say" how deeply the British people felt about the Commonwealth. He further stated that it would be a "tragedy" if British entry into the EEC "forced other members of the Commonwealth to change their whole pattern of their trade and perhaps their political orientation." Britain, Heath warned, could not "join the EEC under conditions in which this trade connection was cut with grave loss and even ruin for some of the Commonwealth countries."[26]

Heath further pointed out that Britain's system of agricultural protection provided the highly satisfactory result of cheap food for consumers and guaranteed incomes for farmers. Britain placed low tariffs on agricultural products and none at all upon those coming from the Commonwealth. Prices in the shops were therefore low. The British farming community was maintained by income support payments that amounted to a large slice of the industry's net income. Britain, in other words, paid a relatively small number of people to till the land and maintain the rural community in exchange for the benefits of world market food prices for the consumers: benefits that the subsequent CAP agreement in January 1962 explicitly renounced. Heath insisted that price rises in foodstuffs would have to be introduced "gradually" and hinted that The Six might contemplate a CAP that incorporated British practices, rather than the reverse: "I am sure that the pooling of ideas and experience will have fruitful results; indeed, some features of our agricultural arrangements may prove attractive to you."[27]

Heath had to insist upon these conditions. Conservative Party opinion objected to harming the interests of the Commonwealth countries, especially Australia, New Zealand, and Canada, the so-called white dominions. Farmers were one of the Conservative Party's key backers. Yet the two key British conditions were bound to tread on de Gaulle's corns. Unlike France and Belgium's former colonies, Commonwealth nations such as India, Pakistan, and Hong Kong were potential competitors in politically sensitive industries such as textiles, while Australia, Canada, and New Zealand were highly competitive agricultural exporters. If the Commonwealth countries had been given the same sort of access to the domestic market of The Six granted to France's former colonies, Dutch and French agriculture would have been subjected to fierce competition; if the dominions' access to the common market was restricted, however, Dutch and French exporters could expect to gain market share in Britain. Since Britain was the biggest importer of foodstuffs in the world at this time, this was a welcome prospect.

Altering the CAP to take British practices into account, or even to allow the UK a lengthy period of adjustment, was also a nonstarter. As we have seen, the CAP negotiations were coming to a close in the fall of 1961, and all The Six were acutely aware that the agriculture issue was capable of disrupting the whole European project. The UK could hardly be granted privileges that were being denied to the farmers or shoppers of the existing member states. Maurice Couve de Murville, the French foreign minister, dryly remarked that he could not see that adaption to the CAP would be "significantly more uncomfortable in the British case than elsewhere."[28]

For these reasons, The Six, in general, and the French, in particular, were insistent that Britain should adapt her domestic agriculture to the same regime as The Six and enter the CAP fully in 1970, and the British, who were under intense pressure from the Commonwealth countries, felt obliged to honor Heath's pledge not to harm trade with the former empire. The two sides' negotiating positions "were too distant for real negotiation to be possible."[29] A summit meeting between Macmillan and de Gaulle on June 2–3, 1962, at Château de Champs failed to break the deadlock. Although Macmillan warmly asserted that Britain's imperial mission was being substituted by a growing European vocation, especially among the young, de Gaulle remained unconvinced. British attitudes, he thought, still had to "evolve further" to be compatible with The Six.[30]

Britain showed by deeds, not words, that it was serious about joining the EEC by significantly softening its negotiating stance in the summer of 1962, which led to real progress being made on some of the less controversial topics (it was agreed, for instance, that the common external tariff on tea would be reduced to zero, which would save Ceylon's main export industry). But progress on "temperate zone foodstuffs," i.e., agricultural exports from Australia, Canada, and New Zealand, were a different matter. The Six, especially France, were unwilling to be generous to such relatively wealthy countries.[31]

The failure to get a deal meant that a Commonwealth summit in London in September 1962 was a public relations disaster for Macmillan as the prime ministers of Australia, Canada, and New Zealand openly accused him of neglecting their interests. A few weeks later, the opposition Labour Party's leader, Hugh Gaitskell, made political capital out of the Conservatives' difficulties by clearly stating that Labour was opposed to any deal that harmed the Commonwealth trade. Gaitskell, moreover, also raised the thorny issue of membership's constitutional implications. Shocking many of his own closest supporters, notably a future president of the European Commission, Roy Jenkins, Gaitskell claimed that British membership of the EEC would threaten "a thousand years of history."[32]

The British membership bid was thus already in deep trouble by October 1962. France, but not only France, considered that Britain would disrupt the economic arrangements agreed by The Six; the UK was constrained by its historical ties to the Commonwealth and by domestic politics. Nevertheless, the way in which negotiations were brought to an end came as a bolt from the blue for everybody concerned. On January 14, 1963, de Gaulle held a damning press conference on the subject of British entry and, without ever pronouncing the word *non*, made clear his rejection of Macmillan's entry bid. The French president's move has become something of an academic mystery story, with historians queuing to decipher his motives.

The still standard interpretation is the so-called Trojan Horse theory. This links de Gaulle's action to the so-called Nassau agreement between Britain and the Kennedy administration on December 21, 1962. The Nassau agreement was a U.S.-British deal to modernize Britain's independent nuclear deterrent. Britain, after failing to make her own nuclear delivery system in the 1950s, had been relying on Skybolt missiles purchased from the United States for the delivery of British-made warheads. Early in December 1962, the Kennedy administration abruptly told the British government that it would be canceling Skybolt for technical and financial reasons. Macmillan was determined to get submarine-launched Polaris missiles in Skybolt's place, but there was strong resistance within the Kennedy administration to making a deal, since many high officials believed that any special treatment for Britain would weaken the prospects for the "multilateral force" (MLF) that was the strategic dimension to Kennedy's Grand Design for an Atlantic Community.

At Nassau, Kennedy and Macmillan's good personal relationship, which had been strengthened during the October 1962 Cuban missile crisis, led the president to override his advisers. Kennedy agreed that Britain should have Polaris, and while Britain's nuclear submarine fleet should be assigned to NATO, Britain would retain the right, when the highest British interests were at stake, to use its deterrent independently.[33] The two countries invited de Gaulle to participate in the multilateral force under similar conditions—although as France was still unable to make her own warheads, and the United States was not prepared to provide France with the know-how—the offer was much less evenhanded than it seemed.

De Gaulle, who had met Macmillan at Rambouillet just a few days before Nassau and who may have understood from Macmillan's elliptical

French that Britain intended to develop nuclear missile technology together with France, was convinced that the deal was evidence that Britain
was a privileged partner of the United States. This, according to the "Trojan Horse" theory, led him to conclude that he had to keep Britain out of
the EEC. As Stanley Hoffmann put it: "Slamming the door on the British
. . . seemed to him less damaging to his policy [of building a strong and independent Europe] than the disaster represented by the entry of England,
the Trojan Horse of the United States, into the Common Market and by the
formation of a loose Atlantic Community directed by and dependent upon
the United States."[34]

The standard interpretation has been challenged by the American political scientist Andrew Moravcsik, who contends, in keeping with his
economics-driven theory of the development of European integration
more generally, that de Gaulle's decision was motivated primarily by
fears for the future of French agriculture if Britain were to be admitted. Geopolitical considerations, in Moravcsik's view, were much less
important for the general's decision. Moravcsik's work has given rise to
a *historikerstreit* that it is unnecessary to discuss here but that has undeniably provoked some intriguing questions about the utility (and pitfalls) of
political science theory when applied to historical data.[35]

Actually, this interpretative battle seems otiose. De Gaulle was frank
about his motivations during the January 14, 1963, press conference. Both
agriculture and geopolitics mattered greatly. The French president began
by asserting that he could not "conceive of a Common Market in which
French agriculture would not find outlets commensurate with its production." The "entry of agriculture into the Common Market" had been
a "formal condition" for French participation. Britain, however, from
the beginning "had requested membership, but on its own conditions."
This was especially true of Britain's agricultural regime, which de Gaulle
termed "obviously incompatible with the system that the Six have set up
for themselves." The question, de Gaulle suggested (and this, in fact, was
the nearest he came to expressing an outright *non*), was whether Britain
could place itself "within a tariff that is truly common, giving up all preference with regard to the Commonwealth." De Gaulle concluded, "One
could not say" that this problem had been resolved. Would it ever be?
Only Britain, de Gaulle averred, could answer that question.

On the other hand, de Gaulle also unquestionably believed that British entry would prevent the EEC from growing into a geopolitical force
independent of American tutelage. He argued, repeating comments that
he had made to Macmillan in their December meeting, that Britain's
entry would be followed by the applications of other states. An influx
of new members would "completely change the series of adjustments,
agreements, compensations and regulations already established between

the Six." In de Gaulle's view, the "eleven-member, then thirteen-member and then perhaps eighteen-member Common Market that would be built would, without any doubt, hardly resemble the one the Six have built." He went on:

> Moreover, this Community, growing in this way, would be confronted with all the problems of its economic relations with a crowd of other states, and first of all with the U.S. It is foreseeable that the cohesion of all its members . . . would not hold for long and that in the end there would appear a colossal Atlantic Community under American dependence and leadership which would soon swallow up the European Community. This is an assumption that can be perfectly justified in the eyes of some, but it is not at all what France wanted, and what France is doing, which is a strictly European construction.[36]

De Gaulle also spent part of the press conference giving a "disdainful rejection of . . . the Nassau accords," but the Nassau agreement was more a symptom of Britain's extraneousness from the French vision of the Community's purpose, not a primary cause for rejection.[37] In his memoirs, de Gaulle in fact says that he and Macmillan spent many hours together "either alone or accompanied by our ministers" discussing the "great subject" of British membership. De Gaulle says that these conversations convinced him that Britain was not yet ready to "moor herself to the Continent." Later, he adds, "a certain special agreement concerning the provision of American rockets and underlining the submission of Britain's nuclear means, concluded separately at Nassau with John Kennedy, was to justify my circumspection."[38] The overall thrust of the press conference, and the tone of de Gaulle's comments on American strategic policy toward Europe, leave no doubt that the general's central preoccupation in 1963—*along* with agriculture—was that the countries of the EEC might lose their independence and become satellites of the United States both economically and militarily. British entrance into the Community could only strengthen this possibility.

De Gaulle nevertheless would not have been able to stand out against British membership, which was desired by all the other member states of the EEC, had he lacked the support of Chancellor Konrad Adenauer, who had become convinced in the early summer of 1962 that Britain would be an uncomfortable partner within the EEC.[39] As Adenauer's biographer says:

> Those who spoke to Adenauer during these weeks [May 1962] gained the impression that he had made up his mind: a definite turning towards France, reserved relations with the United States, a scarcely concealed "no" to Britain's participation in political union and—this was also important—intensive efforts to achieve a modus vivendi with the Soviet Union.[40]

What drove "the Old Man" to take the decisive step of backing de Gaulle? De Gaulle's cultivation of Adenauer (between November 1958 and January 1963, the two men met on fifteen occasions, had one hundred hours of talks, and wrote to each other over forty times) was certainly one reason.[41] When Adenauer made a state visit to France in July 1962, he was hailed by de Gaulle as "a great German, a great European, a great man who is a great friend of France."[42] Flattery on this scale must have been hard to ignore. When de Gaulle made a return visit to Germany in September 1962, moreover, he aroused popular approval by declaring his admiration for the "great German people." In a droll aside, he added: "If they weren't still a great people, they wouldn't be applauding me."[43] Nobody had spoken to the Germans in these tones since 1945. Adenauer also doubted that Britain would bring economic benefits to the Community and was less than impressed by the Kennedy White House. The prolonged Berlin crisis in 1961 had left Adenauer with the conviction that Kennedy was "a weak president surrounded by inexperienced advisors from the professorial class."[44]

Adenauer, in short, had concluded that France should be the keystone of his foreign policy. Backing de Gaulle was nonetheless a very bold decision to take. Adenauer gave his foreign policy a French orientation against the advice of his economics minister (Ludwig Erhard), his foreign minister (Gerhard Schröder), and most of the rest of his government. Adenauer's support for the French government was given, moreover, in the most explicit manner possible—by the signature of the Franco-German Treaty of Friendship on January 22, 1963, just a week after de Gaulle's shock press conference. Although the contents of the treaty had been under discussion for some months, the German foreign ministry staffers were so unprepared to formalize relations that they had not brought any official treaty paper with them, nor did they have the appropriate leather folder. An official was dispatched at the last moment to buy something suitable in rue Faubourg St. Honoré.[45] As a leading German scholar has commented: "It is almost certain that if there had been someone else heading the Federal Government the treaty would not have been signed."[46]

The treaty established close military, diplomatic, and cultural ties between the two countries. The heads of government were to meet each other twice a year; the foreign ministers of the two nations were to meet every three months; "high officials" within the foreign ministry were to meet every month to "survey current problems and to prepare the ministers' meeting." Similar regular contacts were to be initiated in the fields of defense, education, and youth (a particular preoccupation of Adenauer's). In foreign policy, the two countries committed themselves to "consult each other, prior to any decision, on all important questions of foreign policy . . . with a view to arriving, in so far as possible, at a similar position." Such consultation would specifically deal with EEC, NATO, and East–West matters, although the German parliament, upon ratification, insisted upon writing into the preamble of the treaty a commitment that such consultation would not lead to decisions incompatible with West Germany's obligations under the EEC and NATO treaties. In defense, the high commands of the two countries were to "harmonize" strategy and tactics, and the governments were to "endeavor" to organize military procurement projects on a joint basis. In the field of education and youth, every effort was to be made to increase the number of young French people learning German and young Germans learning French. In terms reminiscent of the 1948 Congress of Europe, the two governments called for the institution of exchanges between "pupils, students, young artists and workers" and for cooperation in scientific research.

The Franco-German treaty was Adenauer's last major act as a statesman. Erhard, under strong American pressure, broke into open revolt against his leader, and after intense party infighting, substituted Adenauer as leader of the CDU in September 1963. But from the British viewpoint the damage was done. On January 29, the French foreign minister, Couve de Murville, brought negotiations for British entry to a close. The Benelux governments and press squawked but were unable to go beyond merely voicing their dissent. Macmillan was left to tell the British people in a broadcast: "What happened at Brussels yesterday was bad; bad for us, bad for Europe, and bad for the whole Free World."[47] But not bad for de Gaulle, who had revenged the defeat of the Fouchet negotiations and had asserted his primacy within The Six.

THE "EMPTY CHAIR" CRISIS AND
THE LUXEMBOURG COMPROMISE

The paradox of de Gaulle's rejection of the British application is that he might well have found the UK a welcome ally during the so-called Empty Chair Crisis. If the Fouchet crisis was about the supranational Dutch battling to stop the French domination of The Six, and the 1963 crisis about de Gaulle's opposition to the EEC's Atlanticization, the infighting that rocked the Community between June 1965 and January 1966 was characterized by de Gaulle's desire to keep decision making out of the hands of the Commission and Assembly and in the hands of the member states. Britain would likely have sided with the general on this issue.

The crisis arose directly out of a major success for greater integration. The EEC had spent most of the period between January 1962 and December 1964 wrangling over the small print of the CAP. West Germany, in particular, had defended the interests of her farmers tenaciously against the Commission's desire to accelerate trade in cereals by harmonizing wheat prices throughout the EEC.

In the autumn of 1964, France, the likely main beneficiary of freer intra-Community trade in agriculture, lost patience and set a deadline of December 15, 1964, for reductions in West German wheat prices. Caught between these external pressures and internal resistance in an election year from farmers' groups who feared French competition, the German government eventually agreed to reduce its target price for cereals to 425 DM per metric ton. It was further agreed that the harmonized wheat price would be introduced on July 1, 1967, not in 1966 as the Commission wanted. The 425 DM price was 60 percent over the world market price, and by enabling "all but the most inefficient farmers to go on producing," it ensured that the CAP would be an expensive commitment for The Six.[48]

These decisions opened the way for a completion of the common market. In January 1965, the Commission proposed that July 1, 1967, should become the deadline for the final removal of all intra-Community tariffs and the final harmonization of the common external tariff. Economic union, it seemed, would be realized three years ahead of schedule. Almost simultaneously, The Six, recognizing that the EEC had outgrown Euratom and the ECSC, agreed to unify the three Communities into a single body. The so-called Merger Treaty was signed in April 1965. This move was not an unmixed blessing: "The amalgamation of functions and the doubling of staff necessitated large-scale reorganization . . . as a consequence of which the Commission lost valuable time which could have been spent on its real tasks."[49]

The agreements to complete the common market and unify the Communities turned the Commission, potentially, into a major force. Its president, Walter Hallstein, was determined to give the Commission a higher profile. At the end of December 1964, at Chatham House in London, he gave a forthright speech that reminded his listeners that from January 1966, the Council of Ministers would vote by a qualified majority and, in accordance with article 149 of the EEC treaty, unanimity would be needed among the member states to amend a Commission proposal. These two key "constitutional" powers, Hallstein insisted, would make the Commission the "mediator" of the EEC and end forever any prospect of a single country—read France—dominating the EEC's proceedings.

Hallstein posed the question of whether this fact implied a reduction in national sovereignty. He responded that it did not. The concept of state sovereignty was a myth, at any rate for the relatively small powers of the EEC. Europe had to learn to speak with a single voice if it was to count on the world stage. To this end, the member states would be forced to recognize that economic union was not enough. More integration was needed at the political level, and Hallstein made clear that he regarded the Commission as the agent that would promote integration in the political sphere. What would the foreign policy orientation of this new Europe be? Hallstein underlined that the EEC's link with the United States was fundamental to its future. He scathingly attacked, though not by name, supporters of power politics, arguing that a vision of international politics that reasoned in such categories was "mistaken" and "immoral."[50]

Hallstein's Chatham House speech has been summarized at some length because it illustrates the old adage that it takes two to make a fight. Hallstein, conscious of the fact that de Gaulle had a presidential election within a year and hence was unlikely to wish to seem anti-Community, had decided that the moment was ripe to strengthen the Community's supranational institutions at the expense of the member states. Nevertheless, most historical accounts of the major crisis that paralyzed the EEC in 1965 have cast de Gaulle as the villain of the piece—a role that he admittedly played with relish.[51]

The issue that sparked a conflict between the French government and the Commission was the sensitive one of CAP financing. The January 1962 accord had specified that the CAP would be paid for by national contributions until June 30, 1965. After the December 15, 1964, agreement, the Council invited the Commission to submit proposals by April 1, 1965, specifying how agriculture would be financed from July 1, 1965, until the CAP entered into operation. Hallstein and Agriculture Commissioner Sicco Mansholt drew up the three-point plan that they subsequently submitted to the Council in "utmost secrecy." The other members of the Commission were apparently kept "carefully out of the picture" while the proposals were being drafted.[52]

"Hallstein's gamble" was simple. From July 1, 1967, he proposed that the EEC's running costs would be paid out of the EEC's "own resources." These would derive from the levies imposed upon non-Community agricultural imports and by the proceeds deriving from the common external tariff on industrial goods. Since collecting fees on this scale would produce resources far in excess of what the Community was already spending, the Commission's second proposal was to phase in the amount raised by industrial tariffs—a popular proposal with the Netherlands, which otherwise stood to lose the income from duty on goods imported via Rotterdam and then reexported to the rest of The Six. Nevertheless, by January 1, 1972, the Commission would have been in control of all revenues deriving from the common external tariff.[53]

The Commission also proposed that the Assembly should have a greater say in deciding the Community's budget. The Commission's scheme was that the existing system (by unanimous vote in the Council of Ministers, after the opinion of the Assembly had been heard) should be replaced by a new procedure. The Commission would send a draft budget to the Council of Ministers, which would amend it and send it to the Assembly. The Assembly was empowered to make amendments by a simple majority vote and to send the budget back to the drawing board—the Commission. The Commission could accept or reject the amendments. If the Commission accepted the amendments of the Assembly, the Council could only overturn the decision if five out of six countries voted against on a "one country, one vote" basis. In the event of the Commission disagreeing with the Assembly on a specific point, the support of four countries out of six was needed by the Commission in the Council of Ministers. If a blocking majority of four could not be raised, the Assembly's version was automatically accepted.[54]

This scheme, in short, gave the Assembly much more power and made the Commission, in budgetary matters, a "kind of government of the Community," to quote Marjolin. The Commission would, with the assistance of a mere two states (the profederalist Netherlands and Luxembourg, say), have been in a position to drive through its expenditure plans even if Italy, Germany, and France had been opposed. Robert Marjolin regarded this as an "absurdity" and told his colleagues so.[55] Jean Monnet's Action Committee nevertheless welcomed the Commission's proposals at the beginning of May 1965.

The Commission's plans, however, did not go far enough for the Assembly. On May 12, it adopted a resolution by seventy-six votes to zero, with ten Gaullists abstaining, which would have increased its role in the budget process still further: indeed, it would have made the Assembly the final arbiter of the budget's size.[56]

The issue was thus a fundamental one. From July 1, 1967, the EEC was set to become an institution with substantial resources of its own. Who would decide how the resources would be spent? The Commission and the Assembly were suggesting that the member states should cede control of the EEC's financial future to its supranational institutions. It was a challenge that de Gaulle could not ignore.

Nor did he. The Commission's proposals were debated in the Council of Ministers on June 13–15, 1965. At this meeting, the French simply suggested that the member states should disregard the July 1, 1967, date and continue to fund the Community until January 1, 1970. When the Council met again on June 28, faced with the specific task of deciding how to finance the EEC's agricultural spending before the June 30 deadline, France's partners, prompted behind the scenes by Hallstein, linked approval of the agricultural finance mechanism to the broader question of financing the Community.[57] In effect, they argued that they would only keep their promise to fund the CAP if France struck a deal to give the supranational institutions of the EEC a greater budgetary role.[58] Italy, whose agricultural trade deficit had grown from $203 million in 1961 to $805 million in 1965 (and would reach $1,236 million by 1969, when a single market for agricultural products had been established), was particularly insistent: "The most implacable of de Gaulle's antagonists was to be his sorely tried partner to the South."[59]

In short, France's partners had decided to give the French a taste of their own negotiating medicine: "There was a sense of settling old scores."[60] The first rule of international politics, however, is to pick your fights carefully. The gauntlet having been thrown down, France proceeded to slap the Community in the face with it. On July 6, 1965, the French government withdrew its permanent representative from Brussels and announced that it would not be taking part in the Community's specialized policy committees. The "empty chair" policy had begun. The Five and the Commission soon threw in the towel. At the end of July 1965, the Commission drew up an extremely complicated plan that blurred the agricultural financing issue and shelved the notion of the Assembly's role in determining the budget. This new proposal "gave the French full satisfaction."[61]

De Gaulle, however, decided to up the ante. Hallstein's behavior had convinced him that the Commission "had shown a bias which is in keeping neither with its mission nor with ordinary decency." Hallstein and Mansholt, in particular, had, in de Gaulle's view, "disqualified themselves as neutral senior officials" and had to be "sent packing."[62] On September 9, 1965, press conference diplomacy resumed with a vengeance. De Gaulle spoke his mind about federalists like Hallstein and their plans. France, he said, wanted a "reasonable" Community. That did not mean one "ruled by some technocratic body of elders, stateless and irresponsible." The general emphasized that France had only agreed to the implementation of the second stage of the EEC treaty in 1962 because her partners had finally agreed to "settle the agricultural problem" by June 30, 1965. They had not fulfilled that undertaking and had colluded with the Commission's attempts to make itself "a great independent financial power." This fact, de Gaulle argued, had allowed the French government "more clearly to assess in what position our country risks finding itself if some of the provisions initially laid down in the Rome treaty were actually enforced." Meetings in the Council of Ministers would, from January 1, 1966, be by a qualified majority. Decisions would be made on economic policy or even agricultural policy "without France's let or leave." Altering the Commission's proposals would be impossible "unless by some extraordinary chance, the six states were unanimous in formulating an amendment." The Constitution of the Fifth Republic did not permit "such a subordinate position," de Gaulle averred. Delphically, de Gaulle concluded that the Community would no doubt get under way "after a period of time the length of which nobody can foresee."[63]

The Five vehemently insisted that France should return to the table but took few specific actions to entice her back. They backed off, however, from dragging France before the European Court of Justice for having breached article 5 of the EEC treaty, which states that "[member-states] shall abstain from any measure which could jeopardize the attainment of the objectives of this treaty." Any such decision would surely have prompted de Gaulle to break with the Community permanently.

At this point, however, Hallstein's confidence that de Gaulle could not break too openly with the EEC was verified. In the December 1965 presidential elections, all four of de Gaulle's opponents, especially the Socialist François Mitterrand, overtly campaigned on a pro-European platform and advocated restarting negotiations with The Five. French farmers' associations urged their members to vote against de Gaulle. As a result, Mitterrand, who was endorsed by Jean Monnet, forced de Gaulle into a second ballot that the general only narrowly won.

The week after Christmas 1965, the French government said it would attend a meeting of foreign ministers to discuss the crisis on January 17–18, 1966, in Luxembourg. At this encounter, foreign minister Couve de Murville took a strong line. The French government asked, among other things, that the member states be given a preventive veto over the submission of Commission proposals to the Council, that a rotating presidency of the Commission be introduced, and that a de facto veto over legislation be introduced by giving member states the right, on questions of declared vital national interest, to vote by unanimity on whether or not a policy vote (to be decided by QMV) should be held.

The meeting was adjourned until January 28. Before the renewal of talks, however, an accord was reached on a set of points clarifying the relationship between the Council and the Commission. The question of the retention of the veto proved more intractable. Negotiations continued until late in the evening on January 29, 1966. The ministers finally agreed to differ. The compromise they arrived at—the "Luxembourg compromise"—is worth quoting in full, if only as testimony to the fertility of the negotiators' imagination:

1. When issues very important to one or more member countries are at stake, the members of the Council will try, within a reasonable time, to reach solutions which can be adopted by all members of the Council, while respecting their mutual interests, and those of the Community, in accordance with Article 2 of the treaty.

2. The French delegation considers that, when very important issues are at stake, discussion must be continued until unanimous agreement is reached.

3. The six delegations note that there is a divergence of views on what should be done in the event of a failure to reach complete agreement.

4. However, they consider that this divergence does not prevent the Community's work being resumed in accordance with the normal procedure.[64]

France, in other words, reserved the right to repeat the obstructive actions of the previous six months if she were to be outvoted on an issue of major importance for her national interests. The other member states did not consent to France's right to do so but acknowledged that she would. Marjolin adds in a sardonic aside that the other governments "did not want the majority vote any more than the French government did and they sacrificed it to the French with no great pain, and some even with secret relief."[65] As Ludlow has argued, "The gap between federalist rhetoric and the realities of cooperation in Brussels had been decisively exposed . . . none of the member states shared the belief in a rapid movement towards federation characteristic of Hallstein, the vast majority of Members of the European Parliament, and a vociferous body of opinion within the Dutch, German, Italian and Belgian assemblies."[66]

As the French wanted, moreover, agriculture was to be financed until 1970 through national contributions, and the decision on the Commission's "own resources" was postponed until that date. A free market in foodstuffs, it was agreed, would come into force on July 1, 1968, at the same time as the last stage of tariff cuts on manufactured goods. France had been forced back to the negotiating table by domestic public opinion, but de Gaulle had made his point. Henceforth, the Commission should regard itself as a civil service, not a proto-government of Europe, and big questions were to be decided by unanimity, whatever the EEC treaty might say. This remains the case today.

A CERTAIN VISION OF EUROPE

The Luxembourg compromise left de Gaulle as the arbiter of the Community's development. France opposed Hallstein's renewal as president of the Commission in 1966, and the German was replaced by Belgium's Jean Rey from July 1, 1967. De Gaulle dismissed the second British attempt to gain membership—during the premiership of the Labour leader Harold Wilson in 1967—almost contemptuously. In May 1967, de Gaulle warned of "destructive upheaval" if Britain succeeded in entering the EEC. A visit from Wilson in June 1967, at which the British prime minister bumptiously told de Gaulle that Britain would not "take no for an answer," was to little avail.[67] In November 1967, de Gaulle expressed his absolute opposition to British entry.

In fairness, Britain's parlous economic state turned the general's veto into a normal act of prudence. The travails of sterling in 1967, which culminated in a substantial forced devaluation just before de Gaulle's announcement, meant that absorbing Britain into the EEC would have been a major risk for the other participants. Britain was no longer the haughty world power that was too dignified to cooperate with her neighbors across the channel. She was a postimperial power who was retrenching desperately on overseas' commitments. She was also rapidly becoming a postindustrial power whose manufacturing prowess had been eclipsed by West Germany and was being superseded by the other countries of The Six, notably once-poor Italy. Two generations of high living had left Britain a beggar at Brussels's door: de Gaulle was not alone in believing that British membership could only weaken the EEC, not strengthen it.

De Gaulle also sat on all attempts to further supranational government within the Community. Plans for a directly elected Parliament, for greater economic integration, and for "political cooperation" were firmly put on the shelf for so long as the general remained in power.

Predictably, this stalemate induced academic analysis to swing from optimism about the inevitability of institutional spillover to pessimism over the prospects for an extension of supranational government within The Six. A seminal article by the Harvard scholar Stanley Hoffmann advanced the thesis that international relations experts had underestimated the extent to which the institutions of the EEC could substitute for nation-states. Touchy, postimperial France was never going to accept the advance of supranationalism once it began to impinge upon sensitive areas: its "historical situation" was more influential, politically, than any spillover mechanism. Hoffmann's article was a useful corrective to the euphoria of much of the early literature in political science and international relations about the European experiment. The EEC was not a machine automatically fuelled by passive transfers of national sovereignty.[68]

While Hoffmann was right to caution that reports of the death of the nation-state had been greatly exaggerated, the EEC had still proved its worth by the end of its first decade. The EEC's biggest achievement was undoubtedly trade liberalization. As soon as the national tariff barriers came down, trucks and trains started moving goods to the neighbors. Trade between EEC members increased more than threefold in cash terms between 1958 and 1970, from just under $7 billion to just over $24 billion. The biggest beneficiary of trade liberalization was Germany, which was running a trade surplus of over $1.1 billion by 1970, but in a sense everyone was a winner. Italy's imports from the rest of the Community expanded from $687 million in 1958 to $3,390 million in 1970; its exports, however, surged from $608 million to $3,373 million in the same period. Behind these bare statistics lay millions of real people who were able to escape from poverty, buy themselves a fridge and a television, and splash out on a car, even a foreign-made car, instead of a scooter.[69]

Most of this trade was in capital goods and foodstuffs, however, and even in these sectors, "the completion of the single market started to falter by the end of the 1960s."[70] Trade in services and banking remained at the starting blocks, as did freedom of movement for workers. Regulation 38/64 abolished all discrimination across the EEC against workers with equal qualifications, but who was to say what was equal? Difficulties in obtaining recognition of diplomas, national professional guilds and their arcane rules, lack of transparency in public contracts, and divergent company law all ensured that the labor market was anything but fully integrated.

In an influential article published in 1969, a contemporary analyst of the EEC, the economist John Pinder, called the removal of measures of national preference within the economic space created by the EEC treaty "negative integration." He contrasted such measures to "positive integration," by which he meant, "the formation and application of coordinated and common policies in order to fulfill economic and welfare objectives other than the removal of discrimination."[71] In his view, the experience of the 1960s had shown that it was simply easier to ban discrimination than legislate positively: "A treaty can more easily make effective the 'thou shalt not' commandments than the 'thou shalt' ones."[72]

This is why the CAP looms so large in the EEC story. It was the single most striking act of "positive integration" achieved during the 1960s. By managing to agree on agriculture, the thorniest of subjects, The Six were able to construct the Community mentality that enabled the process of European integration to consolidate itself. In its first decade, "to a great extent the CAP was the EEC, and the EEC the CAP."[73] If one had failed, the other would have, too.

Yet the psychological and institutional gains brought by the CAP came at a price. The CAP might easily have derailed the liberalization of world trade promoted by the Kennedy and Johnson administrations throughout the 1960s. The EEC played a major role during the Kennedy Round trade talks (May 4, 1964–June 30, 1967). Despite the "Empty Chair" crisis, which by paralyzing the EEC held up the Kennedy Round for some months, the Commission, carefully monitored by the Council of Ministers, negotiated on the EEC's behalf and played a significant role in obtaining the substantial reductions in tariffs on industrial goods that were the Kennedy Round's most praised feature.[74]

The EEC was also the chief culprit, however, for the Kennedy Round's dismal failure to liberalize trade in agriculture. The CAP—a policy that was designed to prop up the incomes of an important economic lobby within the Community even if that meant higher prices in the shops and injured relations with important transatlantic trading partners—was called economic nationalism when others did it. Fortunately, U.S. president Lyndon B. Johnson was convinced, like Eisenhower, that the political and economic unification of Western Europe would be an important improvement in the international milieu and was hence in the United States' long-term interests. Historians have agreed that Johnson showed great forbearance in his dealings with The Six, who—like most of the rest of the world—were abusing his policy in Vietnam as well as blocking freer trade.[75] Johnson's successor, Richard M. Nixon, would prove to be much less benign in his approach to the EEC.

Thanks largely to trade liberalization, the EEC's external trade expanded notably in the EEC's first decade. Imports from the rest of the world, $16.2 billion in 1958, rose to nearly $46 billion by 1970. Exports, $15.9 billion in 1958, reached $45.2 billion in the same period. The EEC built up a substantial trade surplus with the EFTA nations (over $4 billion in 1970) but imported $3 billion a year more from North America than it exported.[76] This huge increase in trade with the rest of the world led to more and better jobs, higher disposable incomes, and a notable increase in the amount of foreign (mostly American) investment attracted by Europe's economic dynamism.

De Gaulle resigned from the presidency of France on April 28, 1969, after a plan of his to decentralize government was defeated in a national referendum. His authority had, in any case, been weakened by the events of May–June 1968. As soon as the general was out of the way, the governments of The Six, including France, began to look at ways in which they could promote measures of positive integration in regional development, social issues, and monetary policy. They also reopened the question of British EEC membership and explored the possibility of having a common foreign policy.

De Gaulle had clearly been a bottleneck for the integrationist aspirations of The Six. But he was not a purely negative figure. Looking back over the 1960s, one comes to the conclusion that dealing with de Gaulle compelled the other national leaders to recognize that they did not want their governments to wither away and be replaced by a federal government responding to a European Parliament—the dream of Altiero Spinelli and many other leading intellectuals and politicians across The Six. Political union meant something else. It meant that the Community should acquire more competences—that more decisions should be taken at Community level—but not that national governments should renounce sovereignty.

It was not by chance that The Six took their bold decision to press ahead with measures of positive integration at a summit meeting of their national leaders at The Hague, the Netherlands' administrative capital, in December 1969. They had learned from the experience of the 1960s that major Community initiatives would not stick unless they were taken by the national leaders acting in concert. In the 1970s, this insight was institutionalized in the form of the European Council, regular summit meetings of the member states' heads of state and government. De Gaulle's lasting achievement in the context of European integration was that he ensured that the member states kept their central role in the process of supranational decision making.

5

✛

Weathering the Storm
The EC during the 1970s

The 1970s and early 1980s are often regarded as years in which the integration process stalled or even went backward. This is exaggerated. In institutional terms, the chief innovation of this period was the creation of the European Council—regular summits of the heads of state or government—which (as de Gaulle had foreseen) rapidly became the EC's agenda setter. Yet the supranational institutions of the EC consolidated their position, too. The Court of Justice successfully asserted the supremacy of legislation emanating from the Community over national laws and confirmed its view that the Treaty of Rome had conferred rights on the citizens of the EC's member states. The Assembly obtained the first prerequisite of parliamentary status by being chosen by direct election in June 1979, although its powers remained purely consultative. The EC also experimented with intergovernmental cooperation in the field of foreign policy, although results were mixed.

Perhaps the most striking achievement of the Community in the 1970s, however, was a negative one. It did not fold when the postwar boom came to a crunching end. The EEC, as chapter 3 underlined, owed its creation at least in part to the benign economic environment created by the United States. The U.S. security shield allowed Europe to spend less on defense; the U.S. economy sucked in European imports and was a source of substantial direct investment; trade was conducted in dollars, with the United States leading the way in making trade freer. In the 1970s, some elements of the Pax Americana began to break down. Nevertheless, the Community held together with remarkable tenacity. There was no return to economic nationalism despite the conditions of "stagflation" (high inflation and low, or negative, growth) that prevailed throughout most of the Community for much of this period, and despite the fact that currency fluctuations distorted the newly created common market. The adoption of the European Monetary System in 1979, with its creation of a nominal European currency (the Ecu), was an important symbolic achievement of the 1970s, although it did not work as its authors intended until the mid-1980s. Roy Jenkins, the British Social Democrat who presided over the European Commission from 1977 to 1981, even contended that the EMS "has been the central channel from which most subsequent European advance has flowed."[1]

The truth is that the 1970s are seen as a decade of stagnation for European integration more for the decade's failure to live up to expectations than for its actual shortcomings. The coincidence of Charles de Gaulle's retirement from politics in 1969, Willy Brandt's innovative new government in Bonn, and the election of a "pro-European" British premier in Britain in June 1970 appeared to provide an opportunity for building a European Union, with its own currency and able to act as a significant independent player on the world stage. These ambitions were revealed as vain by the 1970s, a fact that has blinded scholars to the real consolidation that nevertheless took place.

THE HAGUE CONFERENCE AND ITS CONSEQUENCES

Enthusiasts for European integration hoped that the Community, post–de Gaulle, would take immediate strides toward greater unity. The same desire motivated de Gaulle's successor, Georges Pompidou, who was determined to give his own imprint to French policy. One of Pompidou's first acts as president was to propose a meeting of The Six's leaders to discuss how to go beyond the degree of integration already achieved with the common market.

This meeting took place at The Hague on December 1–2, 1969. At The Hague, the gathered heads of government decided to push ahead in five crucial policy areas: financing the Community, which would finally be provided with its "own resources"; strengthening Community institutions, in particular the Assembly; the creation of an economic and monetary union; "political unification," which the foreign ministers were asked to study; and the enlargement of the Community through negotiations with would-be entrants Britain, Ireland, Denmark, and Norway.[2]

The small print of the first of these objectives was decided in April 1970 when The Six decided that the EEC would be funded by levies on imports into the Community and by the transfer from national governments of up to 1 percent of the receipts from value-added tax (VAT). The French government ruled out, however, any suggestion that the establishment of "own resources" should lead to an increase in the budgetary powers of the Parliament.

The next three of these objectives generated detailed reports by distinguished members of the European establishment. A committee chaired by the Christian Democrat prime minister of Luxembourg, Pierre Werner, dealt with an economic and monetary union. The Werner Report was presented at the end of October 1970. Its main conclusion was that "economic and monetary union is an objective realizable in the course of the present decade, provided the political will of the member states to realize this objective, solemnly declared at the Conference in the Hague, is present."[3] The report set tough immediate targets, however. Between January 1, 1971, and the end of 1974, it recommended that the council of economics and finance ministers should become the "center of decision" for economic policy within the Community: national governments would be obliged to conduct fiscal policy within the guidelines laid down by the Council, while member states' central banks were charged with "progressively narrowing" the "margins of fluctuation" between Community currencies by intervening on the financial markets.[4]

The Werner Report left the question of a common currency open. Economic and monetary union could be "accompanied by the maintenance of national monetary symbols" (this ugly phrase is entirely typical of the report's abstract language), but it was suggested that "considerations of a psychological and political order militate in favor of the adoption of a single currency."[5]

In short, the report envisaged the Community's economy being managed at Community level. As the report stated: "The center of decision for economic policy will exercise independently, in accordance with the Community interest, a decisive influence over the general economic policy of the Community."[6] Such a shift of core economic responsibilities from national governments to collective decision making had political implications that entailed "the progressive development of political cooperation," but the report did not specify what this might mean in concrete terms, except to underline that the "center of decision" would have to be subject to the European Parliament.[7] Werner's report was accepted in principle by the Council of Ministers in the spring of 1971, although not without many reservations being aired.

The powers of the European Parliament were the concern of a report by Professor Georges Vedel, a French political scientist, who was asked in April 1971 to propose measures of constitutional engineering to strengthen the legislative and supervisory role of the Community's parliamentary institutions. Vedel proposed a two-stage extension of powers. In stage 1, he urged that the Parliament should be given powers of "codecision" (veto) over all matters concerning the revision of the treaties, the admission of new members, and the ratification of international agreements and actions taken by the Council under article 235 of the EEC treaty. He argued that the Parliament should possess powers of "suspension" over all proposals to harmonize national legislation. In a second stage, codecision powers (for example, the power to block decisions of the Council of Ministers) would be extended to the Parliament in this sphere, too.[8]

The third report to emerge in response to The Hague summit's final communiqué was actually the first to be published. The foreign ministers of The Six outlined proposals for greater cooperation in foreign policy in July 1970, and on October 27, 1970, they issued a four-part plan of action to increase "political cooperation" (EPC) between the states.[9] Despite some leaden rhetoric in the preamble, the plan's actual recommendations were extremely limited. The member states pledged:

> To ensure, through regular exchanges and consultations, a better mutual understanding on the great international problems;
> To strengthen their solidarity by promoting the harmonization of their views, the co-ordination of their positions, and, where it appears possible and desirable, common actions.

In pursuit of these ends, the foreign ministers advised that they should meet "at least every six months," unless the "gravity" or "importance" of the agenda required a summit of heads of state or government. A "political committee" of government-nominated officials should meet four times a year to prepare their masters' agenda. Within two years, the foreign ministers were to issue a second report that assessed how much progress had been made toward political cooperation among The Six—or rather, as Britain, Denmark, Ireland, and Norway had by then begun entry negotiations, among The Ten.

FROM SIX TO NINE

The foregoing description of the developments set in train by The Hague summit is important background for the enlargement negotiations, which began in earnest at the end of June 1970, following the surprise victory of Edward Heath's Conservatives in the British general elections of that month. The would-be entrants were striving to join a club that had great ambitions for its future. Europe intended to become an economic union with strengthened centralized institutions and, perhaps, a common currency.

In the case of Britain, Prime Minister Heath's task was to show his continental counterparts—especially France—that Britain was prepared to go along with such a major expansion in the EEC's activities. Actually, crisis-hit Britain was desperate to join on almost any terms. British GNP per head had declined to three-quarters of the average for The Six ($2,170 versus $2,557).[10] In his book *Missed Chances*, Sir Roy Denman, a senior Foreign Office official who was part of the British negotiating team, commented wryly: "No sensible traveler on the sinking *Titanic* would have said, 'I will only enter a lifeboat if it is well scrubbed, well painted and equipped with suitable supplies of food and drink.'"[11]

The negotiators on the other side of the table drove a hard bargain. Britain (and the other would-be entrants) was asked to accept the *acquis communautaire* (the accumulated body of Community law) in toto. There would be no opportunity to try and remake the Community in Britain's image: Britain had to accept the main Community policies whether she liked them or not (and in many cases, she did not). Nevertheless, Britain strove to find workable transitional arrangements in sensitive areas such as imports of dairy produce from New Zealand and cane sugar from the West Indies, fishing rights, and the size of the British contribution to the Community budget.[12]

Of these, the last was unquestionably the most important. Since Britain was a major importer of non-Community agricultural produce (New Zealand lamb, beef from Argentina, Canadian wheat), she risked having to pay, under the terms of the agreement on financing the Community reached in April 1970, substantial sums into the Community while receiving (since the EC's budget was dominated by the CAP and Britain had a small agricultural sector) little in return. In all, the EC initially proposed that Britain should contribute a fifth of the Community's budget.

Britain's counterproposal was to pay 3 percent of the EEC's budget in the first instance and gradually increase that figure year by year. This suggestion prompted President Pompidou to declare: "The British have three qualities among others: humor, tenacity and realism. I have the feeling that we are slightly in the humorous stage."[13]

The issue was eventually resolved by deciding that Britain's contribution would rise to approximately 19 percent of the budget over five years from a starting point in 1973 of just under 9 percent. The underlying assumption of this deal, however, was that agriculture would decline as a share of the EC's budget and that Britain would also benefit from Community subsidies to help regional regeneration. So long as agriculture dominated the EC's expenditure, the British contribution to the EC's finances was a bomb waiting to explode. It was in fact informally agreed that the budget deal could be renegotiated if an "unacceptable situation" arose later in the 1970s.[14]

The compromise over the budget issue was reached only after a May 1971 summit meeting between Pompidou and Heath.[15] Thereafter, the negotiations proceeded relatively smoothly and reached a successful conclusion in June 1971. Britain promised to harmonize her food prices up to Community levels by "1 January 1978 at the latest" and to abolish duties on EEC products in five stages between January 1, 1973, and July 1, 1977. The Common external tariff was also to be introduced in progressive stages and was to come into full force on July 1, 1977.

The question of entry to the "Common Market," as the EC was habitually dubbed in Britain until the mid-1980s, at once became a political battlefield. British politics is traditionally highly partisan, with cross-party collaboration being rare. Over EC entry, however, tribal loyalties broke down.

This ability of the European issue to upset traditional allegiances was shown in October 1971 when the House of Commons debated the terms of entry obtained by the government. Only a revolt against the party whip by sixty-eight pro-EC Labour MPs enabled Heath to win the vote.[16] In all, the Commons debated EC accession for 173 hours in 1971 to 1972. The European Communities bill passed its third reading by a narrow majority of 301 to 284 on July 13, 1972, and the bill received the royal assent on October 17, 1972. On the eve of British entry, an influential right-wing weekly opined, in an article provocatively entitled "Unconditional Surrender," that "Heath has done what Napoleon and Hitler aspired but failed to do."[17]

Ireland and Denmark, not least because agriculture played a large role in their economies, had fewer doubts than Britain over the wisdom of entering the EEC. In the 1960s, the EC's protectionist stance over agriculture had worsened Denmark's severe balance-of-payments problems and had inflated the country's welfare costs since the Danish state had to prop up flagging farm incomes. Entering the EC thus made good economic sense for the Danes, although the decision to enter was controversial within the country and especially within the ruling center-left coalition headed by Prime Minister Jens Otto Krag. Denmark was a keen Atlanticist and supporter of Nordic unity and was dubious of French ambitions to build a separate European identity in foreign policy. The Danes were also proud of their highly developed welfare state and feared—without justification—that the "Danish model" would be dismantled. Only the reflection that economic necessity would anyway compel Denmark to reduce the generosity of its welfare state, in the absence of the higher national income that EC membership would bring, persuaded Danish voters to agree to membership.[18]

Ireland stood to benefit even more than Denmark from the CAP, since new markets were opened to Irish agricultural products and rural incomes stood to rise considerably. The downside was that membership meant opening up the Irish domestic market to industrial competition, but it was on the whole a price the Irish government was prepared to pay, not least because membership would enable it to attract foreign direct investment: a potential agent of modernization. Politically, Community membership enabled Ireland after 1973 to escape from its economic dependency on Britain (in 1973, two-thirds of Irish exports still went to Britain) and thus, in a sense, complete the break from her colonial past. EC membership would "create interdependence with Europe, rather than establishing the autarky of myth; again, this was preferable to absolute reliance on the UK." Ireland voted by a plebiscitary majority to join the EC just five months after entry terms had been agreed.[19]

Britain, Ireland, and Denmark (but not Norway, whose electorate's opposition to the EC's fishery policy had led to rejection of membership in a referendum in September 1972) entered the EEC on January 1, 1973. Even before formal accession, however, the three new member states were invited to Paris to take part in a major summit confirming the relaunch of the Community.

The declaration issued by the heads of state and government at the end of the conference on October 21, 1972, boldly presented the EC as a self-confident organization of states that was taking a coherent and independent approach to the world's major problems. As the preamble to the declaration said, "Europe must be able to make its voice heard in world affairs, and to make an original contribution commensurate with its human, intellectual and material resources." The Nine committed themselves to the fundamental principles of democracy, to the establishment of monetary and economic union, to an "improvement in the quality of life as well as the standard of living," to "increase [their] effort in aid and technical assistance to the least favored people," and to the development of international trade and to the promotion of détente with the countries of Eastern Europe. Most strikingly of all, The Nine stated:

> The construction of Europe will allow it, in conformity with its ultimate political objectives, to affirm its personality while remaining faithful to its traditional friendships and to the alliances of the Member States, and to establish its position in world affairs as a distinct entity determined to promote a better international equilibrium, respecting the principles of the Charter of the United Nations. The Member States of the Community, the driving force of European construction, affirm their intention to transform before the end of the present decade the whole complex of their relations into a European Union.

This lofty vision of the Community's future was backed up by a sixteen-point plan for action. In the field of economics, The Nine committed themselves to the Werner Report's timetable, to coordinated policies for fighting inflation, and to obtaining greater stability in the world's currency markets. The Nine further agreed to give a "high priority" to correcting the "structural and regional imbalances that might affect the realization of Economic and Monetary Union." To this end, they agreed to set up a regional development fund before the end of 1973. The establishment of this fund had been the British government's chief priority for the summit.

In foreign affairs, they committed themselves to increase the quantity and improve the quality of their aid to the developing nations; to the "progressive liberalization" of tariff and nontariff barriers via the GATT; and to taking a coordinated position in the ongoing Conference on Security and Cooperation in Europe—a negotiation that eventually led, in 1975, to the Helsinki Declaration on Human Rights, which Italian premier Aldo Moro signed on behalf of the EC.[20] The foreign ministers of The Nine would meet four times a year, instead of twice, and would produce, by June 30, 1973, a second report on "political cooperation."

Finally, the nine heads of state or government made several suggestions for the "reinforcement of institutions." The final paragraph of the declaration requested the institutions of the Community to draw up a report, before the end of 1975, on how to transform the EC's existing institutional structure into a European Union.[21]

Edward Heath judged that "overall, the summit provided the impulse for the next stage of the Community's development."[22] The British certainly fully expected to play a leading role in developing the Community. The official diplomatic report on the Paris summit by Ambassador Nicholas Soames gloated that the summit had marked the end of France's "moral ascendancy" within the Community and the dawn of a new phase in which a "central triangle" of Britain, France, and Germany would be a "directoire de fait" of Community policy.[23] Both this characteristic Foreign Office vainglory and the wider hopes raised by the Paris summit and by the enlargement of the Community were to prove a chimera. The Nine were swiftly knocked off course by the perennial instability of the world's currency markets and by the economic forces unleashed by the October 1973 oil shock.

MONETARY TURMOIL 1971–1974

The optimism of the Paris summit with respect to a monetary union flew in the face of the experience of The Nine on the currency markets since the publication of the Werner Report. At the beginning of the 1970s, the industrial economies were characterized by a set of imbalances that made the conduct of macroeconomic policy extremely difficult. A domestic consumption boom in the United States had led to an outflow of dollars as Americans bought freely from Europe and Japan. Investment overseas by American companies added to the outflow.[24]

The EC, as the world's second largest market, was a particular beneficiary of American investment. This outflow of dollars mattered since the United States had committed itself at the 1944 Bretton Woods conference to buy dollar holdings in gold at the fixed price of $35 per ounce. The dollar, in other words, was literally as good as gold. By the early 1970s, however, the gilt was coming off the greenback. Policymakers realized that if foreign countries decided to swap their accumulated dollars for bullion, the United States would risk a run on Fort Knox. Central bankers and private investors around the world held far greater amounts of dollars than the United States could pay in gold (the EC member states alone held about $16 billion in their central banks), and they were beginning to become skittish at the United States' persistent failure to balance its books.[25]

The inflow of dollars presented major domestic problems for the EC countries, especially Germany, the new "number one in Europe," whose currency, the Deutsche Mark (DM), had emerged in 1968 to 1969 as a magnet for footloose international capital. Germany had to revalue the DM upward by 9 percent in October 1969, although the decision had been the cause of prolonged political debate before and during the October 1969 general elections.[26]

Germany took this step because the large trade and investment surpluses being generated by the cheap mark were socially disruptive (profits were running well ahead of wage rises and the workers were unhappy) and potentially inflationary. Germany had endured one of the worst inflations of all time in the 1920s, and the consequent loss by the German middle class of its savings had been one of the key factors that had propelled the Nazis to power. West Germany's 1949 Basic Law therefore made price stability a constitutional imperative. Once Bonn had revalued, however, it began to press the United States to reduce the high levels of public and consumer spending within the American economy, even if this meant slower economic growth for the United States and the world in general.

The Nixon administration took a different view. Nixon's treasury secretary, the Texan John Connally, argued that countries such as Germany and Japan were exploiting the openness of the American economy to amass artificial trade surpluses. The solution, in his view, was for a measure of protectionism for American manufacturers, for America's allies to take on more of the costly burden of their own defense, and for the Europeans and the Japanese to boost growth within their domestic economies in order to suck in American exports. Presidential elections were due in 1972, and neither Connally nor Nixon wanted to risk a recession.

As Diane Kunz commented, "Nixon decided to put the domestic economy first and let the international chips fall where they might."[27] In a broadcast from Camp David on August 15, 1971, President Nixon ended dollar convertibility for gold, imposed a "temporary surcharge" upon imported goods, and gave tax breaks for investment in plant and machinery "made in the USA."

Nixon's action predictably led to a general strengthening of European currencies. But this strengthening was not symmetrical. That is to say, some currencies, notably the DM, increased in value more than others. France, for instance, limited the rise of the franc against the dollar by selling francs on the currency markets and by imposing exchange controls on the movement of capital. This move also improved France's competitiveness against West Germany, since a weaker currency was a de facto trade barrier that decreased the cost of exports from France and made its imports more expensive. In October 1971, the West German finance minister, the notoriously verbose Karl Schiller, publicly (and pithily) attacked France for following "Colbertian" policies.[28]

Nixon's démarche had, therefore, both opened up cracks within the Community and threatened to cause a breach in transatlantic relations.[29] Faced with a trade war in which everybody would be a victim, the industrialized nations sensibly backed away from the brink. On December 17, 1971, a meeting at the Smithsonian museum in Washington of the so-called Group of Ten, the ten largest economies, agreed to across-the-board revaluations against the dollar in exchange for the suspension of the import surcharge. In order to take some of the tension out of exchange rate movements, the Smithsonian meeting agreed that currencies would be free to fluctuate up to 2.25 percent above or below a "central value" against the dollar before central banks intervened in the currency markets. This device became known as the "tunnel."

It was a device that did not satisfy the West German government. The mark was soon bumping against the roof of the tunnel, while other countries, notably France and Italy, dragged along the floor. Accordingly, on March 7, 1972, The Six, joined by Britain, formed the "Snake within the tunnel." EEC states promised to restrict fluctuations between their own currencies to just 1.125 percent above or below their central value by intervening on the currency markets to shadow the DM. The Snake was thus an attempt to lash the EEC's currencies together like boats in a harbor that would rise and fall together as the dollar tide advanced and ebbed.

Britain's economic weaknesses, however, were such that she was not economically robust or politically stable enough to stick to the regime imposed by the Snake. Sterling joined the Snake in May 1972, just as gloomy balance-of-payments figures and the unconvincing figure of Chancellor

Anthony Barber unleashed a storm of speculation against the pound. On June 23, the pound was forced to float free (and promptly plunged, although high British inflation soon eroded any competitive gains that devaluation was able to give British industry).

In March 1973, the falling dollar caused further tensions. Six EC states—West Germany, the Netherlands, France, Belgium, Luxembourg, and Denmark—jointly floated upward against the dollar; only Italy was forced to drop out. This decision to float as a group undoubtedly reflected the European countries' "aspirations for European unity."[30]

Such aspirations retained some residual force only so long as France tied itself to the others. The oil shock in the autumn of 1973, which quadrupled the price of crude to $11 a barrel, put paid to France's membership. Unable to contain market movements against the franc, France left the Snake in January 1974. In a December 1974 meeting in Paris, The Nine bowed to the inevitable and consigned the Werner Report's timetable for monetary unification to the Greek kalends.

The inability of Britain, France, and Italy to peg their currencies to the DM reflected investors' fears about inflation. Any kind of fixed exchange rate regime among states is impossible to maintain if there are gross disparities in inflation rates, since high-inflation countries are bound to suffer an incremental loss of competitiveness—and thus risk losing markets and jobs to their less-profligate trading partners. As Peter Ludlow has felicitously remarked, the inflation performance of the Community states in the mid-1970s bore more resemblance to the final classification in a Western European subgroup in the World Cup–qualifying competition, with Germany at the top and the United Kingdom and Italy no less securely at the bottom, than to an association of more or less equal states progressing harmoniously and happily toward union.[31]

At bottom, this uneven level of economic performance was a question of domestic political stability. The Community was in fact split along ideological lines. In Germany, politics was based upon broad acceptance by all political forces, including, crucially, the trade unions, of a social market economy in which private enterprise coexisted with high levels of state-provided health care, insurance, and social security. In Britain, France, and Italy, such consensus over the fundamental character of the polity did not exist.

In all three countries, political forces committed to the state direction of the economy were a key variable in the equation. Italy had been wracked by violent strikes and labor unrest since the "hot autumn" of 1969: its successful Communist Party, which was exercising a de facto veto over government policy by the early 1970s, actually represented a force for comparative moderation in industrial disputes. The Heath government in Britain was brought down in 1973 to 1974 by striking miners and power workers. The Labour government headed by Harold Wilson (1974–1976) subsequently followed an expansionary policy of boosting public spending, increasing nationalization, appeasing union pay demands, and imposing crippling levels of taxation on the better off. These policies provoked sky-high inflation and a sterling crisis. In October 1976, the British government, like many Third World countries since, was obliged to beg for a substantial loan from the International Monetary Fund (IMF). In France, the opposition Socialists and Communists formed the "Union of the Left" in 1972. Its platform promised the state control of the economy via public ownership of the banks and the introduction of high-cost measures of social welfare. In all three countries, in short, inflation-fighting measures of the kind that appealed to the Bundesbank were a recipe for social unrest. It was this fact, above all others, that took monetary unification off the agenda and dampened the rhetoric of European unity so common at the beginning of the decade.

FOREIGN POLICY INITIATIVES AND THE TINDEMANS REPORT

The levels of political instability in Western Europe and the acrimony induced by the falling dollar were the main reasons that Henry Kissinger—then national security adviser in the doomed Nixon administration (Kissinger became secretary of state in September 1973)—decided to make 1973 the "Year of Europe" for American foreign policy. In a speech given in New York on April 23, Kissinger argued that a new era in transatlantic relations was dawning. Western Europe's economic revival and economic unification was "an established fact"; the USSR had reached "near-equality" in the military balance of power; Japan had emerged as a "major power center." New problems, such as "insuring the supply of energy" were coming to the fore. By the time President Nixon made a scheduled tour of European capitals at the end of 1973, Kissinger wanted the United States and its allies to have worked out a new "Atlantic Charter" in which the Europeans committed themselves to making a bigger contribution to the West's cause. Kissinger considered that Europe's "new generation" was less committed than their parents to "the unity that made peace possible and to the effort required to maintain it." Kissinger emphasized that the United States supported European unity—but expected "to be met in a spirit of reciprocity" in trade matters. The United States would not withdraw unilaterally from Europe—but, in turn, expected "a fair share of the common effort for the common defense."[32]

In his memoirs, Kissinger insisted that the U.S. government had "conceived the speech as a summons to a new period of creativity among the industrial democracies."[33] In Europe, however, this initiative was greeted with a "thundering silence."[34] When, in June 1973, the Nixon administration signed the Soviet-American agreement on the prevention of nuclear war and intensified détente among the superpowers without so much as consulting the Europeans—who, after all, had most to lose if better U.S.-Soviet relations led to American troop withdrawals—relations became still more chilly. French foreign minister Michel Jobert was especially angered by Kissinger's snub.

The EC's commitment to building a common foreign policy, however, only made the situation worse. The Nine's foreign ministers met in Copenhagen on July 23, 1973, and decided to prepare a document responding to Kissinger's initiative by September. This document, which underlined the EC's role as a "distinct entity" in world affairs, was drawn up without consultation with the Americans and was transmitted to the United States via the Danish foreign minister (Denmark was chairing the Council of Ministers). The Nine then refused to have any bilateral or informal conversations with the United States on the issue. Kissinger regarded this attitude as a deliberate bid by the Europeans—and in particular the French—to take advantage of President Nixon's domestic travails to assert its foreign policy independence from the United States.[35] It is at least as likely, in fact, that the episode simply illustrated the empirical limits of the infant EPC process.

Tensions between the United States and Europe intensified in October 1973 when Syria and Egypt attacked Israel in an attempt to recapture territory lost during the 1967 "Six-Day War." The decision by the Organization of Petroleum Exporting Countries (OPEC) to boycott those Western countries that supported Israel in the conflict—the United States and the Netherlands were singled out—tightened the screws still further. The EC was placed in the uncomfortable position of having to choose between its American ally and the suppliers of what had become since the late 1950s its main source of energy generation.[36]

The governments of The Nine chose to back the Arabs. Having almost unanimously forbidden the United States to make use of European bases for military flights to Israel, the EC's foreign ministers declared on November 6, 1973, that Israel should give back the territory it had held since 1967 and should take into account the "legitimate rights of the Palestinians." This position was in line with several UN resolutions on the Palestinian question, but in Washington the EC's stand "conveyed the implication that when faced with the economic, social and political consequences of a sustained oil embargo the Nine had chosen the path of appeasement at any price."[37]

Proponents of greater political cooperation noted, however, that The Nine had for the first time reached a common position on a major issue of foreign policy. A December 1973 summit of The Nine's leaders, called by Premier Anker Jørgensen of Denmark after pressure from Paris and

Bonn, underlined this novelty by asserting The Nine's "common will to see Europe speak with one voice" in foreign affairs. The Nine's leaders approved a "Document on the European Identity" drawn up by their foreign ministers: this document, while long on rhetoric, was adamant about the EC's desire to develop an independent role in world politics.[38] The summit further announced that The Nine intended to press ahead with a dialogue with the oil producers in order to achieve a "global regime" that would balance economic development in the producer countries with a stable oil supply for the industrialized world at "reasonable prices." The Arab countries welcomed this conciliatory approach.

As a respected French commentator subsequently pointed out, the diplomatic crisis provoked by the oil shock "revealed the gap between the ambitions proclaimed for Europe and its capabilities for real action."[39] By backing the Arabs so openly, the EC had chosen to play hardball with the United States. Certainly, it had more than lived up to its aspiration in the 1972 Paris summit to "establish its position in world affairs as a distinct entity determined to promote a better international equilibrium."

The American response was blunt. In December 1973, speaking just before the Copenhagen summit, Kissinger stated, "Europe's unity must not be at the expense of the Atlantic Community."[40] Kissinger, prompted by Helmut Schmidt, subsequently proposed creating a consumers' organization of the largest industrial nations, whose members would pool their oil reserves and would coordinate their responses to any further price hikes by the OPEC producers' cartel.[41] In February 1974, the largest industrial countries gathered in Washington, D.C., to discuss the American scheme.

The Washington conference was a shambles from the European point of view: Bino Olivi records that "nobody who attended [the conference on energy] will easily forget the grim spectacle of disunity and disorder in the Community's ranks."[42] American speakers from President Nixon down drove home the point that isolationism was likely to gain ground in the United States if Europe persisted in appeasing the Arab countries.[43] This hard American line split—as it was clearly intended to—the French (the keenest supporters of EC–OPEC negotiations) from the Germans and resulted in an embarrassing row between Jobert and Helmut Schmidt, who accused the French government of putting Europe's relationship with the United States in jeopardy.[44]

In the end, every EC state except for France joined the American-sponsored International Energy Agency in November 1974. Earlier, in June 1974, The Nine also acknowledged that the United States would be informed and consulted during the formulation of any major European foreign policy initiative.[45]

The political outcome of the oil shock was, in other words, reminiscent of the Fouchet negotiations. Europe was not yet ready for the French vision of an independent European foreign policy. At the first whiff of grapeshot, its ranks had scattered.

By the end of 1974, therefore, the grand design of the October 1972 Paris summit, of achieving a European Union by the end of the 1970s, was looking somewhat battered. Monetary unification was a nonstarter, hamstrung by the inability of The Nine's governments to combat inflation and by the fragile state of social peace in some member states. The objective of a common foreign policy had proved unworkable on its first trial. Europe was looking more like a loose pan-national trade organization than the serious force in world affairs its leaders aspired to create.

It was this state of disarray in the EC's objectives that pushed the new French president, Valéry Giscard d'Estaing, to launch a crucial institutional initiative in September 1974. Giscard in effect dusted off the Fouchet Plan, but in new, informal, communitarian form, by once again proposing what de Gaulle had always insisted was the only way of taking major decisions among the states: frequent, organized meetings of the heads of the responsible governments. Giscard, however, showed more sensitivity to the preoccupations of the Dutch, Belgians, and Danes, not to mention the Commission, than had the general. Over the next three months, Giscard and his team of negotiators laboriously convinced their counterparts in the Community of their good intentions: France was not making a power grab, just seeking to make the EC work better.[46] At a December 1974 summit in Paris, The Nine agreed to institutionalize their occasional summits and hold them more often. The European Council, as the new body was to be called, would meet three times a year, and while not formally part of the EC's machinery, would provide the EC with an agenda-setting forum.

It did this, and it did more. From the off, the European Council became the Community's strategic decision maker. It gave the EC focus—a kind of de facto Cabinet—and hence provided a mechanism for policy innovation, as opposed to policy implementation. Since December 1974, all new treaties, not to mention key decisions on enlargement, monetary union, and foreign policy, have emanated from the European Council. This fact is anathema to many enthusiasts for a federal Europe, who would prefer nation-states to wither away, not run the show, but so it is.

A second important—though some might say somewhat belated—decision taken by the Paris summit was to ask one of their number, the then prime minister of Belgium, Leo Tindemans, to head an inquiry to "define what was meant by the term European Union."

The Tindemans Report, which was sent to the European Council on December 29, 1975, represented a major act of rethinking about the nature of European integration. European Union, Tindemans argued, implied that "we present a united front to the external world" in "all the main fields of our external relations," including foreign policy. It implied that the EC would have a common economic and monetary policy and that Europe would institute regional development programs to "correct inequalities in development and counteract the centralizing effects of industrial societies." It implied "social action" to "encourage society to organize itself in a fairer and more humane fashion" and to protect Europeans' civil rights. To achieve these tasks, European Union implied institutions "with the necessary powers to determine a common, coherent and all-inclusive political view, the efficiency needed for action, the legitimacy needed for democratic control."[47]

Tindemans envisaged a "step-by-step" approach to European unification and essentially placed the onus upon the governments of the member states to launch initiatives through the newly established European Council.[48] Specifically, in the field of foreign policy, Tindemans recommended that the meaningless distinction between "political cooperation" and "Community business" should be abolished. The member states should cooperate among themselves in the European Council to hold down defense costs and monitor crises—Portugal was a particular worry at that time—within the European region.[49]

In the field of economic and monetary unification, Tindemans presciently suggested that monetary integration might be advanced by allowing those countries that were capable of economic and monetary union to press ahead, using the Snake as a starting point. Tindemans further hoped that the European Council would proceed to coordinate its members' internal monetary policy (money supply), as well as budgetary policy and strategies to combat inflation.[50]

Tindemans was anxious to make Europe "a more discernible reality" to its people.[51] He advocated the introduction of a European passport, free movement across frontiers, the simplification of procedures for refunding medical expenses, increased student exchanges, and the harmonization of educational qualifications. In general, the EC, prompted by the European Council, should try to give Europe its "social and human dimension."[52]

Tindemans also advocated limited, but shrewd, reforms to the institutional structure of the EC. At Paris in December 1974, The Nine had agreed, despite British and Danish reservations, to permit the direct election of the European Assembly. Tindemans approved this decision and made several recommendations for extending the Assembly's powers. The Assembly should gradually be given a "power of proposal" by allowing it, in the first instance, to address resolutions to the European Council. It should take a higher public profile by staging "state of the union debates" twice a year, to which prominent national politicians should be invited. Voting by qualified majority, Tindemans argued, should become the norm for the Council of Ministers. The European Council should appoint the president of the Commission, who would appoint the rest of his colleagues in consultation with the Council. The Assembly would gain the right to approve the new Commission in a formal vote of confidence, and the Commission itself—which since the defeat of Hallstein had stagnated somewhat under the presidencies of Jean Rey (Belgium), Franco Maria Malfatti (Italy), Sicco Mansholt (Netherlands), and François-Xavier Ortoli (France)—would become a more activist body.[53]

Europe's federalists would have preferred Tindemans to present a draft constitution for Europe: plainly, his recommendations fell far short of this. His report was still strong beer, however. Tindemans's report was on the agenda for the four meetings of the European Council subsequent to its submission. No concrete action resulted. Instead, the member states would take a number of cautious sips over the next fifteen years until, with the Treaty of Maastricht, a Europe very similar indeed to Tindemans's prescriptions was actually enacted.

THE EUROPEAN MONETARY SYSTEM

The first such sip was the creation of the European Monetary System (EMS). Essentially a more inclusive version of the Snake, the EMS was brought into operation in January 1979 by diplomatic initiatives on the part of key member states within the European Council. The creation of the EMS owed much to the efforts of three key figures. Helmut Schmidt, who had succeeded Willy Brandt as chancellor of the Federal Republic in May 1974, was the decisive actor. Valéry Giscard d'Estaing, who had become president of France in the same month, and Roy Jenkins, a former British finance minister who became president of the European Commission in January 1977, played important supporting roles. A scheme as ambitious as the EMS could not have overcome the many vested interests opposed to it in the late 1970s in the absence of the high quality political leadership that Schmidt, Giscard, and Jenkins provided.

Schmidt was the chief driving force. Schmidt became engaged with the question of monetary unification out of pique with the weak performance of the new American president, Jimmy Carter, whom he describes as "idealistic and fickle" in his memoir *Men and Powers*.[54] Schmidt was alarmed by what he regarded as Carter's amateurish foreign policy and infuriated by the Carter administration's studied neglect of the dollar. In the first half of 1977, the dollar resumed its slide in the currency markets. By mid-1977, it had skidded to DM 2.35 and would decline to below DM 2.0 by the end of the year and DM 1.76 by September 1978 (under Bretton Woods it had been worth DM 4.20). Nobody knew where the dollar's fall would stop. The dollar "seemed not so much to be floating as drowning."[55] The risk was that the OPEC countries, whose coffers were by now awash with dollars, would stash their newly acquired wealth in European currencies and in the DM in particular, thus making Germany artificially uncompetitive.[56]

As usual, the problem was the American trade deficit, which topped $31 billion in 1977. The Carter administration asserted that its deficit was due to the overly cautious policies of the European economies and urged the Europeans to act as a "locomotive" for growth. Schmidt dismissed this theory as a "Loch Ness monster" that "surfaced from the depths" whenever the dollar was in difficulty.[57] Throughout 1977, West Germany came under intense international pressure to stimulate its economy and cut its substantial trade surplus by sucking in imports. At the May 1977 summit of the leading industrial nations, Schmidt was forced to pledge that Germany would aim for 5 percent growth in its economy—a target that was impossible without increasing inflationary pressures within the economy.[58] Nevertheless, the DM strengthened against the dollar disproportionately in 1977 to 1978. The dollar's slump, in short, was pricing German industry out of its main markets.

According to Roy Jenkins, Schmidt's central role in the decision to launch a monetary initiative in Europe was essentially a reaction to his growing conviction of American incompetence. It gave Schmidt "some escape from his frustration at knowing better how to run the world than Carter or Brezhnev or Callaghan [British prime minister 1976–1979], but mostly feeling himself inhibited by his country's past from trying to do so."[59]

Other countries regarded the imposition of a monetary straitjacket in Europe as beneficial for their economies. Certainly, Giscard's support was motivated by this conviction. When Giscard became president of France, he initially tried to impose austerity in order to combat soaring inflation rates. The ensuing surge in unemployment panicked his government, which pumped subsidies into troubled industrial sectors. But this largesse was a temporary blip in policy. Giscard had lost faith in the power of the state to deliver economic growth without inflation. As he wrote in a stimulating 1976 book of prescriptions for French democracy, economic activity was like the human organism: "If each breath we draw, each step we take, had to be the result of conscious decision, illness would soon follow."[60] The trouble with the French economy, Giscard contended, was that the "brain"—the state—was trying to do too much.

When, in August 1976, Jacques Chirac, Giscard's prime minister in France's semipresidential system, resigned over policy differences, Giscard turned for a new premier to former European commissioner Raymond Barre, whom he knew to share his economic liberalism fully. In September 1976, Barre introduced a tough program of tax increases and public spending cuts designed to take demand out of the economy. France had embarked upon the road of making herself authentically competitive as an economy, instead of relying on currency devaluation to do that job for her. Measures of monetary integration could only help this program. They lashed France to the German economy and gave the French government an opportunity to depict its painful reforms as a necessary sacrifice. It was both idealism and realism that led Giscard to state unambiguously that France's "number one task" was to make economic and monetary unification a reality.[61]

In the case of Roy Jenkins, pressing for greater monetary unification was a means of launching his presidency of the European Commission. Jenkins had become president of the Commission as a result of his impressive leadership of the "Britain in Europe" campaign during the referendum on EC membership called by Prime Minister Harold Wilson. The referendum had been Wilson's way—and, probably, was the only way—of reconciling the war to the knife within the Labour government between "pro-marketeers" like Jenkins and the "anti-marketeers" of the left who, in many instances, wanted Britain's withdrawal from the Community to be the prelude to the imposition of a socialist siege economy.[62]

On June 5, 1975, after a lengthy campaign, Britain had voted on whether or not to stay in the Community. To the surprise of many observers, the majority in favor of staying in was strikingly large: 67.2 percent said "yes." Jenkins, who had worked tirelessly for a "yes" vote and had put the case for a positive vote in the final televized debate, emerged from the campaign with his standing as a statesman enhanced.

Jenkins was first sounded out for the presidency of the Commission, on the initiative of Helmut Schmidt, in January 1976. When he failed to succeed Wilson as leader of the Labour Party (and hence prime minister) in March 1976, he indicated his willingness to do the job and was formally appointed by the European Council in June 1976.

Jenkins did not begin his new job well. He was quickly brought face-to-face with some Euro-realities—the first and foremost being that "in Brussels, outside a narrow field of coal and steel and agricultural decisions . . . nothing much happened unless a majority of governments could be persuaded to join in leaning on the lever."[63] By mid-1977, his performance was being belittled by *The Economist*, which seems to have jolted him out of a self-pitying mood of gloom and despair. At the end of July 1977, he decided that his presidency needed a theme and that that theme would be economic and monetary union.[64]

Jenkins's commitment to monetary union was first systematically aired in public in Florence on October 27, 1977, during the first Jean Monnet lecture at the European University Institute. His speech advanced a powerful case for the economic benefits of a monetary union in Europe. Drawing upon the recently published work of a Community-sponsored committee of academic economists, he also sketched a fascinating picture of the political implications of monetary union. Jenkins envisaged a "multitiered," confederal Europe whose heart was a central government, small by the standards of major federal states such as the United States or Germany, which was spending about 5 to 7 percent of gross Community product. This central administration would occupy itself with "those aspects of external relations where intercontinental bargaining power is called for"; a much-increased regional aid policy; high-tech industries such as aerospace; and politically sensitive industries such as steel, shipbuilding, and textiles. A common energy policy would also be required.[65]

Jenkins was under no illusion of the "political implications" of what he was saying. He was proposing as great a step forward in the degree of integration as the "last generation" of European leaders had faced when they signed the Treaties of Rome. Like them, Jenkins believed that such a step was necessary if the EC member states wished to preserve the substance of their national sovereignty:

> Do we intend to create a European union or do we not? . . . There would be little point in asking the peoples and governments of Europe to contemplate union, were it not for the fact that real and efficient sovereignty over monetary issues already eludes them to a high and increasing degree. The prospect of monetary union should be seen as part of the process of recovering the substance of sovereign power. At present we tend to cling to its shadow.[66]

Jenkins's Florence speech was initially dismissed as Euro-rhetoric by a skeptical press. The commissioner for economic affairs, his predecessor as president of the Commission, François-Xavier Ortoli, was far more cautious. A lengthy and somewhat scholarly document on "The Prospect of Economic and Monetary Union" submitted by the Commission to the December 5–6, 1977, meeting of the European Council reflected Ortoli's views rather than Jenkins's by calling for a gradualist five-year program of economic convergence.[67] The Council itself approved the Commission's document "with satisfaction," but it is doubtful that the leaders of The Nine had, at this stage, engaged with the arguments in any detail.

By December 1977, therefore, The Nine had accepted that monetary union, like good health and fine weather, was in principle a good thing. But they had certainly not committed themselves to pursuing the economic policies that would be necessary to bring it into being. Jenkins says in his biography that "reproclamation of monetary union had done well in providing me with a message, but I was far from confident that it was going to provide Europe with a monetary advance."[68] What turned Jenkins's vision into at least partial reality was the intervention of Helmut Schmidt. On February 28, 1978, Jenkins had a routine meeting with the German chancellor. Schmidt startled Jenkins by stating that if the Union of the Left were defeated in the forthcoming March 1978 elections in

France, he would propose in response to the dollar problem "a major step towards monetary union; to mobilize and put all our currency reserves into a common pool, if other people will agree to do the same, and to form a monetary bloc."[69] This decision represented a significant change of direction for Schmidt, who had greeted Jenkins's original speech with skepticism, saying that he was in favor in principle of economic and monetary union but "not if it meant German inflation going to 8 percent."[70]

Having committed himself to pursuing greater integration in the monetary field, Schmidt proceeded with singular individualism to formulate his ideas. His cabinet, the Bundesbank, and most of the governments of the EC, including Britain, were kept in ignorance of his thinking until the Copenhagen European Council on April 7–8, 1978. Only Giscard was let into the secret during a meeting at Rambouillet on April 2, at which the two leaders, "like two dramatists preparing a performance in which they themselves were to be the most important actors," carefully plotted out the strategy and tactics they would use at the summit.[71]

At Copenhagen, Schmidt proposed that the EC should back up the Snake by creating a European Monetary Fund, similar to the International Monetary Fund, with member states pooling approximately 15 to 20 percent of their reserves to provide cash for interventions in support of economic restructuring in member states' economies. He further suggested that EC currencies should be increasingly used instead of dollars for interventions on the exchange markets and that the so-called European Unit of Account (EUA, the instrument used by the EC to calculate members' contributions and farm prices) should become a proto-currency. EC states should settle their debts to each other in EUAs and should issue debt denominated in this notional "Euromoney."

The other European leaders, Britain's James Callaghan aside, welcomed Schmidt's proposal with varying degrees of comprehension and enthusiasm. Schmidt's proposal, which by now had been elaborated upon by a duo of trusted advisers, was formally adopted—and publicized for the first time—at the subsequent Bremen summit in June 1978. In a coup for the French government, the EUA was renamed the "European Currency Unit," or Ecu, at Bremen. The Ecu, Giscard smugly revealed, had been a coin in medieval France.

Between June and December 1978, Schmidt's proposal was nibbled away in the meetings of the finance ministers and central bankers. The final version, agreed at the Brussels European Council on December 4–5, 1978, jettisoned the idea of a European Monetary Fund and limited itself to widening the membership of the Snake and fine-tuning its mechanisms. The core element of the new EMS was the exchange rate mechanism (ERM), which, at any rate, in theory was to be based upon the Ecu. The Ecu was defined as a "composite currency" whose value was determined by merging together the currencies of the member nations according to a complex formula based on three criteria: percentage of gross Community product contributed; percentage of Community exports; and overall size of the economy. Members of the new system would be obliged to limit fluctuations of their currencies to within 2.25 percent above or below their par value against the Ecu. Italy, however, was allowed to join in a special "band" that allowed the lira to fluctuate as much as 6 percent above or below par for a limited period of time. The same offer was made to Britain, which refused to join, and to Ireland, which broke its postindependence currency union with Britain and joined at the same 2.25 percent rate as everybody else.

The Ecu's role, however, was more nominal than real since, at the behest of the Bundesbank, the "central rate" was to be used to "establish a grid of bilateral exchange rates" among participating currencies. In other words, member states' central banks, as well as monitoring their currencies' standing against the Ecu, had also to ensure that they did not breach the 2.25 band against all other participating currencies. The rules of the Snake, in other words, had been slightly loosened. To suit an increased membership, a slightly wider margin of fluctuation was now being permitted. But the member states were still signing up to a system in which they were obliged to tie their currencies to the value of the mark. If the mark continued to rise against the dollar, the rest of Europe's currencies would rise against the dollar, too, and the member states would therefore tend to trade among themselves more, strengthening the Community as an economic force.[72]

This point is very important. Giscard accepted the idea of a bilateral grid of exchange rates during a Franco-German summit in Aachen in September 1978, which was accompanied with a great deal of pomp and ceremony. Giscard and Schmidt visited the tomb of Charlemagne, and Giscard famously said, "Perhaps when we discussed monetary problems, the spirit of Charlemagne brooded over us."[73] This ostentatious "Euroclaptrap," to use the words of one of the EC's most outspoken and well-informed critics, has been interpreted as being a mere device to help sell the EMS in France.[74]

There is no doubt some truth in this, but it is too reductive. Schmidt was, as usual, thinking long term. According to his biographer, the German chancellor "urged skeptics" to see the EMS "in the political context of the next fifteen or twenty years." He did not regard the niceties of the EMS as "technical monetary questions" but as "political, economic and psychological matters of the first importance."[75] The EMS was enabling Germany to stem the tendency of the mark to overshoot in value, and it did provide the franc with a potential framework for austerity (although the version agreed at Brussels left plenty of room for countries to drop in and out of the system and for periodical revaluations of the member currencies). But, at least in the minds of its creators, the EMS was also laying the foundations for a European economy that was less vulnerable to outside shocks. One can see why they regarded such an achievement as one that transcended narrow national interests.

The EMS eventually got under way, three months behind schedule, in March 1979 after a somewhat futile squabble with France over its effects on farm prices. Britain did not join: the Labour government believed that without the weapon of competitive devaluation, British industry would never be able to withstand the full force of continental competition and unemployment would rise to politically unsustainable levels. When the Conservatives, under the leadership of Margaret Thatcher, won the May 1979 election, they were skeptical of entry for the opposite reason: they wanted a virile pound in order to squeeze inflation from the British economy. As Roy Jenkins dryly remarked in his biography: "In fact under both of them Britain enjoyed for several years a higher rate of unemployment and inflation than any participating country."[76]

BEYOND THE COMMON MARKET

The EMS was a far cry from the plans of the Werner Report at the beginning of the 1970s.[77] The Nine were not using a single currency, nor were centralized institutions in Brussels carrying out macroeconomic policy. The national governments and the central banks of the nine member states continued to be Europe's main economic actors. Yet it was not a negligible event either. The Nine (or eight out of the nine) had, with varying degrees of enthusiasm, signed up to the notion that Europe's economic future lay, at any rate in economic terms, in becoming West Germany writ large: an association of social market democracies trading freely among themselves and committed to budgetary austerity.

This cooperation on the economic front was matched by a gradual and, in retrospect, significant consolidation of the legal status of the Treaty of Rome by the Court of Justice. *Van Gend en Loos* (see chapter 3) had established that the treaty conferred rights directly upon the citizens of the member states and that member states were infringing those rights when they passed laws that did not conform to the EEC treaty. The implication of this position was that Community law took precedence over national law. Insofar as Dutch law already acknowledged the primacy of international law over national law, where the direct effectiveness of international law could be shown to exist, for the Netherlands at least the question was now settled. There were, however, other EC states— for example, Italy—where there was a constitutional presumption of the primacy of national law. In *Costa v. Enel* (case 6/64), a case in which a lawyer from Milan refused to pay his electricity bill because he considered that the Italian government had infringed several provisions of the EEC treaty when it nationalized the electricity industry, the Court of Justice ruled, contrary to the arguments put forward by the Italian government, that it was fully entitled to decide whether the law nationalizing the power industry was in conflict with the EEC treaty. The Court argued that by signing the EEC treaty the member states had made "a permanent limitation of their sovereign rights, against which a subsequent unilateral act incompatible with the concept of the Community cannot prevail."[78] None of this helped Signor Costa, however, since the Court also ruled that the Italian government had not in fact breached the treaty.

In the 1970s, this principle of primacy for Community law was reinforced by two other major cases. In *Internationale Handelsgesellschaft v. Einfuhr und Vorratsstelle Getreide* (case 11/70), the ECJ, responding to a German court that regarded an EC regulation incompatible with the German Constitution, controversially ruled that the "validity of a Community measure or its effect within a member state cannot be affected by allegations that it runs counter to either fundamental rights as formulated by the Constitution of that state, or the principles of a national constitutional structure."[79] In *Amministrazione delle Finanze dello Stato v. Simmenthal* (case 106/77), the ECJ clarified the procedural implications of the doctrine of primacy by insisting that national courts, whenever they were faced with a conflict between a national norm and a Community measure, had the duty to give "full effect" to Community regulations without waiting for new legislation or the rulings of national courts of appeal to resolve the question for them.[80] This ruling was intended to guarantee the efficacy of Community legislation in countries such as Italy, where governments might otherwise have kept the offending norms on the statute books pending an appeal to the country's Constitutional Court, or the death of the plaintiff, whichever might be the sooner. The ECJ was not prepared to let countries with byzantine legal systems use procedure as a backdoor form of protectionism.

Nor, indeed, was it prepared to allow legislative lethargy to block the uniform application of Community legislation. Case 148/78, *Pubblico Ministero v. Ratti*, is a good example of the ECJ's attitude in this regard. Signor Ratti, a manufacturer of solvents and varnishes, had packaged and labeled his products in accordance with guidelines contained in two EC directives, which the Italian government had not yet transformed into Italian law. The Italian authorities prosecuted him for not following Italian law in this area. The ECJ ruled that a member state "may not rely, as against individuals, on its own failure to perform the obligations which the directive intends," although it exonerated the Italian government over the directive on varnishes, since the deadline for implementation had still not expired.[81]

One final case from the 1970s should be cited to show the ECJ's willingness to interpret the EEC treaty in defense of the citizen. *Defrenne v. Sabena* (case 43/75), in which a Belgian air hostess sued the national airline because she was being paid less than male stewards doing the same work, led the ECJ to rule that "the principle of equal pay forms part of the foundations of the Treaty." Article 119 of the treaty was unambiguous on this point. The ECJ, moreover, citing article 117 of the treaty, which says improving working conditions and a rising standard of living for workers is a goal of the Community, meant that pay could not be leveled down but had to be leveled up.[82]

The net effect of the ECJ's case law between 1964 and 1978 was, in retrospect, immensely significant. In the first place, it prevented the member states from undermining the liberalizing thrust of the EEC treaty by domestic legal cavils. Member states could not pretend that the treaty's provisions, or legislation passed in accordance with the treaty's procedures, did not have a direct effect on the citizens of the member states, nor could they lawfully obstruct the effectiveness of EC regulations and (well-worded and appropriate) directives with national principles, practices, and procedures. In the second place, in Weiler's words, it meant that "Community norms that produce direct effects are not merely the law of the land, but the 'higher law' of the land."[83] The EEC treaty had obtained "an authority similar to that of a constitution in a federal system."[84]

By comparison with the ECJ, the European Assembly registered an only modest increase in its powers and status in the 1970s. Nevertheless, the institution did secure the gain that it had been most adamantly pressing for since its very formation: direct election. The Paris summit of December 1974 conceded the principle of direct election (for which the Assembly had been actively pressing since 1960). With a nod to the Vedel Report, the summit communiqué also stated that "the competence of the European Assembly will be extended, in particular by granting it certain powers in the Community's legislative process."

Ironically, the failure of the EC to make progress on a common foreign policy and to achieve monetary union in a sense robbed proponents of a larger role for the Assembly of their strongest argument: the need to make the Community's procedures more democratic and more transparent. Had the EC evolved during the 1970s into the European Union envisaged at the 1972 Paris summit, the case for a genuine European legislature armed with powers of scrutiny, veto, and proposal would have become unanswerable. But as David Marquand argued at the time, "Although large numbers of critically important decisions are now taken by the

Community authorities, integration has not yet gone far enough to make the undemocratic nature of the system either obvious or intolerable."[85]

In September 1976, the foreign ministers of The Nine approved the European Elections Act. The Assembly was enlarged from 198 members to 410, and a five-year term between elections was agreed. Seats were distributed to the member states with little regard to the relative size of national electorates: Britain, Federal Germany, and Italy, whose electorates were all just over 40 million voters, were given eighty-one seats apiece—but so was France, whose electorate was only 33.3 million. The Netherlands, with twenty-five seats for 9.3 million voters, could feel hard done by in comparison with Belgium (6.3 million and twenty-four), Ireland (2.1 million and fifteen), and Denmark (3.5 million and sixteen). Luxembourg's mere 200,000 voters were given six representatives in the revamped Assembly.[86]

Article 5 of the act permitted members of the Assembly to belong both to their national parliaments and the European body. Member states were free to draw up their own electoral systems for the vote pending a proposal from the Assembly itself for a uniform electoral procedure. Since these provisions revised certain articles of the EEC treaty, the member states were obliged to submit the European Elections Act to national parliaments for ratification.

In most countries, ratification was a formality. In Britain and France, however, ratification became the center of a major political debate over the threat supposedly posed by direct election of the European Assembly to national sovereignty. Gaullist and Communist opposition meant that the French government was only able to ratify the European Elections Act by making it a vote of confidence.[87] In Britain, ratification took until 1978 and was only passed after a clause was included stating that "no treaty providing for any increase whatever in the powers of the Assembly will be ratified by the United Kingdom unless it has been approved by an Act of Parliament."

There was also a major battle in Britain over the choice of electoral system. The strong anti-Europe faction within the Labour Party meant that premier James Callaghan was reliant on Conservative votes for the passage of the European Elections Act, and the Conservatives' price was retention of the British first-past-the-post electoral system. Direct elections were postponed from the spring of 1978 to June 10, 1979, as a result of this British reluctance to embrace any form of proportional representation and the consequent need for the UK Boundaries Commission to design eighty-one new Euro-constituencies.

The election campaign itself disappointed supporters of European federalism by being predominately "local" in tone. In Italy, the national election took place the previous week, and the two polls inevitably merged into a single campaign. In France, the election became a referendum on the EMS and granted both the Gaullists and the Communists a platform for a frenzied denunciation of the European project—hardly the advertisement for European unity that federalists wanted. The Communists' electoral manifesto said that the country's leaders wanted "France, dismembered and weakened, to be integrated and drowned in a West European conglomeration led by Federal Germany, and ultimately controlled by the United States."[88] Jacques Chirac, the Gaullist leader, not to be outdone, ranted too against "this Europe which is dominated by Germano-American interests."[89]

Turnout varied from country to country. There was 90 percent turnout in Belgium; well over 80 percent in Italy. At the other extreme, turnout in Britain was just 33 percent. Overall, a respectable 60 percent of eligible European citizens voted.

The newly elected Assembly certainly reflected the full diversity of political opinion within The Nine. The Socialists, with 109 seats, narrowly beat the European Peoples' Party (Christian Democrat: 105) to become the largest contingent in the Assembly. The British Conservatives, who took sixty seats, allied with four Danish right-wingers to provide the next largest group. Communists, Liberals, and Gaullists completed the list of major formations within the Assembly. The ideological lineup of the new Assembly, however, was less important than the fact that there was a large majority of Euro-federalists in almost every grouping. The European Parliament, as it now began to be known, would become in the early 1980s a hotbed of activity for more rapid movement toward European political and economic integration and for an increase in its own powers.

These supporters of European federalism, in the European Parliament and outside, were largely responsible for establishing the myth that the 1970s had been a decade of failure for the Community. As Moravcsik has remarked, this characterization is "true only from a federalist perspective that focuses on the institutional centralization of administrative and democratic decision-making."[90] True, the Community had not lived up to the aspirations of The Hague and Paris summits. But politics is the art of the possible, and the wish lists of October 1972 were never going to be attained in the international environment engendered by American domestic crisis, the oil shock, and the collapse of Bretton Woods. What in retrospect is surprising is that Europe survived—survived, moreover, with much of its idealism intact. None of The Nine withdrew from the Community, none established a socialist siege economy, eight signaled their intention to "deepen" their economic cooperation in the EMS and all of them accepted a strongly supranational interpretation of the EEC treaty in relation to national law. Three new members joined the Community (and stayed in it); the new members would shortly be joined by three former Mediterranean dictatorships who regarded the EC as a force that could stabilize and protect their fragile democracies.

The seventies, in short, were, to quote Moravcsik once more, a "decade of both consolidation and innovation."[91] They underlined that Europe's national leaders, working through institutionalized summit meetings, could make substantive progress toward achieving fuller economic integration. The necessity for enhanced economic integration, moreover, seemed evident. If Europe were to insulate herself even partly from an unstable global economy, she had to trade more within her own boundaries—a goal that implied broad agreement over macroeconomic fundamentals. This latter lesson was still imperfectly learned in 1979, but between 1979 and 1986, the commitment to freer intra-Community trade, sound money, and budgetary rigor that was implicit in the EMS bargain became the policy of choice for most of the Community. This agreement on fundamentals was reached, however, only after France had flirted with a form of doctrinaire socialism that was antithetical to Community principles and after Britain's new leader had slammed her handbag on the table and demanded her money back.

6

✛

The 1992 Initiative and the Relaunch of the Community

Between 1979 and 1989, the European Community, after looking briefly as if it were in terminal paralysis, regained the sense of rapid momentum it had possessed before de Gaulle and the adverse economic conditions of the 1970s. The Single European Act (SEA, 1986) was the largest single step toward fuller economic and political integration in Europe since the signature of the EEC treaty in 1957. By the terms of the treaty, the newly expanded twelve-nation EC—Greece joined in 1981; Spain and Portugal, in 1986—committed themselves to achieving a genuinely free internal market in manufactured goods and services by December 1992 by eliminating a host of restrictive nontariff practices that obstructed trade between the member states. The great achievement of Jacques Delors, the French finance minister who became president of the Commission in January 1985, was to place the single market at the heart of Europe's agenda.

The root cause of this liberalizing agenda was one that had underlain the movement toward European economic integration since the 1940s: the belief that establishment of a large domestic market would stimulate steady economic growth. Even during the 1970s, trade among The Nine had continued to grow despite the effects of the recurrent monetary crises.[1] The oil shock of 1979 to 1981, when prices of crude tripled in the space of a year, and the subsequent attempt by the United States to squeeze inflation out of its domestic economy by raising interest rates to record levels, which spilled over into Europe by driving up the price of the dollar and caused European inflation to rise, brought in its wake a period of economic stagnation and rising unemployment in the

Community.[2] While the causes of this stagnation were mostly external, The Nine's sluggish response seemed to indicate that The Nine, for so long an area of extraordinary economic vitality, had become complacent and inflexible. "Eurosclerosis" became the favorite description of the European economy for gung ho Reaganites celebrating the revival of American economic performance in the early 1980s. By the mid-1980s, Europe's leaders were ready to make liberalizing Europe's economy a political priority.

Before then, the political obstacles in the path of a policy of economic liberalization at Community level blocked progress. In the early 1980s, three complex issues—the implications of French domestic policy, the question of British contributions to the Community budget, and enlargement to the Mediterranean countries, especially Spain—dominated The Nine's agenda and left statesmen (and one formidable stateswoman) with little time for major initiatives.

FRANCE SEES THE LIGHT

In the case of France, the issue was its defiant and, with the benefit of hindsight, quixotic attempt to build "socialism in one country." Raymond Barre's austerity programs provoked a backlash among the French electorate in 1981. First, Giscard d'Estaing was defeated in May for the presidency by the Socialist candidate François Mitterrand, and then, the Socialists and Communists won a large majority in the ensuing elections to the National Assembly. The declared objective of Mitterrand's first government, which was headed by Pierre Mauroy and contained several Communists, was to stimulate growth in the French economy while increasing the already generous social benefits enjoyed by French workers.

This strategy flew in the face of most analyses of the French economy's principal weaknesses. Many economists thought that France was already living beyond her means. Throughout the postwar years, France had been loading its productive economy with excessive social burdens. Robert Boyer states: "From 1970–84 French production costs grew faster than those of its competitors."[3] In the 1970s, moreover, France had begun to fall behind Germany and other European countries in the production of high-added-value products for export. These twin failings had led to sliding profits among major French companies and to a decline in the amount of business investment. The oil shock in 1979 compounded these problems by sharply raising production costs and reducing profits still further.

The Mauroy government tried to overcome these problems by boosting domestic demand and centralizing investment decisions in the hands of the state. The poorest households benefited from a policy of "redistributive Keynesianism" worth about 2 percent of GDP; taxes were raised on the wealthy and on business; and the state nationalized key companies and banks.[4] The result of these policies was a predictable increase in imports since the majority of French consumers had more francs in their wallets. But France's industrial partners, who were in the midst of a recession, did not buy more French goods in return.[5] As Ronald Tiersky has written, "Mitterrand's high risk experiment foundered on the too-clever-by-half strategy of trying to use an international capitalist upswing to float the French Socialists' experiment."[6] State ownership, moreover, failed to solve the investment shortfall. Business investment actually fell in 1982, which had a knock-on effect on GDP growth.

France's growing balance-of-payments deficits and sluggish growth provoked a downward lurch in the value of the franc: an event that had European-wide implications since it meant that France was reneging on her commitment, within the EMS, to maintain stable exchange rates. France formally devalued the franc in both October 1981 and June 1982. The devaluations were, moreover, very considerable in size. The franc lost 10 percent of its value in June 1982, while Germany insisted upon a wage freeze in France as the price of her agreement. As Bernard Connolly puts it: "The combination of the ERM and the out-and-out Socialist phase of Mitterrand's government had led to almost total French monetary subjugation to Germany."[7]

By March 1983, Mitterrand's France was faced with an unpleasant choice between the EMS and its ideological commitment to building an economy founded upon socialist principles. The PSF might have elected to solve France's trade deficit by imposing a siege economy, with high tariff barriers in place against both the rest of the world and France's Community partners, but such a strategy entailed "rejection of the EEC," which was the rock upon which French foreign and economic policy had been founded for the previous thirty years.[8] Plenty of Mitterrand's closest advisers nevertheless advocated this course. They were resisted by the finance minister, Jacques Delors, who was convinced that the warm bath of protectionism could only drain the French economy of what vitality it still possessed.

Delors won the argument—just. In exchange for German agreement to a further devaluation of about 10 percent, Delors was authorized to implement cuts in public spending, raise taxes on personal consumption, and reduce taxes on business. Connolly is being provocative when he calls the March 1983 devaluation "a sort of monetary 1940," but the accuracy of his analysis is hard to dispute.[9] By March 1983, the French government had lost control of much of its sovereign power to make economic policy.

The lesson was not lost on Mitterrand. The French president suddenly rediscovered his European vocation and became an ardent proselytizer for further integration. Mitterrand told the European Parliament in May

1984 that it was time for Europe to "put its quarrels behind it and to embark on the road to the future."[10] Mitterrand clearly reasoned that France would regain some measure of economic and political sovereignty only if she pushed for greater political integration within the EC. France had, in short, an impeccably "realist" reason for wanting to see greater integration take place.

Her major European partners, headed by West Germany and Italy, had done their best to keep the European flame burning in France's absence. Shortly after the third French realignment within the ERM, in June 1983, The Ten (Greece had entered the Community in 1981) signed a "Solemn Declaration" on European unification at the Stuttgart European Council (in EC law such declarations are regarded as statements of intent but are not legally binding). This declaration was the outcome of the so-called Genscher–Colombo initiative. In November 1981, Genscher and his Italian counterpart, the Christian Democrat Emilio Colombo, presented to the European Parliament (and subsequently to the European Council) a draft "European Act" with an appended "Statement on Questions of Economic Integration" that made a strong case for a limited, but nevertheless significant, increase in the degree of supranationalism within the Community. The draft act, for example, attached a very high importance to political cooperation, stating that one of the EC's central "aims" should be to "act in concert in world affairs so that Europe will be increasingly able to assume the international role incumbent upon it by virtue of its economic and political importance." Institutionally, it proposed that the European Council should become the "source of political guidance" for the Community and its central decision-making body. On the Parliament, the draft European Act was more timid: it would have remained a chamber that scrutinized and debated the proposals of the governments of the member states rather than an out-and-out legislature. The Commission was referred to as the "driving force of European integration," whose role was to advise and support the European Council on all matters, including foreign policy, with which the Commission would be "closely associated." Within the Council of Ministers, the draft act attached "decisive importance" to the reform of procedures to allow more majority voting. The statement on economic matters was less concrete in its prescriptions. It did affirm, however, that the common market should be "brought to completion" and that the member states should "strive" to obtain "increasing convergence of their economies."[11]

Between November 1981 and June 1983, the draft act was whittled down to size by a "prolonged negotiation" that brought the proposals, by June 1983, "back within the confines of treaty orthodoxy."[12] In particular, the idea of promoting more frequent majority voting in the Council of Ministers vanished from the final text in the face of concerted hostility from several member states, notably Greece and Denmark. The section on the Parliament, moreover, offered such diluted increases in its role that the Parliament passed a motion on June 9, 1983, openly expressing its dissatisfaction. In one regard, however, the Solemn Declaration laid down an important pointer for the Community's future strategy. It indicated the "completion of the internal market" and the "elimination" of nontariff barriers as the most plausible area for concerted Community action in the near future, along with reinforcing the ERM.[13] France's Damascene reconversion to the European cause in March 1983 made this objective a workable one.

In retrospect, the Solemn Declaration's importance was symbolic. The German-Italian venture should be seen less as a "missed opportunity" to secure an advance in European unity than as a restatement of first principles by Bonn and Rome.[14] The early 1980s were arguably the nadir of the EC's fortunes. Summit after summit ended in public acrimony as the British fought relentlessly for a reform in Community financing. It is hard to imagine that two hardheaded statesmen of the caliber of Genscher and Colombo genuinely thought that the time was ripe for an act that possessed even limited supranational overtones. The purpose of the Genscher–Colombo initiative was surely to indicate to Paris and London that two at least of the "big countries" had not lost faith with the European project.

THE BRITISH BUDGETARY QUESTION

Between 1979 and 1984, the British budgetary question was Banquo's ghost at almost every meeting of the European Council. Mrs. Thatcher wanted "her money back" and would not let the Community progress until she had been compensated. The nature of the problem is quite straightforward to describe. Throughout the 1970s, the EC budget grew rapidly, even allowing for inflation. Two countries, Germany and Britain, were paying far more into the Community than they were getting out. In the absence of a budget agreement, Britain's net contribution was scheduled to overtake Germany's in 1981 to 1982 and to rise to over 2 billion Ecu per year.[15] In short, when Mrs. Thatcher took office, Britain was on the verge of becoming the EC's paymaster—though, as Thatcher points out in her memoirs, Britain was only the seventh richest country in income per head.[16]

Britain's excessive contribution was a consequence both of the way in which the Community was financed and of the way in which it spent its money. The Community received 1 percent of the money raised in sales taxes (VAT) by the member states; it received the proceeds of levies on incoming agricultural products and the proceeds of tariffs on extra-Community imports. This was an extremely unsatisfactory formula for Britain, which continued to import large quantities of products from the Commonwealth and the rest of the world. True, British trade with the rest of the EC increased substantially in the 1970s—rising from £6.3 billion in 1972 to £37.3 billion in 1979.[17] But trade with the Community still represented less than half of Britain's total trade. Britain had to pay in a considerable sum in levies and import duties to the Community budget.

This would not have mattered had Britain been benefiting from EC payouts. But she was not. By 1979, the EC was spending three-quarters of its budget on the CAP. Britain, with its limited agriculture sector, received relatively little (£500 to £600 million a year by the early 1980s) in subsidies and price support funds. Since 1973, Britain had been the largest single beneficiary from the European Regional Development Fund (ERDF), receiving 28 percent of all funds committed by the fund until Greece's accession, and 23.8 percent thereafter. But in cash terms these did not amount to much. Between 1975 and 1981, Britain received a measly £720 million from this source.[18]

Britain, in short, was paying lots in, but not taking much out. For many Community officials, this was the membership fee that Britain had to pay if it wanted to be in the club and be part of an area of growing economic prosperity. Obviously, if everybody insisted on treating the Community budget as a ledger in which incomings and outgoings had to be exactly balanced, there would be no point having a Community at all.

Mrs. Thatcher nevertheless had sound political reasons for taking a tough line with Europe. Her government began implementing controversial cuts in programmed public spending as soon as it came to power. Thatcher's cabinet lopped £6.5 billion from planned spending in 1980 to 1981 but were still faced with a public sector borrowing requirement of almost £10 billion.[19] Using British money to keep French farmers in the bucolic idyll to which they had become accustomed was not an option in these circumstances. As Mrs. Thatcher argued in October 1979: "I can't play Sister Bountiful to the Community while my own electorate are being asked to forego improvements in the fields of health, welfare, education and the rest."[20]

The Dublin European Council, on November 29–30, 1979, was "the occasion for Europe's first encounter with Mrs. Thatcher in full flood." During dinner on the first day, Thatcher spoke for four hours "without pause, but not without repetition" about the British budget problem. Helmut Schmidt pretended to sleep; Giscard looked on in unfeigned horror; Francesco Cossiga of Italy "wrung his hands."[21] The other member states were prepared to offer Mrs. Thatcher £350 million a year (about 600 million Ecus); she stood out for a full refund. The British government had a card up its sleeve. In the last resort, it possessed the option of withholding its VAT contributions (in her memoirs, Mrs. Thatcher records that "even the possibility" of this action—which was of dubious legality—caused "satisfactory anxiety in the Commission").[22] On the other hand, if Britain overbid, there was a real risk that the other eight members would make her an offer and tell her to take it or leave the Community.

It gradually dawned upon Mrs. Thatcher's fellow leaders, however, that she was not going to be bluffed. At the end of April 1980, at a meeting of the European Council in Luxembourg, The Eight threw in their cards. Britain was offered a rebate worth 2.4 billion Ecus. Mrs. Thatcher rejected the deal, throwing the Community into potentially its worst crisis since 1965. It was one bluff too many, however. The French and the Germans refused to be "handbagged" any further. Under pressure from the Foreign Office, Thatcher grudgingly accepted an almost identical bargain negotiated at a meeting of the foreign ministers a month later.[23] Ironically, in both 1981 and 1982, the British contribution turned out to be far lower than anticipated, although in 1983 the issue returned once more to the forefront.[24]

It is interesting to note, in retrospect, how the debate over the British contribution swiftly became an exercise in haggling, rather than a discussion of first causes. The British budgetary question arose only because the CAP had succumbed to the logic of its own central design flaw: keeping farmers—all farmers—on welfare. In the late 1960s, farm commissioner Sicco Mansholt had proposed a plan to ensure that the long-term costs of the CAP did not get out of control. Mansholt had argued that there were simply too many farms in the EC that were uneconomic at even the high rates of subsidy that the CAP was prepared to pay. It would be better, Mansholt suggested, to remove land from agricultural production, increase forestation, and shift spending on agriculture to structural measures to improve rural incomes. Perhaps half of the Community's ten million farms should go, the Dutch commissioner warned frankly.[25] This "deliberate and openly admitted plan to reduce the workforce in farming" "roared on to the Community stage like a lion" in 1970. After gigantic riots in Brussels in the spring of 1971 by angry farmers and prolonged dilution of the proposals by the Council of Ministers, the Mansholt plan left the stage a "rather tame and timid mouse."[26] The CAP remained a blank check for farmers, and enlargement to Denmark and Ireland, both of whom, like France, had large agricultural sectors with farms that stood to benefit from the status quo, only made matters worse.

Even the "Comprehensive Agreement" reached with the British carefully stated that the Community, despite pledging itself to "structural changes" to eliminate "unacceptable situations" for any member state, would not "call into question" the "basic principles of the common agricultural policy."[27]

Yet reform was urgently needed. In the early 1980s, the CAP's central design flaw was blatantly obvious: there was constant political pressure to keep farm prices high (in order to keep farmers on the land and to buy rural votes), but higher prices naturally gave an incentive for higher production, which generated huge food surpluses that the Community had to buy.[28] This led to the accumulation of the hugely unpopular "wine lakes" and "grain mountains."

In May 1983, the Commission imposed caps for key products such as milk and grain on the amount of production for which the guarantee price would be paid. Farmers no longer possessed an unlimited license to produce at the taxpayer's expense. This reform to the CAP was the main achievement of the Luxembourger Gaston Thorn, who replaced Roy Jenkins as president of the Commission in 1981 and had the unenviable job of running the Commission during the Community's most litigious period.

What the Commission was not suggesting was a more market-oriented approach to agriculture. In a host of ways, the CAP's interventionism produced negative outcomes. Subsidies, far from enriching Cornish hill farmers or Sardinian shepherds, went disproportionately to already wealthy cereal farmers from Northern Europe, since their yields—helped by large doses of chemical fertilizers and other environmentally damaging practices—had risen faster than anybody's. European consumers, who were being denied access to beef from the Argentine, bananas from Ecuador, and wheat from Canada, had to pay higher prices than necessary in the shops. EC-subsidized exports of grain, meat, and sugar were the source of endless trade friction with the United States, Australia, and South America.[29]

The CAP had not even eliminated domestic subsidies by national governments for farmers. The wild currency fluctuations of the 1970s made a nonsense of the original idea of common agricultural prices almost as soon as the CAP came into force. As a result, from the early 1970s onward, countries had been allowed to pay "monetary compensatory amounts" to farmers to ensure that rivals from weak currency countries did not seize an "unfair" advantage. The French, in particular, were also using a vast range of illegal aids to subsidize agriculture: of fifty-one such subsidies identified by the Commission in 1980, thirty-nine were being used by the French government.[30]

The CAP was moreover an obstacle to enlargement of the EC. Despite the vital political importance of EC membership as a bolster for the still fragile democracies of Portugal and Spain, negotiations were long delayed by fears that the Iberian countries would provide unwelcome agricultural competition and place the CAP under intolerable strain.

A 1982 study of the CAP stated bluntly: "A decade and a half of empirical evidence has confirmed that as an economic policy for the Community as a whole the CAP was irrational."[31] A more recent study has confirmed that the CAP "can hardly be defended from any point of view . . . [it] . . . can really be called the worst agricultural policy in the late twentieth century."[32] A policy can be irrational and indefensible, however, and still have plenty of backers. In the case of the CAP, its supporters were politically powerful farmers' lobbies and the national governments of large agricultural exporters, especially France, Ireland, the Netherlands, and Denmark. It was simply more expedient for Europe's leaders to pay Mrs. Thatcher off than to stop the CAP budget's remorseless growth—growth that Thorn's 1983 measures slowed but did not stop.

MEDITERRANEAN ENLARGEMENT

Greece, Portugal, and Spain all applied for EC membership during a two-year arc in the mid-1970s. Greece, whose military dictatorship crumbled in 1974 after the debacle of the Turkish invasion of Cyprus, formally applied in June 1975; Portugal applied in March 1977, as soon as its own democratic transition had stabilized. Spain, the largest and most problematic of the three would-be entrants, was the last to apply in July 1977. Until the Spanish Socialist Party (PSOE) took power in October 1982, Spain's political instability precluded her from pursuing membership with full vigor.[33]

The three Mediterranean countries presented both a challenge and an opportunity for the EC. In the superb documentation prepared by the Commission for the Copenhagen European Council meeting in April 1978, a clear picture of the chief difficulties consequent upon enlargement emerges.[34] These were

- Economic imbalances: All three would-be entrants had smaller per capita GDP than any member state. This was a particular problem in the case of Portugal, whose income per head, at purchasing power parity, was estimated by the Commission to be just $1,504—less than 50 percent of the per capita incomes of every existing member state except Italy ($2,742) and Ireland ($2,512). Spain ($2,384) and Greece ($2,309) did better by this measure. The relatively good performances of Greece and Spain, however, disguised enormous regional differences. Cities such as Athens, Madrid, and Barcelona enjoyed "European" standards of living; the more rural regions of both countries were as poor as Portugal. The Commission's overall assessment was that The Three possessed a "stage of development lying mid-way between the less-developed countries and the industrialized countries."[35] If The Three entered, it was clear that the rest of the Community was going to have to dig deep into their pockets to pay for infrastructure improvements and to soften the economic costs of entry. It was also assumed that all three countries would become large net exporters of labor once their citizens were at liberty to move throughout the Community: a politically sensitive issue at a time of rising unemployment. Large numbers of Greeks and Portuguese were already working in France and Germany.

- Agriculture and fisheries: All three countries had substantial, none-too-efficient agricultural sectors. The number of people employed in agriculture in the Community would increase by 55 percent if The Three were admitted; agriculture represented 16.6 percent of GDP in Greece, 11.8 percent in Portugal, and over 10 percent in Spain. Admission of The Three raised the specter of deeper wine lakes, a citrus fruit sierra, and overproduction of olive oil. French and Italian producers would face cheaper competition in these areas, as would Irish and British trawlermen, who would have to open their fishing grounds to the gigantic Spanish fleet.

- Trade and industry: All three countries specialized in manufacturing sectors—textiles, chemicals, footwear, food processing—that were already problem industries for the Community. Until the early 1970s, Spanish industry in particular had sheltered behind a formidable array of formal and informal trade barriers. There were serious worries that Spain's coddled industrial sector would not be able to cope with membership of the common market. All three countries possessed worsening current account deficits as their imports of increasingly expensive oil outweighed their surpluses in manufactured exports and "invisible" earnings such as tourism. All three countries had suffered from high rates of inflation throughout the 1970s. The currencies of all three Mediterranean applicants were thus seen as unpromising potential members of the EMS.

- Institutional questions: The Commission warned that "with twelve members, the institutions and decision-making procedures will be under considerable strain and the Community will be exposed to possible stalemate and dilution unless its practical modus operandi is improved."[36] The only way around this problem was to extend qualified majority voting and to weaken the unanimity principle enshrined in the Luxembourg compromise. Deciding how many votes each country should have in the Council of Ministers and how many seats in the Assembly was also no easy matter. Spain was a large country in terms of population (36.2 million), but its total GDP, at the then exchange rate, was not much larger than the Netherlands', which had twenty-two million people fewer. Greece and Portugal were entitled to the same weighting as Belgium (all three had just under ten million inhabitants), but their contribution to the Community's economy was far lower. The Commission was insistent that, as a general principle for regulating such matters, "the Community must . . . avoid any appreciable shift in the existing balance, based on a combination of demographic factors and political considerations, between member states."[37] But this was easier said than done.

Mediterranean enlargement therefore posed a number of difficult questions. The Commission nevertheless argued that "the challenge of enlargement can and must be the start of a new Community thrust towards the objectives set by the authors of the treaties."[38] Its view appeared to be that by anchoring The Three in the Community, democracy would be safeguarded in the applicant states—and the EC itself would obtain a new lease on life as it altruistically sought to bring The Three's levels of development up to rich-country standards.

Despite this high-flown aspiration, negotiations proceeded quickly only with Greece, which signed a treaty of accession on May 28, 1979. President Kostantinos Karamanlis of Greece ably used his personal prestige as the restorer of Greek democracy and skillfully played upon the EC's feelings of guilt about not having opposed the dictatorship of the colonels with sufficient vigor to get Greece a very satisfactory deal. Giscard d'Estaing dryly commented that "it was not Greece that went into Europe but Karamanlis."[39]

Greece was given, with allowance being made for the usual battery of exemptions, five years beginning on January 1, 1981, to implement the *acquis communautaire* (the accumulated legacy of EC law). Greek tariffs and quotas were to be gradually reduced on EC products by January 1986; the Community's agriculture regime (and prices) was to be phased in over the same period; the drachma was to be added to the "basket" of currencies used to calculate the value of the Ecu. The Greek government was to designate which regions would qualify for regional aid under the ERDF. Except for steel products, the member states promised to eliminate all tariff discrimination against Greek products from January 1, 1981. Greece was given five votes in the Council of Ministers and twenty-four seats in the Parliament, and was allowed to nominate one commissioner and one justice on the Court. In return for this settlement, the EC insisted that there should be a seven-year suspension of freedom of movement within the Community for Greek nationals.[40]

Spain and Portugal's accession, by contrast, was still unresolved in 1981 when Mitterrand came to power. The Community quailed at the challenge presented by Spanish entry in particular. The Commission's "Opinion on Spain's Application for Membership," submitted to the European Council at the end of November 1978, was distinctly gloomy. While it was formally favorable to Spanish entry, its opinion largely concentrated on pointing out the "scale and complexities of the problems arising from Spain's accession."[41] The opinion made, moreover, a number of suggestions—the immediate introduction of VAT and a longer transition period for agriculture than industry—that caused "consternation" in Spain, where industrial leaders responded by saying "yes to membership, but not at any price."[42] Spain's grave political problems, which culminated in a tragicomic attempted coup by reactionary army officers in February 1981, hardly strengthened its cause.

There were two other major obstructions, however. The first was French hostility to Spanish entry. Under Giscard d'Estaing, French worries about Spanish agricultural competition and the likelihood that Spanish entry would lead to a reduction in the size of the subsidies paid out to French farmers, bogged down negotiations. By the end of 1981, there had been twenty-five negotiation sessions, including nine at ministerial level, but no single chapter of the accession accords had been completed.[43] French obstruction lessened after the election of Mitterrand—on March 22, 1982, six chapters of the accession instruments were agreed in a single marathon bargaining session—but did not disappear entirely. However, when Spain elected a Socialist government that had placed membership of the Community at the heart of its manifesto, the new prime minister, Felipe Gonzales, hoped that "Socialist solidarity" would weaken France's tenacious defense of her national interests.[44] He was swiftly disillusioned.

It was not until Mitterrand's conversion to a pro-European stance in the spring of 1983 that Spanish and Portuguese entry became a genuine possibility. But it was still clear that the French government would not let the Iberian democracies in at the cost of her farmers' incomes. The June 1983 Stuttgart European Council offered a glimpse of hope when, following a successful visit to Bonn by Gonzales, Germany (who would have to shoulder most of the financial burden) proposed increasing the Community's share of VAT revenues from 1.0 to 1.4 percent, but explicitly linked any such increase to a successful resolution of the enlargement question.[45] But Britain's agreement had to be obtained for any such move, and Mrs. Thatcher was unbending in her determination to limit Britain's EC contribution, which was rising again, to "fair" levels. The December 1983 European Council in Athens was dominated by the budget crisis and ended with the member states being unable even to agree upon a final communiqué.

The crucial act of political will, which made enlargement to the Iberian countries certain, came only at the Fontainebleau summit (June 25–26, 1984), which committed the EC to resolving all the technical problems associated with enlargement within three months—after first resolving the budget problem. This ambitious timetable was not respected—not least because Greece, of all countries, made its "yes" to enlargement conditional upon the institution of "integrated Mediterranean programs" from which it could benefit—but the summit's decision did give decisive impetus to the negotiating process.

Spain and Portugal finally signed their treaties of accession in March 1985. The terms were less generous than the treaty with Greece had been, although the Iberian countries were allowed a longer transitional period than Greece to adjust to membership. Beginning on January 1, 1986, a seven-year transitional period was agreed for the full reduction of all tariff barriers and quotas imposed by the Iberian countries on industrial products. For agricultural products, the transitional period was seven years for Spain and ten years for Portugal. Unlike the Greek case, this accord was to be reciprocal: Spanish wine growers and citrus fruit producers were not allowed immediate access to the Community market but had to wait for the EC's own tariffs to be gradually eliminated over the same time span. Spanish and Portuguese citizens, like the Greeks before them, had their freedom of movement within the Community suspended for seven years; access to northern fishing waters was also to be restricted for the same period. Spain was awarded eight votes in the Council of Ministers; Portugal, five. Sixty deputies were to be elected to the European Parliament by the Spanish electorate; Portugal was awarded twenty-four MEPs. With these additions, the Parliament reached the unwieldy size of 518 members. Three new portfolios were created on the Commission, with Spain being awarded two places and Portugal one.[46]

Overall, membership of the EC did not offer Spain and Portugal the prospect of overnight prosperity. It did, however, symbolize the return of the two states to the democratic mainstream after nearly fifty years at the margins. Both states would prove capable of grasping the political opportunities presented by EC membership with both hands.

THE 1992 INITIATIVE AND THE DOOGE COMMITTEE

The decision to approve the entry of Spain and Portugal into the Community was not the only decision of importance taken at Fontainebleau. First, the Community's leaders finally defused the British question. The preceding Brussels European Council in March 1984 had ended in disarray, when Mrs. Thatcher's demands had enraged the French and Italians. Mitterrand openly warned Britain that she should not assume that the rest of the Community would wait forever. A Europe *à deux vitesses* (two-speed Europe) was thinkable.[47] At Fontainebleau, the Community's desperate need for a bigger overall budget (to pay for an enlarged CAP) coincided with some unexpected flexibility from the Iron Lady. After a day and a half of talks, Britain was guaranteed 1 billion Ecu for 1984 and an automatic 66 percent refund thereafter in return for supporting an increase in the Community's "own resources" from 1 percent of VAT revenues to the 1.4 percent suggested by the Germans at Stuttgart the year before.[48] This refund would be guaranteed so long as the 1.4 percent rate remained. Since Britain possessed a veto over any alteration to this figure, the deal was very acceptable for Thatcher, who had got most of what she was asking for.[49]

The summit also took the key decision to relaunch the project of the European Union—for which the Parliament had been pressing—by appointing two ad hoc ministerial commissions. The first, which was to deal with the question of the "Europe of Citizens," was chaired by the Italian politician Pietro Adonnino. It eventually recommended the introduction of important innovations such as the diffusion of a European driving license and making May 9 "Europe Day." The second, on institutional reform, was chaired by an Irishman, James Dooge.

The Fontainebleau summit ended with an effusion of hope for the future of the Community from the gathered leaders, including Mrs. Thatcher. A document presented by the British government to the European Council pressed for immediate action to "harmonize" market-deforming standards and practices in order to create a "true" single market; urged the abolition of frontiers and all obstacles to the movement of people, capital, or goods; spoke of the need for a "common approach" in foreign affairs; and claimed The Ten should show their "political will" on the world stage. It even recommended more frequent use of qualified majority voting (QMV) in the Council of Ministers.[50]

There was, in fact, enough harmony among the gathered leaders for them to agree on replacing Gaston Thorn with Jacques Delors. The Council realized it needed to appoint a heavyweight figure from a big country that would not be overshadowed by the national leaders. Delors, a technocrat who had also served in the European Parliament before becoming Mitterrand's finance minister, was the ideal choice: so much so that the Germans, who might have been expected to nominate a candidate of their own, were among his strongest supporters. The Commission that Delors and the national governments assembled in the next months was an experienced body, which could boast among its number Lorenzo Natali of Italy, who had served as vice president of the Commission since January 1977, and Claude Cheysson, who had served in the Commission under

Ortoli, Jenkins, and Thorn. Yet the member of the Commission who had the most impact was a newcomer. Lord Arthur Cockfield was a British businessman who had been minister for trade and industry under Mrs. Thatcher. Delors appointed him as commissioner responsible for the internal market, the liberalization of which was made the centerpiece of the new Commission's agenda for 1985.

In retrospect, it can be seen that the time was ripe for an initiative in this field. The leaders had committed themselves to it in the 1983 Solemn Declaration; the British government, so wary usually of initiatives with a "European" flavor, was deregulating its own economy with vigor, and freer trade within the Community offered the prospect of boosting sluggish economic performance and getting unemployment down from the socially dangerous levels (the Community average had soared to above 11 percent during the recession of the early 1980s) to which it had risen. Business groups, the most important of which was the so-called European Round Table, were also lobbying hard for a reduction in nontariff barriers to trade and for enhanced measures of deregulation.[51]

There had also been an important judicial stimulus for reform. In the Cassis de Dijon case (no. 120/78), the ECJ ignored the German government's imaginative defense that under German law Cassis (a black currant liquor) was too strong to be classified as a wine but too weak to be spirits and held that a product lawfully produced and marketed in one member state should normally have access to the others, unless compelling reasons of health and safety could be adduced to the contrary.[52] Quite apart from winning the esteem of German drinkers, the ECJ, by its ruling, also "created a simple standard for resolving trade disputes."[53] This, in turn, weakened the member states' previous resistance to the notion that there should be harmonized standards at Community level, for "mutual recognition would lead to national measures being applied to national products only, while goods produced in member-states with less stringent requirements would have to be admitted freely."[54]

One can exaggerate, however, the extent to which the Court's ruling opened the trade barriers within the EC. In the aftermath of the Cassis de Dijon ruling, the Thorn Commission drafted detailed legislation to achieve common product standards, but most of it never reached the statute books. In the meantime, Germany continued to ban imports of foreign beer by invoking its time-honored beer purity laws, Italy rejected all pasta that was not made with hard grain, and Belgium insisted that margarine should be sold in cubes, not rectangles.[55]

Cockfield's key contribution was to pressure the member states into living up to their rhetoric on the single market and free trade. Upon becoming commissioner, Cockfield bundled together the numerous suggestions for legislation piled up by the Thorn Commission into a single white paper, *Completing the Internal Market*, which contained nearly three hundred proposed regulations and directives.[56] The document also had a compelling rationale (Cockfield called it a "philosophy"), which was that the EC should become a "space without barriers." Customs posts and border controls, the physical symbols of the Community's continued division, should be torn down. But so should the invisible restrictions on trade in goods and services that were equally effective at segregating national economies.

The individual chapters were concerned with specific physical, technical, and fiscal barriers that needed to be abolished if the overall objective of a barrierless Community was to be attained by 1992. In the meantime, the document insisted, member states should conduct trade on the basis of mutual recognition of national standards and should not allow the absence of a European norm to affect the import of any product.

Completing the Internal Market was more than a mere memorandum on technicalities, however. It concluded with a rhetorical flourish that underlined its historical importance. In every politician's favorite cliché, the Commission claimed, "Europe stands at the crossroads." The Community could either press ahead with the plans outlined in the document or "drop back into mediocrity." The free movement of goods was "the indispensable precursor" for a more historic objective: "European unity." Failure to implement a single market in goods, services, and people by the end of 1992 would be to "offer the peoples of Europe a narrower, less rewarding, less secure, less prosperous future than they could otherwise enjoy."[57]

Cockfield and Delors were well aware, of course, that Europe's statesmen were perfectly capable of subscribing to such lofty sentiments about Europe's future while defending national interests tooth and nail. The Commission accordingly distributed the document just two weeks before the Milan summit on June 28–29, 1985, in order to give national governments little time to think up exceptions.

The dedication and energy that Cockfield brought to the task of completing the single market lost him the esteem of his patroness. In her memoirs, Lady Thatcher describes Cockfield as "a natural technocrat of great ability and problem-solving outlook." She adds, however, that he "was prisoner as well as master of his subject." It was "all too easy" for him to "go native" once he got to Brussels and move from "deregulating the market to re-regulating it under the rubric of harmonization."[58]

Thatcher's immediate wrath was directed against Cockfield's proposals to harmonize indirect taxes throughout the Community. Cockfield's defense—that article 99 of the EEC treaty required such harmonization since varying tax rates could distort the market by advantaging countries with low tax regimes—provoked a glacial encounter between the British prime minister and her appointee.[59] Tax harmonization was one aspect of the white paper that did not survive the subsequent negotiating process. Thatcher subsequently explained her position in her memoirs: "Competition between tax regimes is far more healthy than the imposition of a single system . . . in any event, the ability to set one's own levels of taxation is a crucial element in national sovereignty."[60]

Thatcher and the British government had also begun to cool on other aspects of the project launched at Fontainebleau. The Dooge Committee was punctuated by British intransigence. The Fontainebleau communiqué had rashly compared it to the 1956 Spaak committee, and the committee was thus burdened with the expectation that it would present proposals for a historical transformation of the EC's institutions. Pressure for more supranationalism had been growing for some time. In 1983, the European Parliament, ably instigated by the veteran Italian federalist Altiero Spinelli, drafted "Treaty on European Union," which envisaged a greatly empowered European Parliament, effectively equal in status to the Council of Ministers, and a clear division of competences between the Union and its member states. The draft treaty was formally approved by the Parliament on February 14, 1984, and was submitted to the Fontainebleau summit for its reaction.[61]

None of the member states were prepared to countenance the Parliament's proposal. But some countries (the Benelux nations, Italy, Germany) were more willing than others to implement some of the Parliament's recommendations. The British, backed up by the Danes and the Greeks, were much less enthusiastic.

The divergent positions were reflected in the report of the Dooge Committee to the March 29–30, 1985, meeting of the European Council in Brussels. The committee agreed that Europe's "priority objectives" were "a homogeneous internal economic area," "promotion of the common values of civilization," and the "search for an external identity," but they were divided over the means. The committee wanted "efficient and democratic institutions" for the EC but had quite different interpretations of this phrase. The argument raged in particular around the question of whether formal veto power would be retained or dispensed with by member states for all but "exceptional cases." Denmark was determined not to give up her formal veto power in the Council; Britain was equally opposed to relinquishing her sovereign power to say no. The majority of the committee favored an increase in the Parliament's powers of "joint decision making," among other reforms, seeing this as a way of making the Parliament a "guarantor of democracy in the European system": Britain merely urged the Parliament, within its existing treaty powers, to "make a more effective contribution." In all, some thirty-seven different points of dissent were entered as footnotes to the text agreed by the majority.[62]

The British and Danes were actually on the horns of a particularly uncomfortable dilemma. Both wanted to press ahead with market liberalization but without paying a cost in sovereignty. But market liberalization was impossible while the veto remained. Once Cockfield's white paper became public knowledge, the dilemma sharpened. Britain welcomed the laissez-faire thrust of the Commission's proposals and expected to do well from them. But the white paper, in the absence of QMV for single-market legislation, manifestly offered almost three hundred opportunities to use the national veto unless the member states compromised their sovereign rights.

Nevertheless, at the Milan summit, Britain and Denmark stood by their blank refusal to surrender the veto. The British suggestion, that there should be a "gentleman's agreement" that QMV would be used for single-market issues and that member states should have to defend any use of the veto by giving a public statement of their reasons, found little favor among the rest of the Community, who perhaps reflected that one of the gentlemen was a lady of strong convictions.

The impasse was broken by Italian prime minister Bettino Craxi and his foreign minister, the perennial Giulio Andreotti, who realized that article 236 of the EEC treaty allowed them to call, by a simple majority vote, an intergovernmental conference to discuss the amendments to the treaties proposed by the Dooge Committee. The Dooge Committee had itself recommended that its recommendations be discussed by a conference of this type. With the support of all the member states except Britain, Denmark, and Greece, Craxi put the matter to the vote. Mrs. Thatcher found herself in the unusual position of being "bulldozed" into doing the will of others, but she was compelled to acquiesce.[63] Italian historiography has somewhat nationalistically described this diplomatic victory for Craxi and Foreign Minister Andreotti as "one of the most important successes of Italy's European policy"; events would prove that it was no more than a deft procedural move. It was Mrs Thatcher's approach, not the Italian government's, that prevailed once the IGC began.[64]

THE SINGLE EUROPEAN ACT

Britain was in fact more successful than any other country in writing its agenda into the language of the final treaty. During the intergovernmental negotiations that took place in the autumn of 1985, Britain skillfully accepted much greater use of QMV but in return drove a very hard bargain over the single market. In her memoirs, Thatcher makes her negotiating stance perfectly clear:

I had one overriding positive goal. This was to create a single common market. . . . British businesses would be among those most likely to benefit from an opening up of others' markets. For example, we were more or less effectively excluded from the important German insurance and financial services markets where I knew—as I suspect did the Germans—that our people would excel. . . . The price which we would have to pay to achieve a single market with all its economic benefits, though, was more majority voting in the Community.[65]

The internal market was defined as "an area without internal frontiers in which the free movement of goods, persons and capital is ensured," and the Community committed itself to "progressively establishing" this area by December 31, 1992. The treaty made clear that legislation necessary for the achievement of this objective would be decided by QMV in all matters except "fiscal provisions" and matters relating to "the free movement of persons" and "the rights and interests of unemployed persons." Article 17 of the SEA amended article 99 of the EEC treaty to ensure that proposals to harmonize "turnover taxes, excise taxes and other forms of indirect taxation" would henceforth require a unanimous vote in the Council of Ministers.

Thatcher, aided by Germany and the Netherlands, tenaciously resisted any attempt to include economic and monetary union among the objectives of the EC. Article 20 of the SEA, which dealt with general economic policy, merely committed European leaders to "cooperate with each other in accordance with the objectives of article 104 of the EEC treaty" (which requires each member state to pull off the enviable balancing act of ensuring "the equilibrium of its overall balance of payments and to maintain confidence in its currency, while taking care to ensure a high level of employment and a stable level of prices"). The SEA did, however, open up the prospect of an intergovernmental conference being called in the event of further developments in the economic and monetary field becoming necessary. Though this gave Britain a de facto veto over the evolution of the EMS into anything more ambitious (since treaty changes suggested by an IGC had to be approved unanimously), Thatcher would have cause to rue this concession.

Mrs. Thatcher also resisted a determined effort by the Italian government to give the European Assembly (or Parliament as it was for the first time explicitly referred to in a Community treaty) powers of legislative "codecision" (i.e., putting it on a par with the Council of Ministers). In the SEA, the Parliament gained two new powers. First, it was given the right of assent over all treaties of enlargement and association made by the Community. Second, article 7 of the SEA introduced the so-called cooperation procedure for some ten articles of the revised

EEC treaty—the "cooperation procedure" being, in effect, the power to delay, though not veto, legislation. About two-thirds of the proposals in the Commission's "internal market" white paper were to be decided by this new approach.[66]

The SEA, if anything, strengthened the role of the Community's executive in the legislative process. This point was subsequently stressed by the European Parliament when it debated the SEA in January 1986. The distinctly unenthusiastic motion proposed by supporters of the SEA perceptively pointed out that the act had transferred substantial legislative responsibilities from elected national parliaments to the unelected Commission and to national governments.[67] Since 1986, it has been objectively true that in many crucial areas of policy EC governments need to concern themselves more with building a winning coalition within the Council of Ministers than with winning over backbenchers in their own national parliaments. The fact that most EC legislation is made during bargaining sessions between national executives and the Community central administration is the root cause of the EC's (now EU's) notorious democratic deficit. Arguably, it has also been a major contributing factor in the generally acknowledged decline in status of national parliamentary institutions in the EC states. Voters are well aware that the real action takes place in Brussels—but can do little or nothing to influence developments there.

The introduction of the single-market clauses, the wider adoption of QMV, the safeguarding of member states' veto power over tax questions, the adoption of the cooperation procedure, and the suggestion that economic and monetary union might be resolved by a further intergovernmental conference constituted the major elements of novelty in the SEA. But the treaty also contained a series of related articles on social policy, economic and social cohesion, research and technological development, and the environment. In retrospect, it is clear that Mrs. Thatcher thought she was turning the Community into a market economy administered by national governments. Most of the other heads of state or government thought, by contrast, that they were creating a social market economy, on the Rhineland model, that would evolve into a more tightly knit political Community with the passage of time.

Thus article 21 obliged member states to "pay particular attention to encouraging improvements" in health and safety matters and urged them to make "harmonization of conditions" their objective in this area. The Commission was instructed to prepare directives establishing minimum requirements for gradual implementation in the social policy field, although the act was careful to state that such directives should "avoid imposing administrative, financial and legal constraints in a way which would hold back the creation and development of small and medium-sized undertakings." This commitment to harmonized health and safety initiatives, in conjunction with article 18's explicit call for high levels of protection in these areas, was to become one of the major sources of Mrs. Thatcher's subsequent alienation from the EC and its works. The Commission and most of the member states tended to regard this article as legitimating Community action in the general sphere of social policy. The commitment of such countries as Denmark, France, and the Netherlands to top quality standards in social policy was absolute. Such countries were afraid that laissez-faire countries such as Britain would steal a cost advantage once the market became truly free. But they were also alarmed that harmonization might level-down standards to British or American levels: to avoid this fate, article 21 specifically provided for member states introducing "more stringent measures for the protection of working conditions" if they wished.

Economic and social cohesion, at the behest of the Greeks, became a Community priority. Article 23 of the treaty introduced a commitment to "reducing disparities between the various regions and the backwardness of the least-favored regions." The member states were to "conduct their economic policies" with this aim in mind. Overall, the language of the new clauses expressed the fears of the Mediterranean countries—including the two Iberian democracies which, being on the point of entry, had participated in the negotiations—that the internal market, unless it was tempered with rapid investment to enable them to catch up, would only heighten the economic superiority of the richer northern countries.

The environmental provisions of the SEA, by contrast, reflected a fear on the part of the richer countries that boosting economic growth, as the internal market promised to do, meant more pollution and a lower quality of life. They laid down as a principle that Community action on environmental issues should ensure "the polluter should pay" for the pollution caused: a dictum that opened up the prospect of the Commission introducing legislation to tighten fuel emission targets or to compel recycling. It was agreed, however, that on environmental regulations, that although QMV would be used "to define those matters on which decisions are to be taken," the Council of Ministers would make final decisions by a unanimous vote.

The lengthiest provision in the SEA was article 31 on European political cooperation (EPC), which was brought into the treaty framework. To a very great extent, the member states reiterated the positions they had taken since the early 1970s. They promised to "endeavor to formulate" common foreign and defense policies; to "ensure that common principles and objectives are gradually developed and defined"; and to "endeavor to avoid any action or position which impairs their effectiveness as a cohesive force in international relations." Much of the complex machinery coordinating foreign policy discussions between the member states was now formalized into words (and a permanent secretariat of officials seconded from the foreign ministries of member states was established). Yet the integration of foreign policymaking remained in its infancy. Despite this fact, final ratification of the SEA, which was signed in February 1986, was held up until July 1987 because an Irish citizen, Raymond Crotty, argued successfully in the courts that the Irish constitution would have to be changed by referendum before the clauses on political cooperation could be approved.[68] The Irish electorate dutifully did change the constitution, though less than half bothered to vote.

The SEA was only signed, let alone ratified, after some embarrassing argument. In January 1986, the Danish parliament passed a motion rejecting, by a narrow majority, the text of the act and urging its government to renegotiate terms. This demand was obviously impossible, and so Denmark instead held a hastily organized referendum on the SEA on February 27, 1986. When the Danes voted, the SEA passed with a 56 percent vote in favor. By then, nine countries had formally signed the treaty at a ceremony in Luxembourg on February 17; Italy and Greece grouchily opted to wait until the result of the Danish referendum and eventually signed on February 28. The Italians were at pains to underline their "deep dissatisfaction" with the SEA as a worthwhile step toward European integration. Foreign Minister Andreotti, upon signing, placed an official record of dissent in the annals of the intergovernmental conference: in his view, "objective analysis of the results of the conference showed that the SEA was merely a partial and unsatisfactory response to the need for substantial progress."[69]

At the signing ceremony, other advocates of stronger European institutions did their best to put a good face on the results of the conference. Hans van den Broek, the Dutch foreign minister and president of the Council of Ministers in the first half of 1986, said the SEA possessed the merit of striking a balance between "the possible and the desirable"; Frans Andriessen, a vice president of the Commission, described the SEA merely as "the embodiment of what is feasible in Europe" and expressed his wish that the member states had displayed "more courage in their commitment to the completion of the internal market and the enhancing of the monetary dimension."[70]

The European Parliament made even these effusions of faint praise seem like eulogies. Altiero Spinelli said dismissively, "The Council has produced a mouse, a miserable, stillborn mouse." In another cutting remark, Spinelli said, "They have left us with the bare bones."[71] A significant minority of MEPs wanted to make a symbolic vote of rejection; eventually, however, the Parliament approved the treaty by passing a motion that asserted that the intergovernmental conference had been "undemocratic" in keeping the Parliament "at arm's length" throughout the negotiation and described the SEA as being "very far from constituting the genuine reform of the Community that its people need." The Parliament urged the member states and the Commission to "exploit to the very limit the possibilities offered by the Single Act."[72]

EVALUATING THE SINGLE EUROPEAN ACT

There is little doubt, in retrospect, that the doom and gloom that accompanied the signing of the SEA was more angst over dashed expectations than a lucid appraisal of the act's significance. True, the member states had shrunk during the IGC from instituting parliamentary democracy on a continental scale and had chosen to make more policy in negotiations among themselves. However, what is surprising—bewildering is perhaps the correct word—is that anybody should have thought that the federalist option stood even the remotest chance. It is fascinating to read the conclusion on the SEA of the standard Italian history of European integration, Bino Olivi's passionately profederalist work *L'Europa difficile*: "The intergovernmental conference's attempt to arrive at a treaty instituting European Union had failed; the contents of the SEA were inadequate and piecemeal [*inorganico*], less comprehensive than even the most pessimistic predictions on the eve of the talks."[73] This is a good example of how historical writing is inevitably permeated by the author's own values and hopes. That the objective of the IGC might actually be European Union never crossed Mrs. Thatcher's mind. And what crossed Mrs. Thatcher's mind counted a good deal more during the negotiations than any number of draft treaties from the European Parliament.

But the inescapable fact that was missed in the immediate recriminations over the outcome of the SEA negotiation was that the member states had committed themselves to completing the internal market and that even the states most traditionally jealous of their national sovereignty had been willing to relinquish their right of veto in a wide range of policy areas. The case of Britain is particularly striking. Mrs. Thatcher, in pursuit of the economic gains she believed market liberalization would bring for Britain's competitive financial services sector, had approved a document that allowed Britain's European partners to make law applicable to British citizens without, at any rate in theory, the consent of the British government. As Hugo Young has written, the Single Act "surrendered sovereignty, accelerated momentum . . . it seemed to signal Britain's open-eyed engagement with the dominant culture of the Community."[74]

More generally, the SEA was, to use Pinder's terminology, a massive advance in the degree of negative integration present in the Community;

but it also opened the prospect, if the political will existed, of pursuing positive integration in the fields of monetary policy, health and safety, and economic cohesion. This was not small beer. It was wildly unrealistic of European federalists to expect the Iron Lady to give any more. The SEA may have been a lowest common denominator agreement, but the common denominator was a high one.

Moreover, the fact that all twelve member states had put their names to a document of the SEA's importance was in itself an achievement that few academic commentators would have predicted in the late 1970s or early 1980s. Probably the best work of scholarship on the EC in these years was a book by the British international relations theorist, Paul Taylor. Significantly entitled *The Limits of European Integration* (1983), Taylor's book argued that the EC had settled down into little more than a collaborative association of nation-states. Supranational institutions like the Commission had waned in importance, while intergovernmental institutions like the European Council had waxed. The presidency of the Council of Ministers had become a key role, with individual governments using their presidency to obtain a share of the Commission's agenda-setting function. Despite the direct election of the European Parliament, European political parties had not formed; this reflected the fact that Community consciousness at a popular level was nonexistent.[75] The EC was, in short, a useful institutional facilitator of interstate cooperation, but it was not a significant political actor in its own regard.

According to Taylor, the causes of this loss of impetus were inherent in the nature of the project. The ideology of the European movement had posited a "United States of Europe," with centralized institutions and an open economy, to which every democratic European country could belong. But centralizing power in Community institutions had run into the predictable problem of persuading recalcitrant national institutions to give up power. Moreover, there was too great a diversity in the member states' economic and social circumstances for everybody to be included comfortably into a single formula. Policies such as the EMS and the CAP were constantly being amended to take national circumstances into account and had become denatured as a result. Expansion of the Community to include Britain meant that the Community had lost the "dominant core" of France and Germany as a driving force.[76] The Community's efforts and energies had increasingly been diverted toward satisfying British objections to its existing practices rather than pressing on toward greater integration. The only way out of this situation of blockage, Taylor argued, was to allow "Europe à la carte." This was to permit the practice of partial agreements among the member states so long as a specified minimum of states approved.[77]

Taylor's recommendation reflected the frustration felt by many pro-European academics, policymakers, and politicians in the early 1980s.

Britain's behavior over the budget, France's flirtation with a siege economy, and France's watchfulness during the entry negotiations for the Iberian democracies had bred a mood of resignation. Openly pro-integration, Taylor could see in 1983 no other way of regenerating "a stronger sense of Community."[78] If partial agreements were permitted, he argued, there would probably be rapid movement toward economic and monetary union, a passport union, abolition of frontier controls, and the introduction of common welfare policies in a select group of states. Other countries could join when and if they were ready: in the meantime, they could pass "parallel legislation" in their national parliaments whenever a particular regulation struck them as worthwhile.[79]

The SEA proved that the EC could make one last collective leap forward. It did not disprove Taylor's overall thesis; the Schengen and Maastricht treaties, which are discussed in the next chapter, were only possible because the Community renounced a set menu for all its diners. The idea of "Europe à la carte," moreover, has since been dignified with the name of "enhanced cooperation" and written into the Treaties of Amsterdam (1997), Nice (2001), and Lisbon (2007). But, while negotiating the SEA, all of The Twelve did eventually agree upon the same, admittedly restricted, list of courses—much though some of them wanted to taste the splendid, but possibly indigestible, desserts being offered by the European Parliament. Why? What persuaded the national governments to abandon the negativity of the early 1980s and contemplate the substantial reduction in national sovereignty implicit in the SEA?

The SEA was, in retrospect, the outcome of a unique set of circumstances. These were (1) Britain, having resolved the budgetary question, was both relatively open to EC initiatives and ideologically inclined toward free markets; (2) completing the single market, especially after the Cassis de Dijon ruling, was an objective that had wide appeal among the member states on economic grounds; (3) France, having experimented with an overambitious form of domestic socialism, placed European integration at the heart of her policy as a way of regaining some degree of economic sovereignty; (4) the enlargement of the Community to the new democracies of the Mediterranean made institutional reform desirable; (5) the leaders of Germany and Italy, in particular, showed a strong propensity to test the limits of European integration and push for significant renunciations of national sovereignty to Community institutions. Germany, moreover, backed her rhetoric with hard cash. By allowing France to devalue the franc within the EMS and by paying for the British budget rebate, Germany prevented these two more acrimonious partners from wrecking the Community altogether.

Exceptional political leadership also played a crucial role. Two politicians in particular stand out. Margaret Thatcher's preference for free

markets and her underestimated personal pragmatism overcame her ab-
horrence of surrendering national sovereignty and ensured that an agreement was reached among The Twelve. But her willingness to compromise
was limited and ensured that the process of integration remained firmly
in the hands of the national governments—even if those governments
soon found themselves with their hands full.

Jacques Delors convinced Mitterrand in 1983 that France could not go
back on her postwar choice of participating in a wider European market.
When he became president of the Commission, Delors showed subtle
political judgment in making the completion of the internal market,
rather than monetary and economic union, the flagship of the Commission's proposals and charismatic leadership in selling the Commission's
ideas to the national governments. Hugo Young has said, rightly, "The
Single European Act . . . was a fusion between the visions of Margaret
Thatcher and Jacques Delors."[80] The Iron Lady has never lived this uncomfortable fact down.

Although Delors and Thatcher shared a belief in the value of free markets, their intellectual companionship ended there. The internal market,
in the view of Delors, required a social dimension, with high levels of
welfare protection, if it were not to be a mere charter for business. It
also required a mechanism to prevent the competitive devaluation of
currencies—the last major barrier against imports available to member
states. These issues would ignite the conflagration in relations between
Britain and the rest of the EC that soured Community politics between
1988 and 1990 and would lead to Mrs. Thatcher's ousting in November
1990 as leader of the Conservative Party. They would also be the most
controversial elements of the Maastricht Treaty (February 1992), which at
once superseded the SEA as the most important addition to the corpus of
Community law since the EEC treaty.

7

✛

The Maastricht Compromise

The Single European Act deliberately created a space. The question that arose between 1986 and the signature of the Treaty on European Union in February 1992 was what would be built upon the terrain cleared by Cockfield and Delors. Margaret Thatcher wanted the space to be developed by the free market, with the minimum of regulation. Jacques Delors, the quintessential French planner, was disinclined to adopt this solution. He wanted to build a towering edifice—a European construction that would substitute the national governments in most areas of policymaking. At the Maastricht meeting of the European Council in December 1991, The Twelve opted for a lopsided three-pillar structure that no architect would ever have designed. The Treaty on European Union, or, as it is familiarly known, the Maastricht Treaty, was a hard-fought compromise that blended a genuine impulse toward a greater supranational organization with the need to safeguard the interests and preferences of the member states.

The impulse for supranationalism owed much to the challenges raised by German reunification in 1989 to 1990, which unambiguously established Germany as first among equals in The Twelve. United Germany had eighty million people—twenty million more than Britain, France, and Italy—and was the natural reference point for the former Communist countries. The unambiguous support of the Bush administration for unification showed that Washington regarded the new Germany as the key element in its European policy. For the first time since the early 1950s, the prospect of Germany breaking free from French tutelage in Europe became a reality—or seemed a reality to anxious diplomats in London and Paris. The strengthening of European integration represented by the Maastricht Treaty was thus a symbolic affirmation that Germany intended to continue its postwar commitment to pooling sovereign power. Germany would become even more "European."

At the same time, the Maastricht negotiations and events post Maastricht illustrated that the European Community would be more "German" than ever before. The greatest innovation of the Maastricht Treaty—monetary union—was achieved by transferring the principles and practices of German monetary policy onto a continental scale. Much of the popular hostility to the Maastricht Treaty in Britain, Denmark, and France can be traced to the dislike of this prospect. Since Maastricht, the most important country within the EU has been united Germany, not France. Germany cannot get everything it wants in EU negotiations, but nothing meaningful can be achieved against German opposition.

THE "DELORS PACKAGE" AND THE DELORS REPORT

The Single European Act was expected to lead to a substantial increase in the Community's economic output. A Commission-sponsored report asserted in 1987 that the 1992 initiative, if fully implemented, would produce a noninflationary boost of at least 7 percent in the gross economic output of the Community by 1993 and to the creation of five million jobs.[1]

Professional economists were skeptical of the Commission's claims. Nobody disputed, however, that the 1992 initiative was likely to increase economic activity. The question was—for what end? Delors did not regard economic growth as an end in itself. As George Ross has written, "The Delorist vision saw the market as an indispensable allocator of resources, decision-maker and source of economic dynamism. The market by itself could not, however, guarantee equity, a moralized social order, or full economic success."[2] Delors's primary concern between 1987 and 1990 was to ensure that the gains of the single market were fairly shared out.

In particular, Delors was concerned that shortcomings of infrastructure and investment would hamper the efforts of the Community's least-developed regions to compete in the single market. In addition, Delors had been convinced by the Italian economist Tommaso Padoa-Schioppa that the single market required a single currency to function properly.[3]

Third and most important, Delors believed that the single market ought to lead to increased welfare and social cohesion. Raised in the "personalist" tradition of the French Catholic thinker Emmanuel Mounier, Delors rejected the vision of human society promoted by laissez-faire liberalism.[4]

As he affirmed in a 1988 book: "There is no sense in competition developing to the detriment of the standards of social protection and the working conditions upon which the European economic model is founded. Europe will not be built if the workers do not feel involved, if social progress is not part of its final objectives."[5]

The Delors Commission acted swiftly in 1987 to 1988 to address the first two of these concerns. In February 1987, the Commission presented the "Delors Package"—in effect, a five-year plan to increase the amount the Community spent on regional development. In all, the Commission's proposals envisaged spending about 60 billion Ecu before the end of 1992; funding for the regions would by then account for one-quarter of all the Community's expenditure. Most of the new spending (63 percent) was to be concentrated on so-called Objective 1 regions (Ireland including Ulster, most of Spain, Portugal, Greece, southern Italy, Sardinia, and Corsica), where economic activity was much lower than the Community average. A lesser proportion of the new money (12 percent) was to be directed at Objective 2 regions that had been hard hit by industrial decline. Areas "fully eligible" for Objective 2 status included South Wales, northwest England, the Walloon provinces of Belgium, the Saarland, Genoa, and the Basque country.[6] Delors boasted that "the sums invested in the first of these objectives are comparable to those mobilized by the Marshall Plan."[7] The remaining 25 percent was to be spent on measures for alleviating long-term unemployment, providing youth training, and modernizing agriculture in certain designated parts of the Community.

Overall, the Delors Package meant a substantial transfer of wealth from Europe's rich heartland to its poorer fringes. Getting it approved was not easy. Regional development could only be paid for by capping growth in agricultural spending (which was opposed by the French) or by increasing the amount of the Community's "own resources" (which was resisted by the British). Had German Chancellor Helmut Kohl not underwritten the costs of this latest expansion in the Community's budget, Delors's scheme would have failed. As it was, it was only approved in February 1988 after several heated meetings of the European Council.

The Delors Package nevertheless did its intended job. The poorer nations that entered the EC in the 1970s and 1980s prospered after 1987. Ireland, for instance, thanks to generous dollops of cash from the CAP and regional aid budgets, improved its infrastructure and raised income levels in the countryside. By the mid-1990s, Ireland boasted an income per head that was rapidly approaching British levels and an 8 percent annual growth rate. Overall, the "Celtic Tiger's" GNP increased by a startling 140 percent between 1987 and 2000. Although only a fraction of this performance was directly due to the effects of the structural funds, Ireland's stature as a rapidly modernizing country within the single market made the country more attractive to the foreign, mostly American, businesses whose flood of direct investment was what drove Ireland's acceleration in growth.[8]

Portugal, to give another example, enjoyed a substantial rise in affluence after it joined the Community. As in the case of Ireland, EC membership led both to substantial regional aid investment (over 40 percent of public investment was financed by the EC in the run-up to January 1, 1993) and large increases in foreign direct investment as American and German businesses took advantage of Portugal's low wage costs to export to the rest of the EC. By 1993, well over 70 percent of Portuguese exports were going to fellow member states. Portuguese income per head had been just half of the EC average in 1985; by the end of the 1990s, it was three-quarters of the average. The downside of this increased wealth was that Portugal began to import luxury goods from the rest of the Community and to run a current account deficit—something that was sustainable only if its competitiveness improved. Nevertheless, the first decade of Portuguese membership undeniably contributed to making the Portuguese "mainstream Europeans"—an important point of pride for a country whose authoritarian government had turned it into a backwater.[9]

Delors's second concern, economic and monetary union, was addressed at the Hanover summit of The Twelve in June 1988, when the European Council authorized him to chair a committee of the governors of The Twelve's central banks that had the specific remit of evaluating how a single currency could be introduced.[10] The central bankers were thus not asked to say whether a single currency was desirable but to assess how, technically, such a currency might be introduced.

Pressure for a single currency had been growing throughout the 1980s. France and Italy, to name but two countries, had complained about the economic costs of shadowing the Deutsche Mark in the EMS. Delors capitalized upon this sentiment to put the issue on the agenda—although, once again, he needed Kohl's support. Yet, involving the central bankers was a must. As Tommaso Padoa-Schioppa has written, "Had the Central Banks been excluded . . . [from the Delors committee] . . . they might have taken a more negative view of the prospects of monetary union." In that case, the Italian economist added, it would have been "more difficult" to "produce the document that played, both technically and politically, a role comparable to the Spaak report on the Common Market."[11]

The implementation of the 1992 program, the Delors Package for aiding the poorer regions of the EC, and monetary union added luster to the EC's international image. Following the Hanover summit, opinion formers both inside and outside the Community began to focus upon the EC's future as a global economic player rather than on its internal divisions and arguments over the budget process. The *New York Times* expressed the mood well:

> Having set a deadline for lifting all economic barriers by the end of 1992, the European Community has raced ahead in recent weeks to eliminate a large number of obstacles. . . . The Community hopes to remove all border posts so that people can drive from Munich to Malaga without stopping at Customs. And this is only the beginning. Predictions that an all-powerful European president could emerge and hold his or her own against the United States and the Soviet Union are exaggerated, or at least premature. Still, the implications of the economic integration of the 12 nations are immense. . . . Although the unification plan was established with economics in mind, it will inevitably have vast political repercussions. . . . Individually, the nations of Europe find it hard to be seen as equals by the superpowers. It might be a different story with a united Europe of 320 million people.[12]

Nevertheless, had the Delors committee on monetary union finished in recriminations, this wave of optimism in the EC's future would have dissipated as quickly as it appeared. Indeed, there were good reasons for expecting failure. Chairing the committee was by no means plain sailing for Delors, who was no expert on monetary policy.[13] Delors had, moreover, to cope with the attitude of the Bundesbank's chairman, Karl-Otto Pöhl, who was determined to ensure that the committee made no recommendations that might weaken his institution's notoriously rigid stance against cheap money and inflation. Pöhl switched off his earphones and read a newspaper when Delors gave his opening speech in French! Delors dealt with this arrogance by playing "a modest role throughout."[14] His style was "to depoliticize discussions by focusing on very precise technical points, to define the exercise as technocratic."[15] He even spoke in English. Gradually, Pöhl became more cooperative.

Pöhl did not bend on questions of substance, however. The Bundesbank position was based around three cardinal points. First, monetary union would require a central bank that could set interest rates without political interference and that was mandated to keep inflation low. Second, monetary integration should follow general economic convergence: would-be members should have met precise targets for inflation, budget deficits, and currency stability. Third, there should be no fixed timetables that might lead to political pressure for a fudge of the economic criteria for membership. EMU would start when there were enough countries ready to start and not a moment before.[16]

The Delors Report was published in April 1989. Delors himself supervised the published text very closely: "There wasn't a phrase in the final paper which he didn't author."[17] The report advised that the Community should move to EMU in three stages. The first stage would begin on July 1, 1990. By then, all the EC's countries would be members of the ERM and would cooperate, through existing institutions, for an unspecified amount of time, to achieve convergence of the main economic indicators. All remaining controls on cross-border capital movements would be abolished in line with the single-market initiative, but currency realignments within the ERM would still be possible at this stage. Stage 2 would establish the "European System of Central Banks," a coordinating body independent both of national governments and other EC institutions. The ESCB would take over the day-to-day running of the EC's existing arrangements for coordinating monetary policy and would plan its own eventual transformation into a central bank. The Council of Ministers would set nonbinding guidelines, by qualified majority voting, for the member states' budgetary policy at this stage. Exchange rate adjustments, while still legally possible, were to be regarded as "last resort" measures. Stage 3 would imply the fixing of exchange rates, compulsory macroeconomic policy guidelines set down by the Council of Ministers and the European Parliament, to avoid stability-threatening budget imbalances by individual member states and the centralization of hard currency reserves and monetary policy in the hands of the ESCB. A single currency would preferably be introduced at this stage.[18]

The conformity of the Delors Report to the Bundesbank's preferred model is evident from this summary. All involved in drawing up the report knew that the Bundesbank's prestige as the constitutionally enshrined defender of the value of the DM was such that the Bundesbank possessed a de facto veto. EMU without Germany was meaningless, but German political elites would not accept EMU without the say-so of the Bundesbank.

Yet conformity was a price that Delors was ready to pay. Simply by saying that EMU was possible, the Delors Report gave momentum to the idea. At the first EC summit after the publication of the report, in Madrid at the end of June 1989, the heads of government agreed to adopt the report as the basis for an intergovernmental conference, though they postponed the decision on when the conference would actually start.

This sudden acceleration toward monetary union was very unwelcome to the British prime minister. At Madrid, Mrs. Thatcher acquiesced in the Council's decision and—after a tense battle with her chancellor and foreign secretary—also committed Britain to membership of the ERM.[19] She did, however, reserve Britain's right to choose for herself when the economic conditions were ripe for entry to the ERM (and not be constrained by the July 1990 deadline) and emphasized that Britain's adherence to the first stage of the process outlined by the Delors Report did not mean that Britain was prepared to sign up to the second and third stages as well.

Paragraph 39 of the Delors Report stated, "The decision to enter upon the first stage should be a decision to embark on the entire process." In other words: "Taking the first bite committed the diner to swallow the whole meal."[20] Mrs. Thatcher had decided that she would scrutinize the exotic foreign food on offer with care and would pick only the items she was sure she would like.

THE BRUGES SPEECH

The rest of The Twelve were under no illusions that proceeding toward EMU would mean a fight with the British prime minister. They had known for nearly a year what Mrs. Thatcher's vision of the future of the Community was. In the summer of 1988, Delors, newly confirmed for a second term as president of the Commission, had told the European Parliament that he expected that "80 percent" of legislation affecting the Community's citizens would soon be made in Brussels, not the national parliaments. He had compounded this candor by promising the British Trade Unions Congress in August 1988 that social protection and employees' rights would be a primary concern of his second presidency. The Congress, battered by nine years of Thatcherism, greeted Delors's speech with a standing ovation.[21] It was a deliberate challenge that Mrs. Thatcher could not ignore.

Nor did she. On September 20, 1988, she delivered a speech entitled "The European Family of Nations" to the College of Europe in Bruges. The "Bruges speech" is one of the most memorable tirades in contemporary political history—and would have been still more memorable had the Foreign Office not edited out some of the more inflammatory passages of the first draft. But the speech was not merely a tirade. It presented a carefully constructed alternative vision for the development of the EC that the subsequent evolutions of the Community in the 1990s have not entirely eclipsed.

One important point to underline about the Bruges speech is that it was not a nationalist rant. The speech's main thrust was to warn the EC that it was becoming "a narrow-minded, inward-looking club" and was in danger of equating strengthening the EC's institutions with the construction of European identity. For Thatcher, European identity was bound up with the shared experience of the many wars European nations had fought against each other. In these wars, she asserted, Britain had always "fought to prevent Europe from falling under the dominance of a single power." If liberty was today one of Europe's core values, this was largely due to Britain: "Only miles from here in Belgium lie the bodies of 120,000 British soldiers who died in the First World War. Had it not been for that

willingness to fight and to die, Europe would have been united long before now—but not in liberty, not in justice."

In the light of her cultural understanding of European identity, Thatcher
reminded her listeners that the countries "east of the Iron Curtain" were
also "European" and, crucially, so was the United States. The Atlantic
Community, Thatcher stressed in her peroration, was "Europe on both
sides of the Atlantic" and Britain, Thatcher implied, would never permit
the EC to be built at the expense of the relationship individual European
nations enjoyed with their cousin across the Atlantic.

Thatcher's alternative to Delors's vision for Europe was based around
five "guiding principles" for action: "willing cooperation between sovereign states"; "encouraging change"; "Europe open to enterprise"; "Europe open to the world"; and "Europe and defense." Her vision for the EC
was one in which sovereign nation-states cooperated, within the framework of the EC, to inject a dose of free-market principles into the CAP, to
build upon the SEA by accelerating the liberalization of trade within the
Community and the ending of state protectionism in such industries as
telecommunications and banking, to adopt a liberal common policy in the
ongoing "Uruguay round" of trade talks, and to maintain and strengthen
Europe's defense in partnership with the United States. It was, in short, a
very British appeal "not to let ourselves be distracted by Utopian goals."

It was a speech, moreover, that drew three lines in the sand. The first
such line was a rejection of supranational government in Europe. Her
speech's most memorable sound bite was, "We have not successfully
rolled back the frontiers of the state in Britain, only to see them reim-
posed at a European level, with a European super-state exercising a new
dominance from Brussels." The second was an assertion of the British
state's right to police its borders: it was a "matter of plain common-sense
that we cannot totally abolish frontier controls if we are also to protect
our citizens from crime and to stop the movement of drugs, of terrorists,
and of illegal immigrants." The third was a warning that Britain would
not adopt the Rhineland "social market" model of capitalism. The EC
did not need "new regulations which raise the cost of employment and
make Europe's labor markets less flexible and less competitive." Britain
"would fight attempts to introduce collectivism and corporatism at the
European level." [22]

These three anathema were not chosen casually. They were the areas
in which the Commission and the more actively integrationist of Britain's
European partners were most intent on pooling or delegating sovereignty.
When Mrs. Thatcher made her speech, the Delors committee was beginning its deliberations. The second area, the abolition of border controls,
was already proceeding via the so-called Schengen agreement between
the Benelux countries, Germany, and France. In June 1985, in pursuit of a

decision made in principle by the June 1984 Fontainebleau summit, these countries had agreed that they would gradually diminish frontier checks on vehicles crossing their borders—including vehicles from other Community countries or even nonmember states. Despite some of the problems that arose from this policy—the Netherlands had, for instance, much more liberal drug laws than the other Schengen countries and the accord facilitated the circulation of soft drugs purchased in Dutch cities—the original five were determined to press on with this policy. In June 1990, they signed a full-blown treaty that confirmed that they would abolish all internal borders before January 1, 1993, and that made provisions for joint policing of the frontierless zone thus created. The Schengen "group" also committed themselves to gradually harmonizing their laws on immigration, asylum, drugs, and other issues.

The Schengen group's commitment to open borders presented many problems for other EC countries: the issue of IRA terrorism made joining impracticable for any British government in the late 1980s. But Mrs. Thatcher, in the Bruges speech, was intent on underlining a point of principle. In her view, immigration, asylum, and drugs were issues that would be decided by the British Parliament in perpetuity. Moreover, her commitment to the free movement of peoples throughout the single market was not to be taken to mean that she believed movements of people should go unmonitored. Deciding who could, and who could not, enter Britain was a sovereign right of the Westminster Parliament that could not be surrendered.

The third area excluded by the Bruges speech from Community action, social policy, went to the heart of the Thatcherite "revolution" in the British economy. Since 1979, Thatcher had pushed the deregulation of British business. By the late 1980s, British business had the least onerous level of welfare provision in the EC, and the trade unions had been squashed by a series of laws that limited their right to picket and to organize, let alone take part, via German-style supervisory boards, in the management decisions of major companies. For the rest of The Twelve, Britain's position was an unfair competitive advantage—so-called social dumping. Despite the blunt warning of the Bruges speech, the Commission pressed ahead in 1989 to put social rights at the heart of the EC's agenda.

The outcome of this Commission activity was the Community Charter of Basic Social Rights for Workers, a "solemn declaration" of principle that was presented in its final form to the December 1989 Strasbourg European Council and was approved by all the member states, with one predictable dissenter.[23] The Charter identified twelve broad rights that everybody working in the EC ought to possess. These were (1) the right to freedom of movement (EC citizens should be able to move from one country to another and take up jobs on the same terms—social security, tax, and so forth—as locals); (2) the right to employment and fair remuneration; (3) the right to improved living and working conditions; (4) the right to adequate social protection against unemployment, illness, and so forth; (5) the right to freedom of association and collective bargaining; (6) the right to vocational training throughout the worker's career; (7) the right of men and women to equal treatment not only in pay but also in education, training, social protection, and career opportunities; (8) the right to worker information, consultation, and participation; (9) the right to health and safety protection in the workplace; (10) the right to protection of children and adolescents; (11) the right of the elderly to a pension providing a decent standard of living; (12) the right of the disabled to be given opportunities for work training and social rehabilitation.

Mrs. Thatcher described the social charter as "quite simply a socialist charter."[24] In 1990, the Commission proposed draft directives to ensure minimum standards across the Community in the rules concerning the employment of part-time workers, the length of the working day, and the duration of maternity leave. Britain, which was faced with by far the largest bill for introducing this legislation, took the directive on part-timers all the way to the ECJ and strongly resisted the other two in the Council of Ministers. Ultimately, all three directives were implemented, but the British government had made its point. It would fight social policy legislation tooth and nail.[25]

By the time of the Strasbourg summit in December 1989, then, Britain was fighting the rest of the Community on several fronts. Britain was opposed to giving up its currency, opposed to surrendering its right to police its own border, opposed to turning the single market into a social market. It was increasingly clear, moreover, that Britain would have few allies in these struggles. At Strasbourg, in addition to welcoming the social charter, The Twelve took the decision to begin an intergovernmental conference on EMU in December 1990.

GERMAN UNIFICATION AND ITS CONSEQUENCES

Strasbourg was the first European Council since the breaching of the Berlin Wall. At Strasbourg, The Twelve decided to establish a European Bank of Reconstruction and Development (EBRD) to help finance the economic recovery of the nations of Central Europe. More generally, the collapse of communism gave new impetus to the movement toward the political integration of Europe. Convinced federalists now urged the national governments to give the EC a political dimension that would enable it to "act as a stronger unit" and to fill the vacuum left by the end of the Cold War. The European Parliament began agitating for a political dimension to the IGC as early as November 1989. In an unusual event, some 250 MEPs and delegates from the various national parliaments met in Rome on November 27–30, 1989, for a European "assizes" in which proposals to strengthen the Community's central institutions, notably the Parliament, were debated. In March 1990, the Parliament's ideas took shape in the so-called Martin I report, in which a committee chaired by the Socialist deputy David Martin proposed that the treaties should be revised to include European political cooperation (foreign policy), strengthened Community competence in social and environmental policy, systematic use of QMV in the Council of Ministers, European citizenship, and a substantial increase in the power of the Parliament.[26]

Important though the Parliament's pressure was, the most powerful impulse for greater political integration came from President François Mitterrand. French foreign policy was initially dubious at the prospect of German unification, not least because West Germany itself did not initially pay enough attention to French sensibilities. Helmut Kohl's Ten-Point Plan to deal with the collapse of East Germany, announced on November 28, 1989, and envisaging the creation of a "contractual community" between the two Germanies that would gradually advance to confederal status, was not cleared with the French government in advance. Mitterrand was livid at what he saw as an act of disrespect, not least because Kohl had also asked, the day before, that the decision to start an IGC on monetary union be postponed until December 1990. This decision caused "consternation at the Elysée." The French, but not only the French, worried that Kohl was trying to wriggle off the hook.[27]

For these reasons, the Strasbourg European Council, as Kohl underlined in his memoir of German unification, greeted the great events in Germany with diffidence. Only the premiers of Ireland and Spain welcomed the new situation in Germany.[28] On December 31, 1989, Mitterrand called for the construction of a European confederation that included the newly liberated states of Eastern Europe. This proposal put a cat among the pigeons. The president of France was interpreted as suggesting that German unification was so menacing an event that the EC was no longer an adequate institutional vehicle to restrain an enlarged Germany.[29]

German unification, as Karl Kaiser explained at the time, was an issue that raised four major concerns. How could worries about the power of a unified Germany be assuaged? How could Germany be unified while remaining in Western structures of integration? NATO membership was a particularly knotty issue. How could unification be achieved without the imposition of restrictions on German sovereignty? Last but not least, how could unification take place without the convocation of a major international conference featuring all of Germany's wartime adversaries?[30] The solution to this last question was, in February 1990, to institute the so-called 2+4 talks between the two Germanies acting in concert and the four major wartime allies (Britain, France, Russia, and the United States). At the risk of oversimplifying, the solution found to the other three questions—at any rate so far as the nations of Western Europe were concerned—was ultimately accelerated integration of the European Community. Germany would be allowed to reunite so long as it promptly pooled much of its new power in the institutions of a strengthened European Union.

The main architect of this strategy was Chancellor Helmut Kohl. In a key speech in Paris on January 17, 1990, he invoked a metaphor much used by Konrad Adenauer and stated that "the German house must be built under a European roof." This speech was followed up by a series of meetings and telephone calls with Mitterrand (but also with Italy's premier, Giulio Andreotti, who had deeply disappointed Kohl by initially taking a deeply negative view of a united Germany), in which the two leaders and their staffs worked out a plan of action. Following the March 1990 elections in East Germany, which Kohl's Christian Democrats, by turning them into a referendum on unity, won easily, Kohl and Mitterrand put European political integration on the EC's agenda. On April 19, 1990, a week before a meeting of the European Council in Dublin, Kohl and Mitterrand jointly wrote to the Irish prime minister, Charles Haughey, to urge the convocation of a second IGC on political union "parallel with" that on EMU and with the fourfold objective of strengthening the democratic legitimacy of the EC, making its institutions work better, ensuring "unity and coherence" in the EC's political action, and defining and implementing a common foreign and security policy. They further urged that the preparatory work for the IGC on monetary union be accelerated, with the objective of ratifying any changes made by the two IGCs before January 1993.[31]

This move, not least because Kohl accompanied it with a promise that Germany would pay for the costs of unification and would not ask—at any rate immediately—for increased voting rights to reflect united Germany's higher population, defrosted Kohl's peers in the European Council. The Dublin Council "warmly welcomed" German unification and in effect authorized a fast-track enlargement of the Community to admit East Germany, so long as its absorption into West Germany did not disrupt the goal of constructing a single market by December 1992.[32] Adding a new dimension to the colloquial expression "to work like a Trojan," a team of Commission officials labored frantically throughout the summer of 1990 to prepare the legal framework for accession.[33] On August 28, 1990, the Commission presented a legislative package that ensured that 80 percent of extant European law would be effective on the territory of former East Germany upon unification, which took place in October 1990. The remainder would be enacted by January 1, 1993, with some limited derogations being permitted until 1995 for environmental legislation. Thanks to this feat of administrative competence, the Commission became a "major (if silent) actor in the unification process."[34]

It should be said, however, that the decision to absorb East Germany so quickly was based upon heroic assumptions about the strength of its economy. A document submitted to a second Dublin European Council in June 1990 remarkably argued that the "macroeconomic implications" of German unity were broadly benign. Absorption of East Germany was not expected to lead either to increased transfers of resources or to higher inflation. Overall, it was thought that the absorption of East Germany would have "a significant positive impact" on the Community's economic activity.[35] Portugal would never have been treated so leniently or analyzed so superficially (nor, subsequently, were Poland, Hungary, and the other former Communist states). In fact, unification led both to an inflationary consumer boom and the collapse of East German industry—both of which had severe repercussions for the economy of the rest of the Community (see chapter 8).

AN OBSTACLE REMOVED

German unification, and the concomitant push for greater political union, pushed Thatcher into open rebellion against the direction being taken by the Community. In July 1990, a British newspaper published the leaked minutes of a seminar held some months previously between Thatcher and half a dozen academic experts on modern Germany. The minutes of the meeting asserted that "the way in which the Germans currently used their elbows and threw their weight about in the Community" suggested that "a lot still had not changed" from the days of Hitlerism![36]

If anybody was determined to ensure that united Germany did not repeat the errors of the past it was Chancellor Kohl. But it is easy to understand why Thatcher lost her cool. From London, it must have seemed as if events were skidding hopelessly out of control. At the second Dublin summit in June 1990, The Twelve committed themselves to transforming the Community "from an entity primarily based on economic integration and political cooperation into a political union."[37] In addition, the European Council dismissed a British plan to introduce a so-called hard Ecu as a substitute for a single currency. Under this scheme, the Ecu would have had a fixed value against each of the currencies of The Twelve, and banknotes denominated in Ecu would have been freely redeemable in any Community country. Citizens of the Community and businesses could thus get used to working with a common currency and, over time, a climate of opinion favorable to giving up individual national currencies might have asserted itself. Britain's partners, however, regarded the plan as a complication that would only lead to unnecessary delay.

After Ireland, the presidency of the EC passed to Italy. Just before the first summit of the Italian presidency, at Rome on October 27–28, 1990, Britain joined the ERM at a parity of 2.95 DM to the pound. Thatcher went to Rome expecting to be congratulated for having kept her word. Instead, the Italians organized the so-called ambush in Rome. Eleven out of twelve states committed themselves to starting stage 2 of the EMU process on January 1, 1994, thus setting a specific deadline for moving toward currency union. Thatcher flatly refused to accept this development. The summit's final communiqué also made specific suggestions for transforming the Community into a Union, extending the number of areas of competence in which the new Union could act, empowering the European Parliament by adding to its legislative powers, and precisely defining European citizenship. It added that a consensus had emerged on the need for a common foreign and defense policy for the Community. After each of these commitments, the communiqué was punctuated with an asterisk indicating that the British government reserved its position pending the debate due to take place in the IGC.[38]

The Rome summit thus left no one in any doubt that the battle announced in the Bruges speech was about to be joined. It would be Britain against the rest. At a press conference immediately after the summit, Mrs. Thatcher promised that she would use the government's majority in the House of Commons to block ratification of any treaty that was not in British interests. *The Sun* newspaper, in a moment of inspired chauvinistic wordplay, reported her comments with the headline, "Up Yours, Delors!"

Speaking in the House of Commons two days later, Thatcher cranked the rhetoric up further. She claimed that the Commission was trying to "extinguish democracy" and create a federal Europe by the back door: "If you hand over your sterling, you hand over the powers of this parliament to Europe." In front of a House hypnotized by the "sheer force of her presence," she declared that her answer to Europe's federalists was, "No, no, no!"[39]

The British negotiating position was thus clear. Had Thatcher remained as British prime minister, there could have been no Maastricht Treaty—or else, the other member states would have been driven to establish some new treaty arrangement superseding the EC altogether and excluding Britain.

But Thatcher did not remain as prime minister. Her intransigence was the last straw for senior pro-Community members of her government, notably former foreign secretary Geoffrey Howe, who resigned from the government and delivered a stinging parliamentary rebuke of Mrs. Thatcher's European policy. Thatcher's opponents rallied around the candidature of Michael Heseltine, a noted enthusiast for European integration and a former defense minister, when he challenged Thatcher for the leadership of the Conservative Party in November 1990. Heseltine received 152 votes in the contest, Thatcher 204, four votes short of the number (65 percent) required to win on the first ballot.

Thatcher's failure to win outright provoked a cabinet rebellion. Thatcher stepped down and in a second ballot, the chancellor of the exchequer, John Major, beat Heseltine to become leader of the party and hence, given the Conservatives' majority in the House of Commons, prime minister. Had just two of Heseltine's supporters voted for Thatcher in the first ballot, the result might have seemed a vindication of Thatcher's policy on Europe, and the rest of the EC might have faced a revitalized British prime minister in the two IGCs—an instructive reminder of the importance of contingency in political events.

Although there were other important reasons why Thatcher had lost the confidence of her party, Europe was the touchstone issue. Though John Major at once asserted that he wanted Britain to be "at the very heart of Europe," the British government was obliged to negotiate during the IGCs with one eye always on domestic public opinion and the opinion of the Thatcherites in the parliamentary party and in the cabinet.

THE "HOUR OF EUROPE"

The two IGCs were very different from each other. The IGC on EMU, which could work from the template of the Delors Report, was relatively smooth going. Three issues were crucial: When would the European Central Bank be established? What would the criteria of national economic performance be to qualify for EMU, and how rigorously would they be enforced? How would the British question be resolved? In November 1991, the Community's finance ministers agreed that the treaty would contain a specific provision regarding Britain, although the final formulation was left to the decisive Maastricht summit of the heads of government in December. On the other two questions, Germany for the most part got her way.

The IGC on political union was altogether more acrimonious. The Commission and such enthusiastic proponents of European federalism as Belgium, Italy, and the Netherlands pushed hard for institutional changes that would have established the EC's "federal vocation" beyond argument, while France and Britain resisted any alteration to the essentially intergovernmental character of the EC.

The Commission and the more federalist member states preferred the forthcoming treaty to be a "tree." By this, they meant that any innovations would be incorporated, on the model of the single-market clauses of the SEA, into the existing treaty texts as new chapters. France and Britain, by contrast, were insistent that the new treaty should be built around three "pillars," the so-called Greek temple approach. The first of these pillars was the existing EEC treaty, as amended by the SEA and reinforced by the inclusion of EMU. The second pillar would be justice and home affairs; the third, foreign policy. The last two would remain areas of intergovernmental cooperation over which the Commission, the Court of Justice, and the Parliament could exercise no authority.

In the end, the "Greek temple" won this argument hands down, despite a September 1991 move by the Dutch, egged on by the Commission, to start their presidency of the Council of Ministers by presenting an overtly federal draft treaty that demanded increased powers for the European Parliament and incorporated foreign policy into the EC's list of competences.[40] Only the Belgians supported this initiative, which plainly came too late in the negotiations to be feasible. After September 1991, the pillar approach was the only one possible.

Delors's preference for making foreign policy an integral part of the Community framework was linked to the EC's lamentable performance during the Persian Gulf and Yugoslavian crises during 1991. Yugoslavia represented a "tragic failure" in which the Community ended up "aggravating the crisis it was supposed to solve."[41] It is in fact a measure of the scale of the challenges facing the EC's leaders in 1991 that the two IGCs—themselves hugely important developments that required the member states' full attention—were often overshadowed during the year by the twin foreign policy crises dominating the headlines. Both in the Gulf and in Yugoslavia, the EC proved quite unable to frame a common policy and stick to it (or, in the case of Yugoslavia, make it stick).

In the case of the Gulf crisis, which blew up in August 1990 when the Iraqi leader Saddam Hussein invaded Kuwait, the EC unanimously agreed to impose economic sanctions on Iraq. The EC also warned the Iraqi dictator that any attempt to "harm or jeopardize" the safety of the citizens of EC countries in his power (there were several thousand, mostly workers in the oil industry) would provoke a "united response from the entire Community."[42] The EC also pledged substantial sums in aid to the frontline states most directly menaced by the Iraqi army (Egypt, Turkey, Jordan). It nevertheless took the EC until October before the finance ministers agreed to a package worth $2 billion. The Greeks even apparently tried to get their partners to charge interest on the loan to Turkey![43]

The EC's common front soon began to unravel, however. France got its hostages out separately by a murky unilateral deal; Germany tacitly backed the freelance diplomacy of the veteran German statesman Willy Brandt, who flew to Baghdad shortly after the October 1990 Rome European Council had decided that the individual states would not negotiate separately for the release of their hostages. On January 14, 1991, France proposed that the crisis could be resolved, after an Iraqi withdrawal from Kuwait, by a Middle East peace conference. Her Community partners were less outraged by the content of this plan than by the fact that France did not deign to inform them in advance.

When war broke out, the EC countries, Britain and France apart, contributed little to the military effort and France, which was not integrated into NATO's command structure, was the source of a good many problems for the American-led operation. Germany was handicapped by its Basic Law from deploying troops outside the NATO area of command. In the end, Germany sent a token force of air personnel and some fighter aircraft to Turkey, although German checkbook diplomacy did pay for almost one-third of the final cost of the war. Italy similarly had to contend with a vociferous antiwar movement—which included the Church—and a constitutional provision against participation in war. Italy's parliament eventually agreed to participate in an "international policing operation" and dispatched three warships and a fighter squadron to the Gulf, where the airmen in particular took an active operational role and suffered one loss. The Dutch navy made a similar small-scale contribution. Insofar as the ability to project military force is one of the classic distinguishing features of a state, Europe's more gung ho federalists were forced to recognize that in this regard at least a united Europe did not yet begin to exist.

Delors's desire to integrate foreign and defense policy into the Community framework started from this fact. Speaking in London in March 1991, Delors argued that the war against Iraq had shown that "once it became obvious that the situation would have to be resolved by armed combat, the Community had neither the institutional machinery nor the military force to allow it to act as a community." He appealed for the Community to "shoulder its share of the political and military responsibilities of our old nations" by reinforcing the Western European Union (WEU). Delors contended that the EC could "take over" the "mutual assistance" clause of the 1948 Treaty of Brussels (see chapter 2) and incorporate it into the EC treaty framework. The European Council would decide broad foreign policy guidelines by unanimous vote, but specific actions would then be decided by a qualified majority voting in the Council of Ministers. Delors was insistent that the Americans, who had voiced worries that this creation of a European defense identity would become a rival to NATO, need have no fears. The new Europe would be willing "to shoulder a larger burden than before"—which had to be in American interests.[44]

The Americans were skeptical. Delors's speech prompted the United States to reiterate three conditions that its chief defense spokesmen had already presented as limitations upon a future European defense structure: first, there should be no European caucus within NATO; second, that non-EC members of NATO (such as Norway and Turkey) should not be marginalized; third, no European defense structure alternative to NATO should be established.[45] Britain strove during the political union negotiations to find a middle way between Delors's position and the American stance by suggesting that the WEU—kept resolutely free from any entanglement with the EC—might become a forum for European cooperation in "out-of-area" operations such as the Gulf War. In the jargon, the WEU would be a "bridge" to NATO, which would remain the chief forum for defense cooperation among the countries of Western Europe.

The Americans' suspicion of an independent European foreign policy was fueled by the attitude of the French government, and Delors personally, during the so-called Uruguay Round of international trade talks that had begun in 1986. At the end of 1990, the talks were sinking into mutual recrimination over agriculture, textiles, and so-called audiovisual services (television and films). The member states were divided over what line to take during the trade talks. In France, at least, the determination was strong to preserve the amount of subsidies paid to farmers through the CAP and to fight for the retention of the October 1989 "television without frontiers" EC directive that obliged the member states to "ensure, where practicable and by appropriate means" that "a majority proportion of their transmission time, excluding the time appointed to news, sports events, games, advertising and teletext services" were reserved for "European works."[46]

In 1990 to 1991, farming and television became big issues for French public opinion, with accusations of Anglo-Saxon cultural imperialism being bandied by politicians and intellectuals of both the right and left. Delors himself fanned the flames. At a press conference after the Rome II European Council in December 1990, Delors accused the Americans of treating the EC "as if it had the plague" and said that he would not be "an accomplice to the depopulation of the land."[47] It was hardly the ideal moment for Delors to be hinting at European foreign policy independence.

The EC's failure during the Gulf conflict to act as a Community, mixed with the excitement generated by the ongoing political union negotiations, prompted the EC's misguided attempt from the spring of 1991 to settle the brewing crisis in Yugoslavia. To quote Ross: "Yugoslavia . . . was the first real test since the Gulf War of the EC's capacities to act internationally. Much was at stake. The test would be seen as a measure of the Community's ability to practice a common foreign and security policy."[48] Given its track record, one might have expected the EC to approach the boiling cauldron of Yugoslavia with some prudence.

Instead, the Community jumped in with both feet. It decided that it would back the effort of the president of the Yugoslav federation, Ante Markovic, to preserve Yugoslavia as a "confederation of sovereign republics, akin to the European Community of the Balkans."[49] In April 1991, in pursuit of this goal, the first of many EC "troikas," representing past, present, and future EC presidencies (in this case, the foreign ministers of Italy, Luxembourg, and the Netherlands), went to Belgrade and offered a substantial aid package to the Yugoslavs, if only they would stay together.

In retrospect—but not only in retrospect—this policy of dangling carrots before the republics of Yugoslavia was doomed to failure from the beginning. Comparatively wealthy Slovenia and ultranationalist Croatia were determined to split away from Serbia. Moreover, it was obvious that Serbia would not allow these two republics to defect from the Yugoslav federation without safeguarding the considerable Serb minorities in Croatia. On May 30, 1991, Serbian leader Slobodan Milosevic warned, on the eve of a visit to Belgrade by Delors and Luxembourg premier Jacques Santer, that Croatia would have to surrender the territories inhabited by ethnic Serbs if it wanted independence.[50] Civil war was therefore inevitable unless the republics could be prevented from fighting. The carrot of economic aid was manifestly not enough in this regard: Europe needed to wield a big stick as well. But Europe had no stick. All Delors and Santer could offer was aid and closer relations, provided Yugoslavia remained a federation with a single market, currency, and central bank; a single army; a single foreign policy; and a system of guarantees for human rights. In the prevailing political climate in Yugoslavia in the spring of 1991, these conditions were utopian.

Slovenia and Croatia declared independence at the end of June 1991. Fighting broke out immediately between the Serb-controlled Yugoslav army and the insurgent republics. The EC appeared monumentally unaware of its limited ability to influence the conflict. Jacques Poos, the Luxembourg foreign minister and president of the Council of Ministers, triumphantly proclaimed, "This is the hour of Europe. It is not the hour of the Americans."[51]

Poos's rhetoric was a sham. Neither an EC-imposed arms embargo on Yugoslavia, nor the so-called Brioni Agreement, which was signed on July 7 and bound the warring parties to effectuate a cease-fire, stopped the fighting for any length of time. Under the Brioni accords, EC observers were to be allowed into the war zones of Slovenia and "possibly also Croatia." Dressed in white, which won them the sobriquet of "the ice cream men," these brave individuals (they were unarmed and unescorted; several were killed) were well placed to monitor breaches of the Brioni Agreement by all parties throughout the summer of 1991.

On September 1, the EC negotiated "a window of opportunity." The EC threatened the Serbs, whose brutality had by now led to their being widely regarded as the villains of the piece, with "international action" unless they agreed to a new cease-fire and permitted EC monitors to enter Croatia. A peace conference, chaired by Lord Peter Carrington, a respected British diplomat, began on September 7 at The Hague.

Carrington put forward a draft peace plan on October 18, 1991. Backed by the United States and Russia, Carrington proposed independence for all of Yugoslavia's republics on the basis of the existing frontiers in conjunction with comprehensive guarantees for safeguarding the human rights of ethnic and national groups who found themselves on the wrong side of a border. The plan was simply disregarded on the ground, where the Serb minority within Croatia were fighting for union with the Serb motherland and were not willing to accept the restitution of a Croat rule they despised.[52]

From November 1991 onward, the UN and, increasingly, the United States, became the chief outside mediators in the Balkans' crisis. Community action (or inaction) in Yugoslavia had, by the time the heads of government met in Maastricht on December 9, 1991, undermined "any credible common foreign and security policy."[53] The much-vaunted foreign policy pillar of the Treaty on European Union amounted to a set of hopes and half-promises. In the defense field, The Twelve agreed that the common foreign and security policy (CFSP), which superseded European Political Cooperation (EPC), "shall include all questions related to the security of the Union, including the eventual framing of a common defense policy, which might in time lead to a common defense." The WEU was requested to "elaborate and implement decisions and actions of the Union that have defense implications," but the policy of the Union would "not prejudice" the obligations of "certain member states under the North Atlantic Treaty and [shall] be compatible with the common security and defense policy established within that framework."

The treaty did bind the states to "define and implement" a CFSP and to "refrain from any action that is contrary to the interests of the Union or likely to impair its effectiveness as a cohesive force in international relations," but nothing explained how the member states would do this. The treaty merely prescribed that "member states shall inform and consult one another within the Council . . . in order to ensure that their combined influence is exerted as effectively as possible by means of concerted and convergent action." After Maastricht, The Twelve agreed to formulate a common foreign policy toward those areas—Eastern Europe, the Balkans, and the Middle East—that most directly impinged upon them.[54]

Before the treaty had even been signed, however, Germany illustrated just how far rhetoric about "concerted and convergent action" actually extended by unilaterally granting diplomatic recognition to Croatia and Slovenia. The Twelve had already agreed to recognize, by January 15, 1992, the independence of any of the Yugoslav republics that could meet a series of tests concerning their policy toward human rights, guarantees for minorities, democratic government, the peaceful negotiation of border disputes, and so on. An eminent French jurist, Robert Badinter, had been charged with assessing the republics' performance by these standards and with making recommendations. Yet without waiting for Badinter's findings, Germany abruptly recognized Slovenia and Croatia on December 23, 1991, although as a sop to the rest of The Twelve Germany stated that diplomatic relations would only begin on January 15.[55]

Germany's high-handedness was motivated by fear that Badinter would not give semifascist Croatia a passing grade. Indeed, when he reported in early January, he approved only Slovenia and Macedonia. The Community proceeded anyway to recognize the sovereign status of Slovenia and Croatia, but did not recognize Macedonia, because the Greeks, who were nervous about Macedonian irredentism, were opposed.

The EC, in short, after spending more than six months trying to hold Yugoslavia together, had by January 1992 endorsed the U.S. policy of dismantling it. Bosnian president Alija Izetbegović was informed that Bosnia would be recognized, too, if a simple democratic majority of Bosnians voted for independence. Peace in Bosnia had been maintained for the previous forty years by subordinating a majoritarian view of democracy to the constitutional need to preserve the delicate ethnic power balance among Bosniaks, Croats, and Serbs.[56] If Bosnia declared independence, without first allowing its predominately Serb areas to secede, its Serb community, backed by Serbia itself, was bound to revolt. Sure enough, once the referendum had been held on March 1, 1992, and a majority obtained for independence from Belgrade, clashes swiftly began in rural districts. After the EC states and the United States recognized the new Bosnian state on April 5, 1992, the conflict rapidly became the most barbaric military campaign seen in Europe since the downfall of the Nazis.

Yugoslavia was clearly a tragedy waiting to happen. Yet the EC's interventions probably made a bad situation worse. As Simon Nuttall has written, the EC aspired to be the deus ex machina of the Yugoslav crisis: the god that descends from the clouds in a Greek tragedy and sets all to right.[57] But gods possess overwhelming force and the will to use it. The EC had neither. During the Yugoslav crisis, the EC more closely resembled an overcivilized teacher struggling to separate schoolyard bullies. Unable to clip the Yugoslavs around the ear, the EC was reduced to pleading ineffectually for good behavior from the sidelines until its most powerful member state decided the farce had gone on long enough. The authority with which Germany acted in December 1991 was a potent reminder to the rest of The Twelve of the need to bind united Germany tightly within European institutions.

THE TREATY ON EUROPEAN UNION

The treaty that emerged from the last-minute negotiating scramble among Europe's leaders during the Maastricht European Council on December 9–10, 1991 was a constitutional lawyer's delight—and an unreadable nightmare for any normal human being.[58] Yet public opinion in Europe soon grasped that Maastricht—officially the Treaty on European Union (TEU)—meant an unprecedented voluntary cession of national sovereignty. Long used to thinking of themselves as Belgians, Spaniards, Italians, or Germans, individual Europeans discovered that they had been transformed into citizens of a European Union (EU). This pleased some but infuriated others (especially Danes). Under Maastricht, every member state except Britain and Denmark in principle relinquished its long-term right to make its own monetary policy (and, in the short term, committed itself to meeting austere fiscal targets); every state except Britain acknowledged that it would abide by common Community standards in the field of social policy.

Little effort had been made to discover whether the citizens of the new Union actually wanted the innovations of the treaty or even to explain what the innovations were. The Treaty on European Union was a fait accompli dictated by the needs of high politics. Unsurprisingly, the voters in several countries of the Community—notably Denmark and France—decided to punish such presumption (see chapter 8).

This was ironic since one of the negotiators' main concerns had been to render the institutions of European integration less remote from the citizen. The treaty's preamble stressed that the decision to establish a Union would mark "a new stage in the process of creating an ever closer union among the peoples of Europe, in which decisions are taken as closely as possible to the citizen." The buzzword during the negotiations was *subsidiarity*. What this meant was that the Community would take action "only if and in so far as the objectives of the proposed action cannot be sufficiently achieved by the Member States and can therefore, by reason of the scale or the effects of the proposed action, be better achieved by the Community."

The principal innovation of the Maastricht Treaty was monetary union. In substance, the member states agreed that they would move toward EMU in three stages. Stage 1 was held to have begun on July 1, 1990; stage 2 was to start on January 1, 1994, in accordance with the decision of the October 1990 Rome summit. In stage 2, a European Monetary Institute

(EMI) was to be established. The EMI's key task was to monitor, in conjunction with the Commission, the progress being made by the member states toward meeting the convergence criteria in advance of an examination in 1996 of their progress.

There were five criteria in all. Would-be members

- were restricted from running annual government deficits of more than 3 percent of GDP at market prices;
- could possess a national debt no greater than 60 percent of GDP;
- were bound to keep inflation within 1.5 percent of the average of the three "best-performing member states" for a full year prior to the examination;
- could boast a currency that had "without severe tensions" respected the "normal fluctuation margins" of the ERM for at least two years; and
- had maintained for a full year an average nominal interest rate on their long-term government debt that did not exceed by more than 2 percent the average of the three best-performing member states.

The treaty allowed for some flexibility, however. Failure to meet the 3 percent annual deficit criterion could be condoned if the offending state had got its deficit down "substantially and continuously" to a level not much in excess of the 3 percent requirement; alternatively, if a usually prudent state was in breach of the 3 percent rule, allowances could be made. Exceeding the permitted total of national debt could be forgiven if the debt/GDP ratio was "sufficiently diminishing and approaching the reference value at sufficient pace."

If seven out of twelve member states met the five criteria, the European Council could move to stage 3 of EMU in 1997, although the treaty allowed for a delay of one year if too few nations had passed the test. If a critical mass of seven countries had still not been achieved by the end of 1997, the virtuous remainder were committed to press on with stage 3 from January 1, 1999. They were obliged, in short, to take the irrevocable step of fixing the relative value of their currencies and to introduce a common currency. The only way, therefore, that member states with sound macroeconomic fundamentals (e.g., Germany) could wriggle out of their commitment to the common currency was to take the irrational decision to run their economies in deliberate breach of the convergence criteria. By contrast, the only way countries such as Italy, whose annual budget deficit was over 9 percent of GDP and whose accumulated public debt was over 120 percent of GDP, could hope to meet the standards set by the convergence criteria was to tread unaccustomed paths of austerity rapidly.

Britain was the main exception to the iron rule of irrevocability.[59] Britain was specifically given the privilege of "opting in" to stage 3 "by a separate decision of its government and Parliament." The question to join or not to join would become over the next few years an open wound in the body of the British body politic, and in particular in the Conservative Party. But it is difficult to see what alternative Prime Minister Major had. Major had to satisfy his party's Thatcherite wing (and with an election due in 1992, he could not possibly take any step that would split his party) and handle his European partners' reluctance to allow Britain special privileges. The opt-in formula allowed everybody to save face and was something of a personal triumph for the prime minister.

In stage 3 of EMU, the European Central Bank (ECB) and the European System of Central Banks (ESCB) would be finally established. The ESCB was to be composed of the ECB and the central banks of the member states. Its primary objective was to conduct monetary and exchange rate policy in such a way as to maintain price stability, and its institutional independence was to be absolute.

The ESCB was to be governed by the decision-making bodies of the ECB. These were the Governing Council and the Executive Board. The latter of these bodies was to consist of a president, a vice president, and four other members, all appointed for an eight-year term by the European Council. The Executive Board was to be responsible for the implementation of monetary policy in accordance with "the guidelines and instructions laid down by the Governing Council," which was to be composed of the members of the Executive Board and the governors of the participating national central banks. The politically sensitive task of raising or lowering interest rates was the key duty of the Governing Council. Each member of the Governing Council was to have one vote, with decisions being made by a simple majority.

The ESCB's powers also included the right to set minimum reserve requirements for banks and other credit institutions established in member states and "exclusive right to authorize the issue of bank notes within the Community," but it did not contain exclusive power to conduct external exchange rate policy, which was reserved for Ecofin, the finance ministers' committee.[60]

Overall, the new treaty reflected Teutonic principles of monetary rigor. Tough macroeconomic targets had been set for would-be members; the new ECB would be institutionally mandated to deliver low inflation. German policymakers were not entirely happy, however. The decision to set a definitive date for stage 3 of the EMU process raised the suspicion—correctly, as it turned out—that political pressure to fudge the convergence criteria to allow as many countries as possible to join would be immense as stage 3 drew near. But since this concession had been put on the table at Maastricht by Chancellor Kohl, who saw it as a symbolic way for Germany "to demonstrate . . . its will to bind itself to Europe," doubtful German voices could only mutter.[61] It is almost certainly true, too, that Germany's negotiators thought that the convergence criteria could not possibly be blurred enough to allow Italy—the real problem case, since Greece was not even a member of the ERM—to enter.

Insulating the ECB from political pressure unquestionably added to what commentators were beginning to call the EC's "democratic deficit." Unlike the Bundesbank or the U.S. Federal Reserve, the ECB-ESCB was not subjected to the power of a national legislature able to amend—or threaten to amend—its statutory powers.[62] The statute establishing the ECB was a treaty between the member states of the European Union and thus could only be altered by all the member states acting in concert together—a distinctly unlikely hypothesis. The only nod in the direction of accountability was a requirement that the ECB should publish quarterly reports and send an annual report on its activities to the European Parliament, which could then debate it.

It was a thin democratic veneer. At Maastricht, the nations of the new Union had potentially contracted out the task of steering economic output to a clique of bankers whose training, culture, and personal convictions predisposed them to make monetary stability a priority over growth and employment. It was an astonishing thing for the heads of government to do. For if the ECB's pursuit of monetary stability were to lead to economic stagnation, the people who would carry the can for the resulting unemployment would continue to be Europe's politicians.

The ECB-ESCB was by far the most important innovation in the Maastricht Treaty, even though, in 1991, it was still a mirage by comparison with the omnipotent Bundesbank. Nevertheless, the treaty contained other significant novelties. The European Parliament finally obtained the right to codecision it had been denied in the SEA. It was now to have the last word on all legislation dealing with the free movement of workers, the provision of services, culture, education programs such as Community-financed student exchanges, consumer protection, trans-European infrastructure, the Community's highly complex programs to stimulate scientific research and development, and, most important of all, measures harmonizing national legislation for single-market purposes.

The Parliament also obtained the right to request the Commission to submit new policy proposals (though not the right to propose measures itself) and won the right to approve any changes in its own size or composition. The Parliament was given the important new power of being able to pass an initial vote of confidence in a new Commission, and the Commission's own term of office was extended to five years in order to coincide with the life span of the Parliament. In sum, insofar as the Maastricht

Treaty strengthened the supranational institutions of the Community, it did so by giving new authority to the Community's legislature, rather than its executive (the Commission).

The European Council was formally brought into the Community's decision-making structure for the first time. The Council was to "provide the Union with the necessary impetus for its development and shall decline the general political guidelines thereof." The European Council's actions remained outside the EC framework, however, and hence outside the jurisdiction of the ECJ, which itself at Maastricht gained the power to find member states that ignored its rulings in contempt of court and to fine them. Earlier, in 1988, the ECJ had been strengthened by the creation of a "Court of First Instance" to help it cope with the huge growth in cases in the wake of the SEA. Last—and certainly least—a consultative Committee of the Regions was set up to provide subnational tiers of government a voice in the policymaking process.

The number of policies decided at Community level increased. The Commission was given powers to propose legislation in well-defined areas of education, culture, environment, health, transport, and telecommunications. The right of the Community to pass legislation by QMV on workers' rights and other measures of social protection, which Britain flatly rejected and which almost caused the collapse of the summit, was the subject of a special protocol to the treaty, brokered by Dutch premier Ruud Lubbers and signed by the other eleven member states, which thus gave Britain an opt-out to add to its opt-in on monetary union.[63] When one considers that Britain had also ensured that there was no reference to the Union's "federal vocation" and that foreign policy decision making was left firmly in the hands of the member states, the triumphant comment by a British government spokesman that the Maastricht summit was "game, set and match" for Britain becomes comprehensible, though it was much resented by Delors and other European leaders. Prime Minister Major returned to London to cheers from even the most anti-European British newspapers—though that did not stop them subsequently from demonizing the treaty as a sellout of British national sovereignty.[64]

A final feature of the Maastricht Treaty that deserves extended discussion is the inclusion of Justice and Home Affairs (JHA) as the second pillar. The Treaty on European Union agreed that strictly intergovernmental cooperation was to proceed on a wide range of areas. The Twelve agreed that asylum policy, border issues, immigration questions, drug addiction, international fraud, judicial cooperation in both civil and criminal matters, customs cooperation, and the sharing of police intelligence were all matters of common interest and could be the object, assuming the unanimity of the member states, of joint action by the member states. To this end, a JHA Council of Ministers was established after Maastricht.

In the 1990s, JHA, after a slow start, was one of the growth areas of European cooperation. The Union affirmed, in the 1997 Treaty of Amsterdam (see chapter 8) that one of its core objectives was to become "an area of freedom, security and justice."[65] By this, the member states meant, specifically, freedom of movement, security from cross-border crime, and judicial cooperation between national legal systems in criminal and civil cases. Quite a lot has been done in the first two of these areas. By the end of the 1990s, the Schengen Treaty, with its small library of related accords and agreements, had been adopted by almost all the member states (Britain and Ireland remained outside, although Iceland and Norway, despite not being members of the EU, both joined) and had been incorporated into the first pillar of the Treaty on European Union. Just as in the United States, it is now possible for a non-European citizen to fly into any airport within the Schengen area and, once admitted, have passport-free liberty of movement from one member state to another. Increased freedom of movement, of course, potentially benefits criminals more than honest citizens. As a consequence, in 1995, the member states agreed to establish Interpol, an information clearinghouse to facilitate cross-border inquiries into specific crimes (drugs, illegal immigration, money laundering), which began work in October 1998. Interpol's remit has been further added to since 1998 in response to the growing frequency of cross-border crime, and since 9/11 cooperation against terrorism has given a further incentive to construct common policies in the sphere of citizen security. A "European arrest warrant" became law in 2003.

MAKING SENSE OF MAASTRICHT

The Maastricht Treaty left the EU as a remarkable hybrid polity of an entirely new kind. It was not a federal state but a confederation with a unique structure of government. The political scientist Alberta Sbragia made a successful effort to translate the EU's institutional structure into American terms in her book, *Euro-Politics*:

> For Americans to begin to grasp the differences in institutional structure between the United States and the Community, they need to imagine a collective presidency composed of governors, who make the strategic decisions on the development of the constitutional and political system (the European Council); a cabinet (the Commission), which exercises a monopoly over policy initiation as well as considerable leadership, but which is chosen by the states' governors; a very strong Senate (the Council of Ministers), comprising top political leaders chosen by the governors and having the right to amend or veto all proposals made by the cabinet; and a weak House of

Representatives (the European Parliament) elected by voters but having the right neither to initiate nor veto most policy proposals.[66]

Moreover, by the end of the 1990s, when monetary union had been completed, one could add to Sbragia's comparison a powerful Federal Reserve (the European Central Bank) composed of national central bankers and accountable for its actions to no directly elected body. It is worth underlining just how immense the institutional innovation had been since the Fontainebleau European Council in June 1984. In the early 1980s, the EC had been an intergovernmental organization primarily concerned with agricultural questions—which meant, inevitably, that it spent much of its time arguing over matters opaque to ordinary citizens. It had pretensions to higher things, but the gap between the rhetoric of European federalists and the reality of the EC's institutions was an abyss. Less than eight years later, scholars were talking of the "European Union" as a polity of a new kind that would exercise a growing influence and importance in world politics—which is the main reason why "EU studies" became so suddenly fashionable in American universities in the 1990s.

The question is, what prompted this undeniable speed-up in the pace of integration? What led The Twelve to strengthen the Community's supranational institutions so markedly? The answer to this question, as usual, is a combination of national self-interest, genuine idealism, and geopolitical concerns. Andrew Moravcsik is surely right to stress the element of self-interest in the decision to press ahead to monetary union.[67] Europe's nations wanted monetary union not just because it would make the single market more efficient, though that was a consideration, but because it would enable them to regain a measure of monetary sovereignty from the Bundesbank. The German government was prepared to concede this demand, but the price of this major concession was that the Maastricht Treaty imposed German levels of macroeconomic discipline and institutional independence.

The fact that the member states, Britain and Denmark apart, acquiesced in this abdication of sovereignty in such a sensitive area cannot be fully explained, however, without making reference to the European idealism of the leaders who were in charge of the negotiating process. Key leaders were convinced, to use a phrase coined by Jacques Delors in his immediate reaction to the fall of the Berlin Wall, that the EC was the "center of gravity of European history."[68] Leaders such as Andreotti, Kohl, Lubbers, and Mitterrand shared this conviction. When the sudden emergence of a uniting Germany became a reality, their first thought was that "it was necessary to make concessions to sustain momentum towards European political unification and make it irreversible."[69] They responded to German unification in European terms. This is what made

Mrs. Thatcher stand out: as N. Piers Ludlow has commented, Thatcher was as "opposed to European integration as she was to German unification." As he adds, this fact "goes a long way to explaining her essential isolation on both issues."[70]

But underlying the need to make concessions was not just an ideological leaning toward supranational government. The Maastricht Treaty, like the Schuman Plan, was also made with an eye to the changing geopolitical realities of the continent. In the face of the prospect of the reestablishment of a reunited Germany, Europe's leaders considered that they had no choice but to anchor Germany into the West.[71] As a result, they tacked on a series of major innovations in the political sphere to a treaty on economic union to which most of them were already willing in principle to subscribe.

The German government was decisive. Helmut Kohl and other members of the German political elite were acutely conscious of their neighbors' fears. This is why Germany's commitment to the political unification of Europe did not end with the Maastricht Treaty. In December 1992, Germany solemnly amended article 23 of its Basic Law (Constitution) to make the completion of a European Union bound to "democratic, legal, social and federal principles" the official goal of the German state. History should not be written in the subjunctive mood, but there can be little doubt that if the Berlin Wall had not fallen in November 1989, the IGC on political union would not have been put on the table with such abruptness by Kohl and Mitterrand. Monetary union was already a gigantic step forward for the Community. Delors himself subsequently (and perhaps uncharacteristically) admitted that the EC perhaps "shouldn't have made a treaty on political union, it was too soon" and argued that the Community, in addition to monetary union, should have contended itself with a "small treaty" clarifying the role of the EC's main institutions.[72]

Yet after Maastricht, in the 1990s and early 2000s, the European Union's member states raised the bar of their collective ambitions still higher. One might have expected the 1990s to be dominated by digestion of the huge changes explicit in the Maastricht Treaty. Instead, the Union sought both to "deepen" its existing powers (that is, to increase the range of activities decided by the Union) and to "widen" its membership to encompass the new democracies of Central and Eastern Europe. In retrospect, the post-Maastricht decade was characterized by overambition, although at the time the EU's progress often aroused enthusiasm and even euphoria.

8

✝

EUphoria?

Many intellectuals and politicians hoped that the Treaty on European Union would be a staging post for a quick transition to greater political integration. Indeed, between November 1993, when Maastricht was finally ratified by all the member states, and the spring of 2005, the EU launched bold initiatives in four key areas of policy: monetary policy, enlargement of the Union, institutional reform of the EU, and foreign and defense policy. Had the outcomes of these initiatives lived up to the ambitions of their sponsors, the EU would today be a federation whose sway in global politics would be significantly greater than that to which any one of its single constituent members could aspire: indeed, it would rival the United States in its geopolitical influence.

Actual achievements fell short of what ambition might have wished. Nevertheless, the EU's progress in all four of the policy areas mentioned above was such that by the mid-2000s, a climate verging on euphoria about the EU's prospects prevailed in academia, much of the media, and inside the EU's institutions themselves. Commentators on both sides of the Atlantic were convinced that the EU was emerging as a "postmodern" political entity whose values and modus operandi were more appropriate for the challenges of the twenty-first century than those of the neoconservatives in power in Washington. Europe would lead by example, not by the projection of military might.

Even by the overexcited standards of foreign policy punditry, this characterization of the EU's potential role in the world was premature—though not, perhaps, wholly ridiculous. The EU had set itself some heroic goals in the 1990s and for a brief period looked as if it was mostly achieving them. As a result, commentators, especially those dismayed by the intemperance of the Bush administration's ideology and strategy, proclaimed Europe to be a superpower before she was ready.

ADOPTING THE EURO

The introduction of a single currency on January 1, 2002, was greeted with great fanfare in all of the twelve participating countries. But the introduction of Euro banknotes, with their distinctive representations of Europe's rich architectural tradition, was only the last step of a troublesome journey. The Euro finished in the pocketbooks of the Union's citizens only thanks to a series of political decisions to keep the single-currency project on track. Had the Maastricht Treaty's provisions been implemented to the letter, 300 million Europeans would not now use the Euro to buy their daily bread.

The first of these decisions was forced by the implosion of the EMS in the summers of 1992 and 1993. Insofar as one of the key criteria for membership of the single currency was an ability to remain "without severe tensions" within the "normal fluctuation margins" allowed by the EMS, the project of a single currency ought to have been consigned to the scrap heap by August 1993. The project, instead, was preserved.

The origin of the EMS's difficulties was German domestic policy. During reunification in 1990, the Kohl government, anxious to stem the human tide of emigrants from East Germany, hastened to boost living standards in the GDR. East Germans were allowed to exchange a large part of their savings for marks at a "one-for-one" ratio. This decision fueled a boom as East Germans spent freely on the Western consumer goods denied to them by communism.

It soon became apparent, too, that bringing the East German economy up to scratch needed more investment than could safely be raised from taxation. Public borrowing would be necessary on a massive scale. High consumer spending plus deficit spending by the government soon caused inflation rates across Germany to tick upward. Starting in September 1991, the Bundesbank, with its statutory duty to keep inflation low, responded by raising interest rates to almost 10 percent—more than double the rate prevailing in the United States, which had eased monetary policy as a response to the recession then taking place in the U.S. economy. This imbalance in transatlantic interest rates ensured that "a sea of money sloshed from Wall Street" into the European money markets in search of higher returns. The German mark absorbed the lion's share of this money, and its value appreciated even against the French franc and other European currencies whose inflation rates and balance-of-payments figures were healthier than the corresponding German ones.[1]

This situation reversed the logic of the EMS. The EMS was designed to export low German inflation to the rest of Europe; it now began exporting high German interest rates. Member states were obliged to peg their currencies to the soaring mark by raising their own interest rates—hence reducing their rate of growth and provoking the risk of recession. It was only a question of time before the other member states began to resent paying for German reunification with their own unemployment.

The prevailing post-Maastricht euphoria, however, was such that doom mongers obtained little hearing. The markets assumed that the EU was on a "glidepath" to monetary union and that the member states would therefore tighten their belts in order to keep step with the rising mark. Bonds with relatively high yields in francs, lire, pesetas, and other currencies thus seemed like a great deal. Traders figured that they would make "capital gains on the bonds, with no risk of currency depreciation."[2]

When, on June 2, 1992, a narrow majority of Danes (50.7 percent) rejected the Maastricht Treaty in a referendum, the bankers were startled from their daydreams. Although the Lisbon meeting of the European Council (June 26–27, 1992) reaffirmed the national leaders' determination to press on with ratification of the treaty, the fact was that the Danish electorate had cast doubt over its future. But if monetary union was no longer guaranteed, would Spain, Italy, and other member states stick with the Maastricht convergence criteria? Might they not allow their currencies to devalue against the DM in the traditional way, rather than undergo the pain of getting their public finances in order? Money started to flow out of the peseta and lira and was only briefly stanched, in the case of Italy, by a package of harsh austerity measures in July 1992.

Sterling also started to come under pressure. Britain, of course, was not committed to joining a single currency, but the Conservative government of John Major had made membership of the EMS the linchpin of its economic strategy. Unwisely, Major boasted at the beginning of July 1992 that the sterling would in time match the DM as the "anchor" of the system.[3] In the midst of a recession brought on by the popping of a property bubble, Britain was in no stronger position than was Italy to defend her currency with high interest rates.

In the wake of the Danish vote, French president François Mitterrand added to uncertainty over the future of monetary union when he announced that France, too, would hold a referendum on the Maastricht Treaty on September 20, 1992. Mitterrand's goal may have been to relaunch the ratification process by obtaining a popular endorsement for the treaty. It is equally possible that he simply acted "impetuously and unwisely."[4] Support for a "no" vote grew as the summer progressed and as anti-German populism found its voice. The prominent conservative politician Edouard Balladur, a supporter of a "yes" vote, was obliged publicly to underline in August 1992 that "rejection of the Treaty . . . will simply allow Germany to act as it desires, without taking heed of its neighbors or partners, without being constrained by any set of European rules in its role as a military, economic, financial and monetary power in the center of the continent."[5]

Mitterrand made things worse on September 3, 1992, in the course of a debate with the Gaullist politician Philippe Séguin, an opponent of the Treaty on European Union. When Séguin contended that the Maastricht Treaty would transfer crucial economic decisions to unaccountable "technocrats," Mitterrand stated baldly in reply that the future ECB would be subject to the control of the European Council.

This open repudiation of a core principle of the ECB's statute infuriated the Bundesbank's new chairman, Helmut Schlesinger, who believed that independence from political interference was vital for the ECB's future credibility. Two days later, at a meeting of EU finance ministers and central bankers in Bath, England, Schlesinger not only refused to reduce German interest rates but also let his growing frustration with the politicians show. When British chancellor Norman Lamont aggressively pushed for a rate reduction, Schlesinger had to be physically restrained from walking out.[6] Had he left, the other central bankers present would have walked out, too. The repercussions upon the electoral campaign in France would have been immediate and immense: probably the treaty would have been voted down.

As it was, the French recorded a *"petit oui."* By a margin of 51 percent to 49 percent, they approved the treaty. "Yes" voters considered that Maastricht was necessary "to secure a lasting peace in Europe" (72 percent) and because it was "indispensable for building Europe" (63 percent). They were typically better educated and more urban. "No" voters, who were less well educated, rural, and disproportionately Communist, Gaullist, or supporters of the neofascist Front National voted "no" because they feared "loss of national sovereignty" (57 percent), thought France was "in the hands of Brussels technocrats" (55 percent), and feared "German domination of Europe" (40 percent).[7] Not only was the French referendum a "soberingly thin endorsement"; it was also a harbinger of the wave of populism that greater powers for the EU would increasingly engender and, paradoxically, of the divisiveness of the project for European unity.[8]

Schlesinger's refusal to cut interest rates, meanwhile, had set off a currency crisis of 1970s dimensions. On September 16, "Black Wednesday," the lira, the pound, and the peseta were battered by waves of selling. On that day, the British government spent more than £15 billion in a desperate attempt to prop up the pound and raised interest rates twice (from 10 to 12 percent and from 12 to 15 percent). Its efforts were to no avail.[9] Sterling snapped the chains binding it to the other currencies and floated free. Major's government lost its reputation for competence and, despite managing the public finances ably for the remainder of its time in office, never regained public trust.

The Economist, which had said on August 29 that the British were "fond" of "talking about currency crises" but had assured its readers that "this one hardly makes the grade," headlined its September 19 edition with a single word: "Mayhem."[10]

By February 1993, the pound had lost 20 percent of its former value against the mark. The lira was similarly savaged: it fell from 750 lire to the mark to over 900 in the space of a few weeks. The Spanish peseta escaped with a mere 5 percent devaluation. In subsequent days, the Irish, Danish, and even French currencies came under attack. But the narrow French "yes" vote, and a timely financial life belt from the Bundesbank, ensured the attacks were repelled.

The September 1992 currency crisis led a number of influential figures to fly the kite of a two-speed Europe, in which Germany, France, and the Benelux countries would press ahead with rapid monetary and political union. Indeed, in the light of the Bundesbank's hostility to the single currency in the 1980s and the tepidness with which it defended the sterling and the lira, it is not idle to wonder whether this was not the German central bank's preferred outcome. More generally, the crisis reminded Europeans that "the removal of currency fluctuations within Europe has underpinned Project 1992."[11] For hard-pressed British and Italian industrialists, Black Wednesday was a day of rejoicing. They could now export more cheaply to EMS members while benefiting from a de facto tariff on imports. Italy, in particular, began a period of substantial trade surpluses that widened even further in 1994 to 1995 as political upheaval drove the lira to more than 1,200 against the mark—a 40 percent depreciation in less than three years. The question was how long Italy's trading partners would put up with such a state of affairs without resorting to protectionist measures that would put the single market—the Community's raison d'être—into doubt.

The EMS lasted only until the end of July 1993. By then, the new center-right government in Paris was pleading for an end to rigor in Frankfurt.[12] A meeting of the Bundesbank Council (its governing body) on July 29, 1993, was expected to deliver a rate cut. Instead, no reduction occurred. The French and Belgian francs, the peseta, and the Danish kroner crashed uncontrollably upon the news. Impotent in the face of the markets, the EU's finance ministers widened the fluctuation bands of the ERM's participating currencies to 15 percent above or below their central rate. In effect, they put a fig leaf in front of the nakedness of their return to floating exchange rates. They also affirmed their common commitment to the principle of monetary union and to ensuring that their economies met the remaining convergence criteria.

And yet arguably the most important criterion for membership had been abandoned. Nor was it the only criterion that was going by the board. High interest rates, by constraining growth, were boosting welfare spending and the cost of servicing member states' national debts. By 1993, several member states were running deficits in excess of the 3 percent permitted by the convergence criteria. The rapid accumulation of new debt meant that several countries now ran the risk of failing to keep their national debts below the 60 percent specified in the Maastricht Treaty.

These problems worsened in the next two years. In 1995, the Commission estimated that Luxembourg, with less than 500,000 inhabitants, would be the only country to satisfy both the deficit and national debt criteria in 1997! Germany and France would probably, but not certainly, squeeze in; no other country except Britain (who hardly counted) could meet both criteria, and several were expected to meet neither.[13]

These economic difficulties explain why the December 1995 Madrid European Council postponed the third stage of monetary union to 1999, as the Maastricht Treaty permitted. The same summit also made several more positive decisions, however. The would-be currency was to be named the Euro (the only alternative seriously considered was the florin). It was decided that Euro notes and coins would circulate by January 2002 "at the latest" and that the decision on the fitness of potential member states would be made "as soon as possible in 1998."[14]

In 1996, Germany insisted upon the adoption of a "Stability and Growth Pact," which was presented to the Dublin European Council in December 1996 by the Community's finance ministers.[15] Under the pact, every EU member state committed itself to aiming for "a medium-term budgetary position of close to balance or in surplus." Every EU member state would submit annual "stability programs" to the Commission, which would flag problem cases. Countries running a budget deficit of over 3 percent of GDP were to be potentially subject to "agreed sanctions" unless their deficit had been provoked by an "unusual event" beyond their control, or else was due to a "severe economic downturn" that had caused a fall of more than 2 percent in GDP.[16]

For most of the member states, this collective decision in favor of fiscal rigor merely meant tightening their belts by a notch or two. For some states, however, the prospect of Euro membership implied greater sacrifices. Italy was the most dramatic example. Italy had been governed since 1948 by Christian Democracy (DC), a party that had maintained public consent by generous use of the public finances. The state sector was overstaffed and unproductive; too many nationalized industries were the fiefs of the political parties and stuffed with political placemen; pension rights had been distributed liberally; infrastructure spending had too often been driven by the need to satisfy powerful political clients rather than by the objective requirements of the economy. Corruption was widespread.[17] In the 1980s, increased political competition from the DC's partner in government, the Socialist Party (PSI), led to an intensification of these practices as both parties tried to buy votes. Italy's public debt expanded at an unsustainable speed, and investors increasingly demanded high rates of interest on the vast quantities of new government bonds being unloaded on the market every year. Public debt had soared to well over 100 percent of GDP by the time Italy signed the Maastricht Treaty and peaked at 123 percent of GDP in 1994.[18]

In 1992 to 1993, the political system collapsed as a result of judicial inquiries into the corruption of the political elite, leaving the political movements that replaced the DC with the unenviable task of getting Italy into shape for the Euro. The leader of the center-left Ulivo ("Olive Tree") government that won the general elections of April 1996, Romano Prodi, made qualifying for the Euro his central priority. But meeting the Maastricht criteria represented a "Copernican revolution" in the organization of Italy's economy.[19] The state could no longer tolerate structural inefficiencies that boosted inflation and imposed costs on business since Italy, once it was in the single currency, could no longer rely on maintaining its competitiveness by devaluation. Prodi's government accordingly launched an intense program of privatizations, pension reforms, labor market deregulation, and local government reforms. Public spending was frozen, tax collection rates improved, and income taxes were raised, notably by a one-off "Euro tax" levied in fiscal year 1996 to 1997.

These policies squeezed inflation and allowed the rate of interest paid on government bonds to come down. By the beginning of 1998, Italy could boast a primary budget surplus of about 3 percent of GDP. There was nothing inevitable about this turnaround, which was the result of political will and popular support for European unity.[20]

Italy had to make the greatest sacrifices in order to get up to the Euro starting line. But the EU-wide austerity program had measurable effects almost everywhere. When the Commission assessed the state of the EU's economies in March 1998, it found that there was a "very high degree of sustainable convergence." Inflation had been driven down to less than 2 percent throughout the Community; only Greece had failed to reduce its annual deficit to below 3 percent; yields on government bonds had converged everywhere. Admittedly, only four EU countries (Britain, Luxembourg, France, and Finland, which had entered the Union in 1995) had a national debt of less than 60 percent of GDP, but national debt was falling relative to GDP everywhere except Germany (which, in any case, was only marginally above the 60 percent figure).

In light of these results, the Commission promoted eleven countries to the Euro-zone and showed a yellow card to two (Greece and Sweden). Britain and Denmark exercised their option not to participate.[21] At the beginning of May 1998, the heads of state and government accepted the Commission's recommendations and chose, against French opposition, a Dutch central banker, Wim Duisenberg, for the ECB's presidency. On January 1, 1999, the exchange rates of the eleven participating currencies were fixed against the Euro, which debuted on the international money markets with a value of $1.17.

The fact that eleven member states had succeeded in qualifying for the single currency was a remarkable demonstration of collective political will in pursuit of European integration. If the Maastricht tests had been applied rigorously, monetary union would not have happened. But since such a failure would have set the goal of integration back permanently, the member states' leaders were willing both to impose unpopular austerity and to show flexibility with the rules. This willingness to do whatever it took to make monetary union happen was not just a reflection of the leaders' commitment to the European cause. The experience of the 1990s had underlined the Euro's advantages to them. EU nations had learned the hard way that in the absence of a single currency, ultimate sovereignty over monetary policy (and hence of general economic policy) lay in the hands of the Bundesbank—or in the anarchy of the currency markets.

In the run-up to the introduction of the Euro, economists advanced many other reasons for a single currency. The Euro promised significant immediate gains in price transparency (would-be buyers of a Volkswagen could tell at a glance whether the car of their choice was cheaper in Germany than across the border in Belgium), lower inflation (more expensive sellers of Volkswagens would have to reduce their prices), and transaction costs (the customer buying the car would no longer have to pay a bank to change her money). Investment and trade decisions would obviously be facilitated by the removal of exchange rate fluctuations and so, less obviously, would labor market and administrative reforms.

After the introduction of the single currency, the only way that member states would be able to maintain or gain competitiveness was to raise productivity and drive down costs. In theory, this meant that national governments would be forced to embark on a root-and-branch search for structural reforms to the welfare state to reduce costs for business (or else lose economic ground to more efficient competitors). The efforts that Italy had to make just to get up to the starting line were indicative, in the views of many economists, of a competitive pressure that would become generalized and permanent for all the Euro-zone's members.[22]

Probably the most important reason for adopting the Euro, however, was strategic. Adoption of the Euro was a way of insulating the EU's economy from dollar volatility. With the adoption of the single currency, the Euro-zone constituted an internal market comparable in size to that of the United States.[23] Supporters of the Euro contended that this would "reduce the costs of transatlantic monetary conflict for Europe and . . . thereby shield European policy-makers from American pressure."[24]

Objectively, the knock-on effects of fluctuations in the dollar's value have caused deep problems for the European economy in the period since the collapse of the Bretton Woods system. The dollar's fluctuations did not diminish, moreover, after the Euro's introduction. The Euro's price relative to the dollar briefly rose to over $1.20 before sinking in October 2000, at the height of the dot.com boom, to as low as 82 cents. It climbed back to parity as the American economy weakened in the aftermath of 9/11 and the popping of the stock market bubble and then surged to almost $1.60 in 2008 to 2009, when the U.S. economy fell into the "Great Recession." Supporters of the Euro can truthfully claim that these drastic variations in the value of the dollar would have wrought havoc with European exchange rates (and hence intra-European trade) in the Euro's absence.

These powerful arguments adduced in the Euro's favor were not universally regarded as overwhelming, however. Critics suggested that the institutions of monetary governance established at Maastricht were inadequate to manage the Euro-zone. The critics worried that a one-size-fits-all approach to interest rates might lead to monetary policy being too lax in some countries and too high in others: this was not a theoretical concern in a continent where the growth rate of the Italian and German economies was languishing at 1 to 2 percent, while Ireland's was racing ahead as fast as the tiger economies of East Asia.

Losing the ability to devalue one's currency, or to reduce interest rates, can also weaken the ability of member states to respond to "asymmetrical shocks" (economic downturns or events affecting some states more than others). In the United States, the impact of a regional economic crisis can be absorbed by either (or both) federal financial transfers (subsidies or tax breaks) or labor market mobility. In Europe, where the EU has a budget of just 1 percent of the total economic activity produced within the Union, fiscal policy remained mostly a matter for the member states, and workers plainly faced far greater linguistic, cultural, and administrative difficulties preventing them from shifting from one member state to another in search of work.[25]

Writing at the end of 1997, the Harvard economist Martin Feldstein published a much-discussed article entitled "EMU and International Conflict," in which he underlined that a single currency was a "symbol of

sovereignty." Europe was becoming a nation. Its next step might be to develop a separate foreign policy from the United States. The United States
would not, at that point, be able to "count on Europe as an ally in all its
relations with third countries." The Europeans, "guided by a combination
of economic self-interest, historical traditions and national pride," might,
Feldstein feared, "seek alliances and pursue policies that are contrary to
the interests of the United States."[26]

As any citizen of the EU knew, Europe was, in 1998, very far from becoming a federal nation-state able to challenge the United States on the
world stage. But Feldstein was perceptive in pointing out that monetary
union did raise the issue of whether it should be one. What kind of organization did the EU want to be? Should it remain a largely intergovernmental body preoccupied, mainly, with detailed economic questions?
Or should it evolve into a federal state, with a central government with
powers over tax policy, foreign policy, and the spending of substantial
sums of money? Or should some hybrid emerge? The successful launch
of the Euro brought such issues to the fore and was a major cause of the
"EUphoria" of the early and mid-2000s.

ENLARGEMENT

The Euro was a child of the end of the Cold War. As we saw in chapter
7, member states wanted greater political and economic integration as a
way of holding united Germany in check. The German mark was sacrificed to this end. The end of the Cold War also caused the second great
transformative development in the EU of the 1992 to 2004 period: enlargement. In these years, the EU more than doubled in size from twelve
to twenty-five member states, with a queue of other aspirants waiting
more or less patiently to get in. The dramatic success of enlargement
was a major cause of EUphoria. When peoples are beating at your door,
asking to be allowed in, you conclude that you are popular—or, to use
the jargon of international relations theory—that your reserves of "soft
power" are extensive.

Enlargement took place in two acts. In 1995, the EU gained three
wealthy new members when Austria, Finland, and Sweden joined. All
three countries were advanced industrial societies with small (though
expensive) agricultural sectors that did not add greatly to the total
population of the EU. They were also all members of EFTA and in May
1992, along with Norway, had signed an accord creating the European
Economic Area (EEA) with the EU. The EEA was an enhanced free trade
agreement for industrial products (not agriculture, naturally) that meant
adopting some fourteen thousand pages of the EU's *acquis communautaire*.

Membership of the EEA was not enough, however. The "Eftans" had no say over the rules made by The Twelve. Moreover, another reason for their diffidence toward the process of European integration—the fact that all of them except Norway were neutrals and the USSR had vetoed their integration into the West—no longer held sway. Austria applied to join the EC in July 1989; Finland, Norway, and Sweden had followed suit by November 1992.

Negotiations started in early 1993 and were concluded in March 1994: a record pace. Apart from agriculture—all three countries, for climatic and topographical reasons, subsidized their farmers even more egregiously than did the EU—the negotiation did not present major problems. The EU obviously insisted on adoption of the CAP but gave the Eftans a five-year transition period to give national aid to their farmers, permitted special subsidies for farmers working above the sixty-second parallel, and invented a new category of regional aid ("Objective Six") to pump Community cash into areas of low population density. Austria, where ecological concerns were very important, was allowed to keep its "Ecopoint" system of transit licenses on trucks for nine years after entry. The Austrians, not unreasonably, wanted to control the flow of heavy trucks using their roads between Germany and Italy. The "Eftans," unlike Denmark, agreed to "participate fully and actively in the Common Foreign and Security Policy as defined in the Treaty on European Union." Actually, all three states had accomplished diplomats and Sweden and Finland were major contributors of development aid, donating 0.7 percent of GDP to the Third World. Nobody doubted their capacity to run an EU presidency or to put new issues on the EU's agenda.

The four Eftans held referendums on membership between June 12, 1994 (Austria), and November 28, 1994 (Norway). Membership was most popular in Austria, where 66 percent of voters approved. In Finland, the vote was closer but still comfortable (57–43). In Sweden and Norway, the result was almost a tie, with the Swedes voting 52–48 in favor and the Norwegians 52–48 against membership. In all four countries, the "No" campaign was mostly carried on by disgruntled farmers, Greens, and the far left; in Austria the right-wing populist Freedom Party (FPÖ) was also a visible opponent. Norway's Social Democrats, the governing party, were deeply split over Europe, which was one reason why Norway voted to stay out.[27]

Despite the fact that Austria joined with the largest majority, it has been plausibly argued that it has been the society whose politics was changed most by EU membership. Austrian voters, long content to cast their ballot for the Social Democrats (SPÖ) or the Christian Democrats (ÖVP), began to show signs of disaffection after EU entry since membership exposed some of the inefficiencies and corruption engendered in the political class during the long years of neutrality. This disaffection led to the rapid rise in the late 1990s of the Freedom Party, which in February 2000 entered a government formed by the ÖVP's leader Wolfgang Schüssel. Prompted by a misguided political correctness (for despite the Nazi-apologist views of the FPÖ's then leader, Jorg Haider, the party had broken no laws, had been democratically elected, and had not disavowed democratic principles), several member states refused to cooperate with Austria in the institutions of the EU. Schüssel threatened to call a referendum over the issue, which would inevitably have become a plebiscite over continued EU membership. When a group of "wise men" sent to Vienna by the EU reported that democracy and human rights were not at risk in Austria, the issue was defused. But it left a sour taste in the mouth of many Austrians, including many former supporters of European integration.[28]

By contrast with the Eftans, the countries of Central and Eastern Europe (CEEC) presented an altogether different degree of difficulty. They were much poorer than the EU average, were highly agricultural, and possessed a relatively rudimentary legal framework. Yet there were important reasons for wanting to incorporate the new democracies into the EU as swiftly as possible after the end of the Cold War. Entry into the EU, as for Greece, Spain, and Portugal, would be an important act of democratic consolidation. Budapest, Prague, and Warsaw are great bastions of European civilization; it was impossible for the EU countries to turn their backs on their cousins east of the Elbe River. More practically, direct investment from EU firms and banks immediately flooded eastward. The new democracies represented a pool of well-educated, skilled, relatively cheap labor that had the potential to develop as major new markets as their income levels rose. As a Commission report presented to the June 1992 Lisbon European Council stated: "Enlargement is a challenge which the Community cannot refuse."[29]

In the immediate aftermath of the downfall of the Communist regimes, the EU pumped aid into the new democracies via the Bank for European Reconstruction and Development (established at the Strasbourg European Council in December 1989), via the European Investment Bank, and through its "Phare" program for technical and scientific assistance. Phare committed over 1 billion Ecu for education, training, and research between 1990 and 1998; nearly 1.2 billion Ecu for the restructuring of small businesses; and over 2 billion Ecu in spending on infrastructure. Poland, with 2 billion Ecu in Phare funding, was the country that benefited most.[30] The EU also gradually negotiated so-called association agreements with the Eastern European states. These agreements provided for the gradual but asymmetric liberalization of trade between the individual new democracies and the EU, with the EU, naturally, opening its markets in everything except agriculture quicker and further. Once these agreements had come into force, the new democracies were free to join Turkey (which had applied in 1987), Malta (1990), and Cyprus (1990) in the queue to enter the Community.

Before the new democracies could apply, the EU's member states had had to rethink the fundamental principles underlying membership. They were determined to open negotiations with the new applicants, but not at the cost of destabilizing the status quo. As a Commission document presented at Lisbon in 1992 underlined: "Widening must not be at the expense of deepening. Enlargement must not be a dilution of the Community's achievements."[31] All member states, it was decided, would have to accept the full Community *acquis*, which meant, in practice, harmonizing national law to EU law in every major policy field.

This was a major obstacle. EU law is daunting even for member states. For countries emerging from the Communist system, lacking a trained judiciary and administrative prowess, the EU's decision was both a substantial technical obstacle and an erosion of their competitive position vis-à-vis the EU states. The costs of implementing and enforcing EU law on health and safety, or the environment, were bound to eat away some of the cost advantage that made building a plant near Pilsen instead of Pamplona worthwhile for foreign investors.

At the June 1993 Copenhagen European Council, The Twelve outlined three key principles (the so-called Copenhagen criteria) that all entrants would have to meet. First, candidate members had to possess stable democratic institutions that promoted respect for the rule of the law, human rights, and ethnic minorities. Second, they had to possess a functioning market economy and be able to survive the competitive economic pressures of EU membership. Third, they had to be able, eventually, to "take on the obligations" of membership, "including adherence to the aims of political, economic and monetary union."[32] These conditions were a formidable obstacle. Indeed, in 1993, an uncharitable observer might have argued that the Copenhagen criteria ruled out Britain and Denmark (who were not enthusiasts for political union), Greece (whose economy was extremely weak in the early 1990s), and Italy (whose political system was imploding) from membership.

Despite the size of the hurdles placed in their path, the new democracies were ready to bid for membership by the mid-1990s. Hungary, whose association agreement came into force in February 1994, applied for EU membership on March 31, 1994. She was followed just a few days later by Poland. A second wave of applications was received in June–July 1995, when Romania, the Slovak Republic, and Latvia all requested membership. Estonia, Lithuania, Bulgaria, the Czech Republic, and Slovenia had all followed suit by June 1996. Without even counting Turkey, these applications implied an eventual expansion of one-third in the territorial area of the EU and ninety million new citizens.

These new citizens, moreover, would be, even by the standards of the Mediterranean enlargement in the 1980s, much poorer than those in the existing member states. In 1998, the Commission found that only Cyprus, the Czech Republic, and Slovenia had incomes per head of over 60 percent of the EU average, measured at purchasing power parity (PPP). Hungary's figure was 49 percent; Poland, with its forty million inhabitants, just 39 percent. In economic terms, to cite *The Economist's* inspired analogy, enlargement to the CEEC was "Europe's Mexico option." It was as if the United States had decided to accept a proposal for the incorporation of the various Mexican provinces as states of the Union and had committed itself to bringing these provinces to American standards of infrastructure and social provision.[33]

Rapid accession of all these countries plainly promised a future of mass migration from east to west, or else massive investment on a scale to dwarf the amounts invested by the EU in the Delors Package in 1988, to build up the entrants' economies. At the Madrid European Council in December 1995, the Commission was asked to "prepare a detailed analysis of [what] enlargement would mean for the EU" and to assess the readiness of the applicant countries to begin entry negotiations. The Commission responded with the document *Agenda 2000: For a Stronger and Wider Union* in July 1997. In this document, the Commission spelled out the costs of enlargement: "A first wave of accessions will affect the budgetary positions of all the present Member States, reducing the positive balances of net beneficiaries and increasing the negative ones of others."[34] The net beneficiaries, Spain, Belgium, Portugal, Greece, and Ireland, were, when *Agenda 2000* was published, gulping down a new and even larger chunk of regional development spending (the so-called Delors II package agreed after Maastricht). These countries stood to lose their lucrative position as the poor cousins of the EU family.

The Commission nevertheless recommended that entry negotiations should begin with the Czech Republic, Estonia, Hungary, Poland, Slovenia, and Cyprus. Negotiations with these countries duly began on March 31, 1998.

The list of would-be new members conspicuously lacked Turkey, although a customs union between Turkey and the EU had come into force in January 1996, and Washington was strongly in favor of Turkish membership on strategic grounds. Ankara was "outraged" by the decision, although since Turkey had recently experienced a "postmodern coup," when the army, the guardians of its secular constitution, had threatened to act against the growing political power of Islam, the EU's decision, in terms of the Copenhagen criteria, was amply motivated.[35] An irate Turkey nevertheless threatened to withdraw its membership application and even to exacerbate the Cyprus problem by integrating the territory annexed by the Turkish army in August 1974 into its own borders.

The Commission subsequently recommended beginning negotiations with Bulgaria, Latvia, Lithuania, Malta, Romania, and the Slovak Republic, and these talks duly began in February 2000. Turkey was finally approved as a candidate for full membership at the Helsinki European Council in December 1999, ostensibly "on the basis of the same criteria as applied to the other candidate states." It was not, however, until December 2004, after an intense period of political reform (during which Turkey abolished the death penalty and strengthened political control of the military), that the European Council gave Ankara the full seal of approval.

Entry talks began in October 2005, although even then Brussels "foresaw a continuing EU role in determining Turkey's reform priorities through updated accession partnerships . . . and threatening to suspend negotiations in the event of stalling or backtracking in the reform process."[36] The Turks considered, with some justice, that they were being discriminated against. Romania and Bulgaria, both of which were admitted in 2007, were hardly paragons of political stability, administrative efficiency, and probity in public life. Turkey was simply too big, too poor, and too Muslim to be absorbed in a hurry.

There is no need to go into excessive detail about the negotiations with the other candidates except to say that the largest problems, as usual, occurred over agriculture. About 5 percent of the EU-15's population was employed in farming, or farming-related activity. In Poland, the figure was over 20 percent. Farms in Central and Eastern Europe were (and are) smaller, less mechanized, and less productive. Enlargement thus posed the EU with an uncomfortable dilemma. Would it be wiser to extend the EU's generous subsidy regime to the farmers of any new member, thus causing the most substantial budget increase in the EC–EU's history, or would it be better to reduce levels of subsidy to individual farmers but ensure that the new members' peasants got their fair share?

The EU's solution, unveiled in February 2002, was to phase in subsidies to the newcomers, so that they would enjoy equal treatment within ten years of entry. To start with, however, they would receive only a quarter of the cash lavished upon the farmers already in the system (though they still raked in a handy €10 billion for the period 2004 to 2006). EU production quotas would also be imposed, and these would in many cases lower the amount farmers in the candidate countries were already producing. These conditions aroused much disquiet among the candidate countries, which feared that that they would turn economic logic on its head by allowing subsidized agricultural produce from the rich west to gain market share in the east.[37] The absence of agriculture from the association agreements had already led to the new democracies incurring a substantial trade deficit with the EU for the period 1995 to 2000.[38] On the other hand, the applicant countries' preferred option— reduced subsidies and a market in agricultural products determined by producer costs—was a nonstarter. None of The Fifteen supported outright laissez-faire in agriculture.

On December 12–13, 2002, the Copenhagen European Council, after some feverish last-minute haggling over terms, decided that Poland, the Czech Republic, Hungary, Slovakia, Lithuania, Latvia, Slovenia, Estonia, Cyprus, and Malta would be ready to join in 2004 and could sign their accession agreements in April 2003.

Enlargement actually took place on May 1, 2004. The EU now stretched from the windswept Atlantic cliffs of Ireland and Portugal and the arctic tundra of Finland and Sweden to the flat steppes of eastern Poland and the olive groves of Cyprus. Its population, at 450 million, was larger than those of the United States and Russia combined. The 2004 enlargement would bring "more unity and more diversity," the EU's publicists vaunted in a leaflet published for the occasion, although it was also true that the same document showed just how few EU-15 citizens had visited even one of the new member states.[39] On enlargement day, ignorance of the new member states and their histories was all but universal in "old Europe," to borrow Donald Rumsfeld's celebrated formulation.

Still, by 2004 Europe had broadly met the challenge it could not refuse. There were genuine reasons to celebrate. Wim Kok, a former Dutch premier who was chair and author of a 2003 report on enlargement drawn up at the behest of the Commission, proudly asserted that the "enlargement of the European Union . . . is the fulfillment of a vision . . . the reunification of Europe's peoples in a constitutional framework that encourages them to work together in peace and stability." In the same report, he added that enlargement was "the EU's most successful act of foreign policy."[40] Enlargement did in fact compel consideration both of the EU's institutions and of its place in the world and was the main driving force both of the tortuous process by which the EU drew up a "Constitution" in the fall of 2004 and of the EU's increasingly ambitious efforts in the post-Maastricht decade to raise its profile in international affairs.

THE INSTITUTIONAL QUESTION

Enlargement posed the institutional question for the EU since the looming entry of so many new member states meant it was necessary to undertake a fundamental review of its institutions. How many commissioners should there be? How many votes should the applicants get in the Council of Ministers? How many policy questions should be decided by unanimity in the Council of Ministers? Could a Union with well over twenty members decide anything unanimously? How large should the European Parliament become? What should the national division of seats in the Parliament be? Would countries like Estonia (population 1.3 million), Latvia (2.3 million), Lithuania (3.4 million), Malta (400,000), and Slovenia (2 million) have the resources to run an EU presidency? All of these questions were debated constantly throughout the 1990s and the early 2000s.

This debate, moreover, took place at a time when worries about the EU's "democratic deficit" were growing—and not just among peoples traditionally skeptical of greater European integration. The first years of the new European Union were marred by apathy among the citizens of the new Europe, tarnished reputations for some of the EU's principal institutions, and much tedious wrangling in Brussels over the arcane question of how QMV would work in the future.

This situation was gall and wormwood for the EU's leaders, especially the more federalist ones in Belgium, Germany, and Italy, who believed that the EU was a great historical experiment that had brought peace and prosperity to the continent and that it should therefore galvanize Europe's peoples to enthusiasm. For this reason, the EU chose in 2001 to launch a constitutional convention charged with listening to European public opinion and proposing new institutional arrangements to the member states. The fact that this process resulted in the adoption of a "Constitution" unquestionably contributed to the mood of euphoria surrounding the EU by that date.

The road to the Constitution was a tortuous one. The EU's first attempt to update Maastricht, the Treaty of Amsterdam (October 1997), was described by two well-known scholars as a "melting pot of disparate measures lacking a coherent vision of either substantive cooperation in a particular area or the future institutional structure of Europe."[41]

Mixed metaphors apart, it is hard to dissent. At Amsterdam, Britain's newly elected Labour government, represented by a youthful Tony Blair, agreed to end its opt-out from the "social chapter" of the Maastricht Treaty. Liberty, democracy, and respect for human rights were made a condition of EU membership, and member states could be suspended if the other member states unanimously agreed that a member state was in "serious and persistent breach" of these principles. The European Parliament gained the right formally to approve or reject the European Council's nominee as president of the Commission and obtained further powers of codecision. After Amsterdam, only agriculture, foreign policy, justice, and home affairs were not subject to the codecision procedure.

These new powers meant that the legislative process of the EU was "virtually a bicameral system."[42] The Schengen Treaty was absorbed into the EU framework, and a new "high representative" was to be in charge of strategic planning in the field of foreign policy and defense, together with the commissioner responsible for external affairs and the foreign minister presiding over the Council of Ministers.

The Amsterdam treaty, in short, while containing a large number of innovations of interest to scholars of European integration, had thus "failed pathetically" to deal with the institutional questions posed by enlargement.[43] Europe's leaders did, however, acknowledge in a protocol to the treaty that a major reform of the EU's institutions was needed before the new member states could join.

Enlargement was not the only reason why the issue of institutional reform became so salient in the 1990s. The actual performance of the EU's institutions was another. The 1990s provided abundant evidence that the EU had become complacent, overcomplex, and distant from the voters of the member states. By the end of the decade, British and Danish Euroskeptics were no longer alone in pointing to the EU's democratic deficit. Many pro-EU citizens and analysts acknowledged that while European integration has multiplied what the German scholar Fritz Scharpf calls the output side of democratic politics (increased welfare and prosperity), it has undoubtedly weakened the input side (the possibility of democratic participation and accountability).[44]

This was in spite of the efforts of the post-Maastricht European Parliament to act in the 1990s as a democratic check on the decisions of the European Council and to hold the Commission to account. In July 1994, the newly elected Parliament almost refused to endorse the member states' choice of replacement for Jacques Delors, the prime minister of Luxembourg, Jacques Santer. The original favorite to replace Delors had been the Belgian Christian Democrat Jean-Luc Dehaene. For Britain, the problem with Dehaene was that he was another figure in the same mold as Delors: a federalist in favor of extending the role of the EU's institutions. Prime Minister John Major accordingly vetoed his nomination. The Parliament struck back by confirming Santer only after a "nail-biting vote of approval."[45] Santer's nomination passed only by 260 votes to 238, with no fewer than twenty-three abstentions.

Santer's Commission, which was full of high-profile politicians with big egos, became a byword for abuse of public funds, cronyism, and nepotism. Following an investigation by the Court of Auditors (the body that scrutinizes EU expenditure to prevent fraud), the European Parliament threatened in January 1999 to pass a motion of censure against the Commission—although MEPs' own luxurious allowances and expenses frauds made this threat one of the most egregious cases of the pot calling the kettle black in modern political history.

To avoid the humiliation of being the first president of the Commission to be sacked by the Parliament, Santer allowed a committee of independent experts to carry out an inquiry into the Commission's management and agreed to abide by its findings. The committee's report was damning. It highlighted a number of serious lapses in judgment by several commissioners, especially Edith Cresson, a former French premier who had appointed a personal friend, a provincial dentist, as a highly paid political adviser, and painted a general picture of inefficiency and waste in the management of the EU. Most severely of all, it concluded that "it is difficult to find anyone who has even the slightest sense of responsibility" for the abuses the committee had uncovered.[46] This shattering phrase obliged the Commission to resign en masse once the report was published on March 15, 1999. Santer was replaced as president of the Commission by Romano Prodi, who hence reaped a personal reward for having successfully steered Italy into the single currency.

The Parliament's zealous pursuit of the Commission's sins might have been expected to raise its profile with the EU electorate. Shortly after Santer's ouster, in June 1999, the EU's citizens elected a new European Parliament. The elections revealed widespread dissatisfaction and apathy among Europe's voters. Britain recorded the lowest turnout in a nationwide election (24 percent) since democracy began. In traditionally Europhile Germany, under half the electorate (45.2 percent) voted: this was a drop of 15 percent compared to the elections in 1989 and 1994. A negligible 29.9 percent of the Dutch went to the polls (down from 47.2 percent in 1989 and 35.6 percent in 1994). In France, where 47 percent of the electorate voted, more than one million blank ballots were cast in symbolic protest, although the protest was aimed as much at the rampant corruption of the country's elites as at the EU.

Most damning of all, the elections inspired little enthusiasm in the three most recent entrants to the Union. Only 30 percent of the Finns (down precipitously from 60.3 percent in 1996, when the country joined the EU), 38 percent of the Swedes, and 49 percent of the Austrians went to the polls. Overall, turnout was a dismal 49 percent.

There were exceptions to this tendency toward lower participation: 90 percent of the Belgians voted; more of the Spanish (64.3 percent) voted than ever before; Greece's turnout, while down, was still over 70 percent. The Irish and the Portuguese also voted in increased numbers. It was, however, instructive to compare this list of the virtuous with the list of net beneficiaries from the Union budget. Shortly after the European elections, the Danes compounded the perception that the EU project was losing traction among Europe's peoples by voting against membership of the Euro in a national referendum in September 1999.[47]

The looming prospect of enlargement and the apathy—or outright hostility—of Europe's voters to the European project stimulated a flurry of speeches and position papers from the EU's great and good as the new millennium began. How could new life be breathed into the project? Probably the most revealing—revealing, that is, of the cast of mind of the EU's political elites—answer to this question was provided in a speech in Berlin to commemorate the fiftieth anniversary of the Schuman Plan by the then foreign minister of Germany, Joschka Fischer.

Fischer's speech contended that the solution for the EU's problems was the full democratization of European integration. In substance, he reprised the arguments of the early federalists, many of whom had never digested the EEC treaty's choice in favor of intergovernmental institutions and market liberalization at the expense of the sovereignty of an assembly representing Europe's peoples. For Fischer, "introducing increased majority voting," while important, could only be a "first step towards reform." The real question was how thirty states were supposed to "balance interests, take decisions and eventually act" without becoming "utterly intransparent [sic]" and without the citizens' acceptance of the EU from "eventually hitting rock bottom?"

In Fischer's view, there was a "very simple answer" to these questions: "the transition from a union of states to full parliamentarianization as a European Federation." He added that this federation would have to be based on a constituent treaty in which the "competences" reserved for the Union and those of the member states were explicitly stated. Fischer's vision of the future institutional structure of the proposed federation was flexible. The new federation's legislature, he suggested, would have to possess two chambers: one directly elected, one representing the member states. The second chamber might be a senate, on the American model, with directly elected members, or it could be a "chamber of states," on the German model, with representatives from the various national governments. The executive of the federation might be the European Council, or else it could be a directly elected president of the Commission with "far-reaching executive powers." It was in fact clear from Fischer's text that he preferred this latter option since he explicitly worried that a thirty-member European Council might take "days, maybe even weeks" to reach decisions on any issue of importance.

Most of the latter half of Fischer's speech was concerned with the issue of "enhanced cooperation." This was the possibility, originally written into the Amsterdam treaty, for a core group of states to press ahead with common policies in policy areas not currently covered by the treaties. Fischer interpreted enhanced cooperation as an invitation for a core group of federalist states to establish a political union within the EU. Such a group of states, Fischer visualized, "would establish a government which within the EU should speak with one voice on behalf of the members of the group" and would have its own parliament and directly elected president. It would also be open to "all member states and candidate countries," for "it would be historically absurd and utterly stupid if Europe . . . were to be divided once again."[48]

The subsequent Treaty of Nice (February 2001) did indeed loosen the rules on enhanced cooperation by reducing the minimum number of states required for an initiative to eight and by removing the other member states' right to veto such initiatives. The treaty emphasized, however, that such initiatives had to respect "the single institutional framework" of the Union and to satisfy a series of conditions to ensure that the EU's achievements (above all, the single market) remained unharmed.

The Nice treaty otherwise fell far short of Fischer's federalist vision of Europe's "*finalité.*" As always, federalist rhetoric yielded to the hard reality that the member states were reluctant to reduce their relative powers of nomination and voting. The December 2000 summit of EU leaders in Nice was the longest in EU history (four days) and was conducted along the lines of a county horse fair. Key provisions of the new treaty were decided at the last moment by the heads of state and government, not by the "sherpas" from the foreign ministries: "IGC negotiations usually advance in three stages: preparation, negotiation and endgame . . . this time it seemed as if 18 months of preparation had been thrown out of the window and negotiations started from scratch."[49]

The Nice summit made the following decisions. First, it welcomed a Charter of Fundamental Rights drawn up by a panel of jurists without, however, adding the Charter to the treaty. The Charter was essentially an updating of the 1950 Convention on Human Rights to take into account contemporary concerns with generational, environmental, gender, and social rights. Among other articles, it outlawed the death penalty, guaranteed the "right of access" of every individual to education, ruled in affirmative action as a means of obtaining equality between men and women, and insisted that a "high level of environmental protection" was a right that the EU should enshrine in law.[50]

Second, the Nice summit decided to reform the Commission by reducing, from January 1, 2005, the number of commissioners to one per member state (Germany, France, Britain, Italy, and Spain nominated two). When the twenty-seventh member state joined, the treaty promised that the number of commissioners would be reduced to less than the number of member states and a system of rotation introduced. The treaty also foresaw that the president of the Commission would after 2005 be chosen by QMV, not unanimity, in the European Council. The president, in his or her turn, was given the power to allocate portfolios and to demand an individual commissioner's resignation: to act, in short, more as a chief executive. The European Parliament was given the power to approve both the choice of president and of the Commission as a whole.

Third, also effective January 1, 2005, the summit agreed to change the procedure for QMV to a so-called triple majority system. This new procedure was thrashed out at Nice by the principals themselves and "could not have been predicted by anybody in advance."[51] The new system required that for a decision to be taken there should be a specified number of votes (169 out of 237) in favor. The number of votes per country was increased at Nice, and the weighting was changed to strengthen the weighting of the five most populous member states, which were given 60 percent of the votes compared with the previous 55 percent. A decision would not be taken, however, unless there was also a numerical majority of member states in favor. Moreover—and this was the third necessary majority—member states could request verification that a given qualified majority represented at least 62 percent of the Union's population (a decision that gave France and Germany, with 140 million people, a de facto veto so long as they voted together).

Fourth, the summit expanded the Parliament to an elephantine 732 MEPs for the elections held in June 2004. From 2009, the number of MEPs belonging to the EU-15 was to drop to 535, with only Germany, the most populous state, and Luxembourg (the smallest) retaining the same number of deputies.[52]

The Nice treaty was relatively uncontroversial everywhere except Ireland. In June 2001, the Irish electorate voted against the Treaty of Nice by 54 to 46 percent, albeit on a low poll of just 35 percent.[53] As with the Danes in 1992, the Irish were told that their "no" would not hold up ratification elsewhere and that they would have to put the treaty to the voters again. In October 2002, they ratified the treaty by a large majority on a much higher turnout.

The thrust of the decisions taken by the Nice European Council, in short, was to tinker with the mechanisms of intergovernmental cooperation among the fifteen existing member states and to propose integrating all new members into the same structure. As a German political scientist approvingly argued, the Nice treaty carried on the EU's trend toward inventing ever more complex forms of institutional cooperation in an increasing number of public policy areas.[54]

The Union's leaders however decided to try something different. The Laeken (Belgium) European Council in December 2001 set up a "Convention" on the EU's institutional and political future. Chaired by Valéry Giscard d'Estaing, the Convention was composed of two vice chairmen

(Giuliano Amato, a former prime minister of Italy, and Jean-Luc De-haene), fifteen representatives nominated by the national governments, thirty members of national parliaments (two per state), sixteen members of the European Parliament, and two representatives from the Commission. The applicant countries each sent a government representative and two parliamentarians to participate in the Convention, but they were specifically debarred from preventing "any consensus which may emerge among the member states."[55]

The Convention held its inaugural meeting on March 1, 2002. It appointed a "praesidium" to "lend impetus and provide an initial working basis." Between March 2002 and July 2003, the Convention wrestled with the task of simplifying the EU treaty on the basis of hundreds of schemes submitted by enthusiasts for European integration in civil society, as well as with weightier proposals from the Commission and the national governments. As the Convention's work proceeded, public opinion, encouraged by Giscard himself, increasingly referred to the document that the Convention would propose as a "Constitution," a good example of the perennial tendency of statesmen involved in EU initiatives to inflate expectations.

Giscard finally presented the outcome of the Convention's labors to the Thessaloniki European Council on July 18, 2003. The bulky document was presented to a chorus of acclaim from press and politicians across Europe. Academic curriculum vitae all over Europe and the United States were enlarged by thousands of learned disquisitions on the Convention's methodology and conclusions.[56] It was generally agreed that Giscard had found a way of guaranteeing "unity in diversity," as the EU's new motto put it. *The Economist*, which published a picture of the Constitution in a wastepaper basket under the heading "Where to File It," was swimming against the prevailing tide.[57]

What did the would-be "constitution" propose? On the face of it, Giscard's team had been genuinely radical. The draft constitution created a new institutional figure, a permanent president of the European Council, who would set the Council's agenda and organize its meetings during a thirty-month renewable term. The "pillar" structure was to be abolished, and all the EU's activities were to be centralized into the EU. The president of the Commission was to be flanked by a foreign minister. The Commission itself should be reduced to just fifteen members, including the president and the foreign minister, that would "reflect satisfactorily the demographic and geographical range" of the EU but would have a further fifteen nonvoting members—like "candidate" members of the Politburo—chosen by similar criteria. The rules for qualified majority voting would be changed yet again: it was now proposed that a "dual majority" composed of a numerical majority of member states representing at least 60 percent of the Union's population would be required for a measure to pass. The European Parliament's assent was to be required for all measures passed by the Council of Ministers, and all EU legislation was to conform to the principles of the Charter of Fundamental Human Rights. The areas of the EU's exclusive competence (trade, customs, monetary policy for the Euro-zone states, fisheries policy) were spelled out, as were the many areas in which it had shared responsibilities. In a nod to national parliamentary sovereignty, however, the principle of subsidiarity was finally taken seriously: Giscard's draft advocated that national parliaments should be given the opportunity to submit a "reasoned opinion" of Commission proposals before they were discussed in the Council of Ministers and that a negative opinion expressed by a third of national parliaments would compel a rethink in the Commission's stance. The constitution would have been extremely difficult to amend.

Giscard's draft constitution represented a notable effort to conjugate respect for the prerogatives of the member states with a workable decision-making structure that empowered the Union's supranational institutions. The draft constitution proposed, in effect, something akin to the "Union of States" advocated consistently by Jacques Delors in many speeches and articles since he left the presidency of the Commission, or the "United Europe of States" preferred by French president Jacques Chirac. Indeed, if one truly believed that the "European Union must exercise the responsibilities of a world power," as most of the delegates to the Convention certainly did, and if one took heed of the dismal failure of all attempts since 1950 to introduce parliamentary government on a Community scale, then Giscard's draft proposals were both logical and daring.[58] This is why they were greeted with such acclaim.

Over the next year, the member states engaged in a line-by-line renegotiation of Giscard's text. This inevitably fraught process was one that required the country holding the presidency of the EU to show diplomatic nous and political leadership. It was a pity, therefore, that in July 2004 the presidency passed into the hands of Italy, whose premier, the ineffable former media entrepreneur Silvio Berlusconi, was disastrously cast for the role.

Italy's presidency began with a ranting, tragicomic speech by Berlusconi to the European Parliament in which he likened a German deputy who heckled him to a concentration camp "kapo." It went downhill from there. Under the Italian presidency, none of the major stumbling points to adoption of the constitutional treaty, above all Spain's and Poland's dislike of the new "double majority" voting rules, was sorted out. Poland and Spain had been given a generous number of votes in the Council of Ministers in the Treaty of Nice and were reluctant to see their voting weight diminished. It was an issue, however, which a competent presidency could have resolved. Indeed, once the baton had been passed to the safer hands of the Irish presidency from January 2004 onward, this, and other, key issues were resolved.

The final version of the Constitution was agreed on June 18, 2004, at a European Council meeting in Brussels. It maintained the spirit of Giscard's draft, though the member states diluted some key provisions and tinkered with the small print of how existing policies were made, which need not bother us here.

So far as institutions were concerned, the European Council's main alterations to the draft presented by Giscard were in the area of foreign policy, where the Constitution clarified that in most cases the EU would continue to vote unanimously when it came to foreign affairs. The post of EU foreign minister remained, however, with that title and a job description that made him or her the sole face for the EU's external actions. The EU, if authorized by the European Council, was given "legal personality" so that the foreign minister could negotiate and sign international agreements on the member states' behalf.

The notion that the European Council would have a permanent president was retained. The notion of reducing the Commission in size fared less well. It was agreed that the Commission would have one member for each state until 2014, when it would be reduced in size to a number equal to two-thirds of the member states (i.e., in a Union of twenty-seven states, it would have eighteen members).

Qualified majority voting in the Council of Ministers or the European Council would be by a double majority of 55 percent of member states representing at least 65 percent of the Union's population. By the standards of the old EEC, this was still a remarkably accessible qualified majority (and hence a real reduction in national sovereignty).

The European Parliament did not become "colegislator" in every field but crucially extended its power into the area of trade agreements: any future WTO trade deal would have to be ratified by the EP—a prospect to send shivers down the spine of enthusiasts for freer international trade.

All in all, the Constitution remained a bold document in its institutional provisions, and as such it was denounced by Euroskeptics across the EU, although opponents of the EU's ambitions took heart from the fact that the Constitution provided member states with a mechanism for leaving the Union—something that had not previously been possible. In Britain in particular, the anti–European Union press went berserk. *The Sun*, a populist daily newspaper owned by the Australian-American entrepreneur Rupert Murdoch, shrieked that "a thousand years of sovereignty are about to be buried by undertaker Blair. Britain demands the right

to a referendum before our country goes six feet under."[59] Other important newspapers, notably the Murdoch-owned *Times* and the *Daily Mail*,
joined *The Sun*'s campaign.

Since Foreign Secretary Jack Straw had come to approximately the
same conclusions, Blair was forced to concede that a referendum would
be held to ratify the Constitution. Blair proclaimed "let battle be joined"
and promised to campaign hard in the Constitution's favor, but he had,
in fact, reneged on a pledge to President Jacques Chirac of France that
he would not call a poll on the Constitution. Chirac accordingly signaled
that there would also be a referendum in France, too—setting the scene
for a repeat of the nail-biting 1992 referendum, although this was not
realized at the time. The press campaign in Britain, in short, had thrown
the Constitution's future into doubt almost before the ink was dry on the
manuscript.

Open Euroskeptics were a small minority, however. Most of Europe's
elites and public opinion formers were captivated by what they had
achieved. The statement of the EU's values in the first part of the Constitution engendered particular pride. The Constitution asserted that the EU's
fundamental values were respect for human dignity, freedom, democracy,
equality, and rule of law. It added, however, that the Union's aims were to
"promote peace, its values and the well-being of peoples." Specifically, it
would "contribute to peace, security, the sustainable development of the
earth, solidarity and mutual respect among peoples, free and fair trade,
eradication of poverty and the protection of human rights."[60]

The Constitution stated that the EU's anthem was Beethoven's "Ode to
Joy." In October 2004, when the Constitution was signed in Rome, it was
a song that intellectuals around the world, including many Americans,
were willing to hum along to. Jeremy Rifkin, an influential American
social theorist, voiced the thoughts of many when he wrote that "Europe
has become a giant freewheeling experimental laboratory for rethinking
the human condition and reconfiguring human institutions in the global
era."[61] The European dream might replace the more renowned American
dream as the world's favored social and economic model, Rifkin speculated. Its "soft power" appeal made the EU a superpower, even though its
military strength was only a fraction of the United States'.

THE EU'S GROWING WORLD ROLE

The notion that the EU was uniquely placed to influence the post–Cold
War world in positive ways was the fourth factor contributing to the
mood of euphoria by the mid-2000s. Historically, the EU's "external" role
had mainly been confined to two areas: international trade and relations

with the member states' former colonies in Africa, the Caribbean, and the Pacific (the ACP countries).

In the 1990s, both of these areas were themselves the subject of important developments. In trade, the French government finally yielded in the Uruguay Round talks and allowed the EU in December 1992 to make a deal that considerably liberalized world trade and that created the new World Trade Organization (WTO) to act as an independent arbiter of trade disputes.[62] The WTO was immediately the seat for a series of high-level trade disputes between the EU and the United States, which objected strongly to the EU's banana import regime, its opposition to the import of hormone-treated meat and genetically modified wheat, and subsidies of Airbus Industries, Boeing's successful chief rival in the production of commercial airliners. The Europeans, on their side, reacted angrily to the American imposition of tariffs on steel imports in March 2002. The EU's steel industries had rationalized their productive capacity much earlier than U.S. producers, at some cost in unemployment, and they produced high-quality steel more cheaply than U.S. producers could manage. In general, the creation of the WTO has sharply raised the EU's profile on the international stage.

Relations with the ACP countries—who number over seventy—have been governed through the four Lomé Conventions (Lomé is the capital of the African republic of Togo) signed since 1975.[63] Like their predecessor, the Yaoundé agreement (see chapter 4), the conventions have provided a framework for the distribution of Community aid through the European Development Fund (EDF) and have offered signatories to the conventions privileged access to the European market. The failure of the African nations, in particular, to move toward greater democracy and higher levels of economic development has, however, caused EU policymakers to rethink its aid program. The fifth Lomé Convention, signed in June 2000, proposed a free trade area with the EU by 2020 and allocated €13.5 billion in aid for the period from 2000 to 2006. It insisted, however, that aid would be closely linked to constructive policies to build democratic institutions and improve human rights. As a sign that it meant business, in February 2002 the EU imposed sanctions on Zimbabwe following the tyrannical behavior of President Robert Mugabe toward Zimbabwe's white farmers and toward the democratic opposition.[64]

These high-profile developments in the traditional areas of "external activity" were matched by several new initiatives. Growing trade with Asia and China led to the institution of annual EU–China summits.[65] The problem of migration from the countries of North Africa stimulated the EU to launch the so-called Euro-Mediterranean process with twelve Mediterranean and Middle Eastern states at Barcelona in November 1995.[66] The goal of the process was the creation of a free trade area by 2005. In the meantime, the EU contributed €1 billion in annual aid to its partners. Commission president Romano Prodi called the Euro-Mediterranean process "a historic opportunity with economic, political and moral dimensions that the European Union cannot let slip."[67] The EU had a clear interest in ensuring that the problems of demography and Islamic fundamentalism currently straining the political systems of these countries did not spill over into social breakdown and civil disruption.

The Euro-Mediterranean process was subsequently incorporated into the "European Neighborhood Policy" (ENP). As one scholar has argued, the extension of the EU's border is "the most important of all the foreign policy implications of enlargement."[68] Enlargement meant that the EU would border upon a number of poor states with unstable governments. Albania, Belarus, Moldavia, Ukraine, former Yugoslavia, and troubled post-Soviet nations such as Armenia, Azerbaijan, and Georgia were all countries whose internal political upheavals might spill over onto the current or future Union. Relations with Russia—provider of a good part of Europe's energy supplies and an increasingly prickly neighbor—loomed large.

At the Copenhagen European Council in December 2002, it was decided to offer increased economic integration and closer political cooperation with sixteen Mediterranean and East European states.[69] These countries would gain greater access to the EU single market and receive EU aid on condition that they carried out reforms in keeping with the EU's values and laws. The ENP, in conception, was a diluted and somewhat more normative EEA. Normative, because while the EU did not dream of telling Austria, Finland, Iceland, Norway, Sweden, and Switzerland how to conduct their domestic affairs (at any rate until Haider came to power and Austria was already a member), the EU did not hesitate to lay down detailed "Action Plans" for the ENP states (an exception being the one with Israel). As a leading scholar of EU foreign policy has put it, the "number of things to do" by the neighbors was "striking."[70] The Action Plan for Ukraine contained some three hundred priorities for action, fourteen of which were listed as having high priority. Ukraine, in short, in order to continue being a privileged partner of the EU, would have to revolutionize its democracy and domestic economy. This might have made sense if the EU was offering membership as a prize, but membership was not on offer for any of the ENP nations. The ENP was predicated on the idea of "all but institutions": that is to say, access to everything except political integration and membership.

By December 2004, the Commission had published draft Action Plans with seven of the sixteen countries, with others on the way. The EU backed up its words by allocating an average of €2 billion a year to ENP programs in the 2007 to 2013 budget cycle. This sum was only a small fraction of the EU budget and was obviously too small to act as a carrot for improved behavior in countries where dictatorship (Belarus, Syria, Tunisia) was so deeply entrenched.

Programs such as the ENP were ultimately motivated by concerns for the EU's security: "It is in the European interest that countries on our borders are well governed."[71] After the demise of the USSR, Europeans no longer feared a traditional threat to their security. Nobody—the Balts apart—feared Russian tanks rolling across their frontiers. The continued existence, indeed expansion, of NATO since the end of the Cold War in any case provided a guarantee against military attack for the countries of the EU, most of whom are also NATO members.

Security, however, is a broad concept, at any rate as the EU interprets it. In December 2003, the EU published "A Secure Europe in a Better World," its official "European Security Strategy." It is worth looking at this document in some detail for the insight it gave into the worldview of EU policymakers in the first few years of this century.

In essence, the EU identified five key threats to its security: terrorism, proliferation of weapons of mass destruction, regional conflicts, state failure, and organized crime. Europe was "a target and a base" for terrorist cells (an assessment that the subsequent Madrid and London train bombings in March 2004 and July 2005 amply confirmed); regional conflicts and state failure—the Balkans being the nearest but not the only case to hand—had had a direct impact upon Europe; organized crime based in the Balkans was flooding Europe with drugs and was trafficking in immigrants and prostitutes. "A Secure Europe in a Better World" essentially argued for "effective multilateralism" as a solution to these problems. The UN, regional organizations such as the EU itself, and the WTO should direct their activities toward eliminating injustice and poor governance: "The best protection for our security is a world of well governed democratic states . . . a world seen as offering justice and opportunity for everyone will be more secure for the EU and its citizens."[72]

The EU was not a pacifist organization, however, wedded to acting only through institutions. Effective multilateralism contemplated the use of military force. "A Secure Europe in a Better World" asserted that the EU needed to "develop a strategic culture that fosters early, rapid, and when necessary robust intervention."[73] To put it mildly, this open espousal of a military role was a novelty for the EU, which had cast itself, hitherto, as a "civilian power." The confidence with which the EU advocated "robust intervention" derived from the creation between 1998 and 2003 of the European Security and Defense Policy (ESDP) as a reinforcement of the CFSP.

The ESDP was a rare bird among EU projects: it owed its origins to a joint Anglo-French initiative. British premier Tony Blair "crossed a European rubicon" in 1998 by softening British policy toward the concept of independent European forces.[74] The St. Malo Declaration (December 3, 1998) by Blair and French President Jacques Chirac spoke of the need for a European "capacity for autonomous action backed up by credible military forces."[75] During the Kosovo war against Serbia in the spring of 1999, which demonstrated that "though their defense expenditure amounted to two-thirds of that of the Americans, [the Europeans] were capable of delivering only one-tenth of the firepower," the EU realized that it was woefully short of such forces.[76] The EU had to rely on the United States to fight the conflict, even though it was taking place on the EU's doorstep.

At the first meeting of the European Council after the end of fighting in Yugoslavia, and after the entry into force of the Amsterdam treaty (May 1999) at Cologne in Germany on June 3–4, 1999, the EU's leaders pledged that the Union would henceforth "play its full role on the international stage." To that end, the Council announced that it was going to give the EU the "necessary means and capabilities to assume its responsibilities regarding a common European policy on security and defence." These responsibilities, known as the "Petersberg tasks," had been identified in the Amsterdam treaty as the duties of peace building, crisis management, and peacemaking in the European neighborhood, and had previously been the core competence of the West European Union (WEU). The Amsterdam treaty, in fact, provided for the integration of the WEU into the EU. The Cologne Council acknowledged that to fulfill these responsibilities, the EU would have to have the "capacity for autonomous action" backed up by "credibile military forces" and the will to use them.[77]

The next meeting of the European Council, at Helsinki in Finland in December 1999, put flesh upon these bones. It decided to construct a "European Rapid Reaction Force" (ERRF) of approximately sixty thousand troops supported by a fleet of one hundred ships and four hundred warplanes by 2003. This decision set off alarm bells in Washington, which was distinctly skeptical of any European defense action that was "autonomous" of NATO. Secretary of State Madeleine Albright eventually approved of European action in the defense field provided it passed the test of the "three Ds." The European force should not duplicate NATO actions or subtract resources from NATO. It should not discriminate against non-EU NATO members (e.g., Norway, Turkey). It should not decouple the EU from the transatlantic treaty framework.[78]

The EU pressed on with its initiative, however. The European Council's reaction to 9/11, which proclaimed that the EU was "totally supportive of the American people" and affirmed that a military "risposte" against the terrorists or those sheltering terrorists was legitimate, subtly distinguished itself from American policy. The Council's communiqué urged the "international community" to pursue "dialogue and negotiation" in all "international fora" with a view to building a "world of peace, the rule of law and tolerance." It explicitly rejected any "equation of terrorism with the Arab and Muslim world" and asserted that "the integration of all countries into a fair world system of security, prosperity and improved development" was a sine qua non for a "strong and sustainable community for combating terrorism." Promoting such integration was the task of the ESDP.[79]

The EU, in short, believed that bombing was not enough. The tone of the EU's reaction was undeniably different—and deliberately different—from the neoconservative agenda that increasingly prevailed in Washington after 9/11. It is this difference in tone that explains why the EU divided so sharply over the U.S. invasion of Iraq in the spring of 2003. President Jacques Chirac and Chancellor Gerhard Schröder of Germany, who led the resistance to United States and British attempts to get a UN Security Council resolution authorizing intervention against Saddam Hussein, were doing so because they believed (1) that using military means would only exacerbate Third World opinion against the West, and (2) that the EU ought to extricate itself from its subordinate position toward the United States and establish a stronger identity in world affairs.

Tony Blair, Italian Premier Silvio Berlusconi, Spanish leader José Maria Aznar, and almost all the leaders of the soon-to-join states in Central Europe (Donald Rumsfeld's "new Europe") took a different line. Although they shared the EU's objectives of increasing dialogue and aid between the West and the Third World (Blair, in particular, made an absolute priority of this objective), they believed that having a European foreign policy only made sense if it was in step with U.S. priorities. On January 29, 2003, eight European leaders published a letter in the *Wall Street Journal* that stated that the "transatlantic relationship must not become a casualty of the current Iraqi regime's persistent attempts to threaten world security."[80] A second letter signed by leaders from Central Europe and the Balkans followed in early February (the so-called Vilnius letter).

Chirac was infuriated, but in the long run he had the bittersweet satisfaction of being proven right. Chirac told Blair at a summit meeting in February 2003 that he had been a young officer in Algeria in the 1950s, that Iraq was a similar case, and that the invasion would end in a bloody civil war with the Americans caught in the middle. Blair told his staff after the summit, "Jacques just doesn't get it."[81]

In fact, he had got it all too well. And as the situation in Iraq deteriorated, more and more pundits began to argue that "old Europe" understood the realities of the new world order rather better than the neoconservative think tanks in Washington. Perhaps dialogue and poverty alleviation were better weapons than drones and bunker busters after all. An exaggeratedly euphoric book argued that Europe would "run the twenty-first century" largely because it had understood that power politics was merely destructive, while its own ideology of mutual cooperation between nations was more adapted for co-opting nations and persuading them to uphold common rules.[82] The political scientist Ian Manners, in a persuasive study showing how the EU had gently pressured other societies into giving up the death penalty, coined the phrase *normative power* and suggested that "the ability to define what passes for 'normal' in world politics is, ultimately, the greatest power of all."[83] In his view, the "most important factor" shaping the international role of the EU was not "what it does or what it says, but what it is."[84] Above all, the British diplomat and political thinker Robert Cooper, whose groundbreaking ideas shaped much of the debate on foreign policy in Brussels in the early 2000s, thought that Europe could become an "empire of values," one that gradually exported its highly civilized and successful society to its neighbors.[85] The bitter divisions over Iraq, in short, did not seriously disturb the growing consensus, shaped by the introduction of the Euro, the enlargement of the Union to encompass twenty-five states, the adoption of a Constitution, and a nascent values-driven foreign policy, that the EU was the most hopeful political phenomenon of its age, a political force that deserved to be treated as an equal partner by the United States.

9

✢

Toward a
Twin-Track Europe?

The idea that the EU's soft power appeal could supersede that of the United States and enable the EU to build an "empire of values" ultimately rested upon two principal assumptions: first, that the EU, dynamized by the adoption of a single currency, would deliver impressive economic results; second, that the EU's postnational approach to governance would evolve into an institutional model that the rest of the world might want to imitate, and would certainly admire.

In both respects, the EU's performance in the second half of the last decade was poor. While the EU remains the largest economic bloc in the world, and while several of its member states have responded well to the most serious world recession since the 1930s, many other member states have had weaknesses in their economy cruelly exposed by the 2008 financial crisis and its aftermath. The gap between the growth rates attained by the EU's most efficient economies (Germany, above all) and its less efficient ones has widened. The accumulation of previously unimaginable budget deficits by Greece and Ireland, and money market speculation against Spanish, Portuguese, and Italian government debt, have even cast doubt over the future of the Euro, although the disintegration of the single currency would be such a calamity for the EU it can be assumed that the member states will continue to do everything within their power to ensure the Euro survives.

The EU has moreover not solved the question of what kind of polity it wants to be. A federal state? The last five years has shown—if any demonstration was needed—that a "United States of Europe" is a complete nonstarter. The "United Europe of States" proposed by the 2005 Constitution turned out to be anathema for millions of ordinary voters. Both France and the Netherlands rejected the Constitution in referendums (the Dutch by a very wide margin) and by so doing illustrated that doubts about the European project were no longer limited to the "Euroskeptic fringe" of former EFTA states. After a pause for reflection between 2005 and 2007, the member states negotiated a diluted version of the Constitution, signed the new treaty—no one made the mistake of calling it a Constitution again—at a meeting of the European Council in Lisbon, and then mostly relied on national legislatures for ratification.

This is not to suggest that the EU has lost all popularity: a plurality (or small majority) of the EU's citizens regularly continue to support the idea of European integration in the surveys of public opinion carried out by the pollsters of *Eurobarometer*.[1] The EU's single market, especially its labor market, is imperfect, but it is still freer than at any time since the late nineteenth century. Certainly, there is no widespread desire to dismantle the EU or to repatriate significant powers from Brussels. At the same time, institutions, certainly institutions that have no deep roots in national tradition, thrive only if they deliver public goods that their citizens want.

The EU, in short, is marking time. As the second decade of the twenty-first century proceeds, its task will be to reinvent itself, prove its utility, and show that it is essential for future prosperity and democracy in Europe. That has been, after all, its raison d'être since the 1950s.

BROUGHT BACK TO EARTH

The failure of the Constitution at the hands of the French and Dutch electorates in the spring of 2005 came quite out of the blue. The Constitution had already been ratified by the parliaments of several member states and by a successful referendum in Spain (77 percent in favor) when the French cast their votes on May 29, 2005. While it was known that there was growing opposition in France to the consequences of such key EU policies as enlargement, few truly believed that the French would turn down their thumbs to a constitution that was, after all, the brainchild of a former French president and which also closely reflected the preferences of French elites. Nevertheless, after an electoral campaign enlivened by heated claims that the Constitution was a "neoliberal" document that would erode the French welfare state and lead to "Polish plumbers" taking jobs away from indigenous clearers of drains, the French voted against the Constitution by a solid 55–45 percent margin. Last-minute appeals from Europe's great and good for France to vote for the Constitution *"parce qu'elle a été la mère fondatrice de l'Europe unie"* unsurprisingly did little to sway the disenchanted public mood.[2]

The Dutch referendum was naturally more sober in tone, but that made the electorate's June 1, 2005, decision to say *nee* by a staggering 62–38 percent margin all the more dramatic. Nobody could reasonably say that the Dutch had bowed to nationalist passions or populist electioneering. Millions of booklets clearly explaining the Constitution's novelties were distributed to Dutch voters (though they were much criticized for their favorable bias), and public debate was well informed and generally thoughtful in tone. The Dutch, who were already grumbling about the Netherlands' contribution to the EU budget, correctly learned from their booklets that the Constitution would strengthen the voting power of the larger EU states, above all Germany, at the expense of the smaller member states, realized that further enlargement to Turkey was in the offing and decided to send Brussels a message. Since the Dutch had always been a pillar of support for greater Europeanization, the signal came through loud and clear, eclipsing even the French vote in its impact. If the Dutch could turn against more Europe, anybody could.

The reaction of Europe's leaders to the referendum defeats was nevertheless politics as usual. President Chirac of France, German Chancellor Gerhard Schröder, and Jean-Claude Juncker of Luxemburg (which held the EU presidency) chose in the aftermath of the Dutch vote vociferously to back the Commission's appeal for a budget increase to ease adjustment caused by enlargement. They further suggested that Britain, given its long-standing enthusiasm for adding new member states, should pick up the cost by renouncing the "rebate" won at Fontainebleau by Margaret Thatcher in June 1984. The first European Council after the referendum defeats was held in Brussels on June 16, 2005, and was a flashback to the early 1980s, with an "awkward squad" of Britain, the Netherlands, and Sweden flatly refusing to accept a significant increase in the EU budget. Prime Minister Tony Blair, for one, calculated that the British taxpayer risked having to pay as much as €25 billion more over the seven-year budget cycle 2007 to 2013 if plans proposed by the Luxembourg presidency were accepted: political suicide in Britain, where the Euroskeptic press was bound to raise a furor.[3] Blair, who was about to take over the EU presidency, used his opening speech to the European Parliament on June 23, 2005, to challenge what he perceived as Brussels's refusal to accept the facts of life:

> It is time to give ourselves a reality check. To receive the wake-up call. The people are blowing the trumpets round the city walls. Are we listening? Have we the political will to go out and meet them so that they regard our leadership as part of the solution not the problem?[4]

The referendum defeats, Blair argued, had underlined that the EU could not remain wedded to the high-cost CAP and to the EU's sprawling bureaucratic centralism, but should become a slimmer organization primarily dedicated to making the EU states more economically competitive.

Blair had much right on his side. It cannot be said, however, that he articulated an alternative that was enticing to the EU's great and good, or, indeed, to citizens from many important EU countries. Blair's recipe for renewing the EU was to implement the so-called Lisbon Agenda, agreed in 2000 at a meeting of the European Council in the Portuguese capital, whose objective was to make the EU the most competitive knowledge-based economy in the world by 2010. In 2004, a committee of experts chaired by Wim Kok had issued a report chiding the EU's member states, especially the Mediterranean ones, for having done little to meet the Lisbon Agenda's numerous targets on higher workforce participation, greater labor market liberalization, and further deregulation and recommending that the EU should at least nominate priorities for reform by the 2010 deadline.[5] Blair wanted to push ahead with Kok's prescriptions, while also taking heed of another EU report, the so-called Sapir Report, which in July 2003 had—among much else—proposed recasting the EU's budget to reduce the weight of agricultural subsidies and to boost EU spending on research and development.[6] Voters and politicians in France, Greece, Italy, Portugal, and Spain, to name just five EU states, were certainly not blowing trumpets for measures that advocated jolting the European economy into more rapid growth by getting more people, with higher qualifications, to participate in the labor market on more flexible terms, while slashing subsidies to farmers. And, in fact, such ideas have got nowhere, or almost nowhere, since 2005.

Like a middle-aged man shrugging off a heart tremor and returning to his slothful ways, the EU overcame its budget tensions and the broader crisis caused by the rejection of the Constitution by its tried and tested methods of fudge, compromise, and postponement of tough decisions. The budget negotiations were resolved in December 2005 at the end of the British presidency. Ferocious infighting within the British government and between the EU's member states produced a deal that simultaneously left the EU-15's privileges mostly intact, did not imply reform of the CAP, significantly augmented the Commission's budget, gave the new members slightly less than they had hoped (but was still a pot of gold), and kept the EU's budget at 1 percent of the Union's forecast output.[7] Britain had to give up €7 billion of its scheduled rebate over the budget cycle, but the nominal figure would still be higher in 2013 than in 2007. Both Blair and the newly elected German chancellor, Angela Merkel, won kudos from the new member states as a result of their willingness to pay for enlargement with hard cash. Everybody was a winner. Business as usual resumed. The final hours of the December 16, 2005, Brussels European Council were "like a bazaar," with everybody trying to squeeze "an extra few million euros" from the British prime minister for their pet national projects.[8]

The failure of the Constitution led to a lengthy "pause for reflection" as other states continued with the ratification process. Britain and the Czech Republic, however, insisted that the Constitution was dead, while the French and Dutch showed no signs of holding a second referendum. In the second semester of 2007, the EU bowed to the inevitable and proceeded to renegotiate the Constitution, undertaking what was now portrayed as merely the sixth major revision (after the Merger Treaty, the SEA, Maastricht, Amsterdam, and Nice) of the Treaties of Rome.

The eventual Treaty of Lisbon was signed in the Portuguese capital on December 13, 2007. It largely reprised the chief institutional and policy novelties of the rejected Constitution, namely the creation of a permanent presidency of the European Council (which itself became an official institution of the EU) and of a European high representative for foreign affairs (the title of foreign minister was eliminated to soothe national sensibilities); the absorption of the foreign policy and justice and home affairs "pillars" into the European Union; and an increase in the number of policy areas where the Council of Ministers (now called the Council of the European Union) decided by qualified majority voting. Taxation questions, social security, and, of course, foreign and defense policy still required unanimity in the Council, however. The "double majority" voting system proposed by the Constitution was also retained. From November 2014, decisions will be taken in the council of Ministers (or Council of the European Union, as it is now known) by a minimum majority of 55 percent of the member states representing at least 65 percent of the population.[9]

Other provisions relating to the making of legislation were equally significant. The rotating presidency of the Council of Ministers was retained: in the first semester of 2017 the policy priorities of what by then may well be the world's largest economic bloc will be set by Malta (population 410,000). Germany (population 82.5 million and the world's fourth largest economy) will next chair the Council between July–December 2020. In a bid to make the EU's institutions seem more open to its citizens, it was agreed that the Council of Ministers would "meet in public" when they deliberated or voted on a legislative act. This was a potential increase in transparency, although it might merely ensure that the Council's legislative sessions are little more than a public ratification of deals done in private. Codecision, the assent of the European Parliament for legislation, was renamed the "ordinary legislative procedure" and was applied to 95 as opposed to 75 percent of all EU legislation. The Commission, at least until October 31, 2014, was to be composed of one commissioner per member state: a superfluous nod to national concerns if the College of Commissioners was truly motivated by their pledge to pursue the common European interest.[10] Certainly, the Commission's reputation as a sprawling bureaucracy was not repaired by the Lisbon Treaty's provisions. The Lisbon Treaty might have been an opportunity to reorganize the whole range of the EU's projects and administrative structures, to reduce the number of directorate-generals (as EU "ministries" are called), and to give their activities greater focus. It was an opportunity missed.

The Lisbon Treaty jettisoned many of the trappings of statehood that had been included in the Constitution. The treaty dropped all references to the Union's flag, anthem, and motto (though they continue to exist; the anthem was played at the signing ceremony) and, still more significant, excised the Charter on Human Rights, though it retained legal force throughout the Union. Britain and Poland, however, negotiated opt-outs from the Charter's provisions.

Despite these concessions to national sensibilities, the Lisbon Treaty did not have an easy passage to ratification. Ireland voted on June 12, 2008, by 53-47 percent, to reject the treaty and only approved it in October 2009 after concessions had been won. The Czech Republic, whose president, neoliberal economist Vaclav Klaus, was an open advocate of the EU's dissolution into a Gaullist-style "organization of European states," also ratified the treaty with a distinct lack of enthusiasm. Klaus's often-voiced belief that the EU had brought about a "huge gap" between the "common people" and the "political elites" and his equally fervent conviction that the EU's "centralism, interventionism and bureaucratism [sic]" was a menace to the Czech Republic's recently acquired national sovereignty, made him a formidable obstacle since his signature was necessary for his country's adhesion to the treaty. Klaus was also seemingly worried that the Charter of Fundamental Rights would enable German and Austrian citizens who had lost their property after 1945 to sue Prague before the ECJ. In October 2009 he openly stated that he would not sign the treaty unless the Czech Republic was exempted, like Britain and Poland, from the Charter's provisions. This move was popular with Czech public opinion, which was highly suspicious that the treaty would extend German hegemony within the EU. The European Council bowed to Klaus's demands at the end of October 2009. It had, in fact, no choice but to do so if it wanted to avoid a paralyzing crisis. Klaus accordingly signed the treaty, though not without taking the parting shot that the treaty's entry into force meant that the Czech Republic would "cease to be a sovereign state." Actually, his actions demonstrated that the EU, far from being a superpower crushing life out of its member states, was, thanks to the hyper-consensual nature of its decision making on major issues, a polity uniquely at risk of being blackmailed by a single recalcitrant member state.[11]

It should be added, however, that Klaus, despite his boorish behavior, had told Brussels a painful home truth. The Lisbon Treaty's ratification process did indeed underline the huge gap that had appeared between the EU's citizens and its elites. Ireland was the only country to hold a referendum on the treaty. Despite the fact that the treaty contained most of the substance of the Constitution, national leaders invidiously argued that Lisbon was merely a technical amendment of the Nice treaty and therefore required only parliamentary assent. Ratification was rushed through in most countries with the bare minimum of popular discussion. The reason for this collective abstention from democratic debate over the Lisbon Treaty was that the EU's leaders knew full well that it would be defeated in a half dozen different member states, at least, were it put to a popular vote. Even in such strongholds of pro-EU sentiment as Germany and Italy, the treaty was greeted with little enthusiasm. The notion of "more Europe" by December 2009 was dividing the citizens of the EU, not uniting them.

The Lisbon Treaty nevertheless became operational on December 1, 2009. The member states chose the Belgian premier, the Flemish Christian Democrat Herman Van Rompuy, as president of the European Council, while Catherine Ashton of the United Kingdom, the commissioner responsible for trade, was elevated to high representative for external affairs (and vice president of the Commission). The multilingual Van Rompuy had won plaudits for his skillful handling of Belgium's internal conflict between the French and Flemish-speaking communities and was widely esteemed for his shrewdness and negotiating skills. Ashton, by contrast, was no linguist, and unlike her predecessor Xavier Solana, who had been Spanish foreign minister and secretary-general of NATO, she had little claim to be a foreign policy expert. Bigger names, notably a former premier and foreign minister of Italy, Massimo D'Alema, were passed over for the job. It was widely assumed that Ashton had been chosen to compensate Britain. Tony Blair, whose premiership had recently ended, had lobbied hard behind the scenes for the job of president of the European Council.[12]

Whatever the political background to the choices of Van Rompuy and Ashton, the Lisbon Treaty's incorporation of foreign policy into the EU's responsibilities has not raised its standing or prestige. On big issues, the EU has still not learned to speak with a single voice. In 2008, while the Lisbon Treaty was being ratified, the EU split embarrassingly over the question of Kosovo independence, which several EU states, including Greece and Spain, refused to countenance. The rise of China (and to a lesser extent Brazil, India, and Russia) has already led it to eclipse the Europeans' role as the United States' main interlocutor: China's Hu Jintao counts for more in Washington than any elected European leader, let alone Mr. Van Rompuy. It is perhaps a marker of the EU's fading luster that Turkey, upon whose entry the EU has posed stiff rules of "conditionality," is increasingly inclined to turn its back on Europe and search for a role of its own as a major regional power.[13]

The EU, in short, had spent most of the first decade of the new millennium debating its organizational structure and had ended by reaching a constitutional settlement that affirmed the centrality of its member states in the decision-making process, safeguarded the democratic balance between the states, and ensured that the key new supranational positions created by the Lisbon Treaty went to individuals who were unlikely to challenge the status quo. The whole process of "constitutionalizing" the EU, begun at Laeken in December 2001, ended by essentially confirming the Maastricht compromise between supranationalism and the rights of governments within the EU. After Lisbon, the EU is a confederation of sovereign states first and a supranational organization second. It is also likely to remain so for the foreseeable future. Even the most ardent advocate for a federal Europe, or for a United Europe of States, must admit that the peoples of Europe show little enthusiasm for their cause.

A PIGS' BREAKFAST?

The EU's citizens could be excused for regarding the EU's constitutional saga as a distraction from their real concerns. The EU's economy was hard hit by the "Great Recession" that began after the collapse of leading U.S. financial institutions in 2007 to 2008. Countries such as Germany and Italy, where manufacturing exports are a large component of national output, saw their national incomes contract sharply. Other nations, notably Britain, were dragged into recession by their banks' losses. (In Britain, indeed, only a massive emergency recapitalization by the state of some of the country's leading banks staved off a meltdown of the entire financial system, which would have turned the banks' losses into a calamity for society as a whole.) In May 2011, the GDP of the Euro-zone was still 2 percent less than its peak in early 2008, with only Germany of the EU's big economies having surpassed its precrisis figure. Italy's economy was still 5 percent smaller than its peak, and Spain's economy had contracted by 4 percent. Greece's economy was 9 percent smaller than its peak.[14]

The contraction in the economy brought rising unemployment in its wake. In May 2011, there were six million more jobless across the EU than there had been in the first semester of 2008. There are currently twenty-three million unemployed in the EU-27, sixteen million of them in the Euro-zone. In percentage terms, this means that approximately 10 percent of the workforce is out of a job. The overall figure masks substantial national disparities, however. Austria, the Netherlands, and Luxembourg can boast 4 percent unemployment rates—near to what economists regard as full employment; the Baltic states and Spain, by contrast, are facing joblessness rates of nearly or more than 20 percent. Greece and Ireland are suffering from unemployment of over 14 percent, and in both countries the number of the jobless is surging. The situation of under-twenty-fives is especially severe: 20.7 percent are unemployed in the EU-27. More than 40 percent of Spanish youth and 36 percent of Greek and Slovakian youth are unemployed. Bulgaria, Ireland, Italy, Hungary, Poland, and Portugal all have over a quarter of their under-twenty-fives out of work.[15]

The other major consequence of the economic downturn was ballooning government deficits. The Stability and Growth Pact (see chapter 8), which was supposed to restrain government deficit spending, had already been weakened in November 2003. In that month, France and Germany, seconded by Italy, successfully argued for greater flexibility in the application of EU sanctions when they ran deficits over the 3 percent figure permitted by the EU treaty for two successive years. Subsequently, Italy, which was to have reduced its stock of public debt to beneath 100 percent of GDP by 2005, failed to meet its target. No sanctions were imposed. When the economic crisis hit Europe in 2008, deficit spending figures soared. The collective deficit of the sixteen Euro-zone nations in 2007 was €55,723 million (a restrained 0.6 percent of GDP). In 2009, it was over €565 billion (6.3 percent), more than ten times more. The Euro-zone's collective debt stock exploded from 66 percent of GDP to 79 percent in the same two-year period. When non-Euro states were added to the equation, deficit spending looked even worse: total deficits surged from €103,584 million in 2007 to a breathtaking €801,866 million in 2009, with Britain providing most of the extra €250 billion. Like the United States, the EU had a trillion-dollar deficit in 2009.

The cause of these deficits was that EU governments were spending over half their countries' GDP in 2009 (50.7 percent) but could not for either political or economic reasons take half of national income in tax. In 2009, Ireland's budget deficit was 14.3 percent of a rapidly contracting GDP: getting the budget in balance would have made the already bad recession even worse. In Greece, the newly elected Socialist government of George Papandreou revealed on October 20, 2009, that its predecessors had been manipulating Greece's fiscal statistics since the country entered the Euro and that the Greek fiscal deficit would certainly be more than triple the forecast 3.6 percent of GDP. The final figure was estimated by the International Monetary Fund (IMF) to be over 15 percent. Britain's deficit was a huge 11.5 percent of GDP and Spain's 11.2 percent. Even Germany's deficit was outside the 3 percent guideline laid down by the Stability and Growth Pact. This surge of deficit spending ensured that by the end of 2009 no fewer than twelve of the EU's twenty-seven member states, including Britain, France, Germany, and Italy, had accumulated debts that exceeded the 60 percent limit theoretically permitted by the Stability and Growth Pact.[16]

In 2010, these figures worsened. The Euro-zone countries borrowed 6 percent of their collective GDP in 2010; the EU as a whole borrowed 6.4 percent. Ireland was the record holder: in 2010, Ireland borrowed a sum equal to nearly *a third* (32 percent) of its entire annual economic activity as the government paid for the losses, chiefly on property, run up by its reckless banks. Overall, accumulated member-state debt reached 85 percent of the Euro-zone's output and 80 percent of the EU-27's, with Italy and Germany being the two largest debtors in quantitative terms. Member-state spending continued to exceed half of GDP, and no fewer than fourteen of the EU's twenty-seven states had now superseded the 60 percent debt ceiling permitted by the EU's rules.[17]

When the tide goes out you can see who is bathing naked. For most of the decade since the introduction of the Euro in 1999, yields on bonds issued by Euro-zone members had converged toward the figure for German debt. The Euro-zone as a whole, not just its most prosperous and economically competitive member states, was perceived by the markets to be an oasis of fiscal rectitude. This perception had permitted countries such as Italy, Portugal, and Greece to borrow more cheaply than in the past and to retire their public debt at lower rates, and the relieving of the debt burden had hence been widely regarded as one of the Euro's most meritorious features.[18]

Once economies were under severe stress, traditional assessments of fiscal prudence reasserted themselves with a vengeance. Yields on bonds issued by Greece and Ireland rose rapidly throughout 2010 as the markets woke up to their parlous situation: Greek bonds were reduced to "junk" status as early as April 2010. By the end of the year Greece and Ireland had been joined on the blacklist by Spain and Portugal, despite both of these countries boasting public debt loads that were less than the European average. The size of their annual deficits, the sluggishness of their economies, and, in the case of Spain, an undercapitalized banking system facing very heavy losses from property developers were nevertheless more than enough to make the markets alarmed. Ireland and Greece, however, were in a different class. They were simply bankrupt—their public finances were on a par with Argentina's, not the advanced economies of Northern Europe.

The "PIGS" (Portugal-Ireland-Greece-Spain), as they were unflatteringly known, threatened the Euro-zone with catastrophe. If they defaulted on their debt, their bondholders would take a "haircut" on the value of their debt. Since these bondholders were largely banks from elsewhere in the Euro-zone, this option offered the prospect of a Community-wide banking crisis. If they left the Euro (a technical nightmare), their currencies would plunge, giving them a competitive boost but boosting also the value, relative to GDP, of their Euro-denominated debts (and hence making default more likely). Policymakers also feared that allowing the Euro-zone to lose its weaker members would lead to frenzy on the bond markets, as speculators focused on other Euro-zone countries with less than impeccable finances, such as Belgium and Italy.

A third option, and the one eventually taken, was to bail the "PIGS" out. This suggestion, however, exposed the extent of European solidarity: German taxpayers and politicians, in particular, did not see why they should lend their money to save countries that had lived beyond their means. After 2002, Germany had implemented deeply unpopular measures to reduce spending on pensions, make labor markets more flexible, and lengthen the working week. The Greeks had not done these things, or not to the same extent; nor, even more to the point, had they cracked down on rampant tax evasion. Powerful forces in German society, such as the tabloid newspaper *Bild*, bluntly asked why the Greeks should be exempted from making the same sacrifices that the Germans themselves had made. Chancellor Angela Merkel had no choice but to listen.[19]

How, then, has the EU conducted its bailout program? In effect, its institutions have gradually, and not without much uncertainty, evolved a three-pronged strategy. First, the ECB began intervening in the secondary debt market in May 2010 to buy Greek and subsequently Irish and Portuguese bonds. (The ECB is banned by the EU treaty from buying bonds from governments directly.) By the end of 2010, it had accumulated a mountain of dubious government (and bank) IOUs on its balance sheet—a controversial move that amounted to Europeanizing sovereign debt that discerning professional investors were too scared to buy. If these countries' economies recover, the ECB will get its money back; if they default, and it seems probable that Greece at the very least will, then the ECB's substantial paper losses on these IOUs will be realized, and the Frankfurt bank will have to be recapitalized. This high-risk strategy was deeply unpopular with German central bankers, who regarded it as providing an unacceptable moral hazard. What incentive would nations have to reform their finances if they knew the EU would save them anyway? In February 2011, the president of the Bundesbank, Axel Weber, resigned rather than continue to acquiesce to the ECB's strategy. After the ECB intervention in the secondary debt market was extended, on a huge scale, to Italy and Spain in August-September 2011, Jürgen Stark, a German member of the ECB's executive board, resigned on September 10, 2011. Such opposition to the ECB's policy reflected the wider unease within Germany about the future of the Euro. For Germany only signed up to the single currency, as we have seen, on the understanding that it would be as strong as the DM it replaced.[20]

Second, the EU, together with the IMF, has put together loan packages, at competitive rates of interest, for the Greeks (May 2010), Irish

(November 2010), and Portuguese (May 2011). Spain and Italy, while not receiving loans, were compelled by the ECB to implement steep austerity packages in the summer of 2011 in exchange for the central bank's purchases of their debt. In the case of Greece, the EU loans were conditional upon drastic austerity measures to adjust women's retirement age to that of men, to tax luxury goods, to liberalize the professions, privatize publicly owned companies, and increase the retirement age for public sector workers from 61 to 65. In all, over five years, the Greek government will have to impose a fiscal tightening equal to 14.5 percent of the country's 2009 GDP.[21] Papandreou's government has courageously faced down the mass protests, strikes, and occasional street violence that have greeted the EU-IMF package, but it must be doubted whether any Greek government can make austerity on this scale stick.[22] Ireland and Portugal also had to agree to steep packages of cuts before they could get loans, though public opinion in both countries has greeted austerity more with resignation than anger.[23] All three nations, along with Italy and Spain, seem condemned to lengthy periods of economic stagnation as they stagger under the burden of the debt accumulated in the Euro's first decade, and as consumption is deflated by the EU's austerity demands.

Third, in May 2010, the EU announced the creation of the European Financial Stability Facility (EFSF), a "special purposes vehicle" (in effect, a kind of investment bank) incorporated in Luxembourg that is authorized, on request from a member state and after approval of the state's request from the Eurozone's finance ministers, to issue debt backed by the EU-27 as a whole, including those states (Finland, Germany, the Netherlands) with a rock-solid credit rating. The EFSF is empowered to issue up to €440 billion of debt on behalf of the EU; the IMF has contributed €2.5 billion to the Facility. By June 2011, the EFSF had brought two large bond issues (for €8 billion in total) to market on behalf of Portugal. The EFSF's objective was to "shock and awe" the markets into accepting that the EU will throw a lifeline to a country in distress and hence to stay speculation against its weaker member states' bonds.

In fact, the sheer scale of the debt problems of the Mediterranean member states has led to market pressure for an *increase* in the size of the fund. Turning the EU into a "transfer union," in which weaker countries effectively ride on the shoulders of their more robust brethren, is deeply unpopular in Austria, Finland, Germany, and the Netherlands, however. The potential expansion of the EFSF's debt-issuing powers had become a controversial political issue across northern Europe by the summer of 2011. It is easy to grasp why. Germany's pledged contribution to the EFSF's original €440 billion fund was already an astronomical €120 billion (about €1,450 for every German citizen). As it has become evident that the money is quite likely to be disbursed, and not just be a paper commitment, so it has become more and more risky for Chancellor Merkel to ask German voters for more.

The debt crisis of 2010 to 2011 within the Euro-zone has unquestionably strengthened the case of the single currency's critics. First, as some critics feared from the beginning, the Euro has led to a significant loss of both sovereignty and policymaking flexibility for some member states. Member states that had postponed unpleasant reforms have been made to implement them by the markets and by their European Council peers. They no longer possess, moreover, the option of evading such reforms, or buying time to implement them, by devaluing their currencies and boosting economic growth artificially. Second, the low interest rates set by the ECB turned out to be inappropriate for the Euro-zone as a whole. Booming Ireland and Spain should have used higher taxes in the mid-2000s to deflate property markets rising on the back of the cheap money permitted by Frankfurt, but unsurprisingly, since their politicians did not have a death wish, this course of action was not followed. Supporters of "more Europe" argue in fact that the chief problem with the Euro is that there is no central government able to set member states' fiscal policies, only a Commission able to warn and at most cajole the member states into good fiscal behavior and a committee of finance ministers reluctant to criticize one another's performance. In short, faced with the "unfolding Greek crisis," Euro-zone governments and the ECB "displayed slowness, division and ineptness."[24]

For this reason, on March 25, 2011, the European Council approved a so-called Euro Plus package by which the Eurozone nations, plus Bulgaria, Denmark, Latvia, Lithuania, Poland, and Romania, but not Britain and Sweden, committed themselves to driving their budget deficits down to below 3 percent of GDP by 2012, boosting competitiveness and introducing supply side measures to boost growth.[25] Compliance would be monitored by the so-called "open method of coordination," which in effect means that the member states set themselves targets and are benchmarked by the Commission according to how close they come to meeting them. The member states remain extremely reluctant to contemplate national public spending policies being set centrally by the Commission: the implications for sovereignty are too great. On May 28, 2011, the president of the ECB, Jean-Claude Trichet of France, nevertheless warned that an EU finance minister with the power to say yea or nay to national budget deficits might be an advisable step.[26] His appeal fell on deaf ears. Meeting in August 2011, Chancellor Merkel and President Nicolas Sarkozy of France merely envisaged the introduction of a biannual European Council entirely dedicated to budgetary matters in order to monitor and prompt member states' progress in this area. This emphasis on intergovernmental solutions does not mean that Europe's leaders are underestimating what is at stake, however. On September 19, 2011, Chancellor Merkel was widely reported as saying, starkly, "if the Euro goes, the EU goes."

All in all, the 2009 to 2011 debt crisis, like the constitutional saga, has exposed both the EU's ambition in trying to meld into one economic union member states as diverse as Greece and Germany and has highlighted how much preserving nationhood matters to its twenty-seven members. The member states are willing, for a price, to help one another out of a hole—but desperately want to retain their sovereign power to dig themselves into the hole in the first place.

EUROPEAN NORMS

Euro membership, in short, has proven to be more than a mere technical choice of currency. It has proven to be a normative choice that certain nations did their best to ignore but which they can't now go back on, no matter how painful their choice has proved to be. The emergence of the EU as a "normative power" for its own member states, not just for states in its "neighborhood," is perhaps the most significant development in the EU since the introduction of the Euro in 1999. For in addition to the Euro's macroeconomic discipline, over the last decade the EU has become a body that is consciously assimilating its members to a common social and economic model. The EU's blueprint for this model is basically one that has been implemented in Northern Europe since the 1980s and early 1990s and that has enabled countries like Finland, Denmark, and the Netherlands to cope, and indeed thrive, in an age of globalization and increasing competition from low-wage economies. Higher education levels, especially in applied science, mathematics, and languages; free labor markets; flexible, secure welfare systems; and sound public finances represent EU "best practice," to use the jargon of management studies. In the best tradition of Brussels technocratic thinking, there has been too little awareness, however, of the upheaval that such an ethos implies for the southern member states and for some of its new members.

The EU's flagship "2020 Initiative" is a target-based approach whose goal is that of improving the quality of the European economy. Its results so far paint a picture of North European progress, Mediterranean and Central European states lagging behind. Thus, the EU wants to have 75 percent of the population aged twenty to sixty-four in work by 2020: in 2010, the figure was 69 percent, down from just over 70 percent in prerecession 2007. Denmark, Sweden, and the Netherlands have consistently beaten the 75 percent target in recent years. Italy, Spain, and Greece still languish at approximately 60 percent workforce participation, thanks mostly to their dismal rates of female employment and high unemployment among young people.

Another core EU objective is to have a better-educated workforce. Brussels hopes to have 40 percent of its thirty- to thirty-four-year-olds with a bachelor's degree, or equivalent, by 2020 (to put this in perspective, about 38.5 percent of Americans over twenty-five years of age in 2009 possessed a college degree).[27] In 2009, the EU was scoring 32.3 percent. The headline figure was deceptive, however. Denmark, Finland, and Sweden (but also Cyprus and Ireland) were already comfortably over the 40 percent target. Italy (19 percent), Portugal (21), Romania (17), Greece (26), but also Austria (23), by contrast, seemed highly unlikely to make the grade by the set date.

Another laudable goal of the "2020 Initiative" is to make Europe cleaner. The EU has taken a high-profile international role on the question of climate change and, recognizing that it can hardly ask the United States, India, or China to clean up their acts if it does not do so itself, has committed itself to reducing its emission of greenhouse gases by 20 percent compared to 1990 levels.[28] At first glance, the EU is advancing toward this goal: in 2008, the index stood at 88.9. The EU's good performance is almost entirely due, however, to the new member states of Central Europe cleaning up their economies during the accession process: their levels of pollution have dropped drastically since Soviet days. Britain, virtuously, has already cut its emissions to approximately the required figure. Elsewhere, even the Northern Europeans mostly continue to pollute at around 1990 rates, while other countries pollute at far higher levels than in 1990 (Spain 142.3, Portugal 132.2, Greece 122.8, Ireland 123). Turkey, a would-be EU member, has doubled its emissions since 1990.

As part of the 2020 plan, the EU is urging nations to match the United States by investing 3 percent of GDP in research and development by 2020. Once again, Finland, Denmark, Germany, and Sweden are close to or above this figure, while Cyprus (0.4 percent), Spain (1.35 percent), Italy (1.23 percent), and Portugal (1.5 percent) are all doing the bare minimum or less. Central European states do even worse than the Mediterranean ones by this measure: few spend even 1 percent of their national income on research.[29]

The consequences of this failure to invest in research and development are reflected by the mixed performance of Europe's universities. In the 2010 to 2011 *Times Higher Education* rankings for universities, seventy-four of the world's top two hundred institutions of higher learning and research were located in the EU, though only twenty-four made the top hundred and only nine were in the top fifty. No fewer than twenty-eight of the EU institutions in the top two hundred were British, fourteen were German, ten Dutch (though the highest placed Dutch university was only 114th), six Swedish, four French, and three Danish. Spain, or more precisely Barcelona, had two universities in the top two hundred. The rest of the EU's Mediterranean states had none. Central Europe, Austria apart, had none. Italy, the seventh largest economy in the world and the homeland of Galileo, Volta, and Fermi, has become an academic backwater. Accusations that these rankings are culturally biased in favor of the English-speaking world do not hold water: Chinese, Japanese, and Korean universities all did well, as did Bilkent University in Istanbul. The results, moreover, are not a one-off. The same pattern has reproduced itself since such attempts at ranking academic quality began in the mid-2000s.[30]

The EU's data are only confirming what other respected surveys of so-called competitiveness have been saying for some years. The World Economic Forum's (WEF) "Competitiveness Report" is an index based not on how well firms from individual countries manage to sell their products but on an array of indicators such as the quality of public infrastructure, level of workforce education and skills, diffusion of higher and primary education, stability of institutions, environmental quality, and so on. By the WEF's criteria, half the top twenty nations of the world are to be found in the EU: Sweden, in second place, is beaten by Switzerland but is ahead of Singapore and the United States. Germany, Finland, the Netherlands, Denmark, the UK, France, Belgium, and Luxembourg all place well. Countries such as the Czech Republic (thirty-sixth) and Poland (thirty-ninth) are improving on past performance. Spain, however, is only forty-second, Portugal forty-sixth, Italy forty-eighth, and Romania sixty-seventh. Greece is a disconcerting eighty-third, sandwiched between El Salvador and Trinidad.[31]

One could stir other indicators of social and economic efficiency into the mix, but there is no need to belabor the point. The EU is split between a core group of highly developed, flexible, well-educated, environmentally conscious nations (some of which have not adopted the Euro) and an outer fringe of poorer, less well-equipped, dirtier, inadequately educated, and inflexible countries where traditional mores (i.e., toward working women) and social hierarchies still prevail. This is a caricature, but it is not a gross one. Some nations (the Czech Republic, Slovenia, the Baltic states, Spain) may—the use of the conditional is essential, for they have much to do—insert themselves into the core group over the coming decade; other countries seem to have little chance, short of really drastic changes imposed by courageous political leadership of the stamp that George Papandreou is trying to give Greece. Italy, the richest and most important of the laggards, is divided between a north whose quality of life and industrial prowess matches the best in Europe and a south that is becoming less "European"— significantly, the word embarrassed Italian politicians use as a euphemism for "advanced"—with every passing day.[32] Mounds of trash in the streets of Naples testify to this fact more eloquently than any mere statistical analysis. The crisis of the Euro, in this context, may be symptomatic of a deeper—for want of a better word—"cultural" divide within the EU. It is, incidentally, a divide that goes far to explain diffidence toward Turkish entry into the EU. The last thing the EU needs right now, or so many believe, is yet another large Mediterranean country with a dynamic but polluting economy, a large informal sector, conservative social attitudes, nationalistic politicians, and shaky institutions.

Will the EU be able to function if it continues its current trend toward being a replica of Italy on continental scale? Italy's disparities have given rise to a political party, the Lega Nord (Northern League), which advocated secession for a northern Italian republic it baptized "Padania," although the movement now limits itself to calling for a federal reform of the Italian state.[33] Millions of northern Italians, including many fervent opponents of the Lega, share its frustration with the seemingly insoluble problems of the south but acknowledge that such problems are part and parcel of *italianità*.

How likely is it that a similar fatalism will prevail among the peoples and member states of Northern Europe, if they conclude that the Southern European states just don't play by the rules or have no political will even to try to meet some of the targets that they are currently so spectacularly missing? The tone of the public debate in Germany since the debt crisis broke, and the emergence of the "True Finns," a populist party which obtained 19 percent of the vote in the April 2011 Finnish general elections, are straws in the wind that suggest the patience of the wealthy north of Europe will not be inexhaustible. The True Finns' able leader, Timo Soini, made opposition to the EU's bailouts a key plank of his victorious platform.

Just as important, how likely is it that Southern Europeans will rebel at a regulatory and fiscal regime that is requiring them to make unaccustomed sacrifices? Millions of young people are out of work in Greece, France, Italy, Portugal, and Spain. Millions more are "precarious." That is to say they have no job security, work on short-term contracts, and have no welfare safety net except the generosity of their families when their contracts run out. It may only be a matter of time before national political leaders break with the Brussels consensus in order to reach out to *los indignados* of the EU. Certainly, it is hard to avoid the conclusion that the EU is heading at best for a period of profound indecision and dissent over the path it should take, at worse for uncontrollable and even irrational reassertions of national political will.

It is not the historian's job, however, to forecast the future. Historians prefer "retrocasting," an activity that does at least give them the satisfaction of often being right.[34] And it is a matter of historical record that since

1945, Europe has enjoyed peace and prosperity on an unprecedented scale. Economic cooperation has raised standards of living; dictatorship, both red and black, has been banished from the continent; fraught issues such as the German question have been peacefully resolved; new democracies have emerged and flourished. European integration, as this narrative has made clear, has been a common thread woven through the pattern of all these great transformations. Any history of European integration has to show this fact; certainly, this book has tried to do so.

It is equally true, however, that no plausible history can or should imply that the EU is evolving, with the slow inevitability of fate, toward the European Republic that many academics and politicians in Europe regard as the ideal outcome for the European project.[35] This book has emphasized throughout that the undoubted gains brought by European integration have been won by skillful political leadership in the face of often adverse circumstances that might easily have caused the European project to fail. It remains to be seen whether the post–Cold War generation of leaders will show the same savvy as their predecessors, whether the institutions of the current European Union are suited to the purpose of creating more unity from Europe's diverse political cultures, or even whether Europe's peoples still want their leaders to try. Even the most finely woven political triumphs can unravel quickly when leadership fails, or markets crash, or when hard-pressed peoples lose their collective tempers.

Notes

CHAPTER 1. INTRODUCTION

1. Christopher Hill, "What Is to Be Done? Foreign Policy as a Site for Political Action," *International Affairs* 79, no. 2 (2003): 243.

2. The original title of this book, *Surpassing Realism*, was an ironic comment about the member states' behavior. They were surpassing (i.e., going beyond) the realism of traditional power politics, but showing surpassing (i.e., overwhelming) realism in pursuing their immediate commercial and political interests. Nobody got the joke, or even the fact that a joke was being made, so I decided on a more staid title for this edition.

3. Mark Gilbert, "Narrating the Process: Questioning the Progressive Story of European Integration," *Journal of Common Market Studies* 46, no. 3 (2008): 641–62.

4. See, Frédèric Bozo, "Mitterrand's France, the End of the Cold War and German Reunification: An Appraisal," *Cold War History* 7, no. 4, (2007).

5. Jeremy Rifkin, *The European Dream: How Europe's Vision of the Future Is Quietly Eclipsing the American Dream* (New York: Penguin, 2004) was perhaps the most assertive expression of this point of view.

6. T. S. Eliot, *The Wasteland* (New York: Harcourt Brace Jovanovich, 1930), line 43, for Madame Sosostris.

7. Herbert Butterfield, *The Whig Interpretation of History* (London: Pelican, 1973).

8. Butterfield, *Whig Interpretation*, 40, 54, 75.

CHAPTER 2. ENEMIES TO PARTNERS

1. Konrad Adenauer, *Memoirs 1945–1953* (London: Weidenfeld and Nicholson, 1966), 21–22.

2. Adenauer, *Memoirs 1945–1953*, 37.

3. See Richard Mayne, *The Recovery of Europe* (New York: Harper & Row, 1970), 29–37, for a brilliant description of the continent's economic breakdown.

4. Alan Milward, *The Reconstruction of Western Europe* (London: Routledge, 1984), 28–29, for the figures cited.

5. Robert Marjolin, *Architect of European Unity: Memoirs 1911–1986* (London: Weidenfeld and Nicholson, 1989), 228.

6. Diane B. Kunz, *Butter and Guns: America's Cold War Economic Diplomacy* (New York: Free Press, 1997), 50.

7. For Christian Democracy's "hegemony by default," see Wolfram Kaiser, *Christian Democracy and the Origins of European Union* (Cambridge: Cambridge University Press, 2007), ch. 5 passim.

8. For brief details of the French Communists' fall from grace, see Frank Giles, *The Locust Years: The Story of the Fourth French Republic* (London: Secker & Warburg, 1991), 67–70. For Italy, see Paul Ginsborg, *A History of Contemporary Italy* (London: Penguin, 1990), 110–14.

9. See François Duchêne, *Jean Monnet: First Statesman of Interdependence* (New York: Doubleday, 1995), ch. 5 passim.

10. Milward, *Reconstruction of Western Europe*, 36.

11. *Foreign Relations of the United States (FRUS)*, 1947, vol. 3, 230–32.

12. Figures from Milward, *Reconstruction of Western Europe*, 26.

13. Milward, *Reconstruction of Western Europe*, 50–51.

14. Michael Hogan, *The Marshall Plan: America, Britain and the Reconstruction of Western Europe* (Cambridge: Cambridge University Press, 1987), 73.

15. Hogan, *Marshall Plan*, 74.

16. Hogan, *Marshall Plan*, 79.

17. Hogan, *Marshall Plan*, 87.

18. Marjolin, *Architect of European Unity*, 195.

19. Quoted Max Beloff, *The United States and the Unity of Europe* (London: Faber and Faber, 1963), 35.

20. The phrase was coined by Charles S. Maier in his essay "The Politics of Productivity: Foundations of American International Economic Policy after 1945," in *Between Power and Plenty: The Foreign Economic Policies of Advanced Industrial States*, ed. P. Katzenstein (Madison: University of Wisconsin Press, 1978).

21. "Junius" (Luigi Einaudi), *Lettere politiche* (Bari, Italy: Laterza, 1920).

22. R. W. Seton-Watson, *Britain and the Dictators* (Cambridge: Cambridge University Press, 1938), 94.

23. H. N. Brailsford, *Towards a New League* (London: New Statesman & Nation, 1936).

24. Examples of this somewhat naïve belief are G. D. H. Cole, *War Aims* (London: Gollancz, 1939); Kingsley Martin, *100 Million Allies If We Choose* (London: Gollancz, 1940); Richard Acland, *Unser Kampf* (London: Penguin, 1940).

25. H. N. Brailsford, *The Future of Germany* (London: National Peace Committee, 1943).

26. For Roosevelt's policy toward Germany, see Robert Dallek, *Franklin D. Roosevelt and American Foreign Policy 1932–1945* (New York: Oxford University Press, 1979), especially ch. 15, "1944: Victories and Doubts."

27. For an account of the birth of Federal Union, see John Pinder and Richard Mayne, *The Pioneers* (Basingstoke: Macmillan, 1990), especially chs. 1–2.

28. See Walter Lipgens, *A History of European Integration 1945–1947* (Oxford: Clarendon Press, 1987), 53–57 and 114–16, for a fuller account. Charles F. Delzell, "The European Federalist Movement in Italy," *Journal of Modern History* 32, no. 3 (1960): 241–50, gives a still excellent overview of the birth of federalist ideas in Italy.

29. Lipgens, *History of European Integration*, 376.

30. See Lipgens, *History of European Integration*, 380–85, for details of the "Third Force" concept.

31. For the "Keep Left" group, see Alan Bullock, *Ernest Bevin* (Oxford: Oxford University Press, 1985), 395–98.

32. Altiero Spinelli, *Europa Terza Forza*, ed. Piero Graglia (Bologna: Il Mulino 2000), 13.

33. Spinelli, *Europa Terza Forza*, 158.

34. Quotation based upon the text given in Uwe Kitzinger, *The European Common Market and Community* (New York: Barnes & Noble, 1967), 35–37.

35. For Churchill's attitudes on European integration, see most recently Roy Jenkins, *Churchill* (London: Macmillan, 1999), 813–19. Lipgens, *History of European Integration*, gives a short account of the formation of the UEM, 323–34.

36. This is a simplified account of a very complex set of negotiations between the various federalist groups. See Lipgens, *History of European Integration*, 657–84, for further details.

37. G. Sharp, *Europe Unites! The Hague Congress and After* (London: Hollis & Carter, 1949), 38–39.

38. Sharp, *Europe Unites!*, 68–71.

39. Sharp, *Europe Unites!*, 88–89.

40. See Richard Aldrich, "European Integration: An American Intelligence Connection," in *Building Post-War Europe: National Decision-Makers and European Institutions, 1948–1963*, ed. Anne Deighton (Basingstoke: Macmillan, 1995), 159–79, for CIA financing of the European Movement.

41. Bullock, *Ernest Bevin*, 516–19.

42. Paul-Henri Spaak, *The Continuing Battle* (London: Weidenfeld and Nicholson, 1971), 144–46.

43. Kunz, *Butter and Guns*, 51.

44. See A. H. Robertson, *The Council of Europe: Its Structure, Function and Achievements* (London: Stevens, 1961), 6–7.

45. Bullock, *Ernest Bevin*, 82.

46. Spaak, *Continuing Battle*, 266.

47. This paragraph drew mostly upon Gordon L. Weil, *The European Convention on Human Rights* (Leyden: Sythoff, 1963).

48. Henry Ashby Turner, *Germany from Partition to Unification* (New Haven, Conn.: Yale University Press, 1992), 12.

49. Figures quoted in P. M. H. Bell, *The World since 1945* (London: Arnold, 2001), 93.

50. Georges Bidault, *Resistance: The Autobiography of Georges Bidault* (London: Weidenfeld and Nicholson, 1967), 161.

51. Milward, *Reconstruction of Western Europe*, 154.

52. Richard Mayne, *La Comunità europea* (Milan: Garzanti, 1963), 101.

53. Figures from Milward, *Reconstruction of Western Europe*, 367.

54. Hans-Peter Schwarz, *Konrad Adenauer: German Statesman and Politician in a Period of War, Revolution and Reconstruction, vol. 1* (Providence, R.I.: Berghahn, 1995), 496.

55. James Chace, *Acheson* (New York: Simon & Schuster, 1998), 242–43.

56. Duchêne, *Jean Monnet*, 200. See also William Hitchcock, "France, the Western Alliance and the Origins of the Schuman Plan, 1948–1950," *Diplomatic History* 21, no. 4 (1997): 603–30.

57. Duchêne, *Jean Monnet*, 181.

58. This sentence reflects the standard account given by Monnet himself and what Milward calls his "disciples." Milward argues in *The Reconstruction of Western Europe*, 395–96, that there was considerable input from the French foreign ministry. He adds that "ultimate credit for the Schuman plan must go to Schuman himself . . . he had the courage to seize the moment and translate into reality . . . suggestions and ideas which the fearfulness of others had left trembling on the brink of actuality" (396).

59. Schwarz, *Konrad Adenauer*, 504.

60. Acheson quoted in David S. McClellan, *Dean Acheson: The State Department Years* (New York: Dodd, Mead, 1976), 251.

61. Hogan, *Marshall Plan*, 367.

62. Quotation based upon the text in Kitzinger, *European Common Market*, 37–39.

63. Schwarz, *Konrad Adenauer*, 510.

64. Schwarz, *Konrad Adenauer*, 509.

65. Hugo Young, *This Blessed Plot* (London: Macmillan, 1998), 56.

66. Jean Monnet, *Mémoires* (Paris: Fayard, 1971), 316.

67. Quoted Pinder and Mayne, *The Pioneers*, 120.

68. Quoted Edmund Dell, *The British Abdication of Leadership in Europe* (Oxford: Oxford University Press, 1995), 176.

69. Dell, *British Abdication*, 296.

70. Bullock, *Ernest Bevin*, 781.

71. The Labour Party, *European Unity* (London, 1950), 4.

72. Marjolin, *Architect of European Unity*, 213.

73. "The chopped up character of Europe has become an absurd anachronism." Robert Schuman, *Pour L'Europe* (Paris: Editions Nagel, 1963), 19.

74. Kunz, *Butter and Guns*, 51.

75. George W. Ball, *The Past Has Another Pattern* (New York: Norton, 1982), 216.

CHAPTER 3. EVER CLOSER UNION

1. Jean Monnet, *Les Etats-Unis d'Europe ont commencées* (Luxembourg: ECSC, 1952).

2. Hans-Peter Schwarz, *Konrad Adenauer: German Statesman and Politician in a Period of War, Revolution and Reconstruction, vol. 1* (Providence, R.I.: Berghahn, 1995), 619.

3. Political and Economic Planning (PEP), *European Organisations: An Objective Survey* (London: Unwin, 1959), 236.

4. Jean Monnet, *Mémoires* (Paris: Fayard, 1971), 438.

5. Robert Marjolin, *Architect of European Unity: Memoirs 1911–1986* (London: Weidenfeld and Nicholson, 1989), 270.

6. PEP, *European Organisations*, 242.

7. See especially William Diebold's *The European Coal and Steel Community* (New York: Council on Foreign Relations, 1960), and Arnold Zurcher's *The Struggle to Unite Europe* (New York: New York University Press, 1958).

8. For Italy's exemption on steel and its cautious approach to the ECSC negotiation in general, see Ruggero Ranieri, "L'Italia e i negoziati sul Piano Schuman," in *L'Italia e la politica di Potenza in Europa, 1945–1950*, eds. E. Di Nolfo, R. H. Raniero, and B. Vigezzi (Milan: Marzorati, 1986), 547–73.

9. The analysis owes much to the excellent chapter on the ECSC in PEP, *European Organisations*, 229–94. More recently, see John Gillingham, *Coal, Steel and the Rebirth of Europe, 1945–1955: The Germans and the French from Ruhr Conflict to Economic Community* (Cambridge: Cambridge University Press, 1991).

10. This point is a central argument in Marc Trachtenberg, *A Constructed Peace: The Making of the European Settlement 1945–1963* (Princeton, N.J.: Princeton University Press, 1999). See also James Chace, *Dean Acheson* (New York: Simon & Schuster, 1998), especially ch. 23.

11. Pascaline Winand, *Eisenhower, Kennedy and the United States of Europe* (New York: St. Martin's, 1993), 27–28.

12. For details, see Kevin Ruane, *The Rise and Fall of the European Defence Community* (London: Macmillan, 2000). For an interesting contemporary account, see H.G.L., "The European Defence Community," *World Today* 8, no. 6: 236–48.

13. Antonio Varsori, *La Cenerentola d'Europa? L'Italia e l'integrazione europea dal 1947 a oggi* (Catanzaro, Italy: Rubbettino, 2010), 99–105, summarizes Italy's role. See also Piero Graglia, *Altiero Spinelli* (Bologna: Il Mulino, 2008), 345–55, for Spinelli's persuasion of De Gasperi. The Italians, for domestic political reasons (the Communist Party was agitating against the EDC), needed to give the EDC a gloss of political respectability.

14. For the EPC, see Rita Cardozo, "The Project for a Political Community 1952–54," in *The Dynamics of European Union*, ed. Roy Pryce (London: Routledge, 1989), 49–77, and Richard T. Griffiths, *Europe's First Constitution: The European Political Community, 1952–1954* (London: The Federal Trust, 2000).

15. Bino Olivi, *L'Europa difficile* (Bologna: Il Mulino, 2000), 43.

16. In a book published in 1950, Dulles wrote:

> Since disunity is so perilous and unity so precious . . . why, may we ask, does integration not happen? It does not happen because of the tradition of complete national independence has become so deeply rooted . . . vested interests have always been powerful enough to prevent peaceful change to unity. Recurrent efforts have been made to unite Europe by violence. Napoleon tried it; so did the Kaiser; so did Hitler; so, now, does Stalin. . . . The United States now has the opportunity to bring about peacefully what every western leader, without regard to nation or party, recognizes ought to be done, but will not be done unless there is friendly but firm outside pressure. The United States can and should take that opportunity and exert that pressure.

J. Foster Dulles, *War or Peace* (New York: Macmillan, 1950), 213–15.

17. Ruane, *Rise and Fall*, 47.

18. Quoted in Winand, *Eisenhower, Kennedy*, 50.

19. Paul-Henri Spaak, *The Continuing Battle* (London: Weidenfeld and Nicholson, 1971), 157.

20. Ruane, *Rise and Fall*, 92–93.

21. Ruane, *Rise and Fall*, 93. See also Winand, *Eisenhower, Kennedy*, 59.

22. Quoted Frank Giles, *The Locust Years: The Story of the French Fourth Republic 1946–1958* (London: Secker & Warburg, 1991), 177.

23. Quotes are from N. Leites and C. de la Malène, "Paris from EDC to WEU," *World Politics* no. 2 (January 1957): 193–219. See also Raymond Aron, *France Defeats EDC* (New York: Praeger, 1957).

24. Quoted in Winand, *Eisenhower, Kennedy*, 62.

25. Monnet, *Mémoires*, 465.

26. For British diplomacy and the WEU, see Anne Deighton, "The Last Piece of the Jigsaw: Britain and the Creation of the Western European Union, 1954," *Contemporary European History* 7, no. 2 (July 1998): 181–96.

27. Monnet, *Mémoires*, 466.

28. Marjolin, *Architect of European Unity*, 214.

29. Alan Milward, *The Reconstruction of Western Europe 1945–1951* (London: Routledge, 1984), 326.

30. Varsori, *La Cenerentola d'Europa?*, 81–82. For a more extended discussion of La Malfa's policies, see Lorenzo Mechi, *L'Europa di Ugo La Malfa. La via italiana alla modernizzazione, 1942–1979* (Milan: Franco Angeli, 2003).

31. Marjolin, *Architect of European Unity*, 220.

32. For the Beyen Plan, see Richard T. Griffiths and Alan Milward, "The Beyen Plan and the European Political Community," in *Noi si mura: Selected Working Papers of the European University Institute*, ed. W. Maiohoffer (Florence: EUI, 1986), 596–622.

33. The text of the Messina communiqué is taken from U. Kitzinger, *The European Common Market and Community* (New York: Barnes & Noble, 1967), 69.

34. PEP, *Statements of the Action Committee for a United States of Europe* (London: PEP, 1969), 11.

35. PEP, *Statements of the Action Committee*, 16–18.

36. *Rapport des Chefs de Délégation des Affaires Etrangères* (The Spaak Report), Brussels, April 21, 1956, pp. 135. For a short account of the Spaak Committee's work, see Michel Dumoulin, "Le travaux du Comité Spaak (juillet 1955–avril 1956)" in *Il rilancio dell'Europa e i trattati di Roma*, ed. Enrico Serra (Milan: Giuffrè, 1989), 195–210.

37. Spaak, *Continuing Battle*, 240.

38. Robert H. Lieshout, *The Struggle for the Organization of Europe* (Northampton, Mass.: Edward Elgar, 1999), 159–65.

39. Marjolin, *Architect of European Unity*, 281.

40. Andrew Moravcsik, *The Choice for Europe: Social Purpose and State Power from Messina to Maastricht* (Ithaca, N.Y.: Cornell University Press, 1998), 96.

41. Marjolin, *Architect of European Unity*, 281.

42. Marjolin, *Architect of European Unity*, 285.

43. Marjolin, *Architect of European Unity*, 288. There is an enormous literature on how France finally opted for involvement in the EEC. According to Craig Parsons, *A Certain Idea of Europe* (Ithaca, N.Y.: Cornell University Press, 2003), 115, "farm-

ers, technocrats, business and Socialists" were "consistently divided on the EEC's appeal." The two most powerful figures in the French political firmament, Charles de Gaulle and Pierre Mendès-France, were both opposed to the EEC idea. "The impulse to the EEC came from a diverse group of leaders who attached varying substantive goals to a shared model of a desirable Europe." Of these leaders, Guy Mollet was the most important.

44. Hugo Young, *This Blessed Plot* (London: Macmillan, 1998), 88. For more detailed accounts, see Simon Burgess and Geoffrey Edwards, "The Six Plus One: British Policy Making and the Question of European Economic Integration, 1955," *International Affairs* 64, no. 3 (Summer 1988): 393–413; John W. Young, "The 'Parting of Ways?' Britain, the Messina Conference and the Spaak Committee, June–December 1955," in *British Foreign Policy, 1945–1956*, eds. Michael Dockrill and John W. Young (Basingstoke: Macmillan, 1989), 197–220.

45. Quoted Parsons, *A Certain Idea of Europe*, 105.

46. For "Plan G," see Martin Schaad, "Plan G: A Counterblast? British Policy towards the Messina Countries, 1956," *Contemporary European History* 7, no. 1 (March 1998): 39–60.

47. P. M. H. Bell, *Britain and France 1940–1994: The Long Separation* (London: Longman, 1997), 146–50.

48. Thus Hanns Jürgen Küsters writes: "The failure of the Franco-British Suez adventure once again made France's limited role as a great power between the two superpowers abundantly clear to the Mollet government. In a quest for closer co-operation with its European partners it gave up its hesitant attitude to the Common Market in the period that followed." H. J. Küsters, "The Treaties of Rome (1955–57)," in *The Dynamics of European Union*, ed. R. Pryce (London: Routledge, 1989), 90–91.

49. Marjolin, *Architect of European Unity*, 297.

50. See Hans-Peter Schwarz, *Konrad Adenauer: German Politician and Statesman in a Period of War, Revolution and Reconstruction, vol. 2* (Providence R.I.: Berghahn, 1997), 240–45, for Adenauer's visit to Paris in November 1956.

51. Bell, *Britain and France*, 155.

52. Lieshout, *The Struggle*, 168. P-H. Laurent, "The Diplomacy of the Rome Treaty 1955–57," *Journal of Contemporary History* 7 (1972): 209–20; see especially 213.

53. Winand, *Eisenhower, Kennedy*, 93. Pierre Mélandri, *Les Etats-Unis et le "défi" européen, 1955–1958* (Paris: Presses Universitaires de France, 1975), 119, makes the same joke.

54. Moravcsik, *Choice for Europe*, 88.

55. An excellent account of Britain's Free Trade Association proposals and subsequent decision to attempt to enter the EEC is to be found in Roy Denman, *Missed Chances: Britain and Europe in the Twentieth Century* (London: Indigo, 1996), ch. 11. For two contemporary accounts, see Uwe Kitzinger, "Europe: The Six and the Seven," *International Organization* 14 (Winter 1960): 20–36, and Agostino Soldati, "Economic Disintegration in Europe," *Foreign Affairs* 38, no. 1 (1958): 75–83. The quotations are from Soldati.

56. On EFTA, Wolfram Kaiser, "Challenges to the Community: The Creation, Crisis and Consolidation of the European Free Trade Association, 1958–1972," *Journal of European Integration History* 3, no. 1 (1997): 7–34, is splendid.

57. For U.S. support of the Euratom project, see Jonathan E. Helmreich, "The United States and the Formation of Euratom," *Diplomatic History* 15, no. 3 (1991): 387–410. The United States made the new Community its interlocutor in Europe rather than making bilateral deals and also encouraged Euratom to be the priority buyer of Congolese uranium ore from 1960, substituting for Great Britain and the United States itself.

58. PEP, *Statements of the Action Committee*, 22.

59. PEP, *Statements of the Action Committee*, 23.

60. Altiero Spinelli, *Diario europeo vol. 1* (Bologna: Il Mulino, 1989), 310. The original Italian is "gigantesco imbroglio." The federalists' objection was to the intergovernmental character of the EEC treaty, which, Spinelli argued in a 1957 article, "deprived" Europeans of "any institutional instrument that would permit them to be the European people and to act as the European people." See Daniele Pasquinucci, *Europeismo e democrazia: Altiero Spinelli e la sinistra europea, 1950–1986* (Bologna: Il Mulino, 2000), 142.

61. Marjolin, *Architect of European Unity*, 303.

62. Guy Mollet quoted in Frédéric Turpin, "Alle origini della politica europea di cooperazione allo sviluppo: la Francia e la politica di associazione Europa-Africa (1957–1975)," *Ventunesimo Secolo* 6 (October 2007): 137.

63. For the first Commission, see Michel Dumoulin, ed., *The European Commission, 1958–1972* (Luxembourg: European Communities, 2007), especially chs. 1, 2, 5. The other members of the first Commission were Robert Lemaignen (France), Michel Rasquin (Luxembourg), Hans von der Groeben (West Germany), and Piero Malvestiti and Giuseppe Petrilli (Italy). Rasquin was replaced by Lambert Schaus within months; the two Italians were also replaced during the lifetime of the first Commission by Giuseppe Caron and Lionello Levi Sandri, respectively.

64. Anthony Arnull, *The European Union and Its Court of Justice* (Oxford: Oxford University Press, 1999), 79.

65. Arnull, *European Union*, 81.

66. Quoted Arnull, *European Union*, 83. For recent historical scholarship on the ECJ's early decisions, see Bill Davies, "Meek Acceptance? The West German Ministries' Reaction to the Van Gend en Loos and Costa Decisions," *Journal of European Integration History* 14, no. 2 (2008): 76, and Morten Rasmussen, "The Origins of a Legal Revolution: The Early History of the European Court of Justice," *Journal of European Integration History* 14, no. 2 (2008): 77–98. Rasmussen contends that the judges' position was the fruit of federalist legal scholarship that had been steadily gaining ground in the 1950s, but also of sheer happenstance. In 1962, just in time for Van Gend en Loos, Charles de Gaulle appointed Robert Lecourt to be the French judge on the Court. This decision remains inexplicable since he was a prominent federalist and a member of the Action Committee for a United Europe. Together with the contemporaneous appointment of an Italian federalist, Alberto Trabucchi, Lecourt's appointment gave the Court an activist majority.

67. Alan Milward, *The European Rescue of the Nation State* (London: Routledge, 1992), 7.

68. Milward, *European Rescue*, 223.

69. Milward, *European Rescue*, 341.

70. Ernst Haas, *The Uniting of Europe*, 2nd ed. (Stanford, Calif.: Stanford University Press, 1968), 16.

71. Haas, *Uniting of Europe*, 527.

72. Haas, *Uniting of Europe*, 311.

73. Haas, *Uniting of Europe*, 527.

74. Milward, *European Rescue*, 13.

CHAPTER 4. IN THE SHADOW OF THE GENERAL

1. Hans von der Groeben, *The European Community: The Formative Years* (Brussels: European Commission, 1985), 39.

2. See Frances Lynch, "De Gaulle's First Veto: France, the Rueff Plan and the Free Trade Area," European University Institute Working Paper no. 8/98, for background on de Gaulle's decision.

3. Von der Groeben, *European Community*, 84.

4. Still the best study of the EC's policy toward its former colonies since the early 1960s is Enzo Grilli, *The EC and the Developing Countries* (Cambridge: Cambridge University Press, 1994).

5. Andrew Moravcsik, *The Choice for Europe: Social Purpose and State Power from Messina to Maastricht* (Ithaca, N.Y.: Cornell University Press, 1998), 180.

6. Ann-Christina Knudsen, *Farmers on Welfare: The Making of Europe's Common Agricultural Policy* (Ithaca, N.Y.: Cornell University Press, 2009).

7. This account of the CAP relies on European Community Information Service, *A Common Market for Agriculture* (Brussels: European Communities, 1967).

8. Moravcsik, *Choice for Europe*, 180.

9. Moravcsik, *Choice for Europe*, 7.

10. The text of Eisenhower's reply is included as an appendix in Lois Pattison de Ménil, *Who Speaks for Europe? The Vision of Charles de Gaulle* (London: Weidenfeld and Nicholson, 1977), 193–94.

11. Pierre Gerbet, "In Search of Political Union: The Fouchet Plan Negotiations," in *The Dynamics of European Union*, ed. Roy Price (London: Croom Helm, 1987), 114.

12. The text of the French draft is included as an appendix in Pattison de Ménil, *Who Speaks for Europe?*, 195–200.

13. Hedley Bull, "Civilian Power Europe: A Contradiction in Terms?" *Journal of Common Market Studies* 21 (September–December 1982): 149–70.

14. Stanley Hoffmann, "De Gaulle, Europe and the Atlantic Alliance," *International Organization* 18 (Winter 1964): 2.

15. Arthur Schlesinger, *A Thousand Days: John F. Kennedy in the White House* (New York: Houghton Mifflin, 1965), is still relevant. See especially chapters on "The Not So Grand Design" and "Two Europes: De Gaulle and Kennedy." John Newhouse, *De Gaulle and the Anglo-Saxons* (New York: Viking, 1970) is an important book.

16. Brian Crozier, *Charles de Gaulle* (London: Eyre Methuen, 1973), 533.

17. Von der Groeben, *European Community*, 112.

18. Uwe Kitzinger, *The European Common Market and Community* (New York: Barnes & Noble, 1967), 166–68.

19. Frank Costigliola, "The Failed Design: Kennedy, de Gaulle and the Struggle for Europe," *Diplomatic History* 8, no. 3 (1984): 227–52, argues that the Atlantic Community was a way of maintaining U.S. control over the EEC. Denise Artaud, *Révue d'Histoire Moderne et Contemporaine* 29, no. 2 (1982): 235–66, concurs. But see also the work of Pascaline Winand, *Eisenhower, Kennedy and the United States of Europe* (New York: St Martin's Press, 1993) and J. G. Giauque, *Grand Designs and Visions of Unity: The Atlantic Powers and the Reorganization of Western Europe, 1955–1963* (Durham: North Carolina University Press, 2002), which provide a more positive interpretation of Kennedy's policy.

20. The most detailed account of the Fouchet negotiations in English remains Alessandro Silj, Europe's *Political Puzzle: A Study of the Fouchet Negotiations and the 1963 Veto* (Cambridge, Mass.: Harvard Center for International Affairs, 1977). My account of the Fouchet negotiations, however, closely follows Maurice Vaisse, "De Gaulle, l'Italie et le projet d'Union politique européenne, 1958–1963. Chronique d'un échec annoncé," *Revue d'histoire moderne et contemporaine* 42, no. 3 (1995): 658–69. The quotations from de Gaulle are from this source. Joseph Luns' views are reported in J. Vanke, "An Impossible Union: Dutch Objections to the Fouchet Plan, 1959–1962," *Cold War History* 2, no. 1 (2001): 95–112 at 97. A broader account of how the Netherlands saw the political union negotiations is provided by Mathieu Segers, "De Gaulle's Race to the Bottom: The Netherlands, France and the Interwoven Problems of British EEC Membership and European Political Union," *Contemporary European History* 19, no. 2 (2010): 111–132.

21. De Gaulle's press conference is quoted at length in Pattison de Ménil, *Who Speaks for Europe?*, 73–76.

22. Hugo Young, *This Blessed Plot* (London: Macmillan, 1998), 105–6.

23. Charles de Gaulle, *Memoirs of Hope: Renewal and Endeavor* (New York: Simon & Schuster, 1971), 188.

24. See Alistair Horne, *Macmillan 1957–1986* (London: Macmillan, 1989), 256.

25. Heath's speech is reprinted in Kitzinger, *European Common Market*, 151–63.

26. Heath in Kitzinger, *European Common Market*, 158.

27. Heath in Kitzinger, *European Common Market*, 162.

28. Quoted N. Piers Ludlow, *Dealing with Britain: The Six and the First UK Application to the EEC* (Cambridge: Cambridge University Press, 1997), 104.

29. Ludlow, *Dealing with Britain*, 122.

30. Alain Peyrefitte, *C'était de Gaulle* (Paris: Plon, 1995), 299–303 for de Gaulle's account of the Champs summit.

31. See Ludlow, *Dealing with Britain*, 138–53, for a full account of these developments.

32. For a full text of Gaitskell's speech, see *The Eurosceptical Reader*, ed. Martin Holmes (London: Macmillan, 1996), 13–38.

33. For the Nassau conference, see Horne, *Macmillan*, 437–43.

34. Hoffmann, "De Gaulle, Europe and the Atlantic Alliance," 14.

35. Moravcsik, *Choice for Europe*, 189. Moravcsik amplified his views in two lengthy articles in "De Gaulle between Grain and Grandeur: The Political Economy of French EC Policy, 1958–1970," *Journal of Cold War Studies* 2, nos. 1 and 2 (2000), with replies by Stanley Hoffmann, John Keeler, Alan S. Milward, John

Gillingham, Jeffrey Vanke, and Marc Trachtenberg. Moravcsik's original work in *A Choice for Europe* has been criticized by Robert Lieshout, Mathieu Seegers, and Johanna van der Vleuten, "De Gaulle, Moravcsik and the Choice for Europe: Soft Sources, Weak Evidence," *Journal of Cold War Studies* 6, no. 4 (2004): 89–139.

36. I am quoting the translation of de Gaulle's press conference in Kitzinger, *European Common Market*, 185.

37. Jean Lacouture, *De Gaulle: The Ruler 1945–1970* (London: Harvill, 1991), 359.

38. De Gaulle, *Memoirs of Hope*, 220.

39. Oliver Bange, *The EEC Crisis of 1963* (London: Macmillan, 2000), 63–67.

40. Hans-Peter Schwarz, *Konrad Adenauer: A German Politician and Statesman in a Period of War, Revolution and Reconstruction, vol. 2* (Providence, R.I.: Berghahn, 1997), 615.

41. De Gaulle, *Memoirs of Hope*, 180.

42. Schwarz, *Konrad Adenauer, vol. 2*, 621.

43. Lacouture, *De Gaulle*, 341.

44. Schwarz, *Konrad Adenauer, vol. 2*, 605.

45. Schwarz, *Konrad Adenauer, vol. 2*, 672.

46. Bange, *EEC Crisis*, 157.

47. Quoted Horne, *Macmillan*, 448.

48. N. Piers Ludlow, *The European Community and the Crises of the 1960s: Negotiating the Gaullist Challenge* (London: Routledge, 2006), 42.

49. Von der Groeben, *European Community*, 175.

50. Hallstein's speech was subsequently printed in the *World Today*, January 1965, 10–24. All quotations are from the published text.

51. See, most recently, Wilfried Loth, "The Empty Chair Crisis," in *The European Commission, 1958–1972: History and Memories*, ed. Michel Dumoulin (Luxembourg: European Communities, 2007), 91–108.

52. Robert Marjolin, *Architect of European Unity: Memoirs 1911–1986* (London: Weidenfeld and Nicholson, 1989), 350.

53. John Lambert, "The Constitutional Crisis 1965–66," *Journal of Common Market Studies* 4 (1965–1966): 195–228 at 202. The phrase "Hallstein's gamble" is Ludlow's, *The European Community and the Crises of the 1960s*, 65.

54. Lambert, "Constitutional Crisis," 204.

55. Marjolin, *Architect of European Unity*, 350.

56. Lambert, "Constitutional Crisis," 205.

57. Loth, "The Empty Chair Crisis," 94, reprints a May 19, 1965, memorandum from Karl-Heinz Narjes, Hallstein's chef de cabinet, to the president of the Commission in which it is suggested that Hallstein should recommend the German government to "guide the five others from behind the scenes" and that The Five should be "willing to confront France unremittingly with the alternatives of complying with the Treaty or breaking with it on the international stage."

58. N. Piers Ludlow, "Challenging French Leadership in Europe: Germany, Italy, the Netherlands and the Outbreak of the Empty Chair Crisis of 1965–1966," *Contemporary European History* 8, no. 2 (1999): 231–48, argues (p. 233) that The Five were so frustrated at the "unequal distribution of benefits and costs of integration" that they decided to call France's bluff. It was a bad call.

59. John Newhouse, *Collision in Brussels* (London: Faber, 1967), 70. The figures on Italy's agricultural trade deficit are from Ludlow, *The European Community and the Crises of the 1960s*, 63.

60. Newhouse, *Collision in Brussels*, 108.

61. Marjolin, *Architect of European Unity*, 353.

62. Peyrefitte, *C'était de Gaulle*, 292, 297.

63. Lambert's translation, "Constitutional Crisis," 216.

64. Quoted in Lambert, "Constitutional Crisis," 226.

65. Marjolin, *Architect of European Unity*, 356.

66. Ludlow, *The European Community and the Crises of the 1960s*, 123.

67. Young, *This Blessed Plot*, 196. For the second British entry bid, see Helen Parr, *Britain's Policy towards the European Communities, 1964–1967* (London: Routledge, 2006).

68. Stanley Hoffmann, "Obstinate or Obsolete? The Fate of the Nation-State and the Case of Western Europe," *Daedelus* 95 (Summer 1966): 892–908.

69. For statistics, see Eric Bussière, "Not Quite a Common Market Yet," in *The European Commission, 1958–1972*, ed. Michel Dumoulin, 294.

70. Bussière, "Not Quite a Common Market Yet," 297.

71. John Pinder, "Positive and Negative Integration: Some Problems of Economic Union in the EEC," *World Today* (March 1968): 90.

72. Pinder, "Positive and Negative Integration," 98.

73. Kiran Klaus Patel, "Europeanization a Contre-coeur: West Germany and Agricultural Integration, 1945–1975," in *Fertile Ground for Europe? The History of European Integration and the Common Agricultural Policy since 1945* (Baden Baden: Nomos, 2009), 150.

74. For the EEC and the Kennedy Round, see Lucia Coppolaro, "The Six, Agriculture and GATT," in *Fertile Ground for Europe?*, ed. Kiran Klaus Patel, 201–19, and N. Piers Ludlow, "The Emergence of a Commercial Heavyweight: The Kennedy Round Negotiations and the European Community in the 1960s," *Diplomacy & Statecraft* 18, no. 2 (2007) : 351–68.

75. For Lyndon B. Johnson and the Europeans, see Thomas A. Schwarz, *Lyndon Johnson and Europe: In the Shadow of Vietnam* (Cambridge, Mass.: Harvard University Press, 2003).

76. For statistics, see Gérard Bossuat and Anais Legendre, "The Commission's Role in External Relations," in *The European Commission*, ed. Michel Dumoulin, 368.

CHAPTER 5. WEATHERING THE STORM

1. Roy Jenkins, *A Life at the Centre* (London: Macmillan, 1994), 490.

2. For an in-depth assessment of the Hague Conference, see the papers collected in the *Journal of European Integration History* 9, no. 2 (2003).

3. The "Werner Report," supplement to Bull. EC, no. 11/70, 14.

4. "Werner Report," 28.

5. "Werner Report," 26.

6. "Werner Report," 12.

7. "Werner Report," 13.

8. The "Vedel Report," supplement to Bull. EC, no. 4/72.

9. The "Luxembourg Report" of EC Foreign Ministers. Bull. EC, no. 10/70.

10. Uwe Kitzinger, *Diplomacy and Persuasion: How Britain Joined the Common Market* (London: Thames & Hudson, 1973), 29.

11. Roy Denman, *Missed Chances: Britain and Europe in the Twentieth Century* (London: Indigo, 1996), 223.

12. For the negotiation, see Sir Con O'Neill, *Britain's Entry into the European Community* (London: Frank Cass, 2000), edited and with an introduction by Sir David Hannay.

13. Quoted in Edward Heath, *The Course of My Life* (London: Hodder & Stoughton, 1998), 372.

14. *Agence Europe* no. 669, October 20, 1970, quoted the Commission as saying that if in an enlarged Community "unacceptable situations were to appear" then the "very life of the Community would require the Institutions to find a just solution for them."

15. Heath, *Course of My Life*, 366–72.

16. Denman, *Missed Chances*, 240–41.

17. *Spectator* n. 7540 (December 30, 1972): 1037.

18. For Danish membership, see Morten Rasmussen, "The Hesitant European: History of Denmark's Accession to the European Communities 1970–1973," *Journal of European Integration History* 11, no. 2 (2005): 45–76.

19. For Irish membership, see Maurice Fitzgerald, "Ireland's Relations with the EEC: From the Treaties of Rome to Membership," *Journal of European Integration History* 7, no. 1 (2001): 11–24.

20. The EC's role at the Helsinki conference has been the subject of much recent academic interest. Daniel C. Thomas, *The Helsinki Effect: International Norms, Human Rights and the Demise of Communism* (Princeton, N.J.: Princeton University Press, 2001), writing from a "constructivist" perspective, and an Italian historian, Angela Romano, *From Détente in Europe to European Détente: How the West Shaped the Helsinki CSCE* (Brussels: Peter Lang, 2009), have strongly made the case for arguing that the EC Nine, working closely together via the new EPC process, played a decisive role in putting human rights on the agenda. The extent to which this success can be attributed to coordinated action is dubious. See Sara Lamberti, "Il dibattito storiografico sulla Conferenza di Helsinki," *Ricerche di storia politica XIII* (Second Series) no. 2 (2010).

21. The communiqué of the 1972 Paris summit of EC leaders is to be found in Bull. EC, no. 10/72.

22. Heath, *Course of My Life*, 392.

23. Soames's report (Diplomatic Report no. 464/72) is reproduced in the documentary appendix of Ilaria Poggiolini, *Alle origini dell'Europa allargata: La Gran Bretagna e l'adesione alla CEE (1972–1973)* (Milan: Unicopli, 2004).

24. Ironically, this investment by U.S. corporations was seen as a major threat to Europe's future in a book that was very influential throughout Europe, Jean-Jacques Servan-Schreiber's *Le Défi Américain* (Paris: Editions Denoel, 1967), published in English as *The American Challenge* (London: Penguin, 1969).

25. Franco Garino, "Dopo i provvedimenti economici di Nixon," *Relazioni internazionali* (September 5, 1971): 873–74, states that the EEC member states had

total reserves of $37,099 million at the end of July 1971. Forty-four percent of these holdings were in dollars. West Germany's holdings were $17,664 million, 61 percent of which were in dollars.

26. William Glenn Gray, "'Number One in Europe': The Startling Emergence of the Deutsche Mark, 1968–1969," *Central European History* 39, no. 1 (2006): 56–78.

27. Diane Kunz, *Butter and Guns: America's Cold War Economic Diplomacy* (New York: Free Press, 1997), 218.

28. Robert Solomon, *The International Monetary System 1945–1981* (New York: Harper and Row, 1982), 196.

29. William Diebold, "The Economic System at Stake," *Foreign Affairs* 51, no. 1 (1972): 170–72.

30. Solomon, *International Monetary System*, 233.

31. Peter Ludlow, *The Making of the EMS* (London: Butterfields, 1982), 8.

32. Henry Kissinger, *Years of Upheaval* (London: Weidenfeld and Nicholson), 152–53.

33. Kissinger, *Years of Upheaval*, 153.

34. James O. Goldsborough, "France, the European Crisis and the Alliance," *Foreign Affairs* 52, no. 3 (1974): 547.

35. Kissinger, *Years of Upheaval*, 192–94.

36. Fiona Venn, "International Cooperation versus National Self-Interest: The United States and Europe during the 1973–1974 Oil Crisis," in *The United States and the European Alliance since 1945*, eds. Kathleen Burk and Melvyn Stokes (Oxford: Berg, 1999), 71–98 (here, 72–73).

37. Henri Simonet, "Energy and the Future of Europe," *Foreign Affairs* 53, no. 3 (1975): 451.

38. Meeting of the Heads of State and Government, Copenhagen December 14–15, 1973. For preparation, see Bull. EC, 11/73, 25–27. For communiqué, see Bull. EC, 12/73, 6–11.

39. Françoise de la Serre, "L'Europe des neuf et le conflit Israélo-Arabe," *Revue Française de Science Politique* 24, no. 4 (1974): 804.

40. Goldsborough, "France, the European Crisis and the Alliance," 543.

41. Helmut Schmidt, *Men and Powers* (New York: Random House, 1989), 163.

42. Bino Olivi, *L'Europa difficile* (Bologna: Il Mulino, 2000), 160.

43. Venn, "International Cooperation versus National Self-Interest," 86.

44. Goldsborough, "France, the European Crisis and the Alliance," 539.

45. See the section on "European Political Cooperation," in Bull. EC, no. 6/74, for an account of the meeting of the EC foreign ministers in Bonn on June 10, 1974, at which this decision was reached. See also Richard McAllister, *From EC to EU: An Historical and Political Survey* (London: Routledge, 1997), 98.

46. For more detail on the creation of the European Council, see Emmanuel Mourlan-Druol, "Filling the Leadership Vacuum? The Creation of the European Council in 1974," *Cold War History* 10, no. 3 (2010): 315–39.

47. Leo Tindemans, *European Union*, supplement Bull. EC, no. 1/76, 12–13.

48. Tindemans, *European Union*, 30.

49. Tindemans, *European Union*, 16–18.

50. Tindemans, *European Union*, 20–21.

51. Tindemans, *European Union*, 28.

52. Tindemans Report, 29.

53. Tindemans Report, 29–32.

54. Schmidt, *Men and Powers*, 181.

55. Jonathon Carr, *Helmut Schmidt: Helmsman of Germany* (London: Weidenfeld and Nicholson, 1985), 138.

56. Ludlow, *Making of the EMS*, 71.

57. Schmidt, *Men and Powers*, 273.

58. Ludlow, *Making of the EMS*, 74–76.

59. Jenkins, *Life at the Centre*, 473.

60. Valéry Giscard d'Estaing, *Towards a New Democracy* (London: Collins, 1977), 100.

61. Giscard, *Towards a New Democracy*, 140.

62. See Jenkins, *Life at the Centre*, 327–49, and Peter Byrd, "The Labour Party and the European Community 1970–1975," *Journal of Common Market Studies* 13 (1974–1975): 476–78, for the internal struggles within the Labour Party over the referendum.

63. Jenkins, *Life at the Centre*, 459.

64. Jenkins, *Life at the Centre*, 461–63.

65. Roy Jenkins, "Europe: Present Challenges and Future Prospects," Bull. EC, no. 10/77, 12–13.

66. Jenkins, "Europe: Present Challenges and Future Prospects," 13.

67. European Commission, "The Prospect of Economic and Monetary Union," Bull. EC, no. 10/77, 22.

68. Jenkins, *Life at the Centre*, 470.

69. Jenkins, *Life at the Centre*, 470.

70. Jenkins, *Life at the Centre*, 467.

71. Ludlow, *Making of the EMS*, 89. See also Jonathan Storey, "The Launching of the EMS: An Analysis of Change in Foreign Economic Policy," *Political Studies* 36 (1988): 397–412, for a meticulous account of how and why the EMS was adopted.

72. Ludlow, *Making of the EMS*, 92.

73. Ludlow, *Making of the EMS*, 182.

74. The quotes are from Bernard Connolly, *The Rotten Heart of Europe* (London: Faber and Faber, 1995), 17, and Andrew Moravcsik, *The Choice for Europe: Social Purpose and State Power from Messina to Maastricht* (Ithaca, N.Y.: Cornell University Press, 1998), 301–2.

75. Carr, *Helmut Schmidt*, 145.

76. Jenkins, *Life at the Centre*, 484.

77. Emmanuel Mourlon-Druol, "Deus ex Machina? Analysing the Place of the EMS in the History of European Monetary Cooperation, 1974–1979," paper read at the conference From Crisis to New Dynamics: The European Community, 1974–1983, Aarhus University, February 11–12, 2010, emphasizes the "conspicuous failures" of EC monetary policy in the 1970s and argues that the final policy that emerged was as much a result of these failures as from the near divine intervention of Jenkins, Schmidt, and Giscard.

78. Quoted Anthony Arnull, *The European Union and Its Court of Justice* (Oxford: Oxford University Press, 1999), 97; Renaud Dehousse, *The European Court of Justice* (London: Macmillan, 1998), 42.

79. Quoted Arnull, *European Union*, 98. The German Supreme Court has never accepted this principle, and in 1994 it warned in *Brunner v. the Treaty on European Union* that it had a general responsibility for monitoring breaches of the rights guaranteed in the Basic Law by EC institutions. See Arnull, *European Union*, 102–5.

80. Dehousse, *European Court of Justice*, 44–45.

81. Quoted Arnull, *European Union*, 118.

82. See Arnull, *European Union*, 460–67, for a discussion of the case. Ms. Defrenne was involved in three sex discrimination cases before the ECJ in all.

83. J. H. H. Weiler, *The Constitution of Europe* (Cambridge: Cambridge University Press, 1999), 22.

84. Dehousse, *European Court of Justice*, 43. The quotation is in the context of the Simmenthal case, but it reflects his wider view.

85. David Marquand, *Parliament for Europe* (London: Cape, 1979), 88.

86. European Commission, *A Parliament for the Community*, October 1977, 29.

87. Geneviève Bibes, Françoise de la Serre, Henri Ménudier, and Marie-Claude Smouts, *Europe Elects Its Parliament* (London: Policy Studies Institute, 1980), 2–3.

88. Bibes et al., *Europe Elects Its Parliament*, 32.

89. Bibes et al., *Europe Elects Its Parliament*, 39.

90. Moravcsik, *Choice for Europe*, 312.

91. Moravcsik, *Choice for Europe*, 312.

CHAPTER 6. THE 1992 INITIATIVE AND RELAUNCH OF THE COMMUNITY

1. See David R. Cameron, "The 1992 Initiative: Causes and Consequences," in *Euro-Politics*, ed. Alberta Sbragia (Washington, D.C.: Brookings Institution, 1993), 23–74 at 38–39, for figures on the growth of trade between EC member states.

2. For an accessible contemporary account of the effect of the rise of the dollar on the world economy, see Robert Solomon, "'The Elephant in the Boat?': The United States and the World Economy," *Foreign Affairs* 60, no. 3 (1981): 573–92.

3. Robert Boyer, "The Current Economic Crisis and Its Implications for France," in *The Mitterrand Experiment*, eds. George Ross, Stanley Hoffmann, and Sylvia Malzacher (Cambridge: Polity Press, 1987), 44.

4. Peter Hall, "The Evolution of Economic Policy under Mitterrand," in *The Mitterrand Experiment*, eds. Ross, Hoffmann, and Malzacher, 54–56.

5. Alain Muet, "Economic Management and the International Environment," in *Economic Policy and Policy-Making under the Mitterrand Presidency*, eds. Howard Machin and Vincent Wright (London: Pinter, 1985), 73.

6. Ronald Tiersky, *François Mitterrand: The Last French President* (New York: Saint Martin's, 2000), 134.

7. Bernard Connolly, *The Rotten Heart of Europe* (London: Faber and Faber, 1995), 28.

8. Hall, "Evolution of Economic Policy," 63.

9. Connolly, *Rotten Heart of Europe*, 30.

10. Quoted, Elisabeth du Réau, "L'engagement européen," in *François Mitterrand: Les années du changement, 1981–1984*, eds. Serge Bernstein, Pierre Milza, and Jean-Louis Blanco (Paris: Perrin, 2001), 293.

11. All quotes from the text of the draft "European Act" presented to the London European Council, November 1981. The act is included as appendix A in Pauline Neville-Jones, "The Genscher–Colombo Proposals," *Common Market Law Review* 20 (December 1983): 657–99 at 685–90.

12. Neville-Jones, "Genscher–Colombo Proposals," 657.

13. The text of the Solemn Declaration is in Bull. EC, no. 6/83, 24–29.

14. This is the conclusion of Gianni Bonvicini, "The Genscher–Colombo Plan and the Solemn Declaration 1981–83," in *The Dynamics of European Union*, ed. Roy Pryce (London: Routledge, 1989), 186.

15. Germany was the biggest contributor in 1979, giving 1.51 billion Ecu. Britain was second with 1,373 million. The big gainers were the Netherlands (320 million), Ireland (641 million), and Denmark (495 million). For the full figures and the method of calculation, see Joan Pearce, *The Common Agricultural Policy* (London: Royal Institute of International Affairs, 1981), 102.

16. Margaret Thatcher, *Downing Street Years* (London: HarperCollins, 1993), 63.

17. European Commission, *Britain in the Community 1973–83: The Impact of Membership* (London: European Communities, 1983), 7–11.

18. European Commission, *Britain in the Community*, 63.

19. Thatcher, *Downing Street Years*, 52.

20. Thatcher, *Downing Street Years*, 79.

21. Roy Jenkins, *A Life at the Centre* (London: Macmillan, 1994), 498–99.

22. Thatcher, *Downing Street Years*, 79.

23. Bull. EC, no. 5/80, 7–10.

24. Geoffrey Denton, "Re-Structuring the EC Budget: Implications of the Fontainebleau Agreement," *Journal of Common Market Studies* 23 (December 1984): 123.

25. Johan Van Merrienboer, "Commissioner Sicco Mansholt and the Creation of the CAP," in *Fertile Ground for Europe? The History of European Integration and the Common Agricultural Policy since 1945*, ed. Kiran Klaus Patel (Baden Baden: Nomos, 2009), 189.

26. For lions and mice, see Rosemary Fennell, *The Common Agricultural Policy: Continuity and Change* (Oxford: Clarendon Press, 1997), 217.

27. Bull. EC, no. 5/80, 9.

28. Pearce, *Common Agricultural Policy*, 1.

29. Pearce, *Common Agricultural Policy*, 59–61.

30. Pearce, *Common Agricultural Policy*, 48.

31. Pearce, *Common Agricultural Policy*, 9.

32. Giovanni Federico, "Was the CAP the Worst Agricultural Policy of the 20th Century?" in *Fertile Ground for Europe*, ed. Patel, 271.

33. For the domestic policies of Spain's fledgling democracy, see Paul Preston, *Juan Carlos: Steering Spain from Dictatorship to Democracy* (London: Harper Perennial, 2004), chs. 7–10.

34. European Commission, "General Considerations on the Problem of Enlargement," Bull. EC, supplement 1/78 (1978a); "Economic and Sectoral Aspects:

Commission Analyses Supplementing Its Views on Enlargement," Bull. EC, supplement 3/78 (1978b).

35. European Commission, 1978b, 22.

36. European Commission, 1978a, 15.

37. European Commission, 1978a, 15.

38. European Commission, 1978a, 17.

39. Quoted, Susannah Verney, "The Greek Association with the European Community: A Strategy of State," in *Southern Europe and the Making of the European Union*, eds. António Costa Pinto and Nuno Severiano Teixera (New York: Social Science Monographs, 2002), 125.

40. The European Communities, *General Report 1979* (Brussels: European Communities, 1979), 211–15.

41. The European Commission, "Opinion on Spain's Application for Membership," Bull. EC, supplement 9/78, 19.

42. Paul Kennedy, "Spain's Relations with the European Community 1962–1986" (unpublished manuscript, University of Bath, England). More generally, for an excellent overview that gives pointers to the literature in Spanish, see Juan Carlos Pereira Castañares and Antonio Moreno Juste, "Spain: In the Centre or on the Periphery of Europe," in *Southern Europe*, eds. Costa Pinto and Texeira, 41–80.

43. Castañares and Juste, "Spain: In the Centre or on the Periphery," call it the "French blockade," 74.

44. Bino Olivi, *L'Europa difficile* (Bologna: Il Mulino, 2000), 231.

45. Antonio Alonso, *España en el Mercado Común. Del Acuerdo del 70 a la Comunidad de Doce* (Madrid: Espasa Calpe, 1985), 173–75.

46. Bull. EC, no. 3/85, 7–9.

47. Andrew Moravcsik, "Negotiating the Single European Act: National Interests and Conventional Statecraft in the European Community," *International Organization* 45 (Winter 1991): 36.

48. Denton, "Re-Structuring the EC Budget," 123–25.

49. Despite the widespread belief that Britain's budget contribution was small beer, the eventual rebate negotiated by Mrs. Thatcher was sufficient to pay for "the entire family doctor service in Britain." See Hugo Young, *This Blessed Plot* (London: Macmillan, 1998), 323.

50. "Europe: The Future," paper produced for the Fontainebleau European Council by the British government, reproduced in the *Journal of Common Market Studies* 23, no. 3 (1984): 73–81.

51. The European Round Table included the chief executives of such important multinationals as FIAT, Philips, Unilever, Thyssen Steel, Bosch Electronics, as well as industrialists from firms based in countries outside the EC (e.g., Volvo, Ciba-Geigy) and it published a series of influential pamphlets in the early 1980s specifically directed at the political elite.

52. For academic discussions of Cassis, see Martin Shapiro, "The European Court of Justice," in *Euro-Politics*, ed. Alberta Sbragia (Washington, D.C.: Brookings Institution, 1992), 123–56; Karen J. Alter and Sophie Meunier-Aitsahlia, "Judicial Politics in the European Community: European Integration and the Pathbreaking Cassis de Dijon Decision," *Comparative Political Studies* 26 (January 1993): 535–61.

53. David R. Cameron, "The 1992 Initiative: Causes and Consequences," in *Euro-Politics*, ed. Sbragia, 53.

54. Renaud Dehousse, *The European Court of Justice* (London: Macmillan, 1998), 92–93.

55. Richard Griffiths, in Keith Middlemas, *Orchestrating Europe* (London: Fontana, 1995), 92–93.

56. European Commission, *Completing the Internal Market* (Luxembourg: Com [85], 310).

57. European Commission, *Completing the Internal Market*, 55.

58. Thatcher, *Downing Street Years*, 547.

59. Arthur Cockfield, *The European Union: Creating the Single Market* (London: Wiley Chancery Law, 1994), 56.

60. Thatcher, *Downing Street Years*, 553.

61. The complete text of the Parliament's proposals is to be found in Bull. EC, no. 2/84, 7–26.

62. The Dooge Committee's report is to be found in Bull. EC, no. 3/85, 102–11.

63. Thatcher, *Downing Street Years*, 551.

64. Antonio Varsori, *La Cenerentola d'Europa? L'Italia e l'integrazione europea dal 1947 a oggi* (Soveria Mannelli, Italy: Rubbettino, 2010), 351–52. Varsori says the Italian leadership became "too complacent" as a result of the Milan maneuver.

65. Thatcher, *Downing Street Years*, 553.

66. Juliet Lodge, "The European Parliament from Assembly to Co-legislature: Changing the Institutional Dynamics," in *The European Community and the Challenge of the Future*, ed. Juliet Lodge (London: Pinter, 1989), 69.

67. Bull. EC, no. 1/86, 9–10.

68. The strange case of Mr. Crotty is discussed in William Nicholl and Trevor C. Salmon, *Understanding the New European Community* (Hemel Hempstead, U.K.: Harvester Wheatsheaf, 1994), 50.

69. Bull. EC, no. 2/86, 10.

70. Bull. EC, no. 2/86, 8.

71. Quotes from Olivi, *L'Europa difficile*, 301.

72. Bull. EC, no. 1/86, 10.

73. Olivi, *L'Europa difficile*, 301.

74. Young, *This Blessed Plot*, 338.

75. Paul Taylor, *The Limits of European Integration* (London: Croom Helm, 1983), 298–300.

76. Taylor, *Limits*, 302–4.

77. Taylor, *Limits*, 305.

78. Taylor, *Limits*, 307.

79. Taylor, *Limits*, 308.

80. Young, *This Blessed Plot*, 332.

CHAPTER 7. THE MAASTRICHT COMPROMISE

1. See Paolo Cecchini, *The European Challenge, 1992: The Benefits of a Single Market* (Aldershot, U.K.: Wildwood House, 1988), for a summary of the research findings.

2. George Ross, *Jacques Delors and European Integration* (Cambridge: Polity Press, 1995), 18.

3. Tommaso Padoa-Schioppa, *The Road to Monetary Union in Europe* (Oxford: Clarendon, 1994), 4.

4. Mounier's philosophy has come under fire in recent years for its antidemocratic tendencies. See Zeev Sternhell, "Emmanuel Mounier et la Contestation de la Démocratie liberale dans la France des Années Trente," *Revue Française de Science Politique* 34 (December 1984): 1141–80.

5. Jacques Delors, *La France par L'Europe* (Paris: Grasset, 1988), 70.

6. For the "Delors Package," see Gary Marks, "Structural Policy in the European Community," in *Euro-Politics*, ed. Alberta Sbragia (Washington, D.C.: Brookings Institution, 1992), 191–224, esp. 206–7.

7. Delors, *La France par l'Europe*, 54.

8. See Frank Barry, John Bradley, and Aoife Hannen, "The Single Market, the Structural Funds and Ireland's Recent Economic Growth," *Journal of Common Market Studies* 39, no. 3 (2001): 537–52, for a detailed assessment of the structural funds' effects.

9. For Portugal, see Sebastián Royo, "From Authoritarianism to the European Union: The Europeanization of Portugal," *Mediterranean Quarterly* 15, no. 3 (2004): 95–129.

10. Kenneth Dyson and Keith Featherstone, *The Road to Maastricht: Negotiating Economic and Monetary Union* (Oxford: Oxford University Press, 1999), 335–42.

11. Padoa-Schioppa, *Road to Monetary Union*, 8.

12. Steven Greenhouse, "The World Watches Europe, the Power That Will Be," *New York Times*, July 31, 1988.

13. Dyson and Featherstone, *Road to Maastricht*, 716.

14. Andrew Moravcsik, *The Choice for Europe: Social Purpose and State Power from Messina to Maastricht* (Ithaca, N.Y.: Cornell University Press, 1998), 435.

15. Dyson and Featherstone, *Road to Maastricht*, 715.

16. Dyson and Featherstone, *Road to Maastricht*, 343.

17. Ross, *Jacques Delors and European Integration*, 82.

18. *Report on Economic and Monetary Union in the European Community ("The Delors Report")* (Luxembourg: European Communities, 1989). For an acute discussion of the report, see Niels Thygesen, "The Delors Report," *International Affairs* 65, no. 4 (Winter 1989).

19. Margaret Thatcher, *Downing Street Years* (London: HarperCollins, 1993), 709–12, describes a "nasty little meeting" with Howe and Lawson that amounted to "an ambush before Madrid." For further detail, see Philip Stephens, *Politics and the Pound: The Tories, the Economy and Europe* (London: Papermac, 1996), 117–19.

20. Nicolas Colchester and David Buchan, *Europe Relaunched: Truths and Illusions on the Way to 1992* (London: Hutchinson, 1990), 171.

21. Charles Grant, *Delors: Inside the House That Jacques Built* (London: Brealey, 1994), 88–89. The evening before, at a dinner in his honor, union leaders had moved him to tears by singing "Frère Jacques."

22. Margaret Thatcher, "The European Family of Nations" (the Bruges Speech), in *The Eurosceptical Reader*, ed. Martin Holmes (London: Macmillan, 1996), 88–96. All quotations are from this source.

23. For the charter, see Bull. EC, 12/89, 11.

24. Thatcher, *Downing Street Years*, 750.

25. See Mark Wise and Richard Gibb, *Single Market to Social Europe* (London: Longman Scientific, 1993), 190–96, for a discussion of the three directives.

26. Richard Corbett, "The Intergovernmental Conference on Political Union," *Journal of Common Market Studies* 30 (September 1992): 272–73.

27. See, Hans-Dietrich Genscher, *Rebuilding a House Divided* (New York: Broadway, 1998), 308, and Frédéric Bozo, "France, German Unification and European Integration," in *Europe and the End of the Cold War: A Reappraisal*, eds. Frédéric Bozo, Marie-Pierre Rey, N. Piers Ludlow, and Leopoldo Nuti (London: Routledge, 2008), 153.

28. Helmut Kohl, *Je Voulais l'Unité de l'Allemagne* (Paris: Editions de Fallois, 1997), 163–66.

29. Frédéric Bozo, "Mitterrand's France, the End of the Cold War and German Reunification: An Appraisal," *Cold War History* 7, no. 4 (2007), insists that Mitterrand's goal all along was to resolve the German problem by increasing European integration.

30. Karl Kaiser, "Germany's Unification," *Foreign Affairs* 70, no. 1 (1991): 186.

31. For these negotiations and the Kohl-Mitterrand letter, see Frédéric Bozo, "France, German Unification and European Integration," 155–58. Bozo emphasizes that these talks, far from being a hasty reaction to French dismay over accelerating German unification, actually represented "a major contribution to the peaceful end of the Cold War." Helmut Kohl's strategy is analyzed in the same volume by Hans Stark, "Helmut Kohl and the Maastricht Process," 246–58, and Italy's by Leopoldo Nuti, "Italy, German Unification and the End of the Cold War," 191–203.

32. Bull. EC, 4/90, 8.

33. The team was led by a Dutchman, Carlo Trojan.

34. Andreas Falke, "An Unwelcome Enlargement? The European Community and German Unification," in *German Unification: Process and Outcomes*, eds. Donald Hancock and Helga Welsh (Boulder, Colo.: Westview Press, 1996), 183.

35. "The Community and German Unification: Implications of the Staatsvertrag, Brussels 14 June 1990, SEC (90) 1138," paras 13–15. Commission documents on German unity are collected in *The European Community and German Unification*, Bull. EC, supplement 4/90.

36. Bull. EC, no. 7/90, 9.

37. *Independent* on Sunday, July 15, 1990, 1.

38. Bull. EC, no. 10/90, 16–19.

39. Stephens, *Politics and the Pound*, 182.

40. Corbett, "Intergovernmental Conference," 280. The draft treaty prepared by the Luxembourg presidency and the subsequent first Dutch draft are included in F. Laursen and S. Van Hoonacker, eds., *The Intergovernmental Conference on Political Union* (Dordrecht, The Netherlands: Nijhoff, 1992).

41. David Buchan, *Europe, The Strange Superpower* (Aldershot, U.K.: Dartmouth Publishing, 1993), 67.

42. Trevor Salmon, "Testing Times for European Political Cooperation: The Gulf and Yugoslavia 1990–1992," *International Affairs* 68, no. 2 (1998): 246–47.

43. Salmon, "Testing Times," 247.

44. Delors's speech in Ross, *Jacques Delors and European Integration*, 97–98.

45. Anthony Forster, *Britain and the Maastricht Negotiations* (London: Macmillan, 1999), 113.

46. Quoted in Youri Devuyst, "The European Community and the Conclusion of the Uruguay Round," in *The State of the European Union: Building a European Polity*, eds. Carolyn Rhodes and Sonia Mazey (Boulder, Colo.: Lynne Rienner, 1995), 457. The text of the directive is to be found in the *Official Journal of the European Communities*, October 17, 1989, 23–30.

47. Quoted Grant, *Delors: The House That Jacques Built*, 172. Delors was subsequently accused of trying, at the behest of the French government, to wreck the Uruguay Round in November 1992. The commissioner for trade, the Irishman Ray MacSharry, briefly resigned when Delors allegedly told him that the deal he had negotiated on agriculture would certainly be vetoed by the French government. Only massive pressure on Delors from the British, Dutch, and German governments got the talks back on track again and got MacSharry his job back. See Grant, *Delors: The House That Jacques Built*, 174–80.

48. Ross, *Jacques Delors and European Integration*, 168.

49. Jonathan Eyal, *Europe and Yugoslavia* (London: Royal United Services for Defence Studies, 1993), 4.

50. Eyal, *Europe and Yugoslavia*, 13.

51. *New York Times*, June 29, 1991, 4.

52. By asserting the principle of unchanged territorial boundaries, the EC was plainly backing the Croats against the Serbs. It is true, however, as Stanley Hoffmann has pointed out, that the Yugoslav government's position at The Hague conference was illogical. It wanted self-determination for all peoples (and hence the right of Serb-majority areas of Croatia and Bosnia to secede and join Yugoslavia), but it made an exception for the Kosovo, the historic heartland of the Serbs, since it now had a large ethnic majority of Albanians. Stanley Hoffmann, "Yugoslavia: Implications for Europe and European Institutions," in *The World and Yugoslavia's Wars*, ed. Richard H. Ullman (New York: Council on Foreign Relations, 1996), 97–121 at 104–5.

53. Ross, *Jacques Delors and European Integration*, 169.

54. Buchan, *Europe*, 46.

55. For a very able article frankly presenting the German perspective, see Wolfgang Krieger, "Towards a Gaullist Germany? Some Lessons from the Yugoslav Crisis," *World Policy Journal* 11, no. 1 (Spring 1994): 26–38. Krieger plausibly argues (p. 30) that Bonn wanted "to demonstrate that Germany could impose its will on its European partners with respect to foreign policy decisions—despite the huge concessions Germany had made at Maastricht."

56. See Misha Glenny, *The Fall of Yugoslavia: The Third Balkan War* (London: Penguin, 1993), 164–66.

57. Simon Nuttall, "The EC and Yugoslavia: Deus ex Machina or Machina sine Deo?," *Journal of Common Market Studies*, Annual Review of 1993, 32 (August 1994): 23.

58. See R. Corbett, *The Treaty of Maastricht: From Conception to Ratification* (London: Longman, 1993) and Andrew Duff, John Pinder, and Roy Pryce, *Maastricht and Beyond: Building the European Union* (London: Routledge, 1994) for clear accounts of Maastricht's innovations.

59. Following the rejection of the TEU by Danish voters in June 1992 (see chapter 8), Denmark also negotiated a battery of opt-outs in defense and foreign policy from the EU treaty and clarified that she would not be participating in the third stage of EMU, nor would she be bound by the Maastricht criteria for macroeconomic policy. Denmark further asserted in a protocol added to the treaty that the EU citizenship provisions did not "in any way take the place of national citizenship" or imply that EU citizens could automatically become Danish citizens. These changes were agreed by the Edinburgh European Council in December 1992. For text, see *Official Journal of the European Communities*, December 31, 1992.

60. Peter B. Kenan, "The European Central Bank and Monetary Policy in Stage Three of EMU," *International Affairs* 68, no. 3 (1992): 466.

61. Dyson and Featherstone, *Road to Maastricht*, 441.

62. Kenan, "European Central Bank and Monetary Policy," 467.

63. Grant, *Delors: The House That Jacques Built*, 201–2.

64. For press comments, see Hugo Young, *This Blessed Plot* (London: Macmillan, 1998), 433.

65. John Pinder, *The European Union: A Very Short Introduction* (Oxford: Oxford University Press, 2001), 104.

66. Alberta Sbragia, *Euro-Politics* (Washington, D.C.: Brookings Institution, 1992), 5.

67. Moravcsik, *Choice for Europe*, ch. 6, 379–471. Moravcsik treats the negotiations on political union as a "sideshow" (p. 447) when compared with monetary union. This enables him to downplay the importance of federal ideology and the geopolitical concerns raised by German reunification.

68. Jacques Delors, *Mémoires* (Paris: Plon, 2004), 277.

69. Dyson and Featherstone, *Road to Maastricht*, 749.

70. N. Piers Ludlow, "The European Institutions and German Unification," in *Europe and the End of the Cold War*, eds. Bozo, Rey, Ludlow, and Nuti, 167.

71. It is interesting to see how little archive research has added to the thesis put forward by Michael J. Baun, "The Maastricht Treaty as High Politics: Germany, France and European Integration," *Political Science Quarterly* 110, no. 4 (Winter, 1995–1996): 605–24.

72. Quoted in Grant, *Delors: The House That Jacques Built*, 208.

CHAPTER 8. EUPHORIA?

1. See David Marsh, *Germany and Europe: The Crisis of Unity* (London: Mandarin, 1995), 63–99. The quotation in this paragraph is from *John Major: The Autobiography* (London: HarperCollins, 2000), 313.

2. Bernard Connolly, *The Rotten Heart of Europe* (London: Faber and Faber, 1995), 122.

3. Connolly, *Rotten Heart of Europe*, 137.

4. Desmond Dinan, *An Ever Closer Union* (London: Macmillan, 1994), 186.

5. Quoted Marsh, *Germany and Europe*, 149.

6. See Connolly, *Rotten Heart of Europe*, 144–47, for an account of this explosive meeting.

7. Referendum analysis from Byron Criddle, "The French Referendum on the Maastricht Treaty September 1992," *Parliamentary Affairs* 46, no. 2 (1993): 228–38.

8. *The Economist*, September 26, 1992, 15.

9. For blow-by-blow accounts of the events on Black Wednesday and the days immediately before and after, see *The Birth of the Euro*, eds. Dan Bilefsky and Ben Hall (London: Penguin, 1998), 63–74. John Major's direct personal account in *John Major: The Autobiography* (New York: HarperCollins, 1999), 330–41, is fascinating reading. Major went to bed on September 16 "half-convinced my days as prime minister were drawing to a close."

10. *The Economist*, August 29, 1992, 19; September 19, 1992, 1.

11. *The Economist*, September 26, 1992, 15.

12. Sir Leon Brittan, *Europe: The Europe We Need* (London: Hamish Hamilton, 1994), 46.

13. *The Economist*, December 23, 1995–January 1996, 45.

14. Bull. EC, no. 12/95, 25.

15. Background to Germany's economic diplomacy in the mid-1990s can be found in S. Bulmer, C. Jeffrey, and W. Paterson, *Germany's European Diplomacy: Shaping the Regional Milieu* (Manchester, U.K.: Manchester University Press, 2000), 92–103.

16. Bull. EC, no. 12/96, 20–30.

17. Sergio Fabbrini and Mark Gilbert, "When Cartels Fail: The Role of the Political Class in the Italian Transition," *Government and Opposition* 35, no. 1 (Winter 2000): 27–48.

18. See Mark Gilbert, *The Italian Revolution: The End of Politics, Italian Style?* (Boulder, Colo.: Westview, 1995), ch. 1 passim.

19. Michele Salvati, "Moneta unica, rivoluzione copernicana," *Il Mulino*, January 1997, 5–23.

20. Alberta Sbragia, "Italy Pays for Europe: Political Leadership, Political Choice and Institutional Adaption," in *Transforming Europe*, eds. Maria Green Cowles, James Caporaso, and Thomas Risse (Ithaca, N.Y.: Cornell University Press, 2000), 95, and Vincent Della Sala, "Maastricht to Modernization: EMU and the Italian Social State," in *Euros and Europeans: Monetary Integraion and the European Model of Society*, eds. Andrew Martin and George Ross (Cambridge: Cambridge University Press, 2004), 126–49.

21. For the Commission's recommendations, see Bull. EC, no. 3/98.

22. There are some who hold the contrary position and argue that the economic costs of maintaining Europe's welfare state will be so great as Europe's population ages that some of the Euro-zone's member states will exert pressure on the ECB to follow a lax monetary policy that will inflate away their debts. The political tensions that arise from this pressure may cause the Euro to fold like the Latin Monetary Union in the nineteenth century. See Niall Ferguson and Lawrence Kotlikoff, "Can the Euro Survive?" *Foreign Affairs* 79, no. 2 (2000): 110–21.

23. This skim through the pros and cons of the Euro is indebted to John Peet, "An Awfully Big Adventure," survey, *The Economist*, April 11, 1998; *The Birth of*

the Euro, eds. Bilefsky and Hall, 94–158; and an excellent short book by a Euro insider, Lorenzo Bini Smaghi, *L'euro* (Bologna: Il Mulino, 1998).

24. The eleven countries constituting the Euro-zone had a joint product of $6.3 trillion in 1998. The U.S. figure was $8.1 trillion. Vicky Bakshi, "Watch Out Dollar," in *The Birth of the Euro*, eds. Dan Bilefsky and Ben Hall, 254–57.

25. C. Randall Henning, "Europe's Monetary Union and the United States," *Foreign Policy*, no. 102 (1996): 94.

26. Martin Feldstein, "EMU and International Conflict," *Foreign Affairs* 77, no. 4 (November/December 1997): 66–73.

27. For the Eftans, see Fraser Cameron, "The European Union and the Fourth Enlargement," *Journal of Common Market Studies* 33 (annual review of 1995), 7–31, and Francisco Granelli, "The European Union's Enlargement Negotiations with Austria, Finland, Norway and Sweden," *Journal of Common Market Studies* 33, no. 1 (March 1995): 117–41.

28. This paragraph draws upon Michael Gehler and Wolfram Kaiser, "A Study in Ambivalence: Austria and European Integration 1945–1995," *Contemporary European History* 6, no. 1 (1997): 75–99. For the Haider affair, see Desmond Dinan, "Governance and Institutions 2000: Edging towards Enlargement," *Journal of Common Market Studies* 39 (annual review of 2000): 41.

29. See Anna Michalski and Helen Wallace, *The European Community: The Challenge of Enlargement* (London: Royal Institute of International Affairs, 1992), Appendix, pp. 152–67.

30. The statistics on the Phare program are taken from European Commission, *European Union Enlargement: A Historic Opportunity* (Luxembourg: European Union, 2001), 44–45. For the EBRD, see Steven Weber, "Origins of the European Bank for Reconstruction and Development," *International Organization* 48, no. 4 (1994): 1–38.

31. Quoted Michalski and Wallace, *European Community*, 158.

32. The Copenhagen Criteria are discussed in European Commission, *European Union Enlargement*, 9.

33. "Europe's Mexico Option," *The Economist*, October 5, 2002, 36.

34. European Commission, *Agenda 2000: For a Stronger and Wider Union* (Luxembourg: European Union, July 1997), 67. See also Michael Baun, *A Wider Europe: The Process and Politics of European Union Enlargement* (Lanham, Md.: Rowman & Littlefield, 2000).

35. See Andrew Mango, *The Turks Today* (London: John Murray, 2004), 97–100.

36. Nathalie Tocci and Benedetta Voltolini, "Europe, the Mediterranean and the Middle East," in *European Foreign Policies*, eds. Ronald Tiersky and John Van Oudenaren (Lanham, Md.: Rowman and Littlefield, 2010), 112.

37. *The Economist*, February 9, 2002, 33–34.

38. For trade statistics, see European Commission, *European Union Enlargement*, 40–41.

39. European Commission, *More Unity and More Diversity* (Luxembourg: European Communities, 2003). This publication revealed, p. 14, that while 81 percent of Austrians, 71 percent of Finns, and 57 percent of Germans had visited at least one of the new member states, the EU average was only 34 percent.

40. Wim Kok, *Enlarging the European Union* (Florence: European University Institute, 2003), 2 and 66.

41. Andrew Moravcsik and Kalypso Nicolaidis, "Federal Ideals and Constitutional Realities in the Treaty of Amsterdam," *Journal of Common Market Studies* 36 (annual review of 1997): 14.

42. Richard Corbett, "Governance and Institutions," *Journal of Common Market Studies* 36 (annual review of 1997): 39.

43. *The Economist*, June 21, 1997, 15.

44. See Fritz Scharpf, "Community and Autonomy: Multi-Level Policy-Making in the European Union," *Journal of European Public Policy* 1 (1994): 219–42.

45. *The Economist*, July 23, 1994, 35.

46. Bull. EC, no. 3/99, 139–44.

47. For an analysis of the EP elections of 1999 and 2004, and a recipe for making the EU more democratic, see Julie Smith, *Reinvigorating European Elections: The Implications of Electing the European Commission* (London: Chatham House, 2005).

48. Joschka Fischer, "From Confederacy to Federation—Some Thoughts on the Finality of European Integration," speech at the Humboldt University in Berlin, May 12, 2000. English translation at http://www.ena.lu/speech_joschka_fischer_ultimate_objective_european_integration_berlin_12_2000-020005639 .html. All quotations are from this source.

49. Mark Gray and Alexander Stubb, "The Treaty of Nice: Negotiating a Poisoned Chalice," *Journal of Common Market Studies* 39 (annual review of 2000): 13.

50. The Charter of Fundamental Rights was published in the Bull. EC, no. 12/2000.

51. Gray and Stubb, "Negotiating a Poisoned Chalice," 15.

52. This account of the institutional changes introduced by the Treaty of Nice is based upon a January 18, 2001, "Memorandum to the Members of the Commission," document reference SEC (2001), 99, from David O'Sullivan, a member of Romano Prodi's private office.

53. Desmond Dinan, "Ireland Says No," *EUSA Review* 14, no. 3 (Summer 2001): 7.

54. Wolfgang Wessels, "Nice Results: The Millennium IGC in the EU's Evolution," *Journal of Common Market Studies* 39, no. 2 (June 2001): 215.

55. For the "Declaration of Laeken," see Bull. EC, 12/2001.

56. I invite the reader to search for "European Constitutional Convention 2002-2003" on Google Scholar.

57. *The Economist*, June 21, 2003. Inside, a leading article described the Constitution as a "blueprint for accelerated instability."

58. Draft Treaty Establishing a Constitution for Europe, July 18, 2003. The text can be downloaded from the EU Bookshop.

59. Quoted Andrew Rawnsley, *The End of the Party: The Rise and Fall of New Labour* (London: Penguin, 2010), 258.

60. *Treaty Establishing a Constitution for Europe* (Luxembourg: EU, 2004). Quotation from Article I-3.

61. Jeremy Rifkin, *The European Dream: How Europe's Vision of the Future Is Quietly Eclipsing the American Dream* (New York: Penguin, 2004), 83.

62. In addition to establishing the WTO, the agreement cut industrial tariffs by 40 percent, liberalized trade in textiles and services, and opened public procurement to international bidding. The estimated direct economic gain of the deal was $200 to $300 billion in increased economic activity by 2002.

63. For an overview of the Lomé process in the 1990s, see David Lowe, "The Developmental Policy of the European Union and the Mid-Term Review of the Lomé Partnership," *Journal of Common Market Studies* 34 (annual review, August 1996): 15–28.

64. The EU Council of Foreign Ministers suspended EU aid programs and froze the assets held within the EU of several important members of the Mugabe regime in February 2002. Bull. EC, no. 1–2/2002, point 1.6.157.

65. The first of these was held in London on April 2, 1998.

66. The twelve states were Algeria, Cyprus, Egypt, Israel, Jordan, Lebanon, Malta, Morocco, Palestinian Authority, Syria, Tunisia, and Turkey.

67. Romano Prodi, *Europe As I See It* (Cambridge: Polity, 2001), 70.

68. Christopher Hill, "The Geopolitical Implications of Enlargement," in *Europe Unbound: Enlarging and Reshaping the Boundaries of the European Union*, ed. Jan Zielonka (London: Routledge, 2002), 97.

69. Algeria, Armenia, Azerbaijan, Belarus, Egypt, Georgia, Israel, Jordan, Lebanon, Libya, Moldova, Morocco, Palestinian Authority, Syria, Tunisia, and Ukraine. For the Commission's analysis of these countries, see "Wider Europe–Neighbourhood: A New Framework for Relations with Our Eastern and Southern Neighbours," Brussels, March 11, 2003, COM (2003), 104 final.

70. Karen E. Smith, "The Outsiders: The European Neighbourhood Policy," *International Affairs* 81, no. 4 (2005): 764.

71. "A Secure Europe in a Better World," The European Security Strategy, Brussels, December 12, 2003, 7.

72. "A Secure Europe in a Better World," 10.

73. "A Secure Europe in a Better World," 11.

74. Jolyon Howorth, "European Defense and the Changing Politics of the European Union: Hanging Together or Hanging Separately," *Journal of Common Market Studies* 39, no. 4 (November 2001): 767.

75. Quoted Howorth, "European Defense," 772. For detailed background on the St. Malo Declaration, see the same author's "European Integration and Defence: The Ultimate Challenge?" Chaillot Paper no. 43 (Paris: WEU-ISS, 2000).

76. John Pinder, *European Union: A Very Short Introduction* (Oxford: Oxford University Press, 2001), 121.

77. Cologne European Council Conclusions, June 3–4, 1999, Annex Three, 33–35.

78. See, William Wallace, "Europe, the Necessary Partner," and Anthony J. Blinken, "The False Crisis over the Atlantic," both in *Foreign Affairs* 80, no. 3 (2000): 16–48, and Anand Menon and Jonathan Lipken, *European Attitudes towards Transatlantic Relations 2000–2003: An Analytical Survey* (Paris: Notre Europe, 2003), text at http://www.notre-europe.eu/fileadmin/IMG/pdf/Etud26-en.pdf.

79. Conclusions of the Extraordinary European Council, Brussels, September 21, 2001.

80. "Europe and America Must Stand United," *Wall Street Journal*, January 29, 2003. The letter was signed by J. M. Aznar (Spain), J. M. Barroso (Portugal), Silvio Berlusconi (Italy), Tony Blair (Britain), Vaclav Havel (Czech Republic), Peter Medgyessy (Hungary), Leszek Miller (Poland), and Anders Fogh Rasmussen of Denmark.

81. For the Blair-Chirac summit, see Rawnsley, *The End of the Party*, 140. Anthony Seldon, *Blair Unbound* (London: Simon & Schuster, 2007), 160, reports the exchanges in almost exactly the same words. Both books are based on conversations with Blair's close aides.

82. Mark Leonard, *Why Europe Will Run the 21st Century* (New York: Public Affairs, 2005).

83. Ian Manners, "Normative Power Europe: A Contradiction in Terms?" *Journal of Common Market Studies* 40, no. 2 (2002): 253.

84. Manners, "Normative Power Europe," 252.

85. Robert Cooper, *The Post-Modern State and the World Order* (London: Demos, 2002). Cooper became the EU's director general for politico-military affairs in 2002.

CHAPTER 9. TOWARD A TWIN-TRACK EUROPE?

1. *Eurobarometer* is published twice a year. As this book was being concluded, the latest edition was no. 73 (August 2010). In response to the question, "Generally speaking, do you think (our country's) membership of the EU is 1) a good thing; 2) a bad thing; 3) neither good nor bad?," only 49 percent of those surveyed replied that it was a good thing. This was down from highs of 58 percent in August 2007 and a return to the lowest levels of the last decade. Those saying the EU was neither a good nor a bad thing were 29 percent of those polled; outright anti-EU opinion had almost doubled during the decade and stood at 18 percent. "Don't knows" were only 4 percent of the sample. Overall, in short, enthusiasm for the EU is ebbing, although supporters continue to outnumber opponents by a large margin.

2. José Rodríguez Zapatero, "L'Europe, aujourd'hui, plus que jamais," *Le Figaro*, May 23, 2005. The Spanish premier's article was one of a series published by the pro-European *Figaro* in the run-up to the poll. The articles were all content free and rhetoric rich.

3. Arthur Seldon, *Blair Unbound* (London: Simon & Schuster, 2007), 351–59, for the British point of view on the budget clash.

4. http://www.guardian.co.uk/politics/2005/jun/23/speeches.eu.

5. Wim Kok et al., *Facing the Challenge: The Lisbon Strategy for Growth and Employment* (Luxembourg: European Communities, November 2004).

6. André Sapir et al., *An Agenda for a Growing Europe: Making the EU Economic System Deliver* (Brussels: The European Union, July 2003).

7. Thus "Preservation and Management of National Resources" (i.e., mostly agriculture) took €54,016 million in 2007, rising to €58,659 million in 2011. The cost of the EU's administration has increased from €6,640 million in 2007 to €8,173 million in 2011—€1,533 million more. At a time when inflation in the Euro-zone has consistently been less than 2 percent per annum and GDP growth close to zero, a 23 percent nominal increase over five years in spending on the salaries, working conditions, and pensions of Eurocrats does tend to suggest that austerity has not yet been embraced by the Commission. Spending on the EU's foreign policy, or as the budget styles it, the "EU as a Global Player," increased from €7,091 million in 2007 to €8,754 million in 2011 (also a 23 percent increase), for a cumulative total of €38,613

million over the five years—more, say, than the GDP of Tunisia. These funds are supposed to ensure that "stability, security and prosperity" are maintained in the EU's neighborhood. All figures accessed on May 14, 2011, at http://ec.europa .eu/budget/biblio/multimedia/interactive/wherefundsgo/wfg_en.cfm.

8. Seldon, *Blair Unbound*, 412, quoting the British civil servant Kim Darroch.

9. To satisfy Poland, the so-called Ioannina Compromise will be in force between November 1, 2014, and March 31, 2017. This requires the Council of Ministers to suspend a vote if member states representing 75 percent of the number of states required to achieve a blocking minority, or amounting to 75 percent of the population necessary for a blocking minority, express their disagreement to voting by qualified majority.

10. The European Council decided in December 2008 that this rule would be extended even after October 31, 2014.

11. Analysis of Klaus's views and all quotations are from Dan Marek and Michael Baun, *The Czech Republic and the European Union* (London: Routledge, 2011), 47–50.

12. See, Tony Barber, "The Appointments of Herman van Rompuy and Catherine Ashton," *Journal of Common Market Studies*, annual review of 2009, 48 (2010): 55–69, for further analysis.

13. See F. Stephen Larrabee, "Turkey Rediscovers the Middle East," *Foreign Affairs* 86, no. 4 (2007): 103–14.

14. *Financial Times*, May 14–15, 2011, 2.

15. Figures from http://epp.eurostat.ec.europa.eu/cache/ITY_PUBLIC/3 -29042011-AP/EN/3-29042011-AP-EN.PDF. Accessed May 18, 2011.

16. Eurostat, Euroindicators No. 55/2010, April 22, 2010.

17. Eurostat, Euroindicators No. 60/2011, April 26, 2011.

18. For an accessible discussion of this technical point, see Erik Jones, "The Euro and the Financial Crisis," *Survival* 51, no. 2 (2009): 41–54.

19. For overviews of the debate in Germany, see http://www.spiegel.de/ international/germany/0,1518,736680,00.html and http://www.spiegel.de/ international/germany/0,1518,734285,00.html. Accessed May 24, 2011.

20. For a very sharp analysis of this problem, see http://www.spiegel.de/ international/business/0,1518,764299,00.html. Accessed May 24, 2011.

21. *Financial Times*, January 11, 2011, 25.

22. The Greek situation is analyzed in Kevin Featherstone, "The Greek Sovereign Debt Crisis and EMU: A Failing State in a Skewed Regime," *Journal of Common Market Studies* 49, no. 2 (2011): 193–217.

23. The Irish were at least able to vent their feelings in a general election held shortly after the EU loan was approved by the Irish Parliament. On February 25, 2011, the ruling Fianna Fáil party was annihilated at the polls, losing fifty-one of its seventy-one seats and seeing its share of the vote fall from over 40 percent of the electorate to just 17.4 percent.

24. Featherstone, "The Greek Sovereign Debt Crisis," 202.

25. For the "Euro Plus" pact, see European Council Conclusions, March 24–25, 2011. Appendix 1, 13–15.

26. For Trichet's proposal, see: http://www.ecb.int/press/key/date/2011/ html/sp110528.en.html. Accessed June 10, 2011.

27. http://www.census.gov/hhes/socdemo/education/data/cps/2009/tables
.html. Accessed May 24, 2011.

28. One of the EU's most important initiatives in external policy in the period
since 2005 has been in the field of global warming. The much-hyped 2009 United
Nations climate change summit in Copenhagen in December 2009 was a test case
for the EU's normative power. The so-called Copenhagen Accord, signed December 18, 2009, merely committed signatories to keeping temperature rises below 2
degrees Celsius but did not bind the big polluters, the United States and China, to
the kind of specific targets for reducing CO_2 emissions that the EU was prepared
to contemplate. See Bertil Kilian and Ole Elgstrom, "Still a Green Leader? The
European Union's Role in International Climate Negotiations," *Cooperation and
Conflict* 45, no. 3 (2010): 255–73.

29. The statistics cited in these paragraphs on levels of workforce participation,
reduction of emissions, education attainments, and research and development
spending are to be found at http://ec.europa.eu/europe2020/targets/eu-targets/
index_en.htm. Accessed May 20, 2011.

30. http://www.timeshighereducation.co.uk/world-university-rankings/
2010-2011/top-200.html. Accessed May 20, 2011.

31. http://www.weforum.org/issues/global-competitiveness. Accessed May
24, 2011.

32. See, for instance, the speeches on this topic by Italy's unpopular but interesting finance minister, Giulio Tremonti, http://www.giuliotremonti.it/. Accessed
May 22, 2011.

33. For the Northern League, see Anna Cento Bull and Mark Gilbert, *The Lega
Nord and the Northern Question in Italian Politics* (London: Palgrave, 2001).

34. The joke is John Lewis Gaddis's, *The Landscape of History* (Oxford: Oxford
University Press, 2004), 58.

35. For two recent interpretations of this perennial idea, see Guy Verhofstadt,
Les État Unis d'Europe (Paris: Editions Luc Pire, 2006) and Stefan Collignon, *Viva
la repubblica europea* (Venice: Marsilio, 2004).

Bibliographical Essay

Rather than give a full list of books and articles that I have read while writing this book, since many of them are already cited in the notes section, I thought it would be more constructive to give a brief guide to some of the key published sources that, for example, a liberal arts college teacher preparing an undergraduate course in post-1945 European history might wish to read and use as the basis for a syllabus.

GENERAL HISTORIES

The best introduction to the literature produced by historians on European integration is a volume edited by Wolfram Kaiser and Antonio Varsori, *European Union History: Themes and Debates* (Palgrave, 2010). This book is a collection of historiographical essays by specialist scholars on various aspects of European integration. Its huge bibliography is a starting point for both scholars and general readers.

The European Union Liaison Committee of Historians has published twelve bulky volumes of collected conference papers since 1987. The quality of these volumes varies, but the series does contain much work that is important. The same group also publishes the *Journal of European Integration History*.

General histories in English of European integration are less common than one might imagine. Desmond Dinan, *Europe Recast* (Lynne Rienner, 2004) and John Gillingham, *European Integration, 1950–2003* (Cambridge University Press, 2003) are two interesting books that appeared contemporaneously with the first edition of this text. The Gillingham book has a very strong thesis but is marred by the author's predilection for politically incorrect wisecracks, only a few of which are funny. Hagen Schulz-Forberg and Bo Stråth's *The Political History of European Integration: The Hypocrisy of Democracy-Through-Market* (Routledge, 2010) is not, despite its title, a general history of European integration but an interpretative essay that argues that the original European project broke down in the early 1970s and was revived in the 1980s as a project based on "neoliberal ideas of a market-driven European economy and democracy." I have a lot of sympathy for this reading of European integration history and certainly for its antiteleological approach.

Andrew Moravcsik's *The Choice for Europe: Social Purpose and State Power from Messina to Maastricht* (Ithaca, N.Y.: Cornell University Press, 1998) is a work of international relations theory applied to history, but it remains a book that makes the reader think. J. H. H. Weiler's *The Constitution of Europe* (Cambridge University Press, 1999) and Stanley Hoffmann's *The European Sisyphus* (Westview, 1991) remain very important collections of analytical essays by two eminent scholars in the field.

MEMOIR AND BIOGRAPHY

The main protagonists of European unification have left a good stock of memoirs, and biographers have themselves extensively studied them. There is no need to mention all the possible biographical sources here. I found Robert Marjolin's *Architect of European Unity* (Weidenfeld and Nicholson, 1989) to be the single most useful autobiography when writing this book, although Jean Monnet's *Mémoires* (Collins, 1978) is also indispensable. The chapters on European matters in Margaret Thatcher's *Downing Street Years* (HarperCollins, 1995) contain, unsurprisingly, very blunt judgments on what she regarded, by the time she wrote her memoirs, as the Community "Babel Express." Among biographies, Hans-Peter Schwarz's monumental *Konrad Adenauer: German Politician and Statesman in a Period of War, Revolution and Reconstruction* (Berghahn, 1995 vol. 1, and 1997 vol. 2) is a very lucid, informative, and well-structured account of the German statesman's life. Its only weakness is that it takes a fortnight to read! François Duchêne's *Jean Monnet, The First Statesman of Interdependence* (Norton, 1994) and Charles Grant's splendidly readable *Delors: The House That Jacques Built* (Brealey, 1994) are both extremely valuable books. We lack, however, biographical accounts in English of the main Italian protagonists: the absence of a life, times, and policy of Alcide De Gasperi, or at least a well-documented account of his European policy, is a glaring gap in the literature.

EARLY YEARS

The early years of European integration are the subject of Alan Milward's *The European Rescue of the Nation State* (Routledge, 1992), which, by giving eighty pages to the travails of the Belgian coal industry and just over twenty to the "lives and teachings of the European saints," makes its methodological priorities almost excessively explicit. Milward's *The Reconstruction of Western Europe 1945–1951* (Routledge, 1984), however, is a classic. A challenging recent book combining a strong methodological statement and ultraempirical chapters is a volume edited by Wolfram Kaiser, Brigitte Leucht, and Morten Rasmussen, *The History of the European Union: Origins of a Trans- and Supranational Polity, 1950–1972* (Routledge, 2009).

The European movement is chronicled in detail by Walter Lipgens, Alan Milward, and Wilfried Loth's *A History of European Integration 1945–1947* (Clarendon Press, 1987), while U.S. policy to Europe is the main subject of Michael Hogan, *The Marshall Plan: America, Britain and the Reconstruction of Western Europe* (Cambridge University Press, 1987), Marc Trachtenberg, *A Constructed Peace: The Making of the European Settlement 1945–1963* (Princeton University Press, 1999), and Pascaline Winand, *Eisenhower, Kennedy and the United States of Europe* (St. Martin's, 1993). British policy toward European unity is vigorously handled by Wolfram Kaiser, *Using Europe, Abusing the Europeans: Britain and European Integration, 1945–1963* (Palgrave, 1997). Robert Lieshout, *The Struggle for the Organization of Europe* (Edward Elgar, 1999) is very good on the negotiation of the Treaties of Rome. Oddly, it seems to be the only English-language diplomatic history of the subject.

The early years of the European Commission, its policies, personalities, and struggles, is the subject of *The European Commission, 1958–1972: History and Memories* (European Communities, 2007). This Commission-financed work was edited by the Belgian scholar Michel Dumoulin and featured the contributions of a great many important scholars in the field. Inevitably, perhaps, it tends toward official history.

DE GAULLE AND THE 1960S

Works on de Gaulle and Gaullism are legion. The standard biography of de Gaulle in French is Jean Lacouture's three-volume work; the latter two volumes are available in English as *De Gaulle the Ruler 1945–1970* (Harvill, 1991). On the question of British entry into the EEC, Oliver Bange's *The EEC Crisis of 1963* (Macmillan, 2000), while a little fragmented in narrative structure, is very convincingly argued. N. Piers Ludlow's *Dealing with Britain: The Six and the First UK Application to the EEC* (Cambridge

UP, 1996), however, is outstanding. De Gaulle's overall impact on the Community is best surveyed by Ludlow's *The European Community and the Crises of the 1960s: Negotiating the Gaullist Challenge* (Routledge, 2006). The key policy adopted by the EEC in these years was, of course, the CAP. The CAP was the subject of an outstanding collection of essays edited by Kiran Klaus Patel, *Fertile Ground for Europe? The History of European Integration and the Common Agricultural Policy since 1945* (Nomos Verlag, 2009) and of *Farmers on Welfare: The Making of Europe's Common Agricultural Policy* (Cornell University Press, 2009), a monograph by the Danish scholar Ann-Christina Knudsen.

THE 1970s AND 1980s

Specialist historical works tend to follow the release of public documents, and so the period 1969 to 1984 is currently the area of European integration that has seen the largest volume of recent work. The link between European integration and détente was the subject of N. Piers Ludlow, ed., *European Integration and the Cold War, Ostpolitik-Westpolitik, 1965–1973* (Routledge, 2007). Daniel C. Thomas's *The Helsinki Effect: International Norms, Human Rights, and the Demise of Communism* (Princeton University Press, 2001) highlighted the EC's foreign policy role in this period, a point reiterated in greater detail by Angela Romano, *From Détente in Europe to European Détente* (Peter Lang, 2009). Peter Lang's "Euroclio" series, in which Romano's book is included, is the best place to scrutinize the tidal wave of recent research by young scholars, especially from France, Germany, and Italy, on European integration history. This work is more and more often published in English.

The topic of enlargement is, of course, crucial for the EC in the 1970s and 1980s. António Costa Pinto and Nuno Severiano Teixera's *Southern Europe and the Making of the European Union* (Social Science Monographs, 2002) is an excellent collection of essays. The literature on Britain is immense, but Stephen George, *The Awkward Partner: Britain and European Community* (Oxford University Press, 2001, 3rd edition) and Hugo Young's *This Blessed Plot* (Macmillan, 1998) have not really been superseded. A lively, well-sourced book dealing with Britain and European integration since 1973 would be useful.

FROM THE SINGLE EUROPEAN ACT TO MAASTRICHT

On developments within the EC between the SEA and Maastricht, R. Keohane and S. Hoffmann, *The New European Community* (Westview, 1991) and Alberta Sbragia's *Euro-Politics* (Brookings Institution, 1993) are outstanding contemporary collections of essays by leading American scholars of the EU.

Their publication represented a revival of American scholarly interest in the European project and today has a "period piece" value.

George Ross, *Jacques Delors and European Integration* (Polity Press, 1995) was very (too?) kind to its subject, but it gave a compelling picture of what working for the upper reaches of the Commission during Delors's presidency was like. Delors's own *Mémoires* (Plon, 2004) are disappointing. Frédéric Bozo, Marie-Pierre Rey, N. Piers Ludlow, and Leopoldo Nuti, eds., *Europe and the End of the Cold War: A Reappraisal* (London: Routledge, 2008) is a recent collection of essays that is helpful for understanding the economic and diplomatic significance of German reunification. Michael Baun, *An Imperfect Union: The Maastricht Treaty and the New Politics of European Integration* (Westview, 1996) and Richard Corbett, *The Treaty of Maastricht: From Conception to Ratification* (Longman, 1993) are two books written in the immediate aftermath of the Maastricht Treaty that remain valuable. Baun's *A Wider Europe: The Process and Politics of European Union Enlargement* (Rowman & Littlefield, 2000) is the best secondary source on enlargement in the 1990s, though the EU's own documentation is both clear and accessible on this issue.

Kenneth Dyson and Kevin Featherstone's *The Road to Maastricht: Negotiating Economic and Monetary Union* (Oxford University Press, 1999) is a brilliantly researched history of monetary policy within the EC from the Werner Report to the EU. Tommaso Padoa-Schioppa's *The Road to Monetary Union in Europe* (Clarendon Press, 1994) is technical in places but very stimulating. Both of these books are broadly (in the case of Padoa-Schioppa, passionately) sympathetic to EMU. Bernard Connolly's *The Rotten Heart of Europe* (Faber and Faber, 1995) is an engagingly splenetic account of the same subject that casts a good deal of doubt on the purity of the Bundesbank's motives and on the general utility of monetary union. Last, but not least, Dennis Swann's *The Economics of the Common Market: Integration in the European Union*, 8th edition (Penguin, 1999), has an outstanding chapter on monetary policy. Swann's book is a central text for all students and scholars of European integration.

John Major: The Autobiography (HarperCollins, 2000) gives a very illuminating picture of the civil war over Europe within the British government after Maastricht. The best general account of the relationship of the Thatcher and Major governments with the accelerating pace of European integration in the 1980s and early 1990s is Philip Stephens, *Politics and the Pound* (Papermac, 1996).

EUROPE TODAY

Anybody claiming to have read all, or even much, of the literature on the EU since the beginning of this century is delusional. Recent years have seen a quantum leap in the number of EU studies as experts, many of them American, have dissected the strange new polity emerging in Europe. In my opinion, the best textbook on the EU is Ian Bache, Simon Bulmer, and Stephen George's *Politics in the European Union*, 3rd edition (Oxford University Press, 2011). Ronald Tiersky and Erik Jones, *Europe Today: A Twenty-First Century Introduction* (Rowman & Littlefield, 2007) is even more accessible and does not limit itself to the EU.

Andrew Martin and George Ross, eds., *Euros and Europeans: Monetary Integration and the European Model of Society* (Cambridge University Press, 2004) is a dense collection of essays on the political economy of the contemporary EU. David P. Calleo's *Rethinking Europe's Future* (Princeton, N.J.: Princeton University Press, 2001) is a brilliant analysis of the EU's place in the global economy. Foreign policy is handled in a lively, informative way by Karen E. Smith, *European Union Foreign Policy in a Changing World* (Polity Press, 2008). Jeremy Rifkin, *The European Dream: How Europe's Vision of the Future Is Quietly Eclipsing the American Dream* (Penguin, 2004) should be read by anybody wanting to grasp the nature of the extravagant hopes aroused by the EU project in the early years of this century.

The reader who simply wishes to know what the main developments have been within the EU in recent years can rely on the very informative annual reports on the EU published as a supplement to the *Journal of Common Market Studies*, which is the principal academic journal in the field of EU studies. These reports each contain a keynote article on a major topic within the Union during the year in question and empirical, well-researched articles on the EU's institutions, its internal and external policy, legal affairs, major developments within the member states, and the economic situation of the Union and its members, as well as a useful chronology of the year's main events. The EU's website, Europa (http://europa.eu/), the EU's online bookshop, most of whose products are free, and the Bulletin of the European Union are essential sources for published documents.

Index

About the Author

Mark Gilbert was born in Chesterfield (UK) in September 1961. He is visiting associate professor of contemporary European history at the Johns Hopkins School for Advanced International Studies in Bologna, on leave from the University of Trento. He has also taught at Dickinson College and the University of Bath. He is the author of *The Italian Revolution: The End of Politics, Italian Style* (1995) and joint author of *The Lega Nord and the Northern Question in Italian Politics* (2001), as well as many articles and essays on postwar political history. He is a Fellow of the Royal Historical Society.